D0986274

THE FIRST AMENDMENT

FIFTH EDITION

DANIEL A. FARBER
Sho Sato Professor of Law
University of California at Berkeley

CONCEPTS AND INSIGHTS SERIES®

FOUNDATION
PRESS

Concepts and Insights Series is a trademark registered in the U.S. Patent and Trademark Office.

© 1998, 2003 FOUNDATION PRESS
© 2010 by THOMSON REUTERS/FOUNDATION PRESS
© 2014 LEG, Inc. d/b/a West Academic
© 2019 LEG, Inc. d/b/a West Academic
    444 Cedar Street, Suite 700
    St. Paul, MN 55101
    1-877-888-1330

Printed in the United States of America

ISBN: 978-1-68467-250-9

To the memory of my brother,
Michael Richard Farber (1953–2019)

ACKNOWLEDGMENTS

This project was originally suggested by Dick Fenton, who was then in charge of Foundation Press. I am also grateful for the continued support and guidance of his successors at Foundation. In addition, although the book's format allows only limited references to secondary sources, my debt to other First Amendment scholars is incalculable. Readers should consult any of the leading casebooks or treatises for additional citations to the wealth of insightful scholarship on the First Amendment.

TABLE OF CONTENTS

PART II. THE CATEGORICAL APPROACH

PART IV. RELIGION

THE FIRST AMENDMENT

FIFTH EDITION

Part I

FOUNDATIONAL ISSUES

Chapter 1

FREE EXPRESSION AND
THE CONSTITUTION

The text of the First Amendment is deceptively simple. With regard to free expression, it says only that "Congress shall make no law . . . abridging the freedom of speech, or of the press." Almost all of these few words are in some respect misleading as guides to legal doctrine:

> *"Congress."* The First Amendment speaks only of Congress. But free expression is also protected against abridgment by the executive branch and the federal courts. Moreover, since early in the last century, it has been understood that the Fourteenth Amendment "incorporates" the First Amendment, so that free expression is equally protected against state governments.

> *"No law."* Justice Hugo Black was fond of saying that "no law means no law." But the courts have never viewed the First Amendment as an unconditional absolute, and in practice even Justice Black found some regulations of speech to be justified.

> *"Of speech, or of the press."* This sounds as if the First Amendment applies only to oral or printed communication. But other forms of communication are also protected, including not only the electronic media but also unconventional forms of "symbolic speech" like flag burning.

Thus, the bare text of the First Amendment provides only a hint of the ultimate contours of legal protection.

The U.S. Constitution is not unique in protecting free expression. Today, nearly all democracies provide constitutional protection for free expression. But nowhere is the protection taken as far as in the United States. The unique features of U.S. law derive less from the constitutional text than from the gloss provided by the Supreme Court. Particularly in the past half-century, the Supreme Court has aggressively expanded the coverage of the First Amendment to include more types of speech and has raised the barriers to regulation. In general, the Court has sharply restricted government regulation of speech, compared both with our own prior history and with other democracies.

Although it is hard to get an accurate count, the Supreme Court has decided several hundred First Amendment cases, most of them since 1970. They deal with a wide range of factual and legal issues, from libel law to nude dancing to school prayer. It would be impossible to examine fully this enormous body of cases, let alone the complex academic debate that surrounds almost every issue. Instead, we will attempt to cover the main lines of doctrinal development and some of the key points of contention.

In this introductory chapter, we begin by considering the most fundamental issue about the First Amendment: Why speech receives special constitutional protection. We then examine how the current scheme of protection evolved, followed by a quick overview of current doctrine. Finally, we take a closer look at the road ahead in the rest of the book.

I.　Why Protect Speech?

The Supreme Court sometimes seems determined to test our commitment to free expression by finding the most offensive conduct to protect. In 1989, for example, the Court shocked many people with its decision in *Texas v. Johnson*.[1] Johnson had burned an American flag as part of a public protest against the Republican national convention. He was convicted for violating a Texas law against desecrating the flag. Chief Justice Rehnquist observed that the Texas law "deprived Johnson of only one rather inarticulate symbolic form of protest—a form of protest that was profoundly offensive to many— and left him with a full panoply of other symbols and every conceivable form of verbal expression to express his deep disapproval of national policy." It would be ironic, said the Chief Justice, if the government could "conscript men into the Armed Forces where they must fight and perhaps die for the flag" but could not "prohibit the public burning of the banner under which they fight."

But Rehnquist was in dissent. The majority opinion was written by Justice Brennan, who had quite a different perspective. He concluded that the Texas law violated the "bedrock principle" that "the government may not prohibit the expression of an idea simply because society finds the idea itself offensive or disagreeable."

Although the *Johnson* opinion was joined by Justice Scalia, a noted conservative, it was not well-received by most conservatives and outraged many ordinary Americans. Liberals, who generally had no strong feelings about flag burning, were unfazed. But their turn was soon to come. Three years later, the Court decided another incendiary case, *R.A.V. v. City of St. Paul*.[2] The issue this time was

---

[1]　491 U.S. 397 (1989).

[2]　505 U.S. 377 (1992).

limitation of offensive speech

not flag burning but cross burning. In the middle of the night, several teenagers constructed a cross from broken chair legs and burned it on the lawn of a black family. They were convicted for violating a hate crime ordinance that specifically banned burning crosses as well as other extreme racist speech. The Supreme Court unanimously reversed the conviction. Although several Justices voted to reverse on narrow grounds, a majority joined Justice Scalia's sweeping opinion for the Court. Scalia observed that the government had singled out racist ideas for special regulation. He invoked the principle that the government may not regulate speech "based on hostility—or favoritism—towards the underlying message expressed." This principle of "equal time for racists" was not well received by liberal scholars and troubled many other Americans as well.

Why should society tolerate ideas that are not only false but dangerous? This is a question that has intrigued philosophers and legal thinkers for decades. We will briefly survey some of the possible answers. They can be divided into two categories. Some reasons focus on the roles played by free expression in the private sphere, including self-realization and the search for truth. Others focus on the connection between free expression and political democracy.

A.   Self-Realization and the Search for Truth

Countries that do not tolerate free expression are not good places to live, even for the completely apolitical. The arts—not just the "high" arts but also television, movies and popular music—are restricted by the government's views of propriety. Even in private life, people are careful about what they say, for fear that something adverse will be reported. People who have lived in totalitarian countries report a pervasive fear of being different, of doing anything that might attract attention. Restrictions on speech have stunted people's lives, their abilities to define and express who they are.

"Self-realization" theories of the First Amendment stress the relationship between free expression and personal fulfillment. If people lack access to a wide range of ideas, they are prevented from imagining the full range of possibilities in their lives. Even for those who would choose conventional ways of life in any case, repressive societies in some sense reduce their ownership of their lives by making traditional lifestyles an unthinking habit rather than a personal choice. Restrictions on expression also confine the ability of writers and artists to express their perspectives, impoverishing the national culture.

Although these observations seem plausible, particularly in light of the experience of totalitarian countries, there are several possible replies to this argument for free expression. In the first place, it might be argued that speech is not unique in its role in self-realization. Many other kinds of activities are critical to a person's developing a self-identity. The person who wants to pursue a profession but cannot because of unnecessary government licensing and the person whose sexual activities violate government restrictions are both frustrated in their quest for self-realization. Yet the First Amendment does not protect these activities. Also, it is not clear that the need for self-realization requires full protection for all ideas regardless of their social utility. Do we really want to preserve the possibility for people to "find themselves" as bigots or criminals? Why not squelch ideas which might lead down the path toward personal decay rather than growth?

An alternate theory stresses the role of free expression in the search for truth. Again, this idea gains plausibility from the experience of totalitarian countries. For example, in the former Soviet Union, modern genetics was once brutally suppressed because it did not fit Stalin's views. We commonly think that open debate is more likely than government fiat to lead to the truth. But this argument too has its possible weak points. It is easy enough to point to historical instances where the truth did not win out, and where truly horrible ideas held sway for considerable lengths of time. Also, critics say, if we are positive an idea is false—and we *are* positive about the falsity of some ideas, such as genocide—why leave them circulating where they can only obstruct the search for truth? And of course, some theorists question whether there is actually such a thing as "truth" anyway.

The truth-seeking rationale for free expression is often called the "marketplace of ideas." In fact, it is possible to develop the concept in terms of economics. Information is what economists call a "public good," which basically means that its benefits cannot be confined to a single consumer. If you get a good idea from a book, there is really no way to prevent you from telling other people about it, and the author of the book won't get compensated for the full benefit his idea provides to society. Since the "producers" of ideas cannot recover the full social benefits of their product, they have an insufficient economic incentive to produce the product. The result is that, if we simply treat ideas like any other goods legally, we will end up producing fewer good ideas than we need. Instead, the legal system needs to make special provision for the production of new ideas and information. By lightening regulatory burdens, we can offset the flawed incentives for speech.

The marketplace theory works fairly well as a general argument for treating speech differently than other forms of conduct, but it may not explain why we go so far in protecting bad ideas. It is hard to maintain very seriously that individual self-development or society's quest for truth will be impaired if people are unable to consider the possible benefits of genocide, or even innocuous but false ideas like the flat earth theory. The counterarguments to these criticisms take several forms. One classic argument is that a "horrible false ideas" exception to free expression would invite government abuse, while providing relatively little benefit. Another classic argument is that even terrible ideas may serve a useful purpose: we revitalize our understanding of true ideas in the course of attacking the bad ones. Another argument stresses the educational value of tolerating bad ideas as a dramatic example of our willingness to put up with disturbing and unconventional approaches to life. None of these counter-arguments, of course, has gone without criticism. And so the debate continues.

B.   Self-Government and Social Stability

Self-realization theories support protection for a broad range of speech. Another approach stresses the particular relationship between free expression and democratic government. Obviously, if democracy is to function effectively, there must be latitude for criticizing the government and for circulating information relating to public affairs. It doesn't make much sense to have a "free" election if opponents of the government have been gagged. Moreover, the government cannot be expected to be evenhanded in censoring its own critics; whatever powers of censorship it is given are likely to be abused to protect the "powers that be." On these simple observations rests a powerful argument for free speech: Speech related to political issues cannot be suppressed because debate is necessary to our democratic government.

It is hard to quarrel with the basic argument, as far as it goes. The question is whether it goes far enough. According to self-realization theorists, approaches based on self-governance confuse a means with an end: democratic government is really only valuable because it fosters self-realization. Compared with self-realization theories, the self-government theory protects a narrower range of speech. It is difficult to explain how abstract art or subatomic physics relate to election campaigns, so the government would seem to have the right to censor them. Also, once we have put an idea off the agenda for democratic government, it seems no longer to be a legitimate political issue. For instance, one might argue, the constitutional ban on racial discrimination means that racism is legally not a relevant argument for any political position; hence, we lose nothing by banning discussions of the subject.

An additional supporting argument for tolerating hateful ideas is that tolerance works better than suppression in maintaining the democratic order. Repression drives dissidents underground, provides them with martyrs, and gives their ideas the attractive aura of the forbidden. Also, dissidents, however bad their ideas, are early warning signs of popular discontent and mounting social problems, alerting the government to the need for reform before events reach a crisis. At least in some circumstances, this "safety valve" argument seems to fit the facts, but it is hard to tell how accurate it is as a general statement about social stability.

Although there have been recurrent arguments to limit free expression to political speech, these efforts have been unavailing. The impact of the self-governance argument has mostly been to support a higher level of protection for political speech or speech on matters of public concern. We will see throughout this book examples of the impulse to provide such heightened protection. An equally recurrent problem, however, is that it turns out to be hard to define precisely what speech is relevant to politics or involves matters of public concern. Self-governance may do better as a philosophical justification than as a legal doctrine.

C.   The Limits of Theory

Some critics believe that *all* of these theoretical efforts are more useful as philosophy than law. For a while there was a trend toward single-value theories of First Amendment law, in which a scholar would posit a single underlying constitutional value and then attempt to deduce all First Amendment doctrine from that value. Such efforts, whatever their merits, never seemed to persuade many other scholars and were almost entirely ignored by the courts. Do we really need a comprehensive theory for the First Amendment?

If the question is whether we need a comprehensive theory to validate our society's support for free expression, that answer seems to be almost the reverse. We know that societies lacking in free expression are undesirable in *many* ways, including being repressive and undemocratic. The efforts to provide a "foundation" for this view are reminiscent of a joke about economists. "An economist," so the joke goes, "is someone who tries to prove that what happens in practice is theoretically possible." Similarly, a free speech theorist is someone who tries to *explain* a fact that we know already: censorship is bad. The best argument for free expression is to look back in history and around the world at societies that have lacked it—societies that have ranged from dismal to terrifying. The best the theorists can do is to try to account for this obvious fact.

We might also wonder whether the courts would benefit from having a comprehensive theory of the First Amendment. Responses to this question depend in large part on one's overall jurisprudential views. Nevertheless, the assumption that general theories make for healthy law is not beyond dispute. Having diverse normative justifications allows the First Amendment to garner broader support. Some people may support it because they are concerned about political censorship, some because they are libertarians, some because they want vitality in the arts, some simply because it is the American thing to do. Perhaps free expression is such a powerful idea precisely because it appeals to so many diverse values.

The search for a foundational First Amendment "brick" has been unavailing so far. If so many thoughtful legal commentators have failed to identify *the* foundational value that supports a unified First Amendment theory, the prospects for future efforts may be dim. The alternative is to abandon the quest for a foundational brick. Instead of thinking of the First Amendment as a tower, built on a single sturdy foundation, we might do better to think of it as a part of a web of mutually reinforcing values. One value is self-realization, a value that helps support both democracy and free speech. But the converse is also true. Democracy and free speech also provide reasons to embrace self-realization: people who have freedom to develop their own unique lives will make better democratic citizens than mindless conformists. Similarly, democracy and free expression also support each other. Protection for free expression not only safeguards the political process but prevents dominant groups from suppressing minority cultures. On the other hand, one reason to support democracy in the first place is that democracies are much less likely to engage in widespread censorship than dictatorships. All of these values are supported by still other values, such as the utility of scientific research (which would be hindered by censorship).

In short, it can be argued that we do not have a tower of values, with free speech somewhere toward the middle and more basic values underneath. Instead, we have a web of values, collectively comprising our understanding of a free society. Foundationalists may be too ambitious in seeking to reduce the complex relationships among our values to a linear arrangement in which a few values have privileged status and others are derivative.

II. First Amendment History

If it is difficult to supply a philosophical answer to the question of why we protect speech, it is somewhat easier to give a historical answer. American law protects speech because in the late Eighteenth Century it was given a home in the Constitution, because in the mid-Nineteenth Century constitutional protections were extended against state as well as federal actions, and because in the Twentieth Century the Supreme Court embarked on a long (and still continuing) project of implementing the First Amendment.

A. Origins of the First Amendment

When the printing press was invented, governments were quick to respond. The novel ability to circulate thousands of copies of a writing was viewed as a threat to social stability and government authority. The government response was to establish a system of licensing for authors and printers. By the mid-Eighteenth Century, however, the English were proud of themselves for having abolished this system. Indeed, for at least some, the absence of licensing was pretty much the definition of a free press. As Blackstone said, "the liberty of the press" consists of "laying no previous restraints upon publication," rather than "freedom from censure for criminal matter when published." Licensing makes a single censor the absolute authority over what is said. But punishing "any dangerous writings, which, when published, shall on a fair and impartial trial be adjudged of a pernicious tendency, is necessary for the preservation of peace and good order, of government and religion, the only solid foundations of civil liberty." Thus, for Blackstone, freedom of the press meant only freedom from prior restraints on publication.

Even in England, Blackstone's view was not universally accepted. Opposition writers (so-called because they opposed the political group in power) emphasized that freedom of speech was a check on the power of tyrants. One author pointed out that a "constant examination into the characters and conduct of ministers and magistrates should be equally promoted and encouraged," because the government had little fear "beyond the censure of the press, and the spirit of resistance which it excites among the people." Another pointed out that the press had exposed the "dark and dangerous designs," as well as the general incompetence, of officials.

The opposition writers found a ready audience in America, where their theories helped provide the intellectual framework for the Revolution. In the colonies, efforts to repress dissent were less frequent than in England. Probably the most notable example was the Zenger trial. The governor of New York, whom Zenger had criticized, charged him with seditious libel. Contrary to existing English practice as well as the judge's instructions, his lawyers argued that he had a right to have the jury determine the truth of his remarks. In his closing argument, one lawyer defended the right "publicly to remonstrate the abuse of power in the strongest terms, to put their neighbors upon their guard against the craft of open violence of men in authority." The jury disobeyed its instructions and acquitted Zenger, to the accompaniment of loud cheers from the audience.

It is familiar history that the original Constitution did not contain a Bill of Rights and that this was one of the major complaints of its opponents. Supporters of the original Constitution maintained, not very convincingly, that a Bill of Rights was unnecessary because the federal government had only limited powers. For example, they said, it would have no power to regulate the press. Ultimately, however, the Federalists gave in to the demand for a Bill of Rights. After ratification, Madison felt compelled to keep his pledge to introduce amendments, one of which became the First Amendment. Unfortunately, the incomplete materials concerning the legislative history of the Amendment shed little light about just what was meant by freedom of speech and of the press. We do know that the Senate rejected a proposal to qualify freedom of the press with the language "in as ample a manner as hath at any time been secured by the common law." The legislative record is otherwise unhelpful.

Although at one time the contrary view was popular, it seems clear now that the First Amendment was intended to do more than adopt Blackstone's views. Licensing had disappeared from American life before the First Amendment was adopted, and there seems little reason for the Framers to have been concerned about its revival. As we will see shortly, the controversies that did arise in America involved other issues.

Moreover, the constitutional text does not support the Blackstonian interpretation. Rather than using Blackstone's phrase (the "liberty of the press"), the First Amendment speaks of the "freedom of the press" and, more significantly, the "freedom of speech." It also protects the right to assemble and petition for the redress of grievances, which goes beyond any concern with press licensing. The right to petition clearly prevented later punishment, not just prior restraint. It is true that at the time of enactment, some knowledgeable observers did interpret freedom of speech in Blackstonian terms, but this understanding was by no means universal.

Another controversy is whether the First Amendment was meant to preclude prosecution for seditious libel—that is, harsh criticism of the government. The answer essentially depends on how we interpret two highly ambiguous signs: the absence of any specific discussion of the issue when the Amendment was passed, and the bitter disputes among its erstwhile supporters soon afterwards, when Congress passed the Alien and Sedition Acts. (These laws are discussed in more detail in Chapter 4.) Some of the original framers of the Constitution, including Madison, argued passionately that those laws violated the First Amendment. Others, like John Adams, were equally sure they were permissible.

Not surprisingly, the conclusions to be drawn from this ambiguous history seem to depend mostly on the presuppositions of the historian. The only thing we can be sure of regarding the original intentions is that the Framers meant to enact certain language, but what they understood that language to mean is unclear. One reason, no doubt, is that the Amendment was passed in response to general fears of excessive central power rather than to any particular abuses in the immediate past, which would have given focus to the discussion.

B.   Free Speech and the Fourteenth Amendment

The First Amendment forbids Congress to pass certain laws, and we know from the history of its adoption that it was specifically *not* intended to apply to the states. So how did it come to pass that the First Amendment became a limit on the states?

Part of the answer is that freedom of speech became a major issue again as the Civil War approached. Legal writers in the Nineteenth Century viewed freedom of speech as a fundamental right. Chancellor Kent stressed that free speech concerning governmental officials was essential to the "control over their rulers, which resides in the free people of the United States." Another leading scholar argued that the "foundation of a free government begins to be undermined when freedom of speech on political subjects is restrained," and that when such rights are denied, "life is indeed of little value."

But freedom of speech was not merely an intellectual concern. The antislavery movement gained much of its strength from Northern reaction to Southern attempts to limit freedom of speech, including the "gag rule" which prevented antislavery petitions from being received by the House of Representatives. Antislavery northerners were also bitter about restrictions that prevented works opposing slavery from being delivered by the mails in the South. The Kansas controversy in the late 1850s provided an important occasion for Republicans to express civil liberties views. The pro-slavery territorial government attempted to suppress antislavery speech. Its attempts to do so were bitterly attacked by Republicans in Congress. One accused the Kansas government of striking down free speech, imposing "[t]est oaths, against which reason and humanity revolt," and reducing the people of Kansas "to the pitiable condition of conquered menials of the slave power." Another accused the Kansas legislature of making it "a crime to think what one pleased, and to write and print what one thought," thereby borrowing "all the enginery of tyranny. but the torture" from the Stuart kings of England. "Before you hold this enactment to be law," yet another proclaimed, "burn our immortal Declaration and our-freewritten Constitution, fetter our free press, and finally penetrate the human soul and put out the light of that understanding which the breath of the Almighty hath kindled."

One of the key provisions of the Fourteenth Amendment prohibited any person from being deprived of liberty without due process of law. It became established law that this provision not only mandated fair procedures but also protected at least some kinds of "liberty" from being destroyed regardless of procedures. The historical pedigree of this doctrine is debatable; some historians think that the same result would more properly have fallen under another clause of the Fourteenth Amendment, while others find it entirely unsupportable. The history surrounding its adoption does not prove that the framers intended the Fourteenth Amendment to protect freedom of speech. It does show, however, that *if* the framers did intend to protect any substantive rights, freedom of speech was probably one of them. In any event, the application of the First Amendment to the states is now beyond dispute.

C. The Evolving Judicial Role

Although the First Amendment was ratified in 1791 and the Fourteenth Amendment in 1868, freedom of speech did not come into its own as a legal issue until World War I. This is not to say that there were no cases involving the issue or no academic writing on the subject, but it did not receive serious Supreme Court attention until the early Twentieth Century. Thus, as a part of legal doctrine, the First Amendment is only about a century old. But like a late-talking toddler who is never quiet for an instant once he finally gets started, the Supreme Court has more than made up for lost time.

Any way of carving up an evolutionary process is arbitrary, but we can divide the history of First Amendment doctrine into three eras. For about fifty years, the governing test for First Amendment law was the "clear and present danger" standard. As we will see later, Justice Holmes originally derived this standard as a justification for government censorship in wartime, but he soon changed his mind and, along with Justice Brandeis, made it a rallying cry for civil libertarians. The idea was quite simple: to suppress speech, the government had to prove that it posed an immediate danger to society.

The Court waffled in its application of the test. In the early years, the majority found no difficulty in upholding convictions against almost anyone who criticized the government in wartime or called for revolution in peacetime. After the trauma of World War I and the post-war "Red Scare" faded, however, the Court began to adopt a more temperate approach. By the late 1930s, the Court was beginning to hand down decisions protecting the speech rights of labor leaders, Jehovah's Witnesses, and others. But when the Cold

War erupted after World War II, the tide turned again, and the Court seemed willing to find a "clear and present danger" whenever communism was involved. We will recount that history in more detail in Chapter 4.

One of the oddities of First Amendment law is that often the dissenting opinions have proved more important than the majority opinion. The eloquent dissents of Justices Holmes and Brandeis are still read for their articulation of First Amendment values, long after the majority opinions have been forgotten. Similarly, in the 1950s, the dissents of Justices Black and Douglas were a bright spot in a period of repression, and they set the stage for the revival of speech rights in the following era.

The next era was short but pivotal. For about a decade, starting in the late 1950s through the late 1960s, the Warren Court adopted a starkly more protective attitude toward speech. It redefined "clear and present danger" in terms more protective of subversive speech. It also expanded the protections of the First Amendment in unprecedented ways: to libel suits brought by public officials against the press, to the publishers of erotic literature, to civil rights demonstrators and anti-war protestors. Some key doctrines were set during this period, but the Court often seemed less interested in doctrine than results, and many Warren Court opinions turned on specific facts rather than adopting any general rule.

That brings us to what might be called the modern era in First Amendment jurisprudence, which began with the Burger Court in the 1970s and now has extended into the Rehnquist and Roberts Courts. Given the generally more conservative orientation of the Burger Court, many observers expected it to be less protective of free speech than the Warren Court. Although the Burger Court did retrench some constitutional rights (particularly those of criminal defendants), it mostly moved in the opposite direction in the First Amendment area. With regard to free expression, the Burger Court not only accepted the Warren Court legacy but set about expanding it, as did the Rehnquist Court. The Roberts Court has built on this legacy. To a far greater extent than in the past, the Court was interested in elaborating a set of rules to govern speech cases. First Amendment law began to take on something of the "texture" of the common law of torts or contracts, with complicated definitions and multipart tests for every occasion. Despite objections from some Justices, First Amendment law has come to resemble a legal code as much as a flexible set of principles. As shown by its willingness to defend with equal fervor the rights of those who burn flags and those who burn crosses, the Court clearly now views the protection of free speech as one of its core responsibilities.

III. Overview of Current Doctrine

We will spend three hundred pages exploring First Amendment doctrines. Before we become too heavily involved in the details, it may be useful to take a quick look at the overall doctrinal framework presently employed by the Court.

A.   "Unprotected" Speech

Historically, some kinds of speech were considered to be simply outside the scope of the First Amendment. This is sometimes called the two-tier theory (one tier of speech being unprotected, the other protected). The list of unprotected speech included incitements to violence, libel, obscenity, fighting words, and commercial advertising.

These categories of speech continue to receive special treatment today. It is a gross oversimplification, however, to say that any of these categories is currently outside the First Amendment. For each category, the Court has now created a set of rules detailing the boundaries of permissible government regulation. For example, as we will see, libel of a public official is only unprotected if the falsehood was intentional or at least reckless. Within this confined subcategory, one can still stay that certain libels are "unprotected"— they can be the basis for punitive damages, for example. But to say that libel as a whole is unprotected would be untrue.

Similarly, after many years of calling advertising "unprotected speech," the Court reversed its stance in the 1970s and began subjecting advertising regulations to serious constitutional scrutiny. But even today, advertising does not enjoy quite the same degree of constitutional protection as artistic, scientific, or political discourse. Rather, it is subject to a detailed set of constitutional rules governing the extent of permissible government regulation. For example, the state has a free hand to regulate false advertising, without being subject to the same kinds of rules that limit libel actions. Thus, we might want to say that false advertising is unprotected speech. Truthful advertising, however, clearly receives some constitutional protection, though not so much as political speech—some might call it "less-protected" speech. Much the same is true of the other categories of "unprotected" speech.

The Court seems increasingly disinclined to treat any form of speech as being completely without First Amendment value. For instance, in *United States v. Alvarez,*[3] the Court stepped away from statements in earlier opinions that false statements of fact are unprotected speech. The case involved a federal ban on false claims

---

[3]   567 U.S. 709 (2012).

by an individual to having received military awards such as the Congressional Medal of Honor. The Court found that such statements were entitled to at least some level of constitutional protection even if they were deliberate falsehoods.

Just as some "unprotected" speech began to receive constitutional protection, it also became clear that under some circumstances "protected" speech could be the basis of government sanctions. For example, normally it would be considered core protected speech to characterize an elected official as a fool. But if a member of the official's staff says the same thing to another staff member, he can be fired from his government job for insubordination. Thus, under some circumstances, virtually any message might be unprotected in the sense that it could constitutionally be subjected to government sanctions. For this reason, we need to be very careful in referring to unprotected speech. Strictly speaking, a message should be considered unprotected only if it could be made subject to sanctions when communicated from one private citizen to another on private property. Even then, we have to keep in mind that whether the sanction would be permitted probably depends not just on the content of the message but on some of the surrounding circumstances, such as whether it was an intentional falsehood.

Despite all of these qualifications, however, it remains clear that some categories of messages are constitutionally disfavored and may be regulated by the state in a broad range of circumstances. Other kinds of messages can be regulated but only on a more limited basis. This distinction is still important. The first step in analyzing any First Amendment problem is to run through the checklist of "unprotected" categories of speech, to see if any of them covers the message in question.

B.   Regulation of "Fully Protected" Speech

Speech that does not fall into any of these disfavored categories is still subject to some kinds of regulation. Roughly speaking, we can divide the permissible regulations into two classes. First, regardless of the type of speech, the government is entitled to impose some restrictions on *methods* of communication. The classic example is that it can forbid the use of loudspeakers in the middle of the night, whatever the message may be. These restrictions on the "time, place, or manner" of speech are subject to some judicial scrutiny, but are likely to be upheld if at all reasonable.

The other type of regulation is less easy to describe because it tends to involve some combination of the message and the surrounding circumstances, such as the location of the speech or the identity of the speaker. Usually, the regulation involves some special relationship between the government and the speaker, the location, or the medium. For instance, the speaker may be a student in a public high school, or may be seeking to use the internal mail system in a government office, or may be a government-licensed broadcasting station. Because of the nexus between the speech and some specific government activity, the government has special regulatory powers that it would not possess over private individuals having a conversation on private property. The crucial issues in this type of case are the extent to which the Court really regards the situation as falling outside the "normal" First Amendment rules, and how much it is willing to defer to government decisionmakers on factual issues.

The extreme case is probably the military: the Court considers the military to be a separate (and unequal) society with only marginal protection by the First Amendment. It also is highly reluctant to second-guess the Pentagon on any issue of policy. Thus, not only are the tests phrased in ways that are highly favorable to the military, but the Court leans over backwards in applying the tests so as not to impair military discipline. If Congress wanted to pass a statute virtually eliminating the First Amendment, all it would have to do would be to draft the entire population into the military. In less dramatic ways, the rights of high school students, public employees, and broadcasters are all abnormal. These abnormal categories give rise to considerable doctrinal tension, since there are always arguments for bringing them into accord with the "normal rules."

C.   Critiques of Current Doctrine

Naturally, the Supreme Court's First Amendment decisions are subject to the usual run of doctrinal critiques, arguing that specific doctrines need to be rethought or have been misapplied in particular cases. We will be seeing a good deal of this kind of criticism all through this book, much of it from dissenting Justices. But there are also two much broader attacks on the Court's work product.

One critique is that the Court has allowed the First Amendment to degenerate into a mass of technicalities, bearing too much resemblance to the Internal Revenue Code or the Rule Against Perpetuities. There is no doubt that the doctrine has become quite elaborate and technical. The Court's view is that these detailed rules provide instruction to lower courts and give government officials and speakers clear guidelines. At some times this venture seems more successful than at others. But even when it works well, one result of this process is that judicial decisions become more technical, which is to say, more removed from the kinds of arguments that would guide a layperson in assessing the situation. For example, in discussing both flag burning and cross burning, the Court seemed more concerned with how to refine its rule against content discrimination (discussed in the next chapter) than with the commonsense arguments for and against allowing the speech. It would be unfortunate if the Court became so immersed in technicalities that it lost sight of the larger social significance of its work.

The second criticism goes to the substance rather than the form of the Court's decisions. The thrust of the Court's opinions (speaking at a very high level of generality) is to unshackle the marketplace of ideas. Critics argue that this approach raises the same issues as the deregulation of any other market. Like other markets, the marketplace of ideas reflects the current distribution of wealth and power. Those who lack access to these resources have little impact on what is said in the major media. Also, what the market produces is based on the tastes that people already have. Those who are deeply critical of the present distribution of wealth and power, and of the current culture of our society, fear that unrestricted free speech will merely reproduce the existing inequalities. Against these critics, others argue that free speech can be a powerful destabilizing force, operating to foment social change. They also question whether the government, which also reflects the existing distribution of power and wealth, could truly be expected to use its power over speech in order to champion the cause of the downtrodden. Instead, it might simply use the banner of social reform as an excuse to entrench its own power.

Because First Amendment doctrine has become so robust, defining the boundaries of the doctrine is increasingly important. Most human activities involves communication. First Amendment doctrine requires more rigorous scrutiny than is typically applied to economic regulations today. But as the scope of First Amendment coverage expands, there is correspondingly less room for governments to engage in regulation of subjects that they traditionally regulated. Such concerns were raised in *National Institute of Family and Life Advocates [NIFLA] v. Becerra*.[4] In *NIFLA*, the majority struck down a California law that requires clinics that do not provide abortions to advise women that the state California provides free or low-cost services, including abortions, and give them a phone number to call. The four dissenters argued that law fell under the well-established power of the states to regulate health care providers. According to the dissent, "[i]n the name of the First Amendment, the majority today treads into territory where the pre-New Deal, as well as the post-New Deal, Court refused to go." We can expect more disputes about the outer boundaries of First

---

[4] ___ U.S. ___, 138 S.Ct. 2361, 201 L.Ed.2d 835 (2018).

Amendment doctrine, given that in the Internet era, transmission of information is so central to the economy.

IV. The Road Ahead

In most of the remainder of the book, we will probe the Supreme Court doctrine in greater detail. As we do so, we will continually return to the problem of First Amendment values and to the complaints of the Court's critics. Before we begin our voyage, here is a brief preview.

A.   Roadmap to the Book

As you can see from the table of contents, the book is divided into four parts. Part I deals with foundational issues, such as those discussed in this chapter. In Chapter 2, we focus on one of the key principles in current First Amendment doctrine, the rule against content discrimination. Chapter 3 then considers a battery of tools available to the First Amendment lawyer, which more or less cut across doctrinal areas. For example, the overbreadth doctrine is a powerful weapon that can be used in a wide range of contexts.

Part II turns to the categories of "unprotected speech." More accurately, it deals with categories of disfavored messages, which the government can regulate except in certain circumstances. Historically, the most important disfavored category has been advocacy of illegal action. This is the subject of Chapter 4, which also takes a more detailed look at some key First Amendment history. Chapters 5 through 8 deal in turn with defamation; offensive communications and hate speech; obscenity and pornography; and commercial speech.

When it seeks to regulate speech outside of these categories, the government bears a heavier burden of proof. In Part III, we consider the permissible regulation of "protected speech"—that is, of messages that at least in some circumstances are wholly immune from regulation. In other circumstances, however, the same message may be subject to regulation, usually if the circumstances include some nexus with government institutions. Specific topics include the public forum doctrine (Chapter 9), speech in the public sector (Chapter 10), and media law (Chapter 11). Chapter 12 covers the related topics of constitutional protection for group activities and for the electoral process.

Part IV turns to the topic of religion, with the Free Exercise Clause covered in Chapter 13 and the Establishment Clause in Chapter 14. Paralleling the discussion of free speech in this chapter, these two chapters trace historical developments and consider normative perspectives before turning to doctrinal issues.

B. Pervasive Issues

In working through the material ahead, it may be helpful to keep in mind some problems that the Court has found itself struggling with again and again. The following three problems seem ubiquitous in First Amendment doctrine.

First, to what extent should the rules take into account the varying social values of different kinds of speech? Regardless of which list of First Amendment values we adopt, it is obvious that some speech involves those values more than others. So it seems reasonable to provide a higher degree of protection to speech that is, for example, closely related to the political process or to individual self-realization. But the contrary fear is that these subjective distinctions cannot be made in a principled way, so that judges are likely to simply give more protection to speech that fits their own tastes. It also can be argued that it is up to the public to decide which speech it believes valuable, not the judiciary.

Second, how important is it to limit judicial discretion? The answer plainly depends on one's general views about the judicial role, but it also involves some concerns specific to the First Amendment. Opponents of discretion put forward a view of the distinctive dynamics of speech regulation. They argue that firm rules are needed to give judges backbone in times of public hysteria when the First Amendment is most needed. They also worry that small exceptions to rules will create a "slippery slope," inevitably leading to broader repression. Finally, they think that clear rules are needed to give advance notice to speakers, thereby preventing the chilling effect that legal uncertainty might have.

Those who favor discretion do not dismiss these concerns, but believe they are overblown, and that the advantages of more sensitive, nuanced decision-making outweigh those of clear mechanical rules. A related question, to put it somewhat bluntly, is how suspicious judges should be about the intentions of government officials. Some Justices seem to presume that government officials are acting responsibly, not merely using reasonable sounding justifications as pretexts for censorship. Other Justices fear the worst in every case. They want prophylactic rules that will ensure against government abuse.

Third, how seriously do we take the harms caused by speech? Although the language of "balancing" is out of favor, in case after case the Court has had to decide if particular state interests justify regulation of speech, and if so, to what extent. Justices who care passionately about personal reputation may take a different view of defamation law than those who do not; those who think political fundraising is distorting the political process will approach cases differently than those who see no problem. More generally, some Justices tend to be sanguine about the effects of speech, on what could be called the "sticks and stones" principle Others find the harms far more serious, and are correspondingly willing to countenance greater regulation of speech.

Many books have been written about First Amendment theory; this is not one of them. It is primarily aimed at explaining legal doctrine, not at setting forth a philosophy of free expression. As a result, we will spend far more time talking about cases than about what might be considered deeper issues, such as judicial methodology or fundamental philosophical principles.

Although I have attempted to be as even-handed as possible, a book of this kind cannot be value-free. I have had to make numerous choices about how to organize the material, what to include and what to leave out, which arguments are important enough to discuss, and which criticisms of the Court's work to discuss. All of these choices inevitably involve my own viewpoint on First Amendment law. But the book's goals are description and analysis. rather than advocacy.

Ideally, the reader will take away from this book a clear understanding of the Supreme Court's rulings across the full range of First Amendment issues. The reader should also have some sense for how these rulings do or do not fit together. Finally, I hope, the reader will be aware of the scholarly debates in each area. Thus, the reader should be in a position to make an informed judgment about current doctrine. We begin in the next chapter with the central doctrinal concept of content neutrality.

FURTHER READINGS

Michael Kent Curtis, Free Speech, "The People's Darling Privilege": Struggles for Freedom of Expression in American History (2000).

Stanley E. Fish, There's No Such Thing as Free Speech, And It's a Good Thing, Too (1994).

Owen M. Fiss, The Irony of Free Speech (1996).

Richard W. Garnett and Andrew Koppelman, First Amendment Stories (2012).

Jeremy Kessler, *The Early Years for First Amendment* Lochnerism, 116 Colum. L. Rev. 1915 (2016).

Leonard W. Levy, Emergence of a Free Press (1985).

Robert Post and Amanda Shanor, *Adam Smith's First Amendment*, 128 Harv. L. Rev. F. 165 (2015).

David M. Rabban, Free Speech in Its Forgotten Years (1997).

Martin H. Redish, Freedom of Expression: A Critical Analysis (1984).

Frederick Schauer, Speech: A Philosophical Enquiry (1982).

Cass R. Sunstein, Democracy and the Problem of Free Speech (1993).

Adam Winkler, *Free Speech Federalism*, 108 Mich. L. Rev. 153 (2009).

Chapter 2

THE CONTENT DISTINCTION

The content distinction is the modern Supreme Court's closest approach to a unified First Amendment doctrine. Government regulations linked to the content of speech generally receive severe judicial scrutiny. In contrast, when government is regulating speech, but the regulation is unrelated to content, the level of scrutiny is lower. Within the category of content-based regulations, those relating to the viewpoint expressed by the speaker are more severely disfavored than those based on subject matter or other message characteristics. As we will see, these rules are subject to exceptions and qualifications, and are sometimes applied oddly. Nevertheless, they do provide overall principles that apply in a broad range of cases.

We will begin by mapping out these rules, before turning to more technical issues, such as the exceptions to the rules and the definitions of the various forms of content discrimination. We then evaluate the scholarly debate over the content distinction.

I. The Content Distinction in Operation

A stark description of the content distinction, like that given above, can give only a rough idea of its actual operation. In this section, we will examine the case that first clearly articulated the content distinction. Then we will look at sample cases that show how the Court views content-based regulations and the very different approach it takes to content-neutral regulations.

A. Origins

The content distinction found its first clear expression in *Police Department of Chicago v. Mosley*.[1] The facts were simple enough. Earl Mosley, a postal worker, frequently picketed a Chicago high school with a sign accusing the school of having an African American quota and practicing "black discrimination." Seven months after he had started picketing, the city enacted an ordinance prohibiting picketing near any school just before, after, or during school hours. A proviso exempted "the peaceful picketing of any school involved in a labor dispute." Mosley's principal argument was that the ordinance was overbroad because it prohibited even peaceful picketing near a school. The Supreme Court did not, however, reach the overbreadth

---

[1]   408 U.S. 92 (1972).

issue. Instead, it adopted Mosley's fallback argument that the labor picketing exception denied him equal protection.

One of the oddities of the *Mosley* opinion is its reliance on the Equal Protection Clause, rather than the First Amendment. Moreover, the treatment of the equality issue was peculiar. Normally, violations of equal protection can be cured in two ways, either by extending an exemption to cover all situations equally, or by eliminating the exemption, so that the regulation applies equally to everyone. But the Court did not consider the possibility of curing the constitutional flaw by eliminating the labor picketing exemption. This may be an indication that, though it was concerned about the ordinance's unequal treatment of different kinds of picketing, the Court was actually thinking at least as much in terms of free speech as equal protection.

The Chicago ordinance, as construed by the Court, applied only to "labor picketing of a school involved in a labor dispute." Under this interpretation, for instance, the ordinance would not allow picketing by parents opposing a school strike, but only by the strikers. This is a clear-cut example of discrimination on the basis of viewpoint. But the Court's opinion went far beyond condemning viewpoint discrimination. Rather, it proclaimed a much broader principle: "[A]bove all else, the First Amendment means that government has no power to restrict expression because of its message, its ideas, its subject matter, or its content." As the Court explained,

> [U]nder the Equal Protection Clause, not to mention the First Amendment itself, government may not grant the use of a forum to people whose views it finds acceptable, but deny use to those wishing to express less favored or more controversial views. And it may not select which issues are worth discussing or debating in public facilities. There is an "equality of status in the field of ideas," and government must afford all points of view an equal opportunity to be heard. . . . Selective exclusions from a public forum may not be based on content alone, and may not be justified by reference to content alone.

Although serving as the foundation for a new approach to First Amendment law, *Mosley* raised as many questions as it settled. The first question was the scope of the principle. As the Court knew full well, settled law did allow certain kinds of regulation on the basis of content. For example, the government can ban direct incitement to immediate violence. The Court clearly had no intention of overruling all of the prior decisions allowing such types of government regulation, but it failed to explain their relationship to the new rule of content neutrality. It also failed to define exactly how to identify content-based discrimination.

Finally, the Court never really explained the basis for its rule. On the face of things, it is not clear that distinctions based on subject matter should always be considered particularly troublesome. For instance, there seems to be nothing suspicious about the decisions of the drafters of the National Labor Relations Act and the Taft-Hartley Act to regulate labor picketing but not antiwar picketing. One would expect as much from labor statutes. Similarly, restrictions on legal advertising are surely not suspect because they fail to cover dental advertising. Nor did the Court account for a seemingly perverse aspect of its decision: in the name of the First Amendment, it struck down the Chicago ordinance because the ordinance failed to prohibit *enough* speech. Why, in terms of First Amendment values, should we prefer an ordinance that bans all picketing near schools over one that suppresses less speech?

Before we can address these questions we need a better idea of how the Court applies the content distinction. The next two subsections provide an illuminating contrast between how the Court treats content-based regulations and content-neutral regulations.

B. Content Regulation

In Chapter 1, we mentioned two of the Court's most prominent opinions on content discrimination. In *Texas v. Johnson*,[2] the Court reversed the defendant's conviction for burning an American flag. The statute prohibited actions that "deface, damage, or otherwise physically mistreat [the flag] in a way that the actor knows will seriously offend one or more persons likely to observe or discover his action." Justice Brennan viewed the statute as a rank example of content discrimination. The statute did not forbid all deliberate combustion of the flag. For instance, it allowed soiled flags to be burned as a method of ceremonial disposal. Because it allowed the flag to be burned only for patriotic reasons, while banning the same action when conducted as an anti-government protest, the effect of the statute was that "the flag itself may be used as a symbol . . . only in one direction." To uphold the statute would be allow the government to "prescribe what shall be orthodox" by authorizing the use of the flag only to convey patriotic messages.

In Chapter 1, we also considered the cross-burning case, *R.A.V. v. City of St. Paul*.[3] The St. Paul ordinance criminalized any communicative act (specifically including burning crosses and Nazi swastikas), if the speaker "knows or has reasonable grounds to know"

---

[2]   491 U.S. 397 (1989).
[3]   505 U.S. 377 (1992).

that the action "arouses anger, alarm or resentment in others on the basis of race, color, creed, religion or gender." The state court had construed the ordinance to apply only to "fighting words," which the Court has previously held to be outside the protection of the First Amendment. (For more on the fighting words doctrine and a fuller discussion of *R.A.V.*, see the discussion of hate speech in Chapter 6.) Justice Scalia's majority opinion viewed the ordinance as impermissible content discrimination. The ordinance allowed abusive communications, "no matter how vicious or severe," unless they related to one of the prohibited categories. Under the ordinance it was perfectly permissible to use fighting words "to express hostility, for example, on the basis of political affiliation, union membership, or homosexuality." Indeed, Justice Scalia considered the ordinance to be even more fatally flawed, because it prohibited only the use of fighting words to support racist or sexist viewpoints, not to oppose those viewpoints. Thus, it was an example of impermissible viewpoint discrimination.

The Court's distaste for content regulation can be seen especially clearly in the "Son of Sam" case.[4] New York passed a statute to prohibit a serial killer who called himself "Son of Sam" and other criminals from profiting from books about their crimes, at the expense of their victims. This is not on its face an unreasonable regulation. It does not prohibit the criminal from publishing a book about the crime but merely reallocates the profits to the victim. In some sense, the criminal's commercial exploitation of the crime could be considered a second "assault." But the Court unanimously overturned the statute because it was based on content: the criminal could profit from writing a book on any subject except for his crimes. Applying strict scrutiny, the Court found the statute to be poorly connected with the state's "undisputed compelling interest in ensuring that criminals do not profit from their crimes." The statute was also overbroad because it would have reached such works as *The Autobiography of Malcolm X*, Thoreau's *Civil Disobedience*, and even the *Confessions* of St. Augustine, all of which describe crimes. The Court detected hints of "the specter that the government may effectively drive certain ideas or viewpoints from the marketplace."

The crucial point here is not that the law placed a financial burden on authors but that it singled some of them out. Books are not immune from the financial burdens caused by *uniform* government regulations. Alas, there is no First Amendment defense against the application of the Internal Revenue Code to book

---

[4] *Simon & Schuster, Inc. v. Members of New York State Crime Victims Board*, 502 U.S. 105 (1991).

royalties! But a special tax on books on particular subjects would run afoul of the ban on content discrimination.

C. Content Neutrality

In contrast to the cases we have just seen, the Court takes a far more relaxed attitude toward content-neutral regulations. The leading case is *United States v. O'Brien.*[5] The defendant had burned his draft card in front of a large crowd as a protest against the Vietnam war. He was convicted for willfully burning the card. The Court had little difficulty in upholding the ban on draft-card burning as a valid method of ensuring that draft cards would be available when someone needed to check a person's draft status.

In his opinion for the Court, Chief Justice Warren announced the following test, in language that has been frequently quoted: "[W]e think it clear that a government regulation is sufficiently justified if it is within the constitutional power of the Government; if it furthers an important or substantial governmental interest; if the governmental interest is unrelated to the suppression of free expression; and if the incidental restriction on alleged First Amendment freedoms is no greater than is essential to the furtherance of that interest." To rearrange the terms a bit, the *O'Brien* rule is that a content-neutral regulation is valid if it is narrowly tailored to a significant government interest. In a concurring opinion, Justice Harlan suggested an additional requirement, that the regulation avoid "entirely preventing a 'speaker' from reaching a significant audience with whom he could not otherwise lawfully communicate."

A refinement of the *O'Brien* test was applied in *Ward v. Rock Against Racism.*[6] Because of a series of noisy concerts in Central Park, New York City adopted an ordinance requiring musicians to use city sound equipment and a government sound technician. The Court applied the following three-part test:

1. The regulation must be justified "without reference to the content of the regulated speech."

2. It must be "narrowly tailored to serve a significant governmental interest."

3. Finally, it must leave open "ample alternative channels for communication of the information."

The first two elements are derived from Warren's opinion in *O'Brien*, the third from Harlan's concurrence. The Court readily concluded that the government's interest in noise control was content

---

[5] 391 U.S. 367 (1968).

[6] 491 U.S. 781 (1989).

neutral, and that the regulation was a reasonable method of keeping the noise level under control.

The Court emphasized in *Ward* that the "narrow tailoring" requirement does not require the government to use the very least restrictive alternative. A content-neutral regulation is not invalid because there is some imaginable alternative that a judge likes better. Rather, the government needs only to show that its regulatory interest "would be achieved less effectively" without the regulation. "To be sure," the Court added, "this standard does not mean that a time, place, or manner regulation may burden substantially more speech than is necessary to further the government's legitimate interests." Putting these remarks together, the upshot seems to be that a regulation is too broad if it could achieve the government's purposes effectively while covering *substantially* less speech.

Perhaps the most typical aspect of the decisions in *O'Brien* and *Ward* is that they uphold the government regulation. Except for statutes that entirely foreclose a traditional channel of communication such as lawn signs, the Court rarely invalidates a regulation once it has found it to be content neutral. Even the presumption against closing a channel of communication is unreliable: the Court had little difficulty in upholding a ban on attaching posters to utility poles.[7] But content-based restrictions are far less likely to survive judicial review. Thus, the outcome of a given case often turns almost completely on whether the regulation is characterized as content based.

II. Refining the Content Distinction

The preceding discussion illustrates the importance of the content distinction, but leaves basic questions unanswered, such as how to define content neutrality and how to distinguish between viewpoint and subject matter discrimination. Also, we need to consider how the concept of content discrimination applies to "unprotected" speech, where reference to content is sometimes not only permitted but required. Finally, a look at other exceptions is in order.

A. Defining Content Neutrality

Some of the difficulties in defining content neutrality can also be seen in *Barnes v. Glen Theatre, Inc.*[8] The plaintiffs challenged a public indecency law forbidding nudity. The state courts had construed the law to require "go-go" dancers in the plaintiffs' bar to wear "pasties and G-strings." The various opinions in the case took

---

[7] Compare *Members of City Council v. Taxpayers for Vincent,* 466 U.S. 789 (1984) (utility posters), with *City of Ladue v. Gilleo,* 512 U.S. 43 (1994) (lawn signs).

[8] 501 U.S. 560 (1991).

four different positions regarding content neutrality. Chief Justice Rehnquist's plurality opinion found the statute to be content neutral, because the state had "not banned nude dancing as such, but has proscribed public nudity across the board." Hence, he applied the *O'Brien* test, upholding the application of the state law to nude dancing. Justice Scalia agreed that the statute was content neutral, but argued that no constitutional scrutiny at all was required because the ordinance was a "general law regulating conduct and not specifically directed at expression." Justice Souter, the swing voter, considered the state's interest in public morality to be too content-related to satisfy the *O'Brien* test. He found the statute to be justified, however, because nude dancing contributed to prostitution, sexual assaults, and other criminal activities in the vicinity of bars. He considered this to be a "secondary effect" of the dancing, as opposed to the immediate impact on the audience.

The four dissenters, led by Justice White, considered *O'Brien* inapplicable. They argued that the purpose of prohibiting other forms of public nudity was to protect against offense to bystanders, but that this "could not possibly be the purpose of preventing nude dancing in theaters and barrooms since the viewers are exclusively consenting adults who pay money to see these dances." The reason for applying the statute to nude dancing could only be "to protect the viewers from what the State believes is the harmful message that nude dancing communicates." In the dissent's view, the "nudity is itself an expressive component of the dance, not merely incidental 'conduct'."

The Court revisited the issue of nude dancing nine years later, but the Justices once again proved unable to agree on a rationale. In *City of Erie v. Pap's A.M.*,[9] the plurality opinion by Justice O'Connor upheld the ordinance on the basis of the secondary effects of erotic dancing, including its tendency to attract prostitution and crime to the locale. Scalia and Thomas once again concluded that a general ban on public nudity regulates conduct rather than speech and is therefore immune from First Amendment scrutiny. In dissent, Justice Souter found an inadequate factual basis to support the city's concerns. Justices Stevens and Ginsburg argued that the ban was content-based since it was aimed entirely at erotic dancing rather than other nude dancing (such as in serious theatrical productions). Apparently, the Court had made little progress toward agreeing on how to apply the content neutrality rule in this context.

In the nude dancing cases, the Court was unable to agree on a single standard for defining content neutrality. Instead, individual Justices have endorsed various tests, none of which is entirely satisfactory. One test, used by Chief Justice Rehnquist in *Barnes*, is

---

[9]   529 U.S. 277 (2000).

whether the law would equally apply if no message at all was being communicated by the conduct. For example, the draft card law would have applied equally to the use of a draft card to start a campfire, while the public decency law would have applied equally if the unclothed women had been serving drinks instead of dancing. But this test can produce odd discrepancies between various media. A ban on physical nudity is content neutral, but a ban on nudity in videos is not, because the state's interest would not be equally implicated by a blank videocassette. Also, Rehnquist's opinion begs the question of whether a ban on public nudity is always in a sense content-based. The general ban on indecent exposure is based on the offensiveness of public nudity. Offensiveness is usually considered a content-related characteristic, because the degree of offense is likely to relate to the conduct's perceived meaning.

Another test, used by Justice Souter, focuses on the causal theory behind the regulation, and asks whether the persuasive effect of the message is a necessary part of the government's justification for regulating. This approach is problematic. For instance, *Mosley* might not qualify as an example of content discrimination, since the reason for the labor exemption might simply have been the city's desire to avoid interfering with union-management disputes, rather than the persuasive effect of labor picketing on its audience.

Alternatively, we might ask with Justice White whether the real motive of the law is disapproval of the message it communicates. A closely related alternative is to look at whether the law on its face draws distinctions based on content. Both approaches are problematic. The "purpose" approach requires proof of the intentions behind the law, which are often hard to document. Also, it may be debatable whether an otherwise valid law should be invalid because of legislative motivation; the *O'Brien* Court specifically rejected such an argument. Looking at the face of the statute seems both too broad and too narrow—too broad, because as Justice Souter points out, there may be non-suspect reasons for keying the regulation to content, and too narrow, because it allows clever drafters to target disfavored speech, so long as they do so covertly.

The Court refined the test for content neutrality in *Reed v. Town of Gilbert*.[10] The town had adopted a sign code that divided signs into various categories of signs based on the type of information they convey and then subjected each category to different restrictions. For instance, signs directing the public to meetings of a nonprofit had stricter limits than other types of signs such as political signs or ideological signs. As an example of how the categories were delineated, political signs were defined as temporary signs designed

---

[10] ___ U.S. ___, 135 S.Ct. 2218, 192 L.Ed.2d 236 (2015).

to influence the outcome of an election. Political signs could be up sixteen square feet on residential property, while directional signs could be no larger six square feet.

The Court defined a law as content based if it "applies to particular speech because of the topic discussed or the idea or message expressed", either on its face or by defining regulated speech by its function or purpose." In addition, laws are considered content based if they "cannot be 'justified without reference to the content of the regulated speech,' or that were adopted by the government 'because of disagreement with the message [the speech] conveys.' " All such laws are subject to strict scrutiny, which the sign ordinance could not survive.

In dissent, Justice Kagan (joined by Breyer and Ginsburg) argued that the Court's definition jeopardized countless innocuous sign restrictions, such as laws allowing houses to have illuminated address signs but not to illuminate other signs. The dissenters saw little risk that such distinctions were covertly aimed at suppressing ideas.

Note that the majority defines content neutrality very narrowly. To be content neutral, a law must neither (a) draw any distinctions based on communicative content, nor (b) have a purpose related to communicative content. Any other regulation of private speech is subject to strict scrutiny. Absent a compelling interest, if the state allows any category of messages, it must allow all categories of messages equally, even if there seems to be a commonsense justification for treating some messages (such as address signs) differently.

It is not clear how the *Reed* test would be applied to the nude dancing issue discussed above. Dance is a medium in which physical conduct is especially closely connected with the "message" of the dance. On that basis, one might argues that nudity is part of the erotic message of the dancing in question, and that the purpose of the ordinance was precisely to suppress or at least temper that message. On the other hand, one might argue that the state objected to nudity in other contexts as well, making it arguably independent of communicative content.

If taken to its full extent, the *Reed* test might even overturn the *O'Brien* case. It's true that the application of the law did not depend on whether the person burning the card was trying to communicate a message. But the law did depend on the importance of the information contained in the card itself. The government was providing special protection for that document because it considered the information particularly important. If the draft card was a blank piece of paper, the legislative purpose would not apply. The same would be true of a state law that prohibited defacing or altering a license plate. Should those laws really be considered content-based and subject to strict scrutiny? Or what about a law that prohibited defacing address signs in order to avoid confusion to mail carriers or other public services. Should those be subject to strict scrutiny?

Lower courts have tended to apply *Reed* only in similar factual settings, leaving the broader question of how to define content neutrality unsettled. In many cases, however, the various definitions coincide, so there is no practical problem except in the exceptional cases like *Barnes* where they diverge. A rough working test is whether the government's interest would be present even if the speech was in a language unintelligible to listeners or involved completely abstract images. (But this simple test doesn't always work. Consider nude dancing, for instance, or a ban on heckling speakers.)

B. Defining Viewpoint Discrimination

Although the Court disapproves of each category of content discrimination, it disapproves most intensely of viewpoint discrimination. Yet, it has not always been easy to distinguish discrimination based on viewpoint from discrimination based on subject matter. In *R.A.V.*, for example, Justice Scalia considered the St. Paul ordinance to be content-based because of the following hypothetical:

> One could hold up a sign saying, for example, that all "anti-Catholic bigots" are misbegotten; but not that all "papists" are, for that would insult and provoke violence "on the basis of religion" [another prohibited category in the ordinance]. St. Paul has no such authority to license one side of a debate to fight freestyle, while requiring the other to follow Marquis of Queensberry rules.

Justice Stevens, however, did not perceive discrimination on the basis of viewpoint, since all racial groups alike were prohibited from using racist epithets against each other.

A later example of this difficulty is *Rosenberger v. Rector and Visitors of the University of Virginia*.[11] The University provided funding for certain student activities, including printing costs, but excluded any work that "primarily promotes or manifests a particular belief in or about a deity or an ultimate reality." Five Justices considered this to be a viewpoint distinction. The four dissenters, however, considered the regulation to be clearly based on subject matter. Rather than singling out any single religious

---

[11] 515 U.S. 819 (1995).

perspective, it applied to all religious advocacy including that by atheists and agnostics.

The phrase "viewpoint discrimination" is not self-explanatory. Presumably, the idea is that some perspectives on a topic are allowed while opposing views are not. One problem is that the Justices may disagree about the interpretation of the speech regulation. Such disagreements are not surprising, since the Justices are seeking to determine whether hypothetical "opposing viewpoints" would be covered, and it is not always clear how the regulation would be applied to these hypothetical cases.

The other problem is deciding what counts as an *opposing* viewpoint, because this depends on how we conceptualize the relevant debate. The easiest picture involves one person affirming and the other denying a proposition. A statute that distinguishes between a statement and its negation is clearly viewpoint-based. This is the standard used by the dissent in *Rosenberger*. ("God exists" and "God does not exist" were both covered by the funding exclusion.) But sometimes the Justices seem to use a broader concept of what constitutes an opposing view. In *R.A.V.*, Stevens was picturing a dispute between members of two racial groups, and he observed that the St. Paul ordinance would apply equally to both. But Scalia pictured a dispute between supporters and opponents of racism, and he concluded that only the racist would be covered. In *Rosenberger*, the dissent considered the opposite viewpoint of "abortion *is* a sin" to be "abortion is *not* a sin." But the majority apparently considered another opposing viewpoint to be "women have a constitutional right to an abortion." Perhaps the only thing that is truly clear is that the Court has not yet found a satisfactory definition of viewpoint regulation.

C. Application to "Unprotected" Speech

The "rule" against content regulation is violated by all of the speech regulations discussed in Part II of this book. The government constantly regulates speech on the basis of content, with the Court's blessings. Much of the regulation is based not only on subject matter but viewpoint: "George is a liar and a thief" is libelous; "George is honest" is not. Content is used to define all the categories of "unprotected" speech—libel, incitement to violence, obscenity, fighting words, and false advertising. Although these broad categories of speech are no longer considered wholly beyond constitutional protection, nevertheless the Court still allows substantial regulation in each of these content-defined categories. Thus, content can clearly be used to define categories of "unprotected" speech.

More troubling is the question of content distinctions within each of these categories. Suppose the state decides to impose liability only on certain kinds of libel—perhaps those against private citizens, or those including accusations of criminal conduct. If the state can impose liability for a whole class of libels without offending the Constitution, does it always follow that it can limit liability to only a subcategory?

The answer given in *R.A.V.* was "no," or perhaps better, "not necessarily." St. Paul could have prohibited all fighting words, but chose to prohibit only some; it was precisely this restricted scope that the Court found unconstitutional. But *R.A.V.* did articulate two exceptions to the rule against content discrimination within an "unprotected" category. First, when the basis of discrimination "consists entirely of the very reason the entire class of speech at issue is proscribable, no significant danger of idea or viewpoint discrimination exists." Since the trait identifying the entire class is considered a constitutionally permissible basis to regulate, the state can confine its regulation to the most extreme forms of the trait. For example, because one characteristic of obscenity is being "patently offensive," the state can limit the prohibition to the most offensive sexual expression within the obscenity category. But the state cannot limit its coverage to obscene works that contain only certain political messages. On the same theory, a state could single out the most extreme forms of disparagements under its libel laws.

Second, according to *R.A.V.*, the government can define a subclass based on secondary effects. For example, a state could permit all live sex shows except those involving minors. More generally, the state can use any basis for selection of which unprotected speech to regulate, so long as the selection is not even arguably based on disagreement with the speaker's message. The main point, according to *R.A.V.*, is that the type of selectivity must be "such that there is no realistic possibility that official suppression of ideas is afoot." Presumably for this reason, the state can legitimately choose to regulate advertising in one industry but not another, or in particular communication media rather than others.

Although not considered in *R.A.V.*, another type of selectivity would also seem to be possible. In libel law, for instance, the Court has itself drawn distinctions based on content. For instance, the Court permits states to allow recovery for defamation of private individuals on a lesser showing than would be required for defamation of public officials. Presumably, if a state libel law draws this same distinction, it cannot be attacked for engaging in content discrimination.

D. Other Exceptions

Apart from the traditional categories of unprotected speech, there seem to be two clearly established exceptions to the rule of content neutrality, and at least one other possible exception. One established exception, which was unsuccessfully invoked in the "Son of Sam" case, is for compelling government interests. This exception essentially amounts to a "catch-all" addition to the list of categories of unprotected speech. To satisfy the test, the content-based speech restriction must be narrowly tailored to serve a compelling state interest. For instance, as we will see in Chapter 12, the Court has upheld some regulations of campaign speech based on the government's compelling interest in preventing the appearance or reality of corruption. Although the Court has recognized other government interests as compelling, it has generally found speech restrictions to be sufficiently narrowly tailored only in connection with political campaigns. Some of the unprotected categories themselves, however, may be partly based on the existence of a compelling government interest. For instance, the category of incitement to violence may be based on the compelling interest in preventing physical assaults.

A second well-established (if somewhat ill-defined) exception covers speech with some nexus to government operations. For instance, the government is entitled to control the curriculum and atmosphere in the public schools, even by restricting the students' speech. It can also create special forums limited to particular subject matters. Stretching the idea of a government nexus a bit, we might even use this category to cover regulation of radio and T.V., if we consider the airwaves to be a publicly owned resource that the broadcaster is being authorized to use. These situations are covered in Part III of this book. The doctrines are complex, but in practice the courts may be tending toward the use of a reasonableness or proportionality standard.

A third, perhaps more dubious, exception may cover regulations with a sufficiently long historical pedigree. In *Burson v. Freeman*,[12] the Court upheld a state law prohibiting vote solicitation within a hundred feet of the entrance to a polling place. This is seemingly viewpoint-related discrimination—for example, it was entirely permissible to tell voters to go home rather than voting, ask them questions about how they had voted, or engage in other speech on the subject of the election. Nevertheless, the Court (particularly Justice Scalia, the swing voter), seemed impressed by the long history of such restrictions, which go back almost as far as the secret ballot itself.

---

[12]   504 U.S. 191 (1992).

Similarly, in *Marsh v. Chambers*,[13] the Court considered the practice of having paid chaplains open legislative sessions with prayer. The Court rejected an Establishment Clause challenge to the practice on the basis of its long history, going back to the very first Congress. A free speech claim by an atheist who wanted to address the legislature presumably would have been equally unavailing. Yet, the practice embodied outright viewpoint discrimination, since only religious messages were allowed. (No atheists were likely to receive invitations to open the session with celebrations of the purely secular nature of human virtue.) If distinguishing between religious and non-religious perspectives is impermissible viewpoint discrimination, it is hard to see how the state could justify its exclusion of all secular viewpoints from the opening ceremony, except on the basis of long and unquestioned history. No doubt the traditional categories of unprotected speech also rest in part on such history. But whether this should be the basis of a general exception to the rule against content distinctions is doubtful.

III. The Future of the Content Distinction

As we have seen, there are some significant difficulties in applying the content distinction, at least in a number of borderline cases. Should a concept that is so difficult to define play such a central role in First Amendment doctrine? We begin by looking at the scholarly debate over the issue, and then offer some remarks about how the doctrine might be used more constructively.

A.   The Scholarly Debate

The Court has not devoted much effort to discussion of the merits of its approach to content regulation, but a substantial scholarly literature now addresses that issue. Without going into much detail, we will survey some of the major arguments.

Scholars have pointed to four possible justifications for the content distinction. All of these justifications have some degree of plausibility, but they are at best rough generalizations. They point to harmful characteristics that may be more common with content-based regulations, but some content-based regulations are free of the characteristics and some content-neutral regulations are tainted.

One justification is that the First Amendment generally takes an anti-paternalistic attitude toward the recipients of communications. Listeners are expected to decide for themselves what they want to hear and whether they believe it. Those who are offended by speech are expected to take care of themselves. The audience is not considered to be in need of protection. Because there

---

[13]   463 U.S. 783 (1983).

is a strong presumption that communicative impact is "no problem," a statute that relies for its justification on such an impact must carry a heavy burden. The difficulty with this argument for content neutrality is that it is too narrow. It applies to content restrictions only when they are based on the forbidden causal link. But this is quite often not true, especially for restrictions based on subject-matter. For example, the "Son of Sam" law was not based on the idea that the criminal's book would have a harmful effect on the audience. Also, the argument may overstate the breadth of the anti-paternalism presumption.

Another justification is that content-based restrictions distort public discourse. This is obviously true in extreme cases, particularly for viewpoint restrictions. For instance, a law banning criticism of the government's economic policy is in some ways worse than a law banning all economic discussion, since it puts the weight of the state on one side of the debate while silencing the other. This justification seems less persuasive as applied to subject-matter restrictions. It's not clear how banning picketing relating to labor disputes, but allowing other picketing, distorts public discourse, since the two are generally not on opposing sides of the same debate.

Moreover, content-neutral regulations also distort communication. For instance, the Court considered the noise control in *Rock Against Racism* to be content neutral, but the activities of the sound technician clearly shaped (and thereby "distorted") the sound of the music. Often, content-neutral regulations fall more heavily on the poorly financed than on the wealthy. Putting up notices on telephone poles is more important for poorly financed campaigns than for those that can afford media time. The ban on draft-card burning hindered anti-war protestors; it was no problem for supporters of the war effort.

• A final justification is that content restrictions, especially viewpoint discriminations, are likely to rest on improper government motives. Justice Scalia worried in *R.A.V.* that "suppression of ideas [was] afoot." When the legislature picks out certain messages for suppression, it is more likely to be motivated by hostility to ideas than when it regulates more evenhandedly. A related argument is that the legislature may be targeting certain groups, defined on the basis of their ideas. But in *R.A.V.*, it seems unlikely that the legislature was trying to favor the "misbegotten Papist" over the "misbegotten bigot" in Justice Scalia's hypothetical debate. Such debates are probably not common in reality, and advocates of tolerance are presumably less likely to rely on fighting words than are bigots. Thus, it is unlikely that the St. Paul ordinance was actually designed to selectively censor the remarks of one of the two competing sides. It is somewhat more plausible to think that the city council took a dim view of people with racist ideas, and used the ordinance as a way of penalizing the more outspoken members of the group. So the ordinance may have been targeted against a political group, but not by trying to give the opposing side an advantage in the free use of fighting words. Perhaps this motive should also count as illicit, but at any rate it is different than the one posited by Scalia.

To use the Court's own terminology, however, the content distinction does not seem "narrowly tailored" to the goal of preventing improper legislative motivation. Not all content distinctions are improperly motivated. A legislature may simply have been trying to limit the impact of the regulation to the kind of speech that seemed to be causing tangible harms, such as disruption or property damage. Rather than reflecting a bad motive, this kind of content restriction might be considered a commendable effort to restrict as little speech as possible. Also, seemingly content-neutral legislation may very well rest on an improper motive. As everyone knew at the time of the *O'Brien* decision, the ban on draft-card burning was aimed specifically at anti-war protestors. Improper motive seems to be a relevant concern, but trying to explain the content distinction entirely on this basis seems to be strained.

B.   Domesticating the Content Distinction

For most of his stay on the bench, Justice Stevens inveighed against the content distinction. He wrote some well-known opinions attacking the distinction, which sometimes garnered support from other Justices. In his plurality opinion in *Young v. American Mini Theatres*,[14] for example, he argued that the state could reasonably single out non-obscene "adult entertainment" for special regulation, as this expression had less First Amendment value than most speech. In *R.A.V.*, he took the occasion to stress that although the Court had frequently repeated the maxim that content discrimination is improper, it has "quite rightly" adhered to this maxim with less than the "absolutism suggested by my colleagues."

Critics such as Justice Stevens have some substantial arguments on their side. As we have seen, the rule against content discrimination is full of exceptions. Essentially, Parts II and III of this book are devoted to cataloguing some of those exceptions. We have also seen that it is difficult to give a precise definition of content discrimination and that the argument for providing heightened scrutiny for content regulations is based at best on some rough generalizations. Given all these difficulties, a reasonable case could be made that the stringent rule against content discrimination is more trouble than it is worth.

---

[14]   427 U.S. 50 (1976).

Yet the Court is unlikely to abandon this rule. All of the current Justices now seem firmly wedded to the content distinction. Even under Justice Stevens' analysis, the content distinction is a relevant factor in the analysis; he simply gave it less weight than his colleagues. By now there are reams of cases, in a broad range of First Amendment contexts, relying on the rule against content discrimination. Whatever may be said in theory, it may simply be too late in the day to retract such a central legal concept.

If so, it may be more useful to consider how the content distinction could be used more effectively. Given the difficulty of defining the boundaries between viewpoint, subject-matter, and content neutral regulation, it may be a mistake to make the differences in constitutional protection quite so stark. By lowering the stakes, the Court could reduce the significance of these definitional disputes. At least some Justices have shown an inclination toward doing so. In *United States v. Alvarez*,[15] Justices Breyer and Kagan argued for the use of intermediate (rather than strict) scrutiny in reviewing regulation of false statements, providing a compromise between wholly protected and wholly unprotected status.

A more important reason for decreasing the differences in constitutional protection relates to the fuzziness of the justifications for disparate treatment. As we move up the hierarchy from content-neutral regulations to viewpoint regulations, it becomes increasingly likely that a regulation poses a serious threat to First Amendment values. But this is only a difference in degree, not in kind. Perhaps the most vulnerable part of the Court's current approach is its nonchalant attitude toward content-neutral regulations, which are almost always upheld despite their capacity to harm First Amendment values.

Justice Stevens' criticism of the Court also raised a jurisprudential issue. In its First Amendment rulings, the Supreme Court has become increasingly prone to lay down specific rules to govern future cases. In general, Justice Stevens favored a case-by-case examination of issues in the common law tradition, combining a commitment to First Amendment values with flexibility in applying existing law. This dispute is a familiar one in the law, between believers in rules and believers in standards. Most law professors can recite, pretty much by heart, the arguments on both sides of the broader debate. Rules have the advantage of providing clearer guidance for both lower courts and the public. Because they leave less room for discretion, they also provide less of a toehold for subjective biases. These advantages may be particularly important in First

---

[15]　567 U.S. 709 (2012).

Amendment litigation. In cases involving free expression, we have particular reason to want to avoid having the judges' ideological biases enter into the decision, lest those biases then have a distorting effect on public discourse. Because of concern that legal uncertainty will deter legitimate speech, the extra clarity of rules is also an advantage.

Even in First Amendment cases, however, the advocates of standards are not without ammunition. The alleged certainty of rules may be overstated. Some supposedly clear-cut rules suffer from significant definitional problems, rendering their boundaries unpredictable. Also, the more complex the rules become, the harder it is for anyone but a specialist to know what is or is not permitted. Some First Amendment rules may have reached the point of being understandable only to experts. And, as advocates of standards point out, whatever certainty does come with the use of rules is purchased at a price. Sticking to a clear-cut rule requires a willingness to decide some cases differently than we would if we considered all the circumstances. In a sense, in the interests of greater certainty and efficiency, we have to be willing to tolerate some mistaken outcomes. For instance, the result of the content distinction is that some innocuous and perhaps beneficial content-based rules are struck down, while some nefarious content-neutral rules are upheld.

A more serious risk is that mechanically following rules will ultimately erode our understanding of the values that the rules are designed to protect. We may unwisely devote our intellectual energies to refining the definition of viewpoint discrimination, rather than trying to consider whether the exclusion of religious proselytizing from University reimbursement actually threatens First Amendment values. This may be a gain in some ways, because the definitional issue may yield more easily to the intellectual tools most familiar to lawyers. But it is also a loss. Among other costs, it reduces the Court's ability to communicate to the interested public in controversial cases.

At present, the balance in First Amendment law seems to be in favor of those who follow rules rather than those who apply standards. The rule against content discrimination is the most prominent example, but far from the last one we will see. But at least when the boundaries of a constitutional rule are unclear, the Court might do well to adopt a more functional approach.

FURTHER READINGS

Ashutosh Bhgwat, *In Defense of Content Regulation*, 102 Iowa L. Rev. 1427 (2017).

Daniel Farber, *The Categorical Approach to Protecting Speech in American Constitutional Law*, 84 Ind. L.J. 917 (2009).

Elena Kagan, *Private Speech, Public Purpose: The Role of Governmental Motive in First Amendment Doctrine*, 63 U. Chi. L. Rev. 413 (1996).

Heidi Kitrosser, *Containing Unprotected Speech*, 57 Fla. L. Rev. 843 (2005).

Genevieve Lakier, *The Invention of Low-Value Speech*, 128 Harv. L. Rev. 2166 (2015).

Gregory Magarian, *The Marrow of Tradition, The Roberts Court and Categorical First Amendment Speech Exclusions*, 56 Wm. & Mary L. Rev. 1339 (2015).

Barry McDonald, *Speech and Distrust: Rethinking the Content Approach to Protecting the Freedom of Speech*, 81 Notre Dame L. Rev. 1347 (2006).

Note, *Free Speech Doctrine After* Reed v. Town of Gilbert, 129 Harv. L. Rev. 1981 (2016).

Martin H. Redish, *The Content Distinction in First Amendment Analysis*, 34 Stan. L. Rev. 113 (1981).

Lawrence Rosenthal, *First Amendment Investigations and the Inescapable Pragmatism of the Common Law of Free Speech*, 86 Ind. L.J. 9 (2011).

Jed Rubenfeld, *The First Amendment's Purpose*, 53 Stan. L. Rev. 767 (2001).

Geoffrey R. Stone, *Content Regulation and the First Amendment*, 25 Wm. & Mary L. Rev. 189 (1983).

Alexander Tsesis, *The Categorical Free Speech Doctrine and Contextual Regulation*, 65 Emory L.J. 495 (2015).

Chapter 3

THE FIRST AMENDMENT TOOLKIT

Like the content distinction, the doctrines discussed in this chapter are part of the essential toolkit of any First Amendment lawyer. The first step in considering a potential First Amendment problem is to ask whether the government has done anything to put the First Amendment in play. The government wins if the conduct involved in the case doesn't count as "speech," or if the government's action with respect to the speech doesn't count as an "abridgment." The next step is to look at the form of the regulation. A regulation may be basically sound, in the sense that the government is trying to regulate speech that it does have the power to control. But the regulation will nonetheless be unconstitutional if it constitutes a prior restraint, or if it suffers from overbreadth or vagueness. Finally, there is the overall question of judicial deference. Before a case ever gets to the Supreme Court, determinations about the need for a particular speech regulation have been made in various ways by legislatures, enforcement officers, and lower courts. Lawyers need a good sense of how much the Court will second-guess these prior determinations.

I. Has There Been an "Abridgment" of "Speech"?

Suppose that the government makes grants to daycare centers. Among various conditions covering aspects of the programs, one is that each daycare center provide suitable celebrations of national holidays. A multicultural center objects to any celebration of the Thanksgiving holiday, on the grounds that it is offensive to Native Americans as an endorsement of European colonialism. As a compromise, the government offers to allow the center to maintain its funding simply by serving turkey for lunch, but the center refuses. The gist of the center's objection is that, on pain of losing its grant, it is being forced to convey a message of support for Thanksgiving with which it disagrees. The government argues that there is no First Amendment problem: conditioning a government grant on whether someone serves a turkey dinner is not an "abridgment of the freedom of speech."

The Thanksgiving hypothetical illustrates three conceivable defenses to a constitutional claim stemming from the language of the Free Speech Clause. The first defense is that the conduct involved in the case (serving turkey) does not qualify as "speech." The second is that, rather than blocking any messages, the government has only mandated *additional* expressive conduct. The final defense is that rather than restricting speech, the government has only offered inducements for desired types of expression.

A.   Speech Versus Conduct

The constitutional references to "speech" and the "press" could be read to protect only verbal communications. However, people communicate in a variety of other ways, some of which we have already discussed. Some people, for example, express their views by burning flags, draft cards, or crosses. The modern Supreme Court seems to have little difficulty in finding these activities sufficiently communicative to come within the scope of the First Amendment. These non-verbal activities are often called "symbolic speech."

Clark v. Community for Creative Non-Violence[1] illustrates the Court's approach to symbolic speech. The national parks system allows overnight sleeping only in designated campgrounds. The plaintiffs, who were protesting the plight of the homeless, wanted to set up "symbolic tents" on the Washington Mall and in LaFayette Park, which is across from the White House. As Justice Marshall's dissent pointed out, these areas "have served as the sites for some of the most rousing political demonstrations in the Nation's history," and the "primary purpose for making *sleep* an integral part of the demonstration was 'to re-enact the central reality of homelessness.' " The Court was willing to assume for purposes of its decision that "sleeping in the park" might be covered by the First Amendment. The Court observed that "a message may be delivered by conduct that is intended to be communicative and that, in context, would reasonably be understood by the viewer to be communicative." But the Court had little trouble in upholding the ban under the *O'Brien* test, finding a reasonable, non-content justification to limit overnight sleeping in parks.

In the 1960s, the question of "symbolic speech" was hotly contested. For instance, the lower courts were sharply divided over whether male students had a First Amendment right to wear long hair as a form of self-expression. *Clark* illustrates why this debate has faded away. Since the *O'Brien* test is applied so favorably to the government, it makes very little difference in most cases whether conduct is classified as speech or not, so long as the government's regulation is content neutral. Thus, the government is not necessarily hampered in enforcing a general regulation unrelated to the protestor's intended message, even if we do classify the conduct as speech. In contrast, if the government regulation is based on a protestor's intended message, the government cannot very well deny that the protestor is engaged in an act of communication. Either way,

---

[1]   468 U.S. 288 (1984).

the crucial question is no longer, "Does the defendant's conduct constitute speech?", but rather, "Is the government's regulation based on content?".

B. The Right to Remain Silent

The First Amendment prevents the government from silencing an individual. Does it also protect the individual who wants to remain silent, when the government is demanding speech?

The Court decided very early that compelled speech may violate the First Amendment. One of the landmark cases in the development of First Amendment law was *West Virginia State Bd. of Educ. v. Barnette*,[2] a World War II ruling that Jehovah's Witnesses could not be forced to salute the flag and recite the pledge of allegiance at the beginning of school. Overruling an earlier decision made just three years earlier, the Court refused to believe that "a Bill of Rights which guards the individual's right to speak his own mind, left it open to public authorities to compel him to utter what is not in his mind." Justice Jackson used the occasion for a stirring proclamation of the right to free expression. With obvious reference to the totalitarian regimes with which we were at war, he remarked that "[t]hose who begin coercive elimination of dissent soon find themselves exterminating dissenters. Compulsory unification of opinion achieves only the unanimity of the graveyard." He closed with a passage attempting to encapsulate the fundamental command of the First Amendment:

> [F]reedom to differ is not limited to things that do not matter much. That would be a mere shadow of freedom. The test of its substance is the right to differ as to things that touch the heart of the existing order. If there is any fixed star in our constitutional constellation, it is that no official, high or petty, can prescribe what shall be orthodox in politics, nationalism, religion, or other matters of opinion or force citizens to confess by word or act their faith therein.

Relying heavily on *Barnette*, the Court sided thirty-five years later with motorists who taped over the state motto on their license plates. The motorists found the motto, "Live Free or Die," objectionable for religious and political reasons. Chief Justice Burger's opinion stressed that the First Amendment protects "both the right to speak freely and the right to refrain from speaking at all."[3] For similar reasons, the Court has rejected compelled financial support for speech activities. For instance, as we will see in Chapter

---

2   319 U.S. 624 (1943).

3   *Wooley v. Maynard*, 430 U.S. 705 (1977).

10, public employees cannot be forced to pay union dues to support the union's political activities.

Although *Barnette* seems clearly correct, the scope of the principle is less clear. The government does compel speech on many occasions—in court, on tax forms, and in school exams. Moreover, the government also requires various payments that go in part to support expressive activities, ranging from general taxes used to pay for government publications to student activity fees used to pay for campus newspapers. Where is the line to be drawn?

The Court has not been particularly successful in delineating the boundaries of the coerced speech doctrine. The cases, however, highlight four factors.[4] First, the imposition of a fee to support speech is much more likely to be upheld when the fee is an integral part of a larger program, rather than a stand-alone requirement. For example, although the Court upheld a requirement that fruit growers contribute to a fund for generic advertising of their product, it struck down a similar program for mushroom growers. The difference was that the fruit advertising was part of a broader joint marketing scheme, while the mushroom advertising was not.

Second, fees are less objectionable than regulations directly forcing the individual to make a statement, to use property to display a statement, or to provide an endorsement. Still, the Court has generally allowed fees only when "first, there is a comprehensive regulatory scheme involving a 'mandated association' among those who are required to pay the subsidy, and, second, compulsory fees are levied only insofar as they are a 'necessary incident' of the 'larger regulatory purpose which justified the required association.' "[5]

Third, the Court is very sensitive to any hint of ideological bias. For example, the Court upheld the use of student activity fees to fund student groups (including those taking controversial public positions), as ancillary to the university's educational program. But it remanded the case to determine whether the voting procedure for allocating the funds posed a risk of discrimination in favor of majority viewpoints. Finally, the First Amendment protects against coerced support for private speech, but not against the use of taxes to support speech by the government itself.[6]

A compelled speech issue that has divided the Court is whether public employees can be required to pay union dues. In *Abood v.*

---

[4]   See *United States v. United Foods, Inc.,* 533 U.S. 405 (2001) (mushroom advertising fee); *Board of Regents v. Southworth,* 529 U.S. 217 (2000) (student activity fee); *Glickman v. Wileman Bros. & Elliott,* 521 U.S. 457 (1997) (fruit advertising fee).

[5]   *Knox v. Serv. Employees,* 567 U.S. 298 (2012).

[6]   *Johanns v. Livestock Marketing Ass'n,* 544 U.S. 550 (2005).

Detroit Bd. of Education,[7] the Court upheld state laws that require nonmember employees to pay an "agency fee" for the union's collective bargaining services, since they benefit from the collective bargaining agreement. In *Harris v. Quinn*,[8] the Court said that given what it considered the shaky foundation of *Abood*, it would not extend the *Abood* holding to quasi-public workers such as home care workers paid by Medicaid but chosen by the patient. The dissenters defended *Abood* and argued for its extension.

The continued vitality of *Abood* was unclear after *Harris*, and some public employee unions were concerned that their own viability could be threatened if *Abood* were to be overruled. Note, however, that the state could avoid any First Amendment problem by agreeing to pay service fee for all workers directly to the union, so that the union's fee for its members would include only non-bargaining expenses. Assuming this approach was allowed by state law, it would raise no First Amendment problem since the money would no longer be part of the non-member's salary. Because government funds not linked to any individual worker would be used, workers could not complain about compelled speech even though economically the outcome is indistinguishable from an agency fee.

In *Janus v. American Federation of State, County, and Municipal Employees*,[9] the Court deployed the compelled speech doctrine to overturn *Abood*. Under Illinois law, when a majority of public employees vote to form a union, that union becomes the exclusive bargaining agent for all employees, including nonmembers. Nonmembers are required to pay a fee for the union's collective bargaining and related activities. Justice Alito wrote for the conservative majority, overruling *Abood*. He stressed that, in addition to the values involved generally in restrictions on free speech, compelled speech places at risk additional values:

> When speech is compelled, however, additional damage is done. In that situation, individuals are coerced into betraying their convictions. Forcing free and independent individuals to endorse ideas they find objectionable is always demeaning, and for this reason, one of our landmark free speech cases said that a law commanding "involuntary affirmation" of objected-to beliefs would require "even more immediate and urgent grounds" than a law demanding silence.

Because Illinois law required non-union members to pay for speech by the union in collective bargaining with which they

---

[7]   431 U.S. 209 (1977).

[8]   573 U.S. 616 (2014).

[9]   ___ U.S. ___, 138 S.Ct. 2448, 201 L.Ed.2d 924 (2018).

disagreed, it was subject to strict scrutiny. The *Abood* Court had found such laws to be constitutional based on the state's interest in "labor peace," but the Court concluded that collective bargaining by unions could function well without requiring non-members' financial support. The Court also rejected an alternative justification, holding that the state's interest in preventing non-members from free riding on the union's activities on their behalf was not compelling.

Justice Kagan's dissent on behalf of the four liberal Justices stressed stare decisis. Kagan argued that "[r]arely if ever has the Court overruled a decision—let alone one of this import—with so little regard for the usual principles of *stare decisis*." She considered the decision particularly unfortunate because laws implementing *Abood* "underpin thousands of ongoing contracts involving millions of employees."

The government often requires disclosures in commercial settings or mandates payments to actors who may among other activities engage in speech. For instance, the federal government requires firms whose securities are publicly listed to make extensive disclosures about their financial affairs. Many states give monopoly status to utility companies that engage in a wide range of speech activities, including making filings with regulatory agencies that some consumers may disagree with. Thus, *Janus* may have broad implications for a wide range of economic activities, as the dissenters feared. On the other hand, the majority may have considered the activities of public sector unions as distinctively entwined with political issues, suggesting a narrower application of the decision.

C. Inducements Versus Coercion

One of the most vexing questions in First Amendment law concerns the doctrine of unconstitutional conditions. It is clear enough that the government cannot jail someone for expressing an idea the government dislikes. But what about other inducements to steer people away from expressing that idea? Can the government condition some benefit on the applicant's abstention from "undesirable" expression?

At least some types of inducements are unconstitutional, as has been clear since *Speiser v. Randall*.[10] *Speiser* involved a California tax exemption for veterans that required a loyalty oath opposing the forcible overthrow of the government. The Court held that to "deny an exemption to claimants who engage in certain forms of speech is in effect to penalize them for such speech." *Speiser* is part of the general modern trend rejecting the right/privilege distinction, under which the government could not abrogate an individual's rights, but

---

[10] 357 U.S. 513 (1958).

could provide or withdraw a "privilege" on any grounds whatsoever. Under the older approach, the Court would simply have said that no one has a constitutional right to a tax exemption, and that it was the state's business if it chose not to convey its bounty to disloyal citizens.

But *Speiser* does not mean that tax exemptions can never be conditioned on expressive activities. In *Regan v. Taxation with Representation,*[11] the Court upheld a tax law that denied charitable deductions for contributions to organizations engaging in lobbying activities. The Court considered the charitable deduction to be the equivalent of a subsidy. Although "the government may not deny a benefit to a person because he exercises a constitutional right," it can decide what kinds of activities it wants to subsidize. Congress could well decide that it did not want to subsidize lobbying to the same extent as other activities by nonprofit organizations. The Court did suggest, however, that the "case would be different if Congress were to discriminate invidiously in its subsidies in such a way as to '[aim] at the suppression of dangerous ideas.'" But it found no such indication in *Regan*.

The *Regan* opinion actually used two quite different methodologies. The first was the subsidy/penalty distinction: Congress cannot penalize speech but it can refuse to subsidize it. Critics have objected that the difference is simply a matter of perspective. If we take as a baseline the world without a particular government program, then the absence of funding for a particular speaker is simply a refusal to subsidize. But if we take the program as a given, then the exclusion of a particular speaker from the program is a penalty. There is a classic psychology experiment in which the same drawing alternatively looks like a duck and a rabbit. (The duck's open bill turns into the rabbit's ears.) The penalty/subsidy distinction strikes critics as having the same basic character.

But despite the argument that the difference lies in the eye of the beholder, Court nevertheless remains very attached to the distinction between penalties and subsidies. Perhaps the critics are somewhat exaggerating the difficulty of drawing the distinction. There are several factors we can look at: whether the program is well established and is regarded by the public as creating an "entitlement" (like social security); whether the basis for the restriction on speech seems integral to the purpose of the overall program or extraneous to it; and whether the legislative history indicates a punitive intent. But admittedly, the distinction may still in the end be a matter of perspective.

The second methodology is to consider whether the subsidy involves viewpoint discrimination, or as the *Regan* Court said, is

---

[11]   461 U.S. 540 (1983).

intended to suppress undesirable ideas. Sometimes this seems to be the decisive factor. For instance, in *Board of Education v. Pico*,[12] a local school board directed that certain books be removed from the school library, describing them as "anti-American, anti-Christian, anti-Semitic, and just plain filthy." The issue had been raised by parents who had attended a conference by a politically conservative organization, where they received lists of books inappropriate for students, including well-known works by Kurt Vonnegut, Langston Hughes, Richard Wright, and Bernard Malamud. The Court was badly divided on the issue, with Justice White casting a cryptic fifth vote against the school board. The plurality opinion by Justice Brennan stressed that, rather than using "established, regular, and facially unbiased procedures" to review the materials, the Board's decision "rested decisively upon disagreement with constitutionally protected ideas in those books" or on a desire to impose "a political orthodoxy" on students.

It is worthwhile to consider why *Pico* was such a difficult case. Of course, the government had no power to ban the publication or sale of the books. In *Pico*, however, the dissenters emphasized that the government was acting in its role as educator. They argued that the school board's decision was a legitimate part of the government's right to control curriculum. In deciding which books to buy for the school library, the government plainly has to make decisions about what subjects should be emphasized and what approaches to those subjects are most useful to students. Some viewpoint distinctions are permissible. The government cannot ban the sale of books promoting the flat earth theory, but it need not order them for the geography section of the school library. Similarly, it can decide that some works of fiction are inappropriate for young readers. If it makes a mistake and orders books that are educationally inappropriate, it ought to be able to remove them from the shelves once the mistake is discovered.

Yet, the school's control over the library cannot be unlimited. Surely the school could not remove all biographies with favorable portrayals of Democratic presidents, or all books criticizing government policies. But where to draw the line is more than a little puzzling. We will return to this problem in more depth in Chapter 10.

II. What Kind of "Abridgment"?

The first impulse is to focus on the *what* of a free speech case: is what the defendant did protected by the First Amendment? But as modern doctrine has evolved, the *how* of the case is often more important: how has the government written the regulation at issue?

---

[12] 457 U.S. 853 (1982).

Thus, today, the First Amendment is as much about which laws the government can pass as it is about what communications people can make. Contrary to what a lay person might think, the right question to ask is usually not, "Did the defendant have a constitutional right to engage in this conduct?" Instead, it is more often, "Has the government written a valid rule for regulating this conduct?" By emphasizing what the government has done, as much as what the speaker has said, this approach may be unwittingly mirroring the text of the First Amendment itself. After all, the Amendment does speak in terms of what kinds of "laws" Congress can "make," rather than solely in terms of what rights are possessed by speakers.

We have already seen the importance of regulatory form in Chapter 2. O'Brien burned his draft card as a way of communicating his opposition to the Vietnam War. Did he have a constitutional right to engage in this conduct? No, in the sense that the Court upheld his conviction under a general law against draft card destruction. But suppose the statute had specifically prohibited the public destruction of draft cards in a disrespectful manner. We know from the flag burning case that such a statute would have been unconstitutional. So even though O'Brien's conduct was not immunized by the Constitution, the government might still violate the First Amendment by using the wrong kind of regulation. Another way of looking at this is that in regulating expressive conduct, the government must properly define the characteristic of the kind that it is targeting.

In this section, we will explore some important doctrines that a speaker can invoke without having to show that the government lacks the power to regulate her speech. We begin with the rule against prior restraints, which says that the government may not prevent speech from taking place, even if it can punish it after the fact. We then turn to two doctrines that make drafting speech regulations difficult. In different ways, both require exceptional precision in writing such regulations. One rule requires that the language of the regulation be particularly clear. The other doctrine invalidates the entire regulation if it intrudes on too much protected speech. The net effect of the two doctrines is to require almost surgical precision in legal drafting.

A. The Rule Against Prior Restraints

As noted in Chapter 1, Blackstone identified the "liberty of the press" with the absence of prior restrictions on publication. So long as the press was able to publish what it wanted, the government could impose a suitable punishment after the fact for abuses. An early opinion by Justice Holmes also suggested a Blackstonian interpretation of the First Amendment. The defendant had been held in contempt of court for publishing an editorial and cartoon questioning the motives of the Colorado Supreme Court. But Holmes said that the main purpose of the First Amendment was to "prevent all such *previous restraints* upon publication as had been practiced by other governments," not to prohibit the "subsequent punishment of such as may be deemed contrary to the public welfare."[13] By the end of World War I, however, Holmes had clearly changed his mind about this point, and today's Court endorses his later view. Later decisions, for example, limit the use of contempt citations to actual violations of court orders or out-of-court conduct that presents a "clear and present danger" to the integrity of pending judicial proceedings.[14] Thus, the First Amendment is clearly not limited to prior restraints. Nevertheless, it does apply to them with particular vigor.

The seminal case on prior restraints is *Near v. Minnesota*.[15] A newspaper had accused public officials with protecting local gangsters and had demanded a special grand jury. Acting under a state statute, the government obtained an injunction forbidding the defendants from circulating "any publication whatsoever which is a malicious, scandalous or defamatory newspaper." Chief Justice Hughes wrote the opinion for the Court lifting the injunction. He emphasized that unless the publisher can "satisfy the judge that the charges are true and are published with good motives and for justifiable ends, his newspaper or periodical is suppressed and further publication is made punishable as a contempt." Thus, the state had instituted the equivalent of a licensing system, covering only the defendants. "This," said Hughes, "is of the essence of censorship." He stressed the powerful objections to prior restraints voiced by Blackstone, as well as later history: "The fact that for approximately one hundred and fifty years there has been almost an entire absence of attempts to impose previous restraints upon publications relating to the malfeasance of public officers is significant of the deep-seated conviction that such restraints would violate constitutional right."

Hughes admitted that the rule against prior restraints was not absolute, but the exceptions were narrow:

> No one would question but that a government might prevent actual obstruction to its recruiting service or the publication of the sailing dates of transports or the number and location of troops. On similar grounds, the primary

---

[13] *Patterson v. Colorado*, 205 U.S. 454 (1907).

[14] See *Wood v. Georgia*, 370 U.S. 375 (1962); *Bridges v. California*, 314 U.S. 252 (1941).

[15] 283 U.S. 697 (1931).

requirements of decency may be enforced against obscene publications. The security of the community life may be protected against incitements to acts of violence.

The national security exception to *Near* has been narrowly construed, In the Pentagon Papers case,[16] discussed in more detail in the next chapter, the Court rejected an injunction against the publication of purloined government documents, even though the documents related to an on-going military conflict and were classified. (As we will see in Chapter 7, prior restraints are not as tightly limited in obscenity cases, the other *Near* exception.) Injunctions also were sometimes directed against the press in order to prevent pre-trial publicity from impairing the defendant's right to a free trial. But in *Nebraska Press Ass'n v. Stuart,*[17] the Court essentially put an end to such injunctions. Only where used to enforce copyright or contractual rights are injunctions commonly available today. For instance, the Court allowed an injunction against a CIA agent who was threatening to publish a book about the agency, in violation of his contractual agreement to obtain prior clearance.[18]

On the whole, then, the prior restraint rule has remained strong, with only limited exceptions. Indeed, sometimes the rule has been stretched in new directions. In *Bantam Books, Inc. v. Sullivan,*[19] a government commission distributed lists of objectionable books, informing bookstores of its intent to recommend obscenity prosecutions, and also distributed the list to the local police. The Court considered this system of "friendly advice" to be in reality a prior restraint.

Although the Court seems firmly attached to the prior restraint rule, it is not immediately obvious what basis exists for the rule other than history. Is an injunction really so different from a later criminal prosecution? If you violate an injunction, then you can be punished with prison, but the same is true of a criminal statute. At least the injunction provides the advantage of giving you a prior opportunity to be heard by the judge before she enjoins your conduct. With a criminal prosecution, you have no way of knowing in advance whether the judge will find your particular conduct illegal. If anything, then, the injunction is arguably preferable to the prosecution option.

One difference between the two is that enforcement of the injunction is more streamlined. Until recently, the procedural

---

[16] *New York Times v. United States,* 403 U.S. 713 (1971).

[17] 427 U.S. 539 (1976).

[18] *Snepp v. United States,* 444 U.S. 507 (1980).

[19] 372 U.S. 58 (1963).

safeguards were minimal, although the gap between criminal contempt and other criminal charges has narrowed. Even so, it is still easier to hold someone in contempt of court than to win an ordinary criminal case. Moreover, the injunction could short-circuit what would otherwise be a right to a jury determination of whether a work is obscene or defamatory or otherwise unprotected. Those issues will be decided by the judge in issuing the injunction; if there is a jury trial for criminal contempt, it will be limited to the question of whether the defendant violated the injunction. A more critical difference is the so-called collateral bar rule. Under this rule, a person who violates an injunction normally can be held in contempt even if the injunction itself was invalid. The idea is that you are supposed to obey the injunction until it can be appealed. The injunction freezes speech, not merely chills it, at least for the duration of appellate proceedings. Thus, even speech that is constitutionally protected may be delayed, perhaps past the time when it has any relevance. At least in jurisdictions following the collateral bar rule, this is a clear-cut reason for disfavoring injunctions against speech.

Supporters of the prior restraint rule also point to less tangible factors. Judges tend to be severe with respect to criminal contempt, since contempt not only violates the law like any criminal conduct but undermines the stature of the judiciary. Before speech takes place, there is necessarily an element of speculation in any forecast regarding its effects. This may cause the judge to incorrectly evaluate the constitutional issue and perhaps overuse injunctions "just to be on the safe side." (This phenomenon is not unknown in other areas of the law. It is easier to get a judge to authorize seizure of potentially dangerous medications than to bring a criminal prosecution after the fact against the manufacturer, because judges are reluctant to make mistakes that could result in a public health crisis.) In a sense, by pursuing the injunction, the prosecutor has "pre-committed" to pursuing any violations, whereas she might or might not bring an ordinary criminal complaint. Finally, the psychology of the situation may be different. In a regime of prior restraints, speakers feel that they are allowed to speak only on government sufferance, an atmosphere that may have a chilling effect. There is something to the familiar saying that it is always better to ask forgiveness than permission.

Despite the significant arguments against the prior restraint doctrine, the intuitions supporting it are powerful. Moreover, notwithstanding the critics, these intuitions are not without foundation. The purported advantage of the prior restraint is that the speaker can obtain a determination of legality before speaking. But a speaker who really desires such assurances could bring an action for a declaratory judgment. Otherwise, the main difference between the prior restraint and subsequent punishment is that an injunction is a more effective deterrent. Yet if increased deterrence is a genuine need, the legislature can obtain this result more directly by increasing the penalty for criminal violations. So there seems to be little to be said affirmatively for injunctions against speech, and at least some risks to free speech if they are allowed. On balance, we seem to lose little by abandoning them.

B.   Chilling Effects: The Overbreadth and Vagueness Doctrines

A badly drafted regulation can be struck down on its face, without any inquiry into its application to the particular plaintiff challenging the regulation. Thus, even if speech could be restricted under a properly drafted regulation, the overbroad or vague regulation will be invalidated. A striking example is provided by *Board of Airport Comm'rs v. Jews for Jesus, Inc.*[20] The L.A. Board of Commissioners adopted a resolution banning all "First Amendment activities" within the "Central Terminal Area" at Los Angeles International Airport. An airport officer told a minister affiliated with Jews for Jesus that he must stop distributing religious literature in the Central Terminal Area. The plaintiff filed suit, claiming that the resolution was unconstitutional on its face. The Court began its analysis by summarizing the test for overbreadth:

> Under the First Amendment overbreadth doctrine, an individual whose own speech or conduct may be prohibited is permitted to challenge a statute on its face "because it also threatens others not before the court—those who desire to engage in legally protected expression but who may refrain from doing so rather than risk prosecution or undertake to have the law declared partially invalid." A statute may be invalidated on its face, however, only if the overbreadth is "substantial." The requirement that the overbreadth be substantial arose from our recognition that application of the overbreadth doctrine is, "manifestly, strong medicine," and that "there must be a realistic danger that the statute itself will significantly compromise recognized First Amendment protections of parties not before the Court for it to be facially challenged on overbreadth grounds."

This was an easy test to apply in *Jews for Jesus*. The resolution did not simply regulate conduct that might cause obstructions or congestion. Thus, it did not simply reach people passing out leaflets

---

[20]   482 U.S. 569 (1987).

like the plaintiffs themselves. Instead, "it prohibit[ed] even talking and reading, or the wearing of campaign buttons or symbolic clothing." Hence, the Court invalidated the regulation, without pausing to consider whether leafleting in airports is constitutionally protected.

Obviously, you may be thinking, the airport had no intention of punishing talking or reading in the terminal, regardless of the language of the ordinance. But in cases like *Jews for Jesus*, overbreadth is closely related to another problem: unconstitutional vagueness. Anyone reading the ordinance would surely know that it would not be applied across its full literal scope. But what the reader would not know is which particular activities would actually be covered and which would not be covered. Would the airport distinguish between passengers and other speakers? Would it draw a line between verbal communications and written leaflets? Or would enforcement simply depend on how any particular airport employees felt about a specific speaker? In effect, assuming it was not given its full literal scope, the airport rule amounted to little more than a delegation of authority to employees to punish whatever speech they wanted. Such an unlimited delegation obviously presents a major risk of viewpoint discrimination by the enforcers. For instance, the activities of mainstream religious groups or charities might well be received more kindly than those of "kooks and nuts." For this reason, in practical effect, the airport rule was unconstitutionally vague as well as overbroad.

The vagueness rule is related to the Court's longtime concern over standardless administrative discretion in speech cases. In *Lakewood v. Plain Dealer Publishing Co.*,[21] a local ordinance allowed newsracks on public property only with a permit from the mayor, which could be denied on any ground she deemed "necessary and reasonable." The Court allowed a facial challenge to the ordinance. As the Court explained, standardless licensing poses two risks: self-censorship by speakers anxious to avoid any possible difficulty in obtaining a license, and the difficulty of preventing content-based censorship in such case-by-case licensing decisions. On the other hand, a completely content-neutral permit scheme avoids these problems and is therefore permissible.[22] A similar concern about unlimited discretion is presented by the overly vague criminal statute, since it will be up to the prosecutor and jury to decide whether to permit speech, with no standards to guide them and no effective review.

---

[21]   486 U.S. 750 (1988).

[22]   See *Thomas v. Chicago Park Dist.*, 534 U.S. 316 (2002).

The overbreadth and vagueness doctrines have both pluses and minuses. These doctrines have certain benefits: (a) minimizing official discretion in the enforcement of statutes that might curtail speech; (b) expanding the range of people who can bring constitutional challenges beyond those most directly affected (but perhaps reluctant to sue); and (c) generally minimizing the "chilling effect" of rules on people's willingness to speak up, protest, and the like. On the cost side, these doctrines may make it too easy for courts to strike down statutes. They also may result in the invalidation of statutes whose harmful effects on speech may be more hypothetical than real. And by allowing individuals whose conduct is properly subject to state regulation to avoid state rules because of the effect those rules might have on others, the doctrines undercut the ability of the state to pursue legitimate policies and may give some challengers an undeserved windfall.

Jews for Jesus also raises an interesting technical issue pertaining to overbreadth and vagueness. Before the Supreme Court, the state did not (for obvious reasons) attempt to justify the full literal sweep of the airport rule. Instead, it argued for a "saving construction" of the rule. In a case involving a federal statute, the Court could adopt such a saving construction on its own. For instance, in *Yates v. United States,*[23] the Court adopted just such a narrowing interpretation to save the constitutionality of the Smith Act. The Act was written in broad terms. It made it unlawful for any person to "advocate, abet, advise, or teach" the desirability of overthrowing the government. Nevertheless, the Court held that the statute did not apply to mere "abstract teaching," but only applied where the audience was being urged to action rather than belief. In a later case, the Court performed similar surgery on the "membership clause" of the Smith Act. The membership clause made it a crime to "be or become a member" of a group advocating overthrow "knowing the purposes thereof." Nevertheless, the Court held the mere knowledge was not enough; the member had to have a specific intent to further the illegal purposes of the organization.[24]

Because the airport rule came from a state government rather than the federal government, the final word on its interpretation could only come from the state courts. The Court considered but rejected the idea of waiting until the state courts had the opportunity to provide a narrowing interpretation. Because there seemed to be so many possible interpretations, the Court doubted whether the state courts could adopt a clear interpretation without waiting to decide a whole series of cases. Moreover, the Court found that the

---

[23] 354 U.S. 298 (1957).
[24] *Scales v. United States,* 367 U.S. 203 (1961).

interpretation suggested by the airport, limiting the rule only to "expressive activity unrelated to airport-related purposes," was itself overbroad and vague.

This brings us to the most difficult technical question, which is the extent to which it is possible to *retroactively* cure a statute that is plainly unconstitutional on its face. The Court addressed this question in two cases dealing with child pornography. In *Massachusetts v. Oakes,*[25] after the state court upheld an overbreadth challenge, the legislature amended the law to narrow it. The question was whether this amendment retroactively cured the overbreadth problem, allowing convictions under the old law to stand if the defendants' own conduct was unprotected. The Court split 5–4 regarding the effect of the amendment. The dissenters argued that the amendment eliminated any threat of a future chilling effect. But the majority said that legislatures would be encouraged to pass overbroad laws if they knew that they could always cure problems retroactively. In *Osborne v. Ohio,*[26] the interpretative surgery was performed by the state court rather than the legislature. The Court distinguished *Oakes* on the ground that the legislature would be unlikely to count on the help of the state courts to retroactively fix problems. Thus, there was no need to use overbreadth as an incentive to good legislative drafting. Hence, the newly narrowed statute could be applied retroactively "provided such application affords fair warning to the defendant." But even though it found fair warning, the Court reversed because the jury instructions did not accord with the new interpretation of the statute.

Thus, there seem to be three requirements for retroactive use of statutory surgery:

> (a) The surgeon must be the judiciary rather than the legislature.

> (b) The defendant must have "fair notice" of the possible narrowing construction.

> (c) The jury instruction must comport with the "revised" interpretation.

Clearly, it is the "fair notice" requirement that is most difficult to apply. About all that can be said is that the Court is less likely to find fair notice, the more seriously defective the statute, and the more "creative" the solution. Both factors indicate that it would have been hard to anticipate the narrowing construction. But to the extent that the defendant's own conduct clearly falls within the core intent of the

---

[25] 491 U.S. 576 (1989).

[26] 495 U.S. 103 (1990).

prior statute, the defendant has less ground to complain about changes in wording or interpretation.

There's no accepted name for the opposite of a saving construction—perhaps it could be called a "wounding interpretation" of the statute. Although these are less common, when they do occur they tend to be fatal. In *City of Chicago v. Morales*,[27] a Chicago ordinance allowed police to disperse any group containing any "criminal street gang members" who were "loitering" in any public place. Loitering was defined as "remaining in any one place with no apparent purpose." The state supreme court viewed the ordinance as effectively giving the police officer absolute discretion. Not surprisingly, the Supreme Court agreed that the ordinance was void for vagueness.

III. The Question of Deference

Supreme Court cases begin in humbler forums. By the time the Court hears a First Amendment case, legislators and administrative officers have taken a position on the issues; juries and trial judges have made factual findings; and lower courts have ruled on the legal issues. How willing is the Court to second-guess these decision makers? This will be a recurring issue throughout the book, but it is worthwhile to touch briefly on it here. Let us take the various decisionmakers in reverse order.

Lower Courts. The Court today seems to have little hesitation in overruling the legal views of the lower courts, regardless of how many judges have taken the position or how distinguished they may be. In an earlier age, the Court seemed to feel a somewhat greater modesty about its abilities in comparison to those of the rest of the judicial world. Not so today. Thus, if you happen to be writing a Supreme Court brief in a case where every federal circuit court has ruled in your direction, do not get a false sense of security.

Juries and Trial Judges. Normally appellate courts do not second-guess the "trier of fact" unless there has been a fairly unmistakable error. In First Amendment cases, the Court is less shy. For instance, in *Jenkins v. Georgia*,[28] the Court took issue with a jury that found obscene *Carnal Knowledge*, a somewhat sexually explicit but mainstream film.

The Court discussed the issue of factual deference more fully in *Bose Corp. v. Consumers Union*,[29] a defamation action. The Court held that it and other appellate courts must exercise "independent judgment" and determine for themselves whether the trial record

---

[27]   527 U.S. 41 (1999).

[28]   418 U.S. 153 (1974).

[29]   466 U.S. 485 (1984).

establishes the constitutional basis for a valid defamation action, rather than merely checking for the presence of a clear error. Thus, reviewing courts must exercise independent judgment about what might be called the "constitutional facts" in the case. The main rationale is that otherwise judges and juries could cloak their prejudices against particular speakers in the form of adverse fact-findings. As lawyers know, this is a common technique for trial judges anxious to avoid reversal. Also, First Amendment standards often involve a mixture of factual and legal determination. In *Bose*, part of the dispute was about what the speaker had meant and whether there was sufficient evidence of intentional falsity. This was partly a factual inquiry about what had happened when the article was written and partly a judgment about whether those events met the relevant legal standard. Because the constitutional standards are so intertwined with factual issues, it is difficult for the Court to fairly consider one without the other.

Legislatures and Administrators. To what extent does the Court defer to Congress and the President? As to what comports with First Amendment values, the answer is "not at all." As in the flag-burning case, where the statute had passed with overwhelming majorities, the Court seems almost to delight in proving its independence from popular opinion. But what about more factual issues? Often, the constitutionality of a law depends on whether it is sufficiently connected with the purported goal. At one time, at least some Justices seemed inclined toward across-the-board deference to Congress and the President on such issues. If Congress thought a particular statute was needed to prevent the Communists from taking over the country, then the Court was indisposed to disagree. Today, deference is not so automatic, but it does seem to be a significant factor in several specific settings.

First, regulations do sometimes involve highly technical issues which the Court doesn't know very much about. For instance, in *Turner Broadcasting System v. FCC*,[30] the Court reviewed rules requiring cable services to carry local broadcasters. The question before the Court in this phase of the litigation was whether the legislation was "narrowly tailored" to three governmental goals: preserving local broadcasting, promoting diversity in communications, and maintaining fair competition in the media marketplace. This required a judgment, not merely about the existing situations of cable and broadcast television, but about how the media were likely to develop with or without the statute. Congress had conducted extensive hearings on this issue, and not surprisingly, the Court gave significant deference to Congress'

---

[30]   520 U.S. 180 (1997).

findings. Such deference seems especially appealing to the Court in cases involving new technologies whose impacts are not yet well-understood. Even so, the degree of deference is not easily predictable.

Second, the Court also seems willing to defer in at least some situations where the issue is far from technical, such as what kinds of materials are appropriate for high school students. This urge toward deference is particularly strong with respect to relatively authoritarian institutions, such as schools, prisons, and the military. The Court also feels some reluctance to interfere with broadscale national programs, where what seems like a small change might have unexpected repercussions. The more the government seems to be acting as a "manager" rather than a "regulator," the more willing the Court is to defer. Realistically, although the Court does not say so explicitly, its willingness to defer is also undoubtedly related to the amount of confidence it has in the particular decision-making body. In the heyday of the Civil Rights Era, anything done by the Mississippi legislature seemed to carry an unspoken presumption of improper motivation, resulting in little deference to its actions indeed.

Third, in *Holder v. Humanitarian Law Project*,[31] the Court also extended deference to Congressional and Presidential determinations in the area of foreign relations and national security—namely, whether aiding even the peaceful activities of foreign terrorist groups indirectly supported their use of violence. The Court emphasized both the need for deference and its limits. As the Court explained, its "precedents, old and new, make clear that concerns of national security and foreign relations do not warrant abdication of the judicial role." Nevertheless, "when it comes to collecting evidence and drawing factual inferences in this area, 'the lack of competence on the part of the courts is marked,' and respect for the Government's conclusions is appropriate." This is not a surprising position for the Court to take, but it remains to be seen how future cases will strike the balance between independent judgment and deference in future national security cases.

———

This concludes our tour of the cross-cutting themes in First Amendment law. As we have seen, there are some useful doctrines that apply across a broad range of First Amendment situations. In particular, the content neutrality, overbreadth, and vagueness doctrines are relevant to most First Amendment challenges.

Much of First Amendment law, however, is more narrowly focused. In Part II, we will examine the doctrines governing

---

[31]   561 U.S. 1 (2010).

regulation of specific categories of speech, such as incitement to violence and defamation. These doctrines are outgrowths of the old two-tier theory, in which these categories of expression were considered as much outside the protection of the First Amendment as riding a bicycle or baking a pizza. The situation today, as we will see, is quite a bit more complicated. In Part III, we will turn to the government's specific interests in regulating speech in certain contexts, usually when the speaker or the channel of communication has some direct tie to the government. Sometimes, but not always, the government can regulate speech by its employees, grantees, licensees, and "wards," when ordinary citizens would be constitutionally entitled to speak without hindrance.

As you can see from the respective length of their coverage in this book, the overarching portions of First Amendment law are somewhat dwarfed in extent by the doctrines relating to particular types of speech and special settings. It is for this reason that First Amendment law has come to resemble a complicated legal code rather than a unitary set of principles. This is not to say that the remaining body of First Amendment doctrine lacks any internal coherence or consistency. Nevertheless, there are many loose ends and peculiar doctrines covering unusual problems, while the common themes are sometimes hauntingly elusive.

FURTHER READINGS

Stephen R. Barnett, *The Puzzle of Prior Restraint*, 29 Stan. L. Rev. 539 (1977).

Ashutosh Bhagwat, *Posner, Blackstone, and Prior Restraints on Speech*, 2015 BYU L. Rev. 2049.

Caroline Mala Corbin, *Compelled Disclosures*, 65 Ala. L. Rev. 1277 (2014).

Richard H. Fallon, *Making Sense of Overbreadth*, 100 Yale L.J. 853 (1991).

Nathan Kellum, *Permit Schemes: Under Current Jurisprudence, What Permits Are Permitted?*, 56 Drake L. Rev. 381 (2008).

Mark A. Lemley and Eugene Volokh, *Freedom of Speech and Injunctions in Intellectual Property Cases*, 48 Duke L.J. 147 (1998).

Henry P. Monaghan, *Third Party Standing*, 84 Colum. L. Rev. 277 (1984).

Eugene Volokh, *Symbolic Expression and the Original Meanings of the First Amendment*, 97 Geo. L.J. 1057 (2009).

Christina Wells, *Bringing Structure to the Law of Injunctions Against Expression*, 51 Case W. Res. L. Rev. 1 (2000).

Part II
THE CATEGORICAL APPROACH

Chapter 4

ILLEGAL ADVOCACY

Ever since governments have existed, they have used force to suppress their opponents and quell criticism. Tolerance for enemies of the established order, then, is the acid test for free speech. Ironically, although our government was born in a revolution and ours became the first national constitution to protect free speech, it was only after a century and a half that this critical element of First Amendment law was firmly established. Today, however, it is a bedrock principle that the government has no power to ban ideas, no matter how dangerous or undemocratic those ideas may seem. But this was a hard-won victory, as we will see.

I. The Rise of "Clear and Present Danger"

Modern First Amendment doctrine is in large part the intellectual child (or great-grandchild, at least) of a few judges in the early Twentieth Century who took the crucial step of recognizing the centrality of free speech to a democratic society. The modern approach began in a series of dissents by these judges and won partial acceptance during the Depression and the World War II era, only to face new challenges in the 1950s. It was not until the 1960s that, in a somewhat different guise, their approach to the issue was embedded in constitutional doctrine. For the past half century, it has been unchallenged. This section will trace the evolution of their approach and its halting acceptance prior to the McCarthy era, when America was swept by anti-Communist hysteria after World War II.

A. Historical Background

Historically, the most stringent controls on speech have appeared during periods of national emergency. As early as 1798, the first federal restrictions on speech emerged during such a crisis. The Sedition Act was adopted when the country was on the verge of war with France. Members of what would become the Federalist Party (then in power) desired a tool to suppress the Francophile Democratic-Republicans, a number of whom were convicted and imprisoned before the Act expired in 1801. The statute criminalized "false, scandalous, and malicious writing or writings against the government of the United States," as well as Congress and the President, "with intent to defame [them]; or to bring them [into] contempt or disrepute." Although the Supreme Court never adjudicated the constitutionality of the Act, several Justices applied it sitting on circuit, and there is some reason to believe that it would have been upheld by the full Court.

Between the Sedition Act of 1798 and the Espionage Act of 1917, the federal and state governments continued to repress speech, especially in periods of emergency. For example, Southern states suppressed abolitionist literature and speech before the Civil War. Both North and South stifled dissent during the Civil War, and during Reconstruction and the Jim Crow era, the South suppressed political opposition. Later, courts as well as state governors brutally suppressed workers and labor leaders. The Nineteenth Century was in fact filled with repression of speech. Despite ongoing debate and litigation about that repression, the First Amendment did not "come into its own" until World War I.

World War I provided the occasion for a bevy of repressive actions. The most important was the Espionage Act of 1917. The Act made it a crime during wartime to "make or convey false reports or false statements with intent to interfere" with the war effort, to "cause or attempt to cause insubordination, disloyalty, mutiny, or refusal of duty, in the military or naval forces," or to "obstruct the recruiting or enlistment service of the United States." Violations carried heavy penalties of up to twenty years in prison.

The Espionage Act might well have been given a narrow interpretation. It could have been construed to apply only to the transmission of false military information, to incitements to mutiny, or to physical obstruction of recruiting services. Instead, it was given a sweeping interpretation that seemingly covered nearly any disagreement with the war effort. For example, one prosecution was based on the mailing of a book that described patriotism as evil. The book questioned whether anything at stake in the war was "worth the life of one blue-jacket on the sea or one khaki-coat in the trenches." In affirming the conviction, the Ninth Circuit said that "attacking the justice of the cause for which the war is waged" and "undermining the spirit of loyalty" were enough to violate the statute.[1] Thus, it was sufficient if the defendant intended to interfere with the war effort, which the court was willing to infer because his speech had a natural tendency to do so.

One of the few bright rays during this period was Judge Learned Hand's opinion in the *Masses* case.[2] The case arose when the post office refused to mail a magazine called "The Masses" on the ground that its content would hamper the war effort. Judge Hand construed the relevant portions of the Espionage Act narrowly, so as to

---

[1]   *Shaffer v. United States,* 255 Fed. 886 (9th Cir.1919).

[2]   *Masses Publishing Co. v. Patten,* 244 Fed. 535 (S.D.N.Y.1917), rev'd, 246 Fed. 24 (2d Cir. 1917).

criminalize only speech or writings that on their face constituted a "direct incitement to violent resistance" to the law. For example, regarding the provision about causing insubordination, he agreed with the government that arousing public discontent tends to promote an insubordinate attitude among the troops. Yet, this broad interpretation of the word "cause" would contradict "the normal assumption of democratic government that the suppression of hostile criticism does not turn upon the justice of its substance or the decency and propriety of its temper." Similarly, with regard to the draft-resistance provision, Hand distinguished between language that might "arouse a seditious disposition," which was not forbidden, and "language that directly advocated resistance to the draft," which was illegal.

Unfortunately, Hand was a voice crying in the wilderness. His opinion was promptly reversed by the Second Circuit, and the Supreme Court also adopted a sweeping interpretation of the Espionage Act. In *Schenck v. United States*,[3] the defendant had mailed a leaflet to draft-age men arguing that the draft violated the Thirteenth Amendment. Justice Holmes wrote the opinion of the Court. He first observed that the leaflet "would not have been sent unless it had been intended to have some effect, and we do not see what effect it could be expected to have upon persons subject to the draft except to influence them to obstruct the carrying of it out." Admittedly, Holmes said, in ordinary times the leaflet would have been protected by the First Amendment. But context was crucial: "The most stringent protection of free speech would not protect a man in falsely shouting fire in a theatre and causing a panic." Then Holmes announced a new test. The question, Holmes said, "is whether the words used are used in such circumstances and are of such a nature as to create a clear and present danger that they will bring about the substantive evils that Congress has a right to prevent." He had little trouble in finding that this standard had been satisfied in *Schenck*. But Holmes would soon change his views on how to apply the standard.

B. The Great Dissenters

The year 1919—a century ago at this writing—was one of the great turning points in the development of First Amendment doctrine. It would be many years before a majority of the Court was prepared to give any real protection to free speech, but for the first time powerful dissenting voices were raised. In time, these dissents were to prove far more persuasive than the majority opinions.

---

[3]   249 U.S. 47 (1919).

Abrams v. United States[4] marked the emergence of these dissents. The defendants had been charged with violating the Espionage Act by criticizing the Allied invasion of Russia. (The invasion, a historical incident which is seldom stressed in American history courses, was an effort to unseat the Bolsheviks, who had withdrawn from the war effort against Germany.) The defendants' pamphlets, which they scattered out of the window of an office building, warned workers that munitions might be used against Russia instead of Germany. The majority found little difficulty in upholding the conviction: "Men must be held to have intended, and to be accountable for, the effects which their acts were likely to produce." Even if the primary purpose was to aid the Bolsheviks in Russia rather than the Germans, the pamphlet would obstruct munition production for the war with Germany as well.

This was too much for Holmes. Congress, he said, "certainly cannot forbid all effort to change the mind of the country," and "nobody can suppose that the surreptitious publishing of a silly leaflet by an unknown man, without more, would present any immediate danger." Holmes then moved on to an impassioned defense of free speech. Although the desire to suppress dissenters is perfectly natural, it should be resisted: "when men have realized that time has upset many fighting faiths, they may come to believe even more than they believe the very foundations of their own conduct that the ultimate good desired is better reached by free trade in ideas— that the best test of truth is the power of the thought to get itself accepted in the competition of the market, and that truth is the only ground upon which their wishes safely can be carried out." Hence, he said, "we should be eternally vigilant against attempts to check the expression of opinions that we loathe and believe to be fraught with death, unless they so imminently threaten immediate interference with the lawful and pressing purposes of the law that an immediate check is required to save the country."

Note the transformation of Holmes's views from *Schenck*, where he upheld a conviction that seemed little different from the one in *Abrams*, where he dissented. Essentially, Holmes had moved toward the libertarian approach urged by Professor Zechariah Chafee in criticizing the Court's earlier decisions. Even though both judges were influenced by Chafee, Holmes's clear and present danger approach was different from the incitement approach taken by Hand in *Masses*. Holmes focused on the proof that speech was dangerous, whereas Hand focused on its content. Thus, Holmes would protect even direct incitement when the situation rendered it harmless, but would punish any kind of speech posing enough of a risk to society.

---

[4]   250 U.S. 616 (1919).

Hand was critical of the Holmes approach. He considered its contextual determination of danger too subjective to constrain lemming-like judges from banning speech in times of national crisis. Apparently, Holmes developed this approach out of his analysis of the law of criminal attempt, where a similar line is drawn between an actual attempt and mere preparation.

Holmes's dissents were joined by Justice Brandeis, who emerged in his own right as a ringing voice for free speech in *Whitney v. California*.[5] In *Whitney*, the majority upheld the conviction for "criminal syndicalism" of a member of the Communist Labor Party, whose only individual activities had been attending meetings. Brandeis' opinion was technically a concurrence because he felt that the defendant had failed to preserve the crucial argument for appeal. But he rejected the majority's reasoning entirely. One of the most famous passages in First Amendment law comes from that Brandeis opinion. It begins with the assertion that "[t]hose who won our independence believed that the final end of the State was to make men free to develop their faculties," believing "liberty to be the secret of happiness and courage to be the secret of liberty." Thus, "freedom to think as you will and to speak as you think are means indispensable to the discovery and spread of political truth." And hence, he continued, "[b]elieving in the power of reason as applied through public discussion," the Founders "eschewed silence coerced by law—the argument of force in its worst form." To support a criminal conviction, "it must be shown either that immediate serious violence was to be expected or was advocated, or that the past conduct furnished reason to believe that such advocacy was then contemplated," bearing in mind the critical difference "between advocacy and incitement, between preparation and attempt, between assembling and conspiracy."

Although it is tempting to repeat the whole passage, which gains much of its power from an almost Biblical rhythm, these excerpts suggest the tone of Brandeis' argument. In his confidence in the power of public discussion to winnow out truth, he shared Holmes's basic belief in the "marketplace of ideas." But Brandeis seemed to have a less individualistic tone, focusing less on the individual speaker and more on the importance of free discussion to the political health of the community. Both Holmes and Brandeis admitted that free speech carried certain risks, and both viewed the willingness to face these risks as exemplifying an important kind of courage. For Holmes, it was the courage of the skeptic willing to make an existential gamble in favor of freedom. For Brandeis, it was the courage of a political community that expresses its identity by

---

[5]　　274 U.S. 357 (1927).

accepting the dangers that come with liberty. Brandeis was a great admirer of the classical Greeks. For him, free speech meant choosing the risks of the open Athenian community over the security of Sparta's regimentation.

C.   Free Speech Takes Root

Brandeis and Holmes did not enjoy immediate success. World War I was followed by the "red scare," during which the country panicked at the thought of an American Bolshevik revolution. In 1925, for example, the Court upheld a conviction under New York's law prohibiting the advocacy of criminal anarchy. The offense was helping to publish a manifesto that advocated class struggle, general strikes, and the establishment of a "revolutionary dictatorship of the proletariat." The Court held that "utterances inciting to the overthrow of organized government" could be punished, because a "single revolutionary spark may kindle a fire that, smoldering for a time, may burst into a sweeping and destructive conflagration."[6] This "fire prevention" approach to the First Amendment was the subject of another strong dissent by Holmes.

But the tide was beginning to turn. Indeed, in retrospect, the most important fact about the 1925 decision was that the Court assumed for purposes of argument that the First Amendment was part of the "liberty" protected by the due process clause of the Fourteenth Amendment. This was the first time that the First Amendment was applied to the states. Over the next 25 years, the Court began applying the First Amendment to strike down state "syndicalism" laws and other restrictions on free speech. By the end of World War II, the Court appeared to have abandoned the "bad tendency" approach of the World War I era, under which evil intent could be inferred from the tendency of an utterance to cause social harm.

For instance, in *Terminiello v. Chicago,*[7] the Court reviewed the conviction of a strident right-wing speaker at a turbulent public meeting, which was described by the dissent as a mob scene. The speech was far more graphic than the pamphlets the Court had found so objectionable in the earlier cases. Rather than dropping anonymous leaflets out a window, the speaker was addressing an angry crowd in a building surrounded by protesters. Yet, the Court reversed the conviction. In an opinion by Justice Douglas, the Court focused on a jury instruction that invited the jury to convict if the speech "stirred people to anger, invited public dispute, or brought about a condition of unrest." But one of the functions of free speech,

---

6   *Gitlow v. New York,* 268 U.S. 652 (1925).

7   337 U.S. 1 (1949).

said Justice Douglas, is to invite dispute—speech "may indeed best serve its high purpose when it induces a condition of unrest, creates dissatisfaction with conditions as they are, or even stirs people to anger." That is why freedom of speech is protected "unless shown likely to produce a clear and present danger of a serious substantive evil that rises far above public inconvenience, annoyance, or unrest." Since it was impossible to tell whether the defendant was convicted under the broad language of the ordinance or because the specific circumstances constituted a clear and present danger, the conviction could not stand. This decision is certainly a far cry from *Abrams* and *Schenck*.

Thus, the "clear and present danger" test seemed to have fulfilled its promise of becoming a sturdy protection for dissenters. As events were to prove, however, the barrier was not rugged enough to survive the onslaught of a new wave of public alarm.

II. The McCarthy Era and Its Aftermath

Students of constitutional law might have felt some cautious optimism after World War II that the Supreme Court's embrace of the "clear and present danger" test would provide secure protection for political dissenters. Unfortunately, the eruption of the Cold War severely tested this optimism. Senator Joseph McCarthy was one of a number of political actors who were willing to make exaggerated claims of communist influence, including charges against individuals on the basis of flimsy evidence. Just as the Court had seemed to give way to popular sentiment during World War I and the following "red scare," its initial response to the McCarthy era seemed equally unhelpful to the cause of free speech. But the Court's surrender to the repressive tide during the 1950s was never as complete, and within a few years it began to reclaim the lost ground.

A. The *Dennis* Ruling

Stalin's tight grip on Eastern Europe, political and economic unrest in much of Western Europe, and Russian acquisition of nuclear weapons all combined to trigger a new fear of communist aggression. During the Great Depression, many liberal intellectuals and labor leaders had flirted with socialism, sometimes becoming members of the Communist Party. In the early days of the Cold War, it was easy to portray these individuals as communist "moles" burrowing away within American institutions, and some actual cases of espionage were uncovered. Whatever the causes, there was a repetition of the post-World War I "red scare," leading to new repressive legislation. The most important law was the Smith Act, which made it unlawful to "knowingly or willfully advocate, abet, advise, or teach the duty, necessity, desirability, or propriety of overthrowing or destroying any government in the United States by force or violence, or by the assassination of any officer of such government."

Dennis v. United States[8] upheld the convictions of Communist Party leaders under the Smith Act. Chief Justice Vinson's plurality opinion and the concurrences left in doubt whether the clear and present danger test retained any vitality, and if not, what other protection remained for speech. Some language in the various opinions suggests that the harm of future revolution is so serious that *any* speech increasing its probability can be punished. Other language suggests instead that the gap between speech and future harm was bridged by the existence of a criminal conspiracy to overthrow the government, and that the speech was closely tied to the operation of the conspiracy.

Vinson adopted the approach taken by the lower court, ironically in an opinion by Learned Hand, author of the *Masses* opinion some thirty years earlier. Hand had argued that the clear and present danger test required a consideration of the degree of harm multiplied by its probability, so that speech causing even a small probability of harm could be banned if the possible harm was great enough. Surely, Vinson said, the government need not wait "until the putsch is about to be executed, the plans have been laid, and the signal is awaited." If a group is indoctrinating its members and preparing them to strike when the time is ripe, the government may step in. Given the nature of the world situation, the majority found ample reason for Congress to conclude that communism posed a legitimate threat. The dissenters argued quite cogently, however, that the defendants were not charged with a conspiracy to overthrow the government, but only with a conspiracy to advocate the desirability of doing so by distributing Marxist tracts. If the government wanted to prove that an actual plan for violent revolution was afoot, it should have made that the basis of the prosecution rather than the defendants' speech.

Dennis left the law in some confusion. On the one hand, the Court obviously was not about to question the threat of domestic communist subversion. On the other hand, the statute was not merely upheld on the basis that Marxist works would infect public thinking, but rather on the basis of an assumed connection between the defendants' speech and an on-going conspiracy that the Court found threatening enough to justify government intervention. The Court's rejection of a facial attack on the Smith Act left considerable question about future application of the statute: Was any advocacy of Marxist doctrine enough, given the congressional findings about

---

[8]   341 U.S. 494 (1951).

the general threat posed by communism? Or was some more specific connection with conspiratorial activity required?

B. Post-*Dennis* Opinions

Yates v. United States[9] was the Court's first attempt to clarify *Dennis*. The government argued that *any* advocacy of forceful overthrow was illegal; the statute permitted only "mere discussion or exposition of violent overthrow as an abstract theory." The trial judge agreed. He relied on language in *Dennis* saying that "advocacy of violent action to be taken at some future time was enough" to justify a conviction, if coupled with an intent to overthrow the government. Apparently, in the trial judge's view, *Dennis* obliterated the line between advocacy of doctrine and advocacy of action. Writing for the Court, Justice Harlan rejected the government's position and narrowly defined the class of speech punishable under the Smith Act. The trial judge, he said, had misread *Dennis*, which Harlan interpreted to apply only to "language of incitement" used to prepare members of a group for future violent action. Even then, such language could only be proscribed "when the group is of sufficient size and cohesiveness, is sufficiently oriented towards action, and other circumstances are such as reasonably to justify apprehension that action will occur." Hence, Justice Harlan remarked, for the statute to apply, "those to whom the advocacy is addressed must be urged to *do* something, rather than merely to *believe* in something." He then proceeded to examine the record, finding too little evidence of a "call to forcible action at some future time," as opposed to advocacy of forcible overthrow as an abstract doctrine.

In addition to banning advocacy, the Smith Act also made it a felony to be a knowing member of any group advocating forceful overthrow of the government. In *Scales v. United States*,[10] Justice Harlan's opinion for the Court gave the membership clause a narrow reading. *Scales* held that membership in the Communist Party could be punished only if the member was active in the Party, knew of the Party's illegal aims, and had a specific intent to further those aims. Because the Party was not named in the statute, the government had to prove anew in each case that the Party was devoted to illegal advocacy. In *Scales* such evidence was present. But in *Noto*,[11] a companion case, the conviction was reversed because the record in that case did not contain substantial evidence of present illegal advocacy by the Party. As Harlan explained in *Noto*, "the mere abstract teaching of Communist theory, including the teaching of the moral propriety or even moral necessity for a resort to force and

---

[9]   354 U.S. 298 (1957).

[10]   367 U.S. 203 (1961).

[11]   *Noto v. United States,* 367 U.S. 290 (1961).

violence, is not the same as preparing a group for violent action and steeling it to such action." The heavy standard of proof established in *Scales* and *Noto* put an end to Smith Act prosecutions. By then, the McCarthy era had faded away. New social issues, rather than communism, would provide the major source of free speech litigation.

C.   Assessing "Clear and Present Danger"

Up through the early 1960s, a cynical observer might have remarked that the First Amendment seemed to evaporate just when it was needed most, in times of public hysteria, while functioning to protect a few harmless cranks during more peaceful periods. Critics of the "clear and present danger" test have argued that this test contributed to the problem because it was too subjective and prone to manipulation. Under Vinson's interpretation, the test amounted to little more than a deferential balancing test. This seems far removed from the original intentions of Brandeis and Holmes, who were attempting to identify emergencies where suppression of speech was the only viable alternative. But Vinson could have replied that communism in the early 1950s did present an emergency situation, and that international experience had shown that the threat of communist conspiracy was just as urgent as a speaker inciting a mob to riot.

The McCarthy era cases prompted a renewed debate about First Amendment methodology. Justices Black and Douglas attacked the "clear and present danger" test as a pernicious example of balancing, which they said served only to sacrifice protected rights to momentary expediency. The "clear and present danger" test, they said, had simply become an invitation to the Court to decide whether it was reasonable to suppress speech in particular circumstances, and it had turned out to be all too easy for the Court to say "yes." In their view, "pure" speech should be absolutely protected from *any* government regulation; regulation should be only allowed where expression was intertwined with "conduct." In reply, the "balancers" accused the "absolutists" of fostering an absurd approach to free speech. This approach was unworkable, they said, because the Constitution can't possibly protect all communicative behavior, and unfounded, because there is no historical evidence that the Framers intended such a sweeping result.

Clearly, the extreme versions of each position were unworkable. Under a pure balancing approach, a judge would approach each case anew, striving to balance the government interest in regulating speech against the individual interest in free speech. This approach would provide little predictability, leaving speakers to guess about what a future judge might consider reasonable. It would also be an open invitation for judges to endorse popular repressive actions at the expense of unappealing, marginalized dissidents. Predictably, judges would be tempted to defer to the political branches of government, as they do in assessing the constitutionality of other kinds of government regulations. Thus, a pure balancing approach would provide only tenuous protection for freedom of speech. Moreover, as the experience of the McCarthy era seemed to show, that protection would be all the more tenuous just when it was needed the most—in periods when public indignation was focused on the elimination of dissent.

But absolutism seemed equally unappealing. As we saw in Chapter 1, there is questionable historical warrant for the idea that the Framers intended such sweeping protection for speech. Historically, some restrictions on speech such as obscenity and libel laws were well entrenched and little questioned. Moreover, society clearly has a legitimate interest in regulating many kinds of communicative activities, such as false advertising, solicitations of bribes by public officials, and agreements to fix prices. Other communicative activities, such as parades, broadcasting, and picketing, seem to require government regulation because of their ability to interfere physically with the activities of others. Supporters of the absolutist approach attempted to deal with these situations in several ways: by saying that the government was regulating the "conduct" aspect of the behavior rather than the "speech" aspect, by classifying certain activities as non-speech even though they involved communication, or by calling them "speech brigaded with action." Balancers found these distinctions metaphysical if not contrived.

Like many great debates, this one faded away without ever being explicitly resolved. At least by the 1960s, there was general agreement that the balancers were partially correct: freedom of speech cannot be an absolute, and legitimate government interests deserve a hearing. On the other hand, the absolutists were right that open-ended balancing provided inadequate protection for speech. The problem, then, was to craft doctrines that provided firm protection for speech without the rigidity of the absolutist approach.

III. *Brandenburg* and Beyond

The 1960s were a time of ferment in American society. Once the perceived threat of domestic subversion had been put to rest, free speech increasingly became intertwined with the Warren Court's crusade against segregation. Many of the free speech cases of the period involved civil rights demonstrators. The case that the Court used to settle the issue of subversive speech, however, came from the other end of the spectrum, for it involved a virulent form of racism. Perhaps this was mere coincidence, or perhaps the Court was pleased to have the opportunity to prove its willingness to support free speech even for its own enemies. In any event, the Court was later to have the opportunity to apply its approach to protect civil rights advocates as well. In a triumph of the idea of "neutral principles," the same test that had served to protect the Ku Klux Klan proved equally serviceable for the NAACP.

A.   The Current Test

The use of the clear and present danger test in *Dennis* raised considerable doubt about whether it offered sufficient protection to subversive speech. After the McCarthy era, however, the test was applied with greater bite. In *Watts v. United States*,[12] the defendant had proclaimed at a public rally that he had received his draft notice but he wasn't going, and "if they ever make me carry a rifle the first man I want to get in my sights is L.B.J. [who was President then]." His conviction, under a federal statute making it a crime to threaten the life of the President, was overturned on the ground that he had merely engaged in political hyperbole.

The current test for illegal advocacy was announced shortly afterwards in *Brandenburg v. Ohio*.[13] A Ku Klux Klan leader had been convicted under the Ohio criminal syndicalism statute for advocating violence as a means of political change. He spoke at a rally where a large cross was burned by hooded figures, some of whom were armed. At the rally, he gave a somewhat incoherent speech in which he proclaimed that the Klan was "not a revengent organization, but if our President, our Congress, our Supreme Court, continues to suppress the white, Caucasian race, it's possible that there might have to be some revengence taken." He also stated that "[p]ersonally, I believe the nigger should be returned to Africa, the Jew returned to Israel."

Despite this hateful language, the Court unanimously reversed the conviction. Although the opinion appeared as a *per curiam*, it was actually drafted by Justice Fortas before he resigned from the Court under congressional pressure. The Court observed that the Ohio statute was quite similar to the law upheld by the majority in *Whitney*, but reasoned that *Whitney* had been discredited by later cases. "These later decisions," the Court said, "have fashioned the principle that the constitutional guarantees of free speech and free press do not permit a State to forbid or proscribe advocacy of the use of force or of law violation except where such advocacy is directed to inciting or producing imminent lawless action and is likely to incite or produce such action." Quoting Justice Harlan's opinion in *Noto*, the Court emphasized that "the mere abstract teaching . . . of the

---

[12]   394 U.S. 705 (1969).

[13]   395 U.S. 444 (1969).

moral propriety or even moral necessity for a resort to force and violence, is not the same as preparing a group for violent action and steeling it to such action." Thus, under *Brandenburg*, advocacy of violence can be prohibited only when (1) it is directed to inciting imminent lawless action, and (2) it is likely to produce such action.

Later cases, though sparse, steadfastly maintain this approach. In *Hess v. Indiana*,[14] the Court reversed the conviction of an antiwar demonstrator who yelled "[w]e'll take the fucking street later (or again)." The Court held that this language amounted at most to the "advocacy of illegal action at some indefinite future time." Since the evidence showed that his statement was an exclamation rather than being directed specifically at any group, and since there was no evidence that his statement was intended and likely to produce imminent disorder, the statement was constitutionally protected.

Similarly, in *NAACP v. Claiborne Hardware Co.*,[15] the Court set aside an award of damages based on an NAACP boycott of white merchants in a Mississippi town. In the course of the boycott, one NAACP official had proclaimed in a public speech that if "we catch any of you going in any of them racist stores, we're gonna break your damn neck." Finding that the speech essentially was an impassioned plea for support of the boycott, the Court admitted that strong language had been used, and that if acts of violence had followed, there would have been a substantial question about whether the speaker could be held liable. But because the only acts of violence were weeks or months later, the Court said, no liability could attach. Advocates must be free to make spontaneous emotional appeals without carefully weighing their words, and such appeals are protected speech when they do not incite lawless action. If anything, *Claiborne* seems to go beyond *Brandenburg* by holding that, at least under the circumstances of the case, it was not only necessary to demonstrate that immediate violence was a likely result of the speech but also to show that it actually materialized.

Brandenburg raises some interesting doctrinal questions. First, it is not clear whether the first element of the test ("directed to producing" lawless action) is a reference to the content of the speech, the subjective intent of the speaker, or some combination of the two. If the test is content (as suggested by the language contrasting abstract teaching with incitement), a subsidiary question is how explicit the meaning must be. A clever speaker might incite a crowd to violence without ever explicitly directing them to break the law; indeed, he might ironically direct them not to do so in terms leaving little doubt about his real intent. (The classic example is Mark

---

[14]   414 U.S. 105 (1973).
[15]   458 U.S. 886 (1982).

Antony's funeral oration, purportedly seeking to "bury Caesar not to praise him," but actually a plea for revenge for Caesar's murder.) It seems obtuse for a court to blind itself to the real meaning of the words; on the other hand, the more the court is allowed to depart from the literal dictionary meaning, the more room for manipulation of the test.

Second, it is not clear whether the test applies beyond the setting of suppression of political dissent. What about advocacy of law breaking in more ordinary settings, such as one gang member trying to talk another into killing a rival? To the extent that *Brandenburg* is aimed at providing expressive room for political radicals, it would seem to have no application, but trying to draw a line between ideological and non-ideological advocacy might be difficult. Finally, what about advocacy of nonviolent crimes? Could a person be prosecuted for incitement to jaywalking, if the *Brandenberg* test was satisfied? More realistically, what about incitement to tax evasion by a tax protestor? All of the decisions to date have involved risks of grievous harm, immediate or otherwise, rather than other kinds of damage that society might be better able to sustain.

The Court has had no real occasion to address these questions, and it seems doubtful that a microscopic parsing of the language of the existing opinions will provide firm answers. Although a number of commentators seem convinced that these questions have obvious answers (which they disagree about, of course), it seems apparent that present law simply does not provide any clear-cut solutions. As we will see in the next chapter, somewhat analogous questions have arisen in the context of libel law, where rules designed to protect vigorous criticism of the government have been invoked in private settings and where the problem of interpreting ambiguous language has also arisen.

B.   Is *Brandenburg*'s Approach Justified?

It does not seem self-evident to many people (perhaps most people) that the Constitution should protect those who would, if given their way, resort to violence in order to suppress their own opponents. It would be no loss if Stalinists, Nazis, and others of their ilk were to fade away from our society. Why should we protect ideas that are, as Justice Holmes put it, "fraught with death"? Advocacy of violence—an idea "fraught with death"—receives considerable protection from the *Brandenburg* approach, which frees their advocates to spread evil so long as there is no proof of immediate physical danger.

The traditional way to address this question is to invoke the First Amendment values discussed in Chapter 1. Thus, proponents of the self-realization theory proclaim the right of individuals to express their ideas, however horrible, so long as no one else is actually injured. Proponents of the marketplace of ideas rely on public debate to eliminate harmful ideas, and in the meantime hope that the debate against them will invigorate more acceptable viewpoints. Tolerance and safety-valve theorists hope to increase social stability, either by demonstrating society's commitment to putting up with disgusting people or by giving them an opportunity to blow off steam rather than doing something more harmful. There is nothing wrong with these arguments, but they seem unlikely to convert skeptics.

Here, to quote another Holmes-ism, a line of history may be worth a page of logic. Slippery slope arguments have always been popular in First Amendment law. Their logic may be suspect; after all, the law does often manage to draw workable lines rather than taking ideas to their logical conclusions. But, at least in the area of subversive speech, there is much historical support for the existence of the slippery slope. Beginning with World War I, the spectacle of American efforts to suppress subversive speech has not been appealing. Rather than limiting itself to genuinely dangerous people, the apparatus of speech control has swept up an array of characters ranging from harmless cranks to those guilty of little more than an offhand remark, not to mention tainting through guilt by association many others whose basic commitment was to democratic politics. Worse, some of the targets of repression have actually been right about what they were saying—in retrospect, World War I didn't make a great deal of sense and the abortive Allied intervention in Russia may have done more harm than good. The threats prompting censorship seem in retrospect to have been chimeras, such as the fear of a successful domestic Communist insurrection. To the extent that Communist activities posed a threat, it involved genuine espionage, not passing out copies of the tedious writings of Marx and Lenin. Surely, we can learn something from this history.

In short, we have awoken "the morning after" some of these censorship binges with more than a little embarrassment. There seems to be no need to repeat the experience. The same experience gives us some reason to doubt, unfortunately, how effectively courts can function to restrain genuine public hysteria. But at least we might as well adopt legal doctrines that provide courts some support in that effort. The *Brandenburg* test may or may not be the ideal formulation. It grows out of some sixty years of effort by judges to forge some workable standard. *Brandenburg* has worked reasonable well, and it seems unlikely that any other formulation would be a dramatic improvement.

IV. Other Restrictions on Subversive Speech

So far, we have been concerned with the use of criminal sanctions to protect public order and national security. To round out the picture, we should at least briefly consider some of the other techniques that the government has used for these repressive purposes from time to time. The judicial responses to these government efforts were different from *Brandenburg*, but shared the commitment to providing a wide zone of protection for "subversive" speech.

A. Prior Restraints

As we saw in Chapter 3, prior restraints are greatly disfavored. The Court has adamantly stuck to this principle in the area of national security. In the *Pentagon Papers Case*,[16] the government attempted to enjoin the New York Times and Washington Post from publishing a classified study about U.S. policy in Vietnam. The Court heard the case at breakneck speed. The arguments were held within three days of the lower courts' decisions, and the briefs arrived only two hours before the argument. A terse *per curiam* opinion, issued only five days after argument in the case, affirmed the refusal of the lower courts to grant the government relief. In addition to the *per curiam*, each Justice filed a separate opinion.

The government's case had several appealing features. First, the material had been classified as top secret, and the government presented some evidence that release of the information would be damaging to foreign relations. Second, the case took place during an ongoing (though undeclared) war, when the government's authority to protect the national interest is particularly strong. And third, the material was not rightfully in the hands of the newspapers; it had been misappropriated by a disgruntled government consultant and turned over to them.

Nevertheless, five Justices firmly rejected the injunction on First Amendment grounds, joined by a sixth who relied on the absence of explicit statutory authority for the government's suit. Not surprisingly, Justices Black and Douglas relied on their sweeping view of the First Amendment. Black argued that "the history and language of the First Amendment" demonstrate that "the press must be left free to publish news, whatever the source, without censorship, injunctions, or prior restraints." In his view, "every moment's continuance of the injunctions against these newspapers amounts to a flagrant, indefensible, and continuing violation of the First Amendment." Douglas argued that government secrecy, in general, is "fundamentally anti-democratic," and that the delays in

---

[16] *New York Times Co. v. United States*, 403 U.S. 713 (1971).

publication during the litigation were a "flouting" of the First Amendment.

Three other Justices agreed, though in less sweeping language. According to Justice Brennan, only proof that publication would "inevitably, directly, and immediately cause the occurrence of an event kindred to imperiling the safety of a transport already at sea" would justify even an interim restraining order. Justice Stewart applied a similar test, and said that judicial relief would be justified only if disclosure of the material "will surely result in direct, immediate, and irreparable damage to our Nation or its people." Although Justice White believed, based on his examination of the materials, that publication would "do substantial damage to public interests," he found this insufficient to carry the government's "very heavy burden" to obtain an injunction.

The Pentagon Papers Case is a firm rejection of governmental authority to obtain a prior restraint, even in a relatively appealing case. The most notable prior restraint case since that time never reached the Supreme Court. It involved an effort to publish material that had been mistakenly declassified but would allegedly make it much easier for a foreign power to build nuclear weapons. The district court issued an injunction against publication, which was later dissolved when other newspapers (not covered by the injunction) published the material.[17] So far, the sky hasn't fallen as a result of the release of the material.

B. Investigations

Efforts to obtain prior restraints based on national security claims are rare in our history. A much more common technique, particularly popular in the McCarthy era, is the use of legislative investigations to expose dissenters to public disapproval. The Warren Court invalidated some of the resulting convictions for refusal to testify on due process grounds, because the witnesses were not given adequate notice of the basis for the legislators' questions. The Court was initially less receptive to First Amendment challenges. In *Barenblatt v. United States*,[18] a former teaching assistant refused to answer questions about his alleged Communist Party membership in hearings before a subcommittee of the House Un-American Activities Committee (better known as HUAC). The Court concluded that investigating communist infiltration into universities was permissible because of the "close nexus between the Communist Party and violent overthrow of [the] government." The Court also found no indication in the record of "other factors" that

---

[17] *United States v. Progressive, Inc.*, 467 F.Supp. 990 (W.D. Wis. 1979).

[18] 360 U.S. 109 (1959).

might support the witness's position, such as indications that the committee was trying to "pillory" witnesses, that the committee had followed an indiscriminate "dragnet" procedure by calling witnesses without any probable cause, or that the relevance of the questions was doubtful.

In later opinions, the Court fastened on some of these factors as a basis for restricting legislative investigations. In *Gibson v. Florida Investigation Committee*,[19] the Court reversed the conviction of the president of a local branch of the NAACP, who had refused to reveal whether fourteen individuals identified as Communists were members of the NAACP. The Court held that when an investigation intrudes on protected expressive activity, the state must "convincingly show a substantial relation between the information sought and a subject of overriding and compelling state interest." *Barenblatt* was found distinguishable because it involved an inquiry into membership in the Communist party, which was not a legitimate political organization, unlike the NAACP. Nor was there any evidence of a connection between the NAACP and communist activities (as opposed to possible overlap of membership). The Court seemed troubled both by the lack of any good reason for the state to seek the information and by the absence of any probable cause to believe that the information would be found. This "probable cause" concept was reinforced in a later decision.[20]

Part of the Court's difficulty in this area stems from the fact that it is dealing with an individualized activity (calling a specific witness for a specific purpose) rather than the application of a general rule. Many of the Court's most powerful tools, like the overbreadth doctrine and the content distinction, are geared toward assessing general rules. Thus, in considering legislative investigations, the Court has been forced to strike a balance in individual cases between the government's need for information and the possible chilling effect of abusive investigations on First Amendment rights.

C. Loyalty Oaths

Another popular technique in the McCarthy era was the loyalty oath. The same pattern was repeated here: early decisions upholding the practice were followed by decisions in the 1960s firmly reining in the government's activities. For example, in *Garner v. Board of Public Works*,[21] the Court upheld a requirement that public employees swear that they did not advocate the violent overthrow of the government or belong to any organization advocating such

---

[19]   372 U.S. 539 (1963).

[20]   See *DeGregory v. Attorney General of New Hampshire*, 383 U.S. 825 (1966).

[21]   341 U.S. 716 (1951).

overthrow. But in 1966, the Court took a much different approach.[22] Arizona required all state employees to take an oath to the effect that they were not "knowingly" members of the Communist Party or any other organization seeking the overthrow of the government of Arizona. The Court found that mere membership, even knowing membership, is insufficient under *Scales* to provide a basis for punishment. A member who does not share the organization's unlawful purposes or participate in unlawful activities poses no threat, but the Arizona oath was not limited to individuals having a specific intent to overthrow the government.

Loyalty oaths seem a particularly apt arena for application of the overbreadth doctrine. It is true that some of the activity proscribed by an overbroad oath is not constitutionally protected, but the employee has no way of limiting the oath to unprotected activity—she must either take the oath as is, or forego the job. Without rewriting the oath entirely, there is no way the court can give it any effect without upholding it entirely.

Loyalty oaths have a bad reputation, going back to Henry VIII's use of oaths to winnow out Catholic sympathizers. Apart from their capacity to impinge on protected rights, they seem uncomfortably close either to self-incrimination (to the extent that refusal to take the oath is a confession) or to compelled speech (to the extent that taking the oath is an ideological pledge). Fortunately, this method of curtailing dissent seems to have fallen out of favor today.

D. True Threats

Particularly in a public setting, there can be a thin line between incitement and threat. *Brandenburg* itself involved a statement that "it's possible that there might have to be some revengence taken" if the President, Congress and the Supreme Court "continues to suppress the white, Caucasian race." The Court treated this as advocacy of violence, but it could equally have been seen as a threat against those federal officials

As with incitement, the key issue is the line between concrete criminality and political advocacy. The Court attempted to define that line in *Virginia v. Black*.[23] The case involved several defendants who were separately convicted of violating Virginia's cross-burning statute. The statute made it a crime to burn a cross with the intent to intimidate. Under the statute, burning a cross was prima facie evidence of the required intent to intimidate.

One of the cases before the Court involved political speech. Black led a Ku Klux Klan rally in an open field near a public highway, at

---

[22] *Elfbrandt v. Russell*, 384 U.S. 11 (1966).
[23] 538 U.S. 343 (2003).

which a cross was burned. The other case arose out of a personal dispute. The other defendants drove a truck onto the property of an African American, planted a cross, and set it on fire.

Virginia v. Black defines a category of unprotected speech consisting of "true threats." According to the Court, "true threats" are not protected speech. This category encompasses "those statements where the speaker means to communicate a serious expression of an intent to commit an act of unlawful violence to a particular individual or group of individuals." Intimidation occurs "where a speaker directs a threat to a person or group of persons with the intent of placing the victim in fear of bodily harm or death." Note that there is no requirement of a probability that the intimidation will succeed or that the defendant have any means of carrying out the threat.

Within the category of true threats, the Virginia statute proscribed only a subset consisting of cross-burning. This selectivity would appear to raise a problem under *R.A.V.* (which was itself a cross-burning case). The Court held, however, that the state could legitimately single out the use of cross-burning for purposes of intimidation because cross-burning is one of "those forms of intimidation that are most likely to inspire fear of bodily harm." Thus, unlike the targeting of racist use of fighting words in *R.A.V.*, targeting cross-burning as a form of intimidation was legitimate. But the Court held that Virginia could not make cross burning prima facie evidence of intent to intimidate, which required a reversal of Black's conviction for cross-burning at the rally and a remand of the other cases.

E.   Material Support for Terrorists

In *Holder v. Humanitarian Project*,[24] the Court dealt with a case on the borderline between freedom of association and freedom of speech. *Holder* involved a statute banning "material support" for foreign terrorist groups, which would suggest that any issue would involve freedom of association. However, the "support" in question in the case involved speech, such as teaching members of the group how to use international law and U.N. petitions as methods of seeking relief for their grievances. The Court upheld the statute in a somewhat guarded opinion. In his opinion for the Court, Chief Justice Roberts identified a compelling government interest— prevention of terrorism—and held that the statute was carefully drawn to cover only a narrow category of speech to foreign groups that the speaker knows to be terrorist organizations. The Court stressed, however, that it was not upholding application of the law to

---

[24]   561 U.S. 1 (2010).

domestic organizations nor was it upholding any possible ban on independent advocacy on behalf of an organization or its goals.

V. *Brandenburg* as Paradigm

Brandenburg is not simply a single case. Rather, it is emblematic of the entire post-1960 development of the law to protect subversive speech. Because repression of subversive speech is so central to the history of censorship, the resolution of the issue in *Brandenburg* became something of a paradigm for other speech problems. As we will see, First Amendment law is full of formulas like the *Brandenburg* test, setting the standards for some class of government speech regulations. Current First Amendment law is replete with "tests," from *Miller* for obscenity and *Sullivan* for libel, to *Perry* for public forums and *Central Hudson* for commercial speech—most of them, like *Brandenburg* itself, sporting multi-part standards. As a result, far more than other areas of constitutional law, First Amendment law resembles a complex code or one of the American Law Institute's detailed Restatements of the Law. Thus, the *Brandenburg* methodology turns out to be quite popular for other areas of First Amendment law, perhaps because of the Court's desire to combine some form of firm guidelines with a degree of flexibility, just as *Brandenburg* compromises between absolutism and balancing.

Brandenburg also changed the psychological stakes in other First Amendment cases. Since the government's interests are so weighty in subversion cases, the severe restrictions placed on its ability to achieve its goals also raise questions about other kinds of government speech regulations. If "let's kill the governor" is protected speech, why not also "the governor is a crook" or simply "fuck the governor"? Subversive speech has been the historical stronghold of censorship, and once the stronghold started to fall, the rest of the domain was immediately at risk. This effect was intensified because, compared with subversive speech, most other areas of speech regulation were not as strongly ideologically charged. Once the Justices had reached a consensus on subversive speech, it was much easier for them to agree on other areas.

Perhaps the most notable aspect of *Brandenburg* is how easily it has attained the standing of an unquestioned tradition. Later cases proclaim as central to the First Amendment the principle that every idea, no matter how hateful, is entitled to full constitutional protection. This is a concept that might not have made much sense to the majority in the *Schenck* case, or perhaps even to some members of the *Dennis* majority, but today it is uncontroversial. The burden is now placed on advocates of government regulation to show that the "suppression of ideas" is not their agenda.

The reasons for this complete acceptance of the new standard probably go beyond the legal system. Although some areas of speech law are still controversial, it is hard to find any serious academic or political voice demanding the elimination of subversive thoughts or organizations. Perhaps the emphatic support of the Supreme Court for free speech has played a role in this change from long-standing American political practice. But there are probably other reasons as well. Today, we have more confidence in the resilience and strength of our system, and less reason to fear that extremists will undermine the entire system. Experience has shown that the system can function well despite widespread dissent and highly pluralist perspectives. Moreover, the government seems to be strong enough to cope with actual threats of violence or criminal conspiracies. In a sense, censorship is a sign of weakness, because it suggests a fear that society may crumble from harsh words.

Many people may experience distress from the weakening of the sense of community involved in this greater degree of pluralism, and from the sheer amount of hateful nonsense in circulation at any given time. Still, the system seems to function well enough. In the meantime, much more repressive systems have crumbled into the dust. In any event, the stakes no longer seem to be as high—we have learned that we can live rather comfortably while accommodating a fair amount of political craziness around the fringes of society. Whatever the sociological causes, the societal urge to hunt down and eliminate subversives seems to have faded away, at least for the moment.

FURTHER READINGS

Vincent Blasi, *The First Amendment and the Ideal of Civic Courage: The Brandeis Opinion in* Whitney v. California, 29 Wm. & Mary L. Rev. 653 (1988).

David Cole, *The First Amendment's Borders: The Place of* Holder v. Humanitarian Law Project *in First Amendment Doctrine*, 6 Harv. L. & Pol'y Rev. 147 (2012).

Gerald Gunther, *Learned Hand and the Origins of Modern First Amendment Doctrine: Some Fragments of History*, 27 Stan. L. Rev. 719 (1975).

Philip Hamburger, *The Development of the Law of Seditious Libel and the Control of the Press*, 37 Stan. L. Rev. 661 (1985).

Thomas Healy, *Brandenburg in a Time of Terror*, 84 Notre Dame L. Rev. 655 (2009).

Leslie Kendrick, *Free Speech and Guilty Minds*, 114 Colum. L. Rev. 1255 (2014).

S. Elizabeth Willborn Malloy and Ronald J. Krotoszynski, Jr., *Recalibrating the Cost of Harm Advocacy: Getting Beyond* Brandenburg, 41 Wm. & Mary L. Rev. 1159 (2000).

Richard Polenberg, Fighting Faiths: The Abrams Case, the Supreme Court, and Free Speech (1987).

Richard A. Posner, *The Constitution in a Time of National Emergency* (2006).

L.A. Powe, Jr., *The H-Bomb Injunction*, 61 U. Colo. L. Rev. 55 (1990).

Alexander Tsesis, *Inflammatory Speech: Offense Versus Incitement*, 97 Minn. L. Rev. 1145 (2013).

William M. Wiecek, *The Legal Foundations of Domestic Anticommunism: The Background of* Dennis v. United States, 2001 Sup. Ct. Rev. 375 (2002).

Timothy Zick, *Falsely Shouting Fire in a Global Theater: Emerging Complexities of Transborder Expression*, 65 Vand. L. Rev. 125 (2012).

Chapter 5

DEFAMATION AND OTHER TORTS

Recall Justice Holmes's assertion that the First Amendment did not protect the person who falsely yelled "fire" in a crowded theater. Indeed, the traditional view was that the First Amendment generally did not protect false statements of fact. For centuries, the common law has provided a generous cause of action to individuals whose reputations have been harmed by false statements, especially published statements. Constitutional lawyers simply took for granted that this remedy raised no First Amendment concerns. If questioned, they might have said either that the right to free speech did not preclude compensation for those injured by abuses, or more simply that slander and libel had never been considered part of the "freedom of speech" protected by the First Amendment.

Today, the situation is quite different. Public officials can file defamation actions only under very limited circumstances. Even ordinary private individuals must bring their defamation actions within the boundaries established by the Supreme Court. Other causes of action for injurious speech are similarly hampered, and in some cases eliminated. For example, it is nearly impossible for a public official to sue for outrageous speech designed to cause severe emotional distress.

This chapter tells the story of this remarkable legal change. It also explores some themes that are directly relevant to current debates about free speech—in particular, how the courts have made the protection of vigorous public debate an overwhelming priority, compared with protection of injured individual reputations and psyches.

I. The *New York Times* Case

More than most areas of the law, constitutional defamation law stems from a single dramatic case. Until that case was decided, lawyers specializing in defamation law could safely ignore the possibility of any constitutional issues; afterwards, the entire field was rapidly subsumed within constitutional law. We begin with a careful examination of that case and its background.

A. Background

The common law provided a generous remedy for plaintiffs whose reputations were harmed by false accusations, whether verbal (slander) or written (libel). It was unnecessary for the plaintiff to show that the falsehood was negligent or deliberate, and the rules about damages were unusually favorable to the plaintiff. Thus, to make a negative statement about a well-known figure was to take a legal gamble.

Prior to *New York Times v. Sullivan*, defamation law had only fitfully received attention as a possible constitutional problem. Undoubtedly, the most important historical controversy related to the Sedition Act of 1798, which made it a crime to print "false, scandalous, and malicious writing" about the government. The great disputes at common law had been over whether truth was a defense or whether the jury was limited to deciding the mere fact of publication. The Sedition Act resolved both of these issues in favor of the defendant, which made it a somewhat progressive piece of legislation, at least compared with the English common law. Nevertheless, the Sedition Act served as a powerful tool for the Federalist Party to attack its enemies, and in return the law was vigorously attacked as a violation of the First Amendment. In the Virginia Resolutions of 1798, which were drafted by James Madison, the Virginia legislature criticized the statute as a violation "of the right of freely examining public characters and measures, and of free communications among the people thereon, which has ever been justly deemed the only effectual guardian of every other right." The constitutionality of the Act never reached the Supreme Court, though it might well have been upheld. But the political verdict was that the Act violated basic constitutional norms. When the Federalists lost the White House, President Jefferson pardoned the offenders, and their fines were refunded by a federal statute.

When the First Amendment began to receive serious judicial attention in the first half of the Twentieth Century, the issue of libel was not at the forefront. Instead, in what became known as the "two tier" theory, libel was considered to be below the plane of constitutionally protected speech (along with some other types of expression), so that it could be regulated by the states with impunity.

In *Beauharnais v. Illinois*,[1] the Court went so far as to uphold a statute prohibiting public exhibition of any publication portraying "depravity, criminality, unchastity, or lack of virtue of a class of citizens, of any race, color, creed or religion." The defendant had organized distribution of a leaflet calling upon the city government to halt the flow of blacks into white Chicago neighborhoods, referring to the "rapes, robberies, knives, guns, and marijuana of the negro." The Court observed that libel is one of the "well-defined and narrowly limited classes of speech, the prevention and punishment of which have never been thought to raise any constitutional problem." The Court concluded that if the state had the power to punish lies about

---

[1]   343 U.S. 250 (1952).

a single individual, it also had power to punish lies against a "defined group." In language which is relevant to present-day discussions of "hate speech," the Court added:

> [T]he Illinois Legislature may warrantably believe that a man's job and his educational opportunities and the dignity accorded him may depend as much on the reputation of the racial and religious group to which he willy nilly belongs, as on his own merits. This being so, we are precluded from saying that speech concededly punishable when immediately directed at individuals cannot be outlawed if directed at groups with whose position and esteem in society the affiliated individual may be inextricably involved.

(We will return to the problem of hate speech in Chapter 7.) Nor was the defendant entitled to litigate the truth of the statements, because Illinois like many other states allowed such a defense only for statements made "with good motives and for justifiable ends." The defendant's motives did not qualify. Because libel was not subject to the First Amendment, the Court held that it was unnecessary for the state to demonstrate the existence of a "clear and present danger," which was then the general standard for speech regulations.

Beauharnais was unusual not only because it involved a group rather than an individual plaintiff, but also because it was a criminal action. During the past century, defamation has almost always been a matter for civil litigation. But even civil defamation law is somewhat punitive. The liability rules are harsh. Unlike most common law torts, defamation liability is based on strict liability rather than intentional or negligent wrongdoing. The plaintiff does not have to be named in order to be defamed; it was enough if a reasonable reader could infer his identity. Truth is a defense, but the defendant had to show that the statement was true in all significant respects to gain the benefit of this defense. Moreover, it is unnecessary at common law for the plaintiff to prove any actual damages in order to recover significant amounts for libel, because harm to reputation was considered to be a basis for compensation even without proof of more tangible harm. Most states did provide a privilege for statements of opinion on matters of public concern, but only a few allowed an exemption for good faith factual errors about public officials.

With this background in mind, we turn to *New York Times v. Sullivan.*[2] The *Sullivan* case exemplified some of the shortcomings of libel law. Sullivan was one of the city commissioners in Montgomery, Alabama, and was in charge of the police department. He sued the

---

[2]   376 U.S. 254 (1964).

New York Times and four black clergymen because of an ad which had run in the Times. A jury awarded him damages of $500,000 (equivalent to several million dollars at today's prices.) The newspaper ad had run in 1960, as an outgrowth of nonviolent demonstrations against segregation taking place in the South. These demonstrations, according to the ad, were being met by a "wave of terror." Among the examples were events taking place in Montgomery.

Although Sullivan wasn't named, the state courts said that negative descriptions of the Montgomery police in the article would naturally reflect on him as the chief administrator. Since in fact he had no connection with these events, the inference that he was involved was erroneous. For example, the ad said "they have arrested" Martin Luther King, Jr. several times. Sullivan claimed that the normal inference would be that he was responsible for the arrests as chief of the police force, and that this implication was false and defamatory.

Also, the text of the ad contained some minor and largely irrelevant inaccuracies, so that the defense of truth was unavailable. For example, on one occasion when demonstrators were alleged to have sung "My Country, Tis of Thee," they had actually sung the national anthem; nine students were expelled from a state college, but for a different demonstration than the one described; and police were "deployed near the campus in large numbers on three occasions" but did not actually "ring the campus" as the ad alleged.

The *Times* was subject to suit in Alabama because 394 copies of this particular edition of the Times were sold there, of which about 35 copies circulated in Montgomery County where they allegedly damaged Sullivan's reputation. The suit was not an isolated incident. In Alabama, there were eleven libel suits by officials seeking over $5 million in damages from the *Times*, and five more suits against the CBS television network seeking $1.7 million.

This litigation was a vivid example of the dangers of libel law. There was no reason to think that Sullivan had suffered any substantial reputational damage. Most of his friends and neighbors would probably have applauded him, if they did happen to see one of the few copies of the *Times* circulating in the county and inferred that he was responsible for brutality against the civil rights movement. The case was brought in Alabama, where Sullivan was guaranteed a partisan jury (not to mention favorable judicial treatment), even though the paper had almost no circulation in the state. Moreover, the errors in the article were relatively inconsequential, and certainly could not have resulted in damaging Sullivan to the tune of $500,000. Yet, the Alabama courts did not have to distort defamation law in order to uphold the jury verdict against the newspaper. On the contrary, the doctrines applied by the state courts were within the mainstream. Traditionally, liability for defamation required only that the defendant make a factually flawed statement, which a reasonable person might view as having a meaning harmful to the plaintiff's reputation.

B. The Court's Opinion

In one stroke, the Supreme Court turned the previously unprotected domain of libel into an area of core First Amendment concern, federalizing an entire field of state tort law. As one noted torts scholar pointed out, during an era in which torts law as a whole was shifting in a highly pro-plaintiff direction, defamation law was the only success story for defendants, thanks to the Supreme Court. The Court's opinion is of interest not only because of its foundational importance in this area of the law, but also because its methodology and reasoning set the tone for other decisions. In some sense, it was the seed from which modern doctrine grew.

Justice Brennan's opening paragraph bluntly explains the issue in the case: "We are required in this case to determine for the first time the extent to which the constitutional protections for speech and press limit a State's power to award damages in a libel action brought by a public official against critics of his official conduct." The opinion then proceeds to a lengthy statement of the facts, whose dramatic interest stems from its connection with the civil rights struggle in the South. As we have seen, the alleged libel was against the Commissioner of Police, who was nowhere named in the publication, and whose reputation could scarcely have been injured by the trivial inaccuracies found in a few copies of the New York Times sold in Alabama. The suit was plainly an attempt to muzzle Northern critics of segregation. After laying out the facts in the introductory section, a brief Part I of the opinion disposes of a couple of insignificant threshold issues.

Part II is the heart of Justice Brennan's opinion. It begins by pulling together a number of prior judicial statements on the role of free speech in American society. This passage culminates in the Court's famous reference to "a profound national commitment to the principle that debate on public issues should be uninhibited, robust, and wide-open, and that it may well include vehement, caustic, and sometimes unpleasantly sharp attacks on government and public officials."

The following eight pages of the opinion are dedicated to establishing that neither falsity, defamatory nature, nor the combination of the two traits are necessarily sufficient to justify suppressing speech. Much of this portion of the opinion is drawn directly from the newspaper's brief. Here, the opinion builds on previous cases recognizing the need for "breathing room" for free speech, on contempt cases dealing with insulting comments about judges, and on the history of seditious libel (which shows that even utterly false statements are constitutionally protected when the target is the government). Indeed, in *United States v. Alvarez*,[3] the Court later held that even false statements of fact (in that case, about the defendant's military service) are not completely lacking in First Amendment value.

At this point, the reader may well have expected a holding that criticism of government officials is absolutely immune from liability. However, the opinion then goes on to consider the defendant's intent:

> The state rule of law is not saved by its allowance of the defense of truth. A defense for erroneous statements honestly made is no less essential here than was the requirement of proof of guilty knowledge which . . . we held indispensable to a valid conviction of a bookseller for possessing obscene writings for sale.

After a discussion of the effects of requiring the defendant to prove truth as a defense, the opinion concludes that such a requirement chills criticism of official conduct. It then announces the now famous *New York Times* test:

> The constitutional guarantees require, we think, a federal rule that prohibits a public official from recovering damages for a defamatory falsehood relating to his official conduct unless he proves that the statement was made with 'actual' malice—that is, with knowledge that it was false or with reckless disregard of whether it was false or not.

The closing portion of Part II bolsters this test with a discussion of the leading state case establishing a similar rule. Finally, the Court analogizes to an earlier case in which the Court granted immunity to federal officials for libels made in the course of their official duties. The reason for this immunity was to avoid inhibiting vigorous action by officials. " 'Analogous considerations support the privilege for the citizen-critic of government. It is as much his duty to criticize as it is the official's duty to administer.' "

Part III of the opinion goes on to consider the particular facts of the case. The Court first holds that the record below did not suffice to establish malice with the "convincing clarity which the constitutional standard demands." Note that "malice" refers in this context to the defendant's knowledge of the facts, not the defendant's ill-will toward the plaintiff. Then the Court goes on to consider

---

[3]   567 U.S. 709 (2012).

another essential element of the tort, the defamatory nature of the material. The Court concludes that general criticism of the police department cannot constitutionally be considered defamatory of the Commissioner of Police as an individual. Otherwise, any criticism of government could be transmuted into a libel of a government official. Oddly, this discussion does not refer to the earlier, quite relevant, discussion of seditious libel. On the whole, this section of the opinion is less successful, perhaps because it was the result of prolonged, difficult negotiations between Brennan and several other Justices.

Justice Brennan did not rest his malice test on any single constitutional foundation. Probably, he could not have done so and gotten the support of a Court that included such varying views of free speech. Instead, he built a web supporting his legal test from many sides. On the other hand, the case is not truly an example of eclectic balancing. It is strongly informed by an overall vision of free speech.

In the course of bringing this vision to bear on a particular case, Brennan also brought order to earlier cases. He drew examples from several cases of judicial concern over chilling speech, and he derived a general principle that free speech needs breathing room. By the time he finished, he had added several things to the First Amendment canon: a new appreciation of the generality of the "chilling effect" principle, a rediscovery of the relevance of the seditious libel debate, an eloquent restatement of the value of free speech, and—of course—a new constitutional rule of libel law.

C.   Appraising the *New York Times* Rule

Given its transformative effect on defamation law, it is not surprising that the *New York Times* rule has been the subject of much scholarly attention. (To avoid confusion, I will use *Sullivan* to refer to the case and *New York Times* to refer to the legal rule.) Of all the aspects of First Amendment law, it is probably the most surprising to foreigners, particularly the British (who have had stringent defamation laws). Against the Court's ruling, it could be argued that the Court undervalued the individual interest in reputation, encouraged careless journalism, and promoted an increased public focus on scandal in public life. From this point of view, the Court went too far. It could have dealt with the possibility of real abuses of libel law by tightening the rules about what constitutes defamation and requiring proof of actual damage. From another viewpoint, the Court did not go nearly far enough. Newspapers and blog sites must still defend expensive libel suits, and the mere threat of litigation may be enough to cause self-censorship. The empirical evidence, however, does not seem to support fears that *New York Times* fails to give the press adequate protection.

It may be helpful to take a somewhat different perspective on the issue. Today, product manufacturers are generally responsible for harm caused by defective products, regardless of whether they were negligent (let alone guilty of "malice" in some sense.) One might well wonder why the press should not have to face the same kind of tort liability as other industries. Economic analysis does, however, provide a justification for imposing a lower liability burden on the press, because information is a different kind of good than most products.

For most products, the seller of the product receives compensation from the buyer for the full value of the product. When you buy a meal in a restaurant, you receive and pay for the full benefit of the meal. But when you read a newspaper or blog, the benefits of the information flow to other people as well as to you, for two reasons. First, if you read something interesting, you may well pass the information along to others, whereas a meal can only be eaten once. Second, the information may affect other behavior, such as how you vote, which in turn affects others through its contribution to the outcome of the election. For this reason, unlike an ordinary consumer product, information is what economists call a "public good." Generally, markets tend to underproduce public goods because the sellers cannot recover the full value of the good from the buyer.

For ordinary consumer goods, it may make sense to make the seller pay for all the damages caused by the goods, however unintentionally. For a public good like information, however, this kind of liability could deter the production of information. Because the newspaper's profits do not reflect the full social value of the publication, strict liability would cause it to strike the wrong balance between the harm done by inaccurate information and the benefit of producing additional accurate information.

Perhaps the most troubling consequences of the *New York Times* rule is not that it deprives plaintiffs of damages, but rather that it deprives them of any forum in which to establish the falsity of the claims against them. For this reason, there have been calls for the establishment of a new judicial procedure that would allow the plaintiff to "set the record straight" but not to recover substantial damages. So far, however, state legislatures have not implemented these proposals. The constitutionality of these proposals remains a moot question, but arguably they would eliminate much of the chilling effect that concerned the *Sullivan* Court, while providing a safeguard for individual reputation.

II. Applying the *New York Times* Rule

Because of the nature of tort litigation, the Supreme Court was soon faced with a plethora of cases requiring it to apply the *New York*

Times rule in various factual settings. For this reason, a rich body of common law doctrine evolved that defines the parameters of the rule. The three most critical issues have been what plaintiffs are covered by the rule, what statements can provide a basis for defamation liability, and what conduct by the defendant qualifies as "malice."

A. Who Is a Public Figure?

New York Times v. Sullivan involved a public official, the police commissioner. It was easy to foresee the extension of the rule to candidates for public office. A few years later, the Court was faced with the question whether the *New York Times* rule applied to other prominent individuals who were not on the state payroll. In two tandem cases, the Court ruled that at least some such individuals were covered by the rule.[4] One of the cases involved allegations of misconduct by the athletic director at a state university. He was technically an employee of a privately incorporated athletic association. The other involved a retired general who had become active in national politics, and was accused of haranguing a mob to resist a desegregation order. As "public figures," the Court held, these plaintiffs were subject to the same rule as public officials.

This ruling immediately raised the question of who constitutes a public figure. These two plaintiffs were not only prominently featured in the public eye, but were also directly involved in political or governmental affairs. A broad reading of the opinion might suggest coverage for any person in the public eye in connection with any newsworthy event. Celebrity status (even if only temporary) would ensure access to the media for purposes of rebutting false accusations, while the newsworthiness of the event would demonstrate its relevance to uninhibited public discussion. Even more broadly, any person involved in public events might be considered a public figure, on the theory that the public must have unrestrained access to information about participants in these events. Later cases make it clear, however, that the category of public figures is much more limited.

For example, involvement in well-publicized litigation is not enough to make a person a public figure. In one case, the plaintiff was a well-known "society" figure who had been involved in a messy divorce from a member of one of the country's richest families. In another, the plaintiff had been convicted some years earlier of contempt of Congress for refusal to appear before a grand jury investigating Soviet espionage. Neither was considered a public figure because neither had voluntarily stepped into the forefront of a

---

[4]   *Curtis Publishing Co. v. Butts,* 388 U.S. 130 (1967) (also presenting the opinion in the companion case of *Associated Press v. Walker*).

public debate.[5] Nor does a lawyer become a public figure by representing a client in civil rights litigation.[6] Similarly, a government researcher was not considered a public figure when a U.S. Senator attacked his work as a waste of public funds. The researcher had not assumed any role of public prominence in the debate over government research expenditures and had not otherwise invited a high level of public attention.[7]

Apart from providing coverage for individuals like the state football coach, who was a public official in everything but name, it is not clear what function the public figure doctrine performs today. The Court's basic idea is one of "assumption of risk"—if you choose to be in the public limelight, you have to expect unpleasant publicity. But there is an element of circularity here: people who enter the public limelight have to expect a greater exposure to defamation only because the Supreme Court has licensed the press to be more careless in discussing their affairs. In any event, it is not clear why someone who chooses to participate in public discourse should be penalized by losing his rights under tort law. Libel actions by such individuals, who are not government officials, are not tainted by the history of seditious libel on which the Court relied in *Sullivan.* Perhaps the Court has in mind a kind of even-handedness rule. It would be unfair to allow open-season on incumbent public officials while restricting criticism of their opponents, so it seems reasonable to say that everyone involved in a political campaign should be subject to the same rules. But this rationale would suggest a fairly narrow scope for the public figure doctrine.

In effect, the Court seems to envision dual spheres—a world of public debate, in which no holds are barred, and a world of ordinary life in which individual reputation continues to receive protection. By entering the public world, the individual exposes himself to free-wheeling attack, but in return either enjoys the opportunity to exercise public authority, or the privilege of engaging in similar attacks on his own opponents. This doctrine is somewhat reminiscent of tort rules regarding athletes. Normally, deliberately knocking someone down would be a tort. But by entering an athletic event, a player in effect consents to the normal rough-and-tumble of the game.

B. What Is Defamatory?

In most situations, there is little doubt whether a statement is defamatory. For example, it is clearly defamatory to accuse an

---

[5] See *Wolston v. Reader's Digest Ass'n,* 443 U.S. 157 (1979); *Time, Inc. v. Firestone,* 424 U.S. 448 (1976).

[6] *Gertz v. Robert Welch, Inc.,* 418 U.S. 323 (1974).

[7] *Hutchinson v. Proxmire,* 443 U.S. 111 (1979).

innocent person of committing a crime. But the courts have sometimes had to wrestle with more difficult definitional issues. Suppose a reviewer describes a book as "poorly researched." If the author can show that many hours of research assistant time went into the writing of the book, can she recover for defamation? Similar questions would be raised about a description of a public official as incompetent or biased.

Lower courts had addressed such issues by asking whether the statement in question involved "fact" or "opinion." The Supreme Court rejected this approach in *Milkovich v. Lorrain Journal Co.*[8] The plaintiff was a high school wrestling coach whose team was placed on probation for misconduct. The local courts overturned the ruling against the team. The coach sued because of press coverage implying that he had lied at the hearing. The Court rejected the newspaper's argument that this statement was merely a matter of opinion and therefore not defamatory under the *New York Times* rule. As the Court pointed out, rephrasing "Jones is a liar" as "in my opinion, Jones is a liar," does not affect the essence of the defamation. Rather than using the "opinion" label, the Court preferred to ask whether a statement has provably false factual implications, and whether the speaker used language in a loose, figurative, or hyperbolic sense that might dispel the factual implications. Although *Milkovich* rejects the idea of a separate privilege for "opinion," it provides the functional equivalent of such a privilege by careful tailoring of the plaintiff's duty to prove falsity.

The hard question remains, however, of determining what constitutes a "factual implication." Consider again the caustic book reviewer who calls a work "poorly researched." (Experience in academic life suggests that the problem may have been that the reviewer's own work wasn't cited in the book!) The book's author claims that this description suggests that either little time was spent on research, or that the research was not performed in accordance with professional standards—a kind of "malpractice" claim, like saying that a surgeon did a sloppy job. Is this actionable under *Milkovich*?

The first question under *Milkovich* appears to be whether the statement can be reasonably interpreted as stating false facts about an individual. But is "sloppy research" a "false fact" or something else? One issue is what research took place. This kind of "historical fact" is the sort of thing we try to determine in litigation all of the time. If the reviewer had said that the author performed no research at all, we could confidently view this as a factual statement. But suppose there is no dispute about what research actually took place,

---

8   497 U.S. 1 (1990).

but only about whether to classify this research as "sloppy." Then the answer might depend on whether there are clear professional standards that were clearly violated. If there is any room for disagreement about the application of the professional standards (or their existence), then the reviewer should be free to offer her own view without fear that a jury will later disagree. It is unclear whether this dispute about standards involves what the *Milkovich* Court considered "actual facts."

The second question under *Milkovich* is whether the factual implication, if any, should be taken literally. Given the general tone of many book reviews, it is hard to know whether harsh language should be taken as anything more than a general statement of dissatisfaction with the book. (And the statement "I hated the book" is clearly not defamatory.) It is commonplace to describe books under review as poorly analyzed and researched, not to mention badly written, biased, and stupid. It seems unlikely that a reader would take a statement that "this book is idiotic" to be a factual assertion about the author's I.Q. Similarly, a statement that the book was badly researched may be little more than an assertion that the book is less detailed than the reviewer would prefer or differs from the reviewer's own preferences about which sources to consult and how to evaluate them. On balance, after *Milkovich*, it seems fair to conclude that the book reviewer cannot be charged with libel.

C.   What Is Malice?

If the author of our hypothetical book is a public figure, the reviewer would also have additional protection, because it would be very difficult to show that this statement was made with the requisite malice. In common usage, malice means personal animosity. This is clearly not the meaning of the term under *New York Times v. Sullivan*. Rather, the plaintiff must prove by clear and convincing evidence that the defendant knew the statement was false or acted with reckless disregard of the truth. And "recklessness" here means something more than a high degree of negligence, as the cases also indicate.

In *Harte-Hanks Communications v. Connaughton*,[9] the plaintiff was a county judge who was under investigation by a grand jury. The defendant ran a front page story alleging that the judge had used "dirty tricks" to influence a witness, and had offered her and her sister a trip to Florida in appreciation of their help during the investigation. The Court held that a showing of "highly unreasonable conduct constituting an extreme departure from the standards of investigation and reporting ordinarily adhered to by responsible

---

[9]   491 U.S. 657 (1989).

publishers" is not enough to show malice. The Court found a sufficient basis for a finding of malice, however, in the newspaper's failure to attempt to contact the witness' sister, the testimony of the editor that he did not bother listening to taped interviews, and the jury's rejection of testimony that the paper found the witness' story credible. Thus, as the Court indicated in another case, the crucial point is whether *in fact* the publisher had serious doubts about the accuracy of the statement, not whether a prudent publisher *would* have had such doubts.[10]

To show malice, it is not enough to show that the journalist knew that a story was not literally accurate in all regards. In *Masson v. New Yorker Magazine*,[11] a published interview contained lengthy passages in quotations, which were not transcripts of the subject's statements. The question, according to the Court, was whether the jury could find that the quotations had substantially the same meaning as the plaintiff's actual statements, or whether they had been changed in ways that rendered them defamatory.

To return to our hypothetical about the book reviewer, assuming the author was a public figure so that the *New York Times* standard applied, it would not be enough to show malice that the reviewer deviated from professional standards common among book reviewers (assuming such standards exist). Instead, it would be necessary to show that the statement about sloppy research was made with knowledge that it was false or with disregard for its truth or falsity. It's hard to imagine what would constitute proof of such malice short of an actual admission by the reviewer that she really thought the book was very well researched—perhaps evidence that the endnote pages in the reviewer's copy of the book were still uncut and thus had never been opened?

III. Private Libels

Even under the broadest interpretation, not everyone who is involved in a libel action is a public figure. Some defamation actions involve purely private disputes—for example, a bad recommendation for a former employee. But others involve newsworthy matters of concern to the public. Despite arguments by some commentators that all expressive statements should receive the same degree of constitutional protection, the Court has refused to apply the *New York Times* rule to all defamation actions, or even to all actions involving matters of concern to the public. It has, however, placed other restrictions on defamation actions involving nonpublic figures.

---

[10]   *St. Amant v. Thompson*, 390 U.S. 727 (1968).

[11]   501 U.S. 496 (1991).

A.   The *Gertz* Rule

Gertz v. Robert Welch, Inc.[12] was a libel suit brought by a Chicago lawyer against the publisher of a right-wing magazine. The lawyer had represented black clients in a civil rights action against a Chicago policeman; the magazine accused him of orchestrating a "frame-up" of the policeman and claimed he had a criminal record and communist affiliations. The Court rejected the argument that *New York Times* should apply to all matters of public concern, despite suggestions to the contrary by several Justices in an earlier case. The Court found two reasons for giving greater protection to private individuals than to public figures. First, public figures have greater media access and therefore a greater ability to resort to "self-help" in response to defamatory accusations. Second, public figures have voluntarily assumed roles of special prominence in society, either by occupying positions of great persuasive power and influence, or by "thrust[ing] themselves to the forefront of particular public controversies." Either way, they "invite attention and comment," whereas the private individual who has not accepted public office or "assumed an 'influential role in ordering society' " has "relinquished no part of his interest in the protection of his own good name." Hence, the state's interest in protecting the reputation of private individuals is stronger, and the balance tips in favor of allowing tort liability.

The Court also considered, but rejected, the option of extending *New York Times* to all matters of general or public interest, concluding that this option would unduly abridge the state interest in protecting individual reputation and would also require judges to make difficult decisions about which publications address matters of public concern.

The *Gertz* Court did not, however, leave private defamation law completely unrestrained. Even in suits involving private individuals, two rules apply. First, to collect compensatory damages, the plaintiff must at least prove negligence. Second, to obtain punitive damages, the plaintiff must prove *New York Times* malice. Of course, it is still necessary that the statement be defamatory, so *Milkovich* and *Masson* remain relevant even for nonpublic figures.

B.   Does the Defendant's Identity or the Nature of the Topic Matter?

Gertz and other libel cases have emphasized the identity of the plaintiff rather than other potentially relevant factors. But the identity of the defendant or the topic might also matter, leading us to distinguish between an op-ed column and a neighborhood gossip. *Sullivan* stressed the importance of robust public debate. Not all

---

[12]   418 U.S. 323 (1974).

defamation actions equally implicate this interest. Because of the special function of the press in covering public disputes and checking government abuses, the press arguably should have greater freedom of action than the private gossiper. Also, where the subject under discussion is one of public concern, a greater degree of leeway might be appropriate.

On the whole, the Court has avoided any reliance on these factors. Despite the special mention of the media in the "press" clause of the First Amendment, the Court has generally declined to provide media with any greater rights than other speakers, as we will see in Chapter 11. Doing so would, among other problems, make it necessary to provide a fairly precise definition of who constitutes the press, and the nature of the distinction is not altogether clear. (Is a xeroxed newsletter "the press"? What about a blog that is visited by thousands of people?) Defining which matters involve "public concerns" is also problematic. If defined narrowly to include only explicitly political speech, much discussion of public affairs would be left out. If defined broadly to include any example of a phenomenon affecting society as a whole, the term would seem all-encompassing. Since sexual mores are an important sociological phenomenon affecting society as a whole, any individual's sexual practices arguably would be relevant to an issue of public concern.

Thus, it is understandable that the Court generally has been reluctant to rely on distinctions between the press and other speakers, or between matters having or lacking public significance. Nevertheless, the distinctions have such great intuitive appeal that the Court understandably has been drawn toward them on occasion.

The concept of "public concern" resurfaced in *Dun & Bradstreet, Inc. v. Greenmoss Builders, Inc.*,[13] in which a credit reporting agency had erroneously given confidential information to some of its clients that the plaintiff corporation was bankrupt. A plurality opinion by Justice Powell refused to apply *Gertz*, even though the jury had apparently awarded punitive damages without finding *New York Times* malice. Concluding that the kind of speech involved in the case to be peripheral to the First Amendment, Justice Powell could find "no credible argument that this type of credit reporting requires special protection to ensure that 'debate on public issues [will] be uninhibited, robust, and wide-open.'" Chief Justice Burger and Justice White concurred on the ground that *Gertz* was wrongly decided. Justice Brennan wrote for four dissenters, insisting that *Gertz* had correctly rejected any reliance on the "public concern" concept, a concept which he insisted was amorphous and could even cover such matters as the potential bankruptcy of an important local

---

[13]   472 U.S. 749 (1985).

firm. (Or a national concern: consider the Lehman Brothers collapse that set off the Great Recession.) As a common sense matter, there may be some appeal to Justice Powell's assessment that First Amendment values usually have little to do with private credit reporting. Nevertheless, his resurrection of the idea of "public concern" made a bit of a hash of libel doctrine, which had previously avoided reliance on this concept.

One point that had clear majority support in *Dun & Bradstreet* is that the media enjoy no special privileges under libel law. But this point too was later called into question. In *Philadelphia Newspapers, Inc. v. Hepps*,[14] the Court considered whether in a private libel case, the state may apply the common law rule that puts the burden of proof on the defendant to establish truth as a defense. Rejecting the common law rule, the Court said that to "ensure that true speech on matters of public concern is not deterred, we hold that the common-law presumption that defamatory speech is false cannot stand when a plaintiff seeks damages against a *media defendant* for speech of public concern."

Thus, although the *New York Times* rule seems to be well-settled, the situation for private libel is less clear. There seems to be a broad consensus that at least some private defamation cases should be subject to constitutional restraints. What is unclear is whether there are some examples of defamation that are so truly private, and so far removed from public discourse, that they should be exempted altogether from these restraints. Much of the dispute turns on whether it is possible to draw an intelligible line distinguishing these wholly private cases from those that raise stronger First Amendment concerns.

IV. Other Torts

Defamation is not the only tort action available to the offended subject of a publication. The Supreme Court has had occasion to consider the interplay between the First Amendment and several other tort actions, finding in each instance that the First Amendment places restraints on tort law.

A. "False Light"

Some of these lawsuits fall under the broad rubric of "privacy torts," a label which covers a cluster of loosely related causes of action. In *Time, Inc. v. Hill*,[15] the plaintiffs had been held as hostages a number of years earlier by escaped convicts. A press account about a theatrical production erroneously described the play as a

---

[14] 475 U.S. 767 (1986).
[15] 385 U.S. 374 (1967).

reenactment of those events, in the process significantly misstating the facts of the earlier episode. The misstatements were not defamatory—none of them implied any fault or misconduct by the hostages—but they were embarrassing. The plaintiffs filed suit under a New York statute that was originally designed to protect celebrities whose faces and names were used for commercial advertising. As construed by the state court, however, the statute also provided a cause of action in cases where the plaintiff was "put in a false light" by the defendant's statements.

Justice Brennan's majority opinion concluded that the plaintiffs had to establish *New York Times* malice in order to prevail. This result was dictated, he said, not by a straightforward application of the rule in libel cases, but by an independent assessment of the First Amendment interests at stake. The Court rejected a negligence test because it would be difficult for the press to guess "how a jury might assess the reasonableness of steps taken by it to verify the accuracy of every reference to a name, picture, or portrait." (In contrast, in a defamation case, the negative content of the statement puts the press on notice that it may be called to account, and that therefore additional care may be warranted.) But this concern does not apply to "calculated falsehood," which the Court described as falling outside the protection of the First Amendment.

Justice Brennan was quite explicit that he was being guided by the First Amendment principles announced in *Sullivan*, but that those principles might apply differently in *Hill* than in a defamation action. Thus, *Time* anticipated the possibility that a later case might give private libel less constitutional protection than a requirement of actual malice, as came to pass in *Gertz*. Nevertheless, since *Gertz*, there has been considerable dispute about whether the *Hill* rule remains valid. The alternative would presumably be to apply a negligence standard in "false light" actions (at least if the matter is of public concern), with the degree of reasonable care depending on how much the publisher was on notice regarding the sensitivity of the topic. It seems far from clear that the social interest in allowing recovery for this tort is sufficiently great to justify such a complex and speculative inquiry about journalistic practices. Perhaps, however, it would be possible to draft a statute covering some specific types of disclosure that are blatant enough that the media would necessarily realize that the same care is required as for defamation.

B. Disclosing Private Facts

Falsity is critical to the "false light" tort, making defamation law a ready analogy. Another privacy-related tort imposes liability for revealing true but highly intimate facts about the plaintiff (such as publishing a nude photo). Here, *New York Times v. Sullivan* provides little assistance, even by analogy. But the general rule seems to be harsh but clear: once information has lawfully become public, the press cannot be penalized for publishing except in extraordinary circumstances (which the Court has never actually found to be present).

The rule is exemplified by *The Florida Star v. B.J.F.*[16] A Florida newspaper was found liable for publishing the name of a rape victim, in violation of a state law prohibiting "any instrument of mass communication" from printing the name of a victim of a sexual offense. The newspaper had obtained the name from a police report, which was inadvertently released to the press without deleting identifying information. As a result of the publication, the victim and her mother were exposed to anonymous phone calls, and they had to seek police protection and obtain mental health counseling. The jury awarded $75,000 in compensatory damages and $25,000 in punitives. Justice Marshall's opinion for the Court reversed the damage award, but refused to go as far as to say the press can *never* be held liable for publishing truthful information. Rather, the Court applied the principle that, if a paper lawfully obtains truthful information about "a matter of public significance," no sanction can apply "absent a need to further a state interest of the highest order." The paper had clearly obtained the report lawfully from the police. Moreover, the news article covered a matter of public significance, according to the Court—"the article generally, as opposed to the specific identity contained within it, involved a matter of paramount public import: the commission, and investigation, of a violent crime which had been reported to authorities."

The most difficult issue presented by *Florida Star* was the significance of the state interest in protecting the privacy of rape victims. The Court conceded that the state had a strong interest in protecting the privacy of rape victims. It did not rule out the possibility that imposing civil sanctions for publishing the name of a rape victim might be "so overwhelmingly necessary" as to pass First Amendment scrutiny. But the Court found serious flaws in the suit against the paper: the paper had been entitled to assume that it could publish the information in a report released to the public, the statute banned publication regardless of the degree of potential harm in any given case, and the statute only covered the mass media. Justice Scalia concurred on the basis of this third point, calling the statute "a prohibition that society is prepared to impose upon the press but not upon itself."

---

[16]   491 U.S. 524 (1989).

The Court's reluctance to allow recovery for invasions of privacy by the media was underscored by *Bartnicki v. Vopper*.[17] The suit had been brought under a federal anti-wiretapping law, which makes it illegal to intercept cell phone calls and other electronic communications. The statute provides a private cause of action against anyone who discloses the contents of illegally intercepted material. The plaintiff, who was the chief negotiator for a local teacher's union, had used the cell phone in her car to call the union's president. During a discussion of the negotiations, the union president had said, "If they're not gonna move for three percent, we'll gonna have to go to their, their homes. . . . To blow off their front porches, we'll have to do some work on some of those guys." After the school district entered into a contract favorable to the union, a radio talk show broadcast a tape of the conversation. The difference between this case and *Florida Star* is that in *Bartnicki* the information was not initially obtained lawfully, though in both cases the press was innocent of any wrongdoing,

Justice Stevens' majority opinion conceded that individuals have a strong interest in the privacy of their communications. But in this case, "privacy concerns give way when balanced against the interest in publishing matters of public importance." In a concurring opinion, Justice Breyer (joined by Justice O'Connor) stressed that the Court's holding was limited to the "special circumstances present here," including the radio station's complete lack of involvement in the original interception itself and the unusual public significance of the information (involving a threat of physical harm). Dissenting, Chief Justice Rehnquist, joined by Justices Scalia and Thomas, defended the statute as a deterrent to the illegal interception of private conversations. The Court's decision, argued Rehnquist, "diminishes, rather than enhances, the purposes of the First Amendment: chilling the speech of the millions of Americans who rely upon electronic technology to communicate each day."

Given *Florida Star*, the result in *Bartnicki* is not a surprise. The Court's use of the "public concern" standard in *Bartnicki,* however, suggests that there may be limits to the Court's willingness to subordinate privacy to free speech, even when the media is involved. If so, however, those limits have not yet been reached.

C.   Infliction of Emotional Distress

In ordinary life, outrageous conduct designed to inflict emotional harm may be subject to tort recovery. It is not surprising that efforts have been made to apply this theory against vituperative public attacks. The Court rejected this effort, however, in *Hustler Magazine*

---

[17]   532 U.S. 514 (2001).

v. Falwell.[18] The magazine had published a parody of a popular series of liquor ads containing interviews with celebrities. The parody purported to be an interview with a well-known fundamentalist minister, in which he allegedly revealed that his "first time" was a drunken rendezvous with his mother in an outhouse. The minister's libel claim failed because the jury found that no reasonable person would have understood the parody as a factual assertion. The jury did, however, award $100,000 in actual damages and $50,000 in punitive damages for intentional infliction of emotional distress. The Court unanimously reversed, holding that intentionally inflicting emotional distress on public opponents is a time-honored American tradition, so that the First Amendment prohibits such liability in the area of public debate about public figures. After all, caricatures are often based on exploiting unfortunate physical traits or handicaps, or on embarrassing events, often calculated to injure the feelings of the subject. "The art of the cartoonist," the Court remarked, "is often not reasoned or evenhanded, but slashing and one-sided." Nor did the Court accept the invitation to use an "outrageousness" standard to limit liability. At least in the area of public and social debate, this standard "has an inherent subjectiveness about it which would allow a jury to impose liability on the basis of the jurors' tastes or views, or perhaps on the dislike of a particular expression."

If the Court had ruled the other way in *Falwell* (or in *Time*, for that matter), it would have created a tremendous loophole in the *New York Times* standard. Almost all serious accusations against individuals could be said to be calculated to cause emotional harm or to put them in a false light. The outrageousness standard seems far too easily manipulated to work as a restraint. (For example, suppose that the minister had won the case, and the magazine publisher turned around and sued him for describing in graphic detail in a televised sermon how the publisher would suffer the torments of hell. Actionable?) Thus, the *Falwell* decision seems harsh but correct.

The Court reinforced *Falwell* in *Snyder v. Phelps*,[19] *Snyder* involved a group of pickets at a military funeral, who carried signs proclaiming that "God hates the United States" for its tolerance of homosexuality and signs saying "Thank God for dead soldiers." The deceased's father sued for intentional infliction of emotional distress as well as intrusion on seclusion. The Court held, however, that the signs addressed a matter of public concern and were constitutionally protected. Justice Alito protested in dissent that "[o]ur profound national commitment to free and open debate is not a license for the vicious verbal assault that occurred in this case." But the majority

---

[18]   485 U.S. 46 (1988).

[19]   559 U.S. 990 (2011).

was unswayed, as it has generally been in cases that rest regulation on emotional harm.

Though these cases involving non-defamation torts may not directly apply the *New York Times* rule, they reflect a similarly protective attitude toward speakers. None of these cases show any strong sympathy with the victims of ridicule or misrepresentations. Although the Court is willing, somewhat grudgingly, to allow compensation in a few situations, it obviously puts a much higher priority on untrammeled speech.

V. Conclusion

Perhaps more than in any other area of First Amendment law, the rules relating to defamation and other torts stress the function of speech in public deliberation. *New York Times v. Sullivan* emphasizes the crucial role of free speech in democratic self-governance. In later cases, such as *Gertz*, the Court has offered protection to a broader range of speech. But *Dun & Bradstreet* illustrates the lingering concern with the public benefits of free speech, as do cases like *Falwell*. The value of speech for purposes of self-expression plays a decidedly marginal role—nowhere do we find an opinion, for example, worrying that defamation law could hinder the vital role played by gossip in expressing and defining social identities. Quite the contrary: It is private speech, by and about private individuals, that the Court finds least subject to First Amendment protection. Thus, this area of the law is something of a triumph for the "public deliberation" school of First Amendment thought.

We saw in the last chapter that the 1950s and 1960s witnessed a great debate between absolutists and balancers. Like *Brandenburg*, *New York Times v. Sullivan* and its progeny are something of a fusion of these approaches. The Court has attempted to strike a balance between the needs of free public debate, generously conceived, and the state's interest in protecting individuals from recognized forms of legal harm. But rather than allowing this balance to be struck in individual cases on an ad hoc basis, the Court has constructed a series of rules governing various categories of speech regulation, ranging from libel suits by public officials to privacy suits by crime victims. In this way, the Court has federalized defamation law. In doing so, it has attempted to make room for legitimate state interests without leaving First Amendment values to the mercy of individual juries and judges.

In establishing these rules, the Court has been keenly aware of the need for clear-cut rules embodying readily enforceable standards. Thus, the Court has sought a certain kind of objectivity in its legal tests. In part, the goal has been to prevent lower courts and juries from enforcing their own norms (and at worst implementing their own political biases). But the goal has also been to provide speakers (the press in particular) with predictable guidelines, so as to avoid potential chilling effects. Indeed, the effort to avoid chilling speech is one of the primary forces at work in this area of doctrine. The Court has been anxious to ensure that sanctions against this unprotected speech do not inhibit speakers from offering their own versions of the truth.

If this area of doctrine represents a kind of accommodation between balancing and absolutism, it is a compromise in which the absolutists have fared much better than the balancers. For while the Court has left some room to control abuses of speech rights, it has been far more anxious to protect the space for public debate. Public officers and figures can recover for libel only in the most outrageously blatant cases; inevitably, many who are the victims of deliberate lies receive no remedy. Even private individuals must confront substantial hurdles before recovering damages, at least if the topic involves any public concern. As to other torts involving abusive speech in the public arena, either the door has been slammed entirely (infliction of emotional distress) or left open only a crack (disclosure of personal information). Across the board, the goal of robust, uninhibited debate has taken priority over the interests of injured individuals, who receive only a bare minimum of protection.

In the next chapter, we turn to other kinds of harm that can be caused by speech that offends and insults its audience or others. As might be expected on the basis of the defamation cases, the Court has given only limited sanction to regulation based on such concerns. The overwhelming consideration has been preserving the vitality of public debate.

FURTHER READINGS

Albert Chen and Justin Marceau, *High Value Lies, Ugly Truth, and the First Amendment*, 68 Vand. L. Rev. 1435 (2015).

Richard A. Epstein, *Was New York Times v. Sullivan Wrong?*, 53 U. Chi. L. Rev. 782 (1986).

Daniel Farber, *Free Speech Without Romance: Public Choice and the First Amendment*, 105 Harv. L. Rev. 554 (1991).

Paul Gewirtz, *Privacy and Speech*, 2001 Sup. Ct. Rev. 139 (2001).

Steven J. Heyman, *To Drink the Cup of Fury: Funeral Picketing, Public Discourse, and the First Amendment*, 45 Conn. L. Rev. 101 (2012).

Harry Kalven, Jr., *The New York Times Case: A Note on "The Central Meaning of the First Amendment,"* 1964 Sup. Ct. Rev. 191.

Lyrissa Barnett Lidsky, *Silencing John Doe: Defamation & Discourse in Cyberspace*, 49 Duke L.J. 855 (2000).

David A. Logan, *Libel Law in the Trenches: Reflections on Current Data on Libel Litigation*, 87 Va. L. Rev. 503 (2001).

Robert M. O'Neil, The First Amendment and Civil Liability (2001).

Robert C. Post, *The Constitutional Concept of Public Discourse: Outrageous Opinion, Democratic Deliberation, and* Hustler Magazine v. Falwell, 103 Harv. L. Rev. 601 (1990).

Rodney A. Smolla, Dun & Bradstreet, Hepps, *and* Liberty Lobby: *A New Analytic Primer on the Future Course of Defamation*, 75 Geo. L.J. 1519 (1987).

Daniel J. Solove and Neil M. Richards, *Rethinking Free Speech and Civil Liability*, 109 Colum. L. Rev. 1650 (2009).

Chapter 6

OFFENSIVE LANGUAGE AND HATE SPEECH

One of the enduring controversies involving the First Amendment relates to speech directed against racial and other minorities. Such speech includes a broad range of racist, sexist, and homophobic expressions, including face-to-face insults, graffiti, cross-burning, and various kinds of publications. The problem of hate speech has given rise to an extensive body of scholarly commentary. Some scholars have argued for far-reaching changes in First Amendment doctrine in order to expunge such speech from our society. Some of their critics connect these efforts to ban hate speech with what they call the "political correctness" movement on campus. Other critics view the problem as genuine but argue for narrower responses that require less change in First Amendment doctrine.

This chapter attempts to put this controversy in perspective. The first section begins with a discussion of the First Amendment doctrines covering government regulation of offensive expression. As we will see, the Court has narrowly defined the situations in which hate speech may be regulated. As discussed in the second section, even where offensive speech is subject to regulation, the Court has made it difficult to single out racist or sexist statements for special treatment. The third section of the chapter explores some contexts in which regulations targeting racist speech may be permissible under current law. The chapter closes by considering scholarly critiques of current doctrine and proposals for new forms of hate speech regulation.

I. Regulation of Offensive Expression

The simplest argument for regulating hate speech is that racist epithets and expressions are appalling, and that members of racial minorities have the right not to be exposed to them. As we will see, however, the Supreme Court has left only very limited room for the government to protect individuals from exposure to assaultive speech.

A. Fighting Words and Hostile Audiences

Consider the following situation: One man steps up to another in a bar and begins addressing him with a hostile stream of four-letter words. Not only is this conduct likely to provoke violence, but it seems unlikely to make much of a contribution to public discourse. Indeed, this particular situation seems quite close to meeting the

Brandenberg incitement test, if we define "incitement" to include deliberately provoking an attack on the speaker himself.

Not surprisingly, the Supreme Court has long taken the position that such "fighting words" are unprotected by the First Amendment. In *Chaplinsky v. New Hampshire*,[1] the defendant was a Jehovah's Witness who had been haranguing an unfriendly crowd with the message that certain religions are "rackets." When a disturbance occurred, the traffic officer on duty at the intersection hustled the speaker off to the police station, but without ever telling him formally that he was under arrest. On the way, they encountered the city marshal, who had earlier warned the speaker about the restive crowd. (The marshal had also told hostile crowd members that the defendant had the right to speak.) The marshal had heard that a riot was underway and was hurrying to the scene. When he met the traffic officer and the speaker, he repeated his earlier warning about the crowd, whereupon the speaker called him a "God damned racketeer" and a "damned Fascist."

The prosecution was brought under a statute that prohibited the use of insulting language. The Court upheld the statute, which had been construed to cover only language "plainly tending to excite the addressee to a breach of the peace." As the lower court had said, "[t]he English language has a number of words and expressions which by general consent are 'fighting words' when said without a disarming smile. . . . Such words, as ordinary men know, are likely to cause a fight." According to the Court, fighting words—"those which by their very utterance inflict injury or tend to incite an immediate breach of the peace"—are "no essential part of any exposition of ideas, and are of such slight social value as a step to truth that any benefit that may be derived from them is clearly outweighed by the social interest in order and morality."

The Court's language in *Chaplinsky* seems broad enough to cover a great deal of what is now called hate speech. But since *Chaplinsky*, the Court has taken a very narrow view of the fighting words doctrine, to the point where it is no longer clear whether the doctrine retains any vitality. In *Gooding v. Wilson*,[2] the defendant had been participating in an antiwar protest which had blockaded a military draft center. While the police were trying to restore access to the draft center, he said to one of them: "White son of a bitch, I'll kill you," and "You son of a bitch, I'll choke you to death." He was convicted under statutory language like that in *Chaplinsky*. The Court held that the statute was unconstitutionally overbroad. The state courts had failed to limit the statute to utterances tending to

---

[1]   315 U.S. 568 (1942).
[2]   405 U.S. 518 (1972).

cause an immediate breach of the peace. For example, the state courts had upheld convictions even when the target of the speech was unable to respond violently at the moment, so long as violence at a later time was possible. According to the Court, this interpretation went beyond the proper scope of the fighting words doctrine, which was limited to utterances tending to incite an immediate assault. (Does this mean that insulting language against a physically helpless target is never punishable, so that the fighting words doctrine protects only individuals who are ready and able to break the law by assaulting the speaker?)

In fact, since *Chaplinsky*, the Court has never upheld a conviction under the fighting words doctrine. Consequently, it is unclear whether the doctrine still has any independent vitality, except perhaps as a kind of adjunct to *Brandenburg* where the incitement is to a brawl with the speaker rather than to an attack on a third party.

These doubts about the current status of *Chaplinsky* are reinforced by the decline of the "hostile audience" doctrine. The police intervention in *Chaplinsky* was originally motivated by a fear that the speaker would provoke a riot by the unfriendly audience. In *Feiner v. New York*,[3] the Court upheld a conviction on that theory. The speaker had referred to the President as a bum, the American Legion veterans' group as the Gestapo, and the city's mayor as a bum who "does not speak for the negro people." He also said that "negroes don't have equal rights; they should rise up in arms and fight for their rights." Fearing that the crowd would get out of control and attack the speaker, the police arrested him for disorderly conduct. Like *Chaplinsky*, *Feiner* has not been overruled, but its current vitality is doubtful, since no later case has utilized this theory in order to uphold a conviction.

The Court's current attitude is indicated by *Texas v. Johnson*.[4] The defendant was convicted for burning a flag during a public demonstration. One of the state's arguments was that the conviction was justified because of the interest in preventing breaches of the peace. Although the protestors themselves had engaged in disruptive behavior, no actual breach of the peace by on-lookers occurred at the time of the flag burning. Several members of the audience, however, were extremely upset by the demonstration. According to the Court, the state's asserted interest reduced to the claim that "an audience that takes serious offense at particular expression is necessarily likely to disturb the peace." The Court remarked that one function of free speech is to "invite dispute" and that "[i]t may indeed best serve

---

3   340 U.S. 315 (1951).

4   491 U.S. 397 (1989).

its high purpose when it induces a condition of unrest, creates dissatisfaction with conditions as they are, or even stirs people to anger." Hence, the Court said, it would be "odd indeed" to conclude that the government can ban speech on the "unsupported presumption" that certain offensive ideas will provoke violence.

Johnson does not completely eliminate the possibility that a conviction for use of fighting words may be upheld. Flag burning has an inherent ideological content that distinguishes it from purely personal insults. Perhaps even flag burning might be punishable in a situation where the act was targeted at a specific individual. (Imagine a case in which the defendant burns a flag in front of a veteran as a means of expressing contempt for the veteran's personal military activities.) Even so, it would apparently be necessary to show that a violent reaction was likely. Yet, it is hard to imagine circumstances in which prosecution for use of fighting words would be useful and in which the state could carry this burden of proof. Originally, the fighting words doctrine meant that certain expressions are so inherently likely to cause fights that they could be banned regardless of whether a fight was likely in a particular situation. But the later decisions seem unwilling to embrace this presumption. If the fighting words actually do provoke a fight, the state can avoid any constitutional issue by basing the prosecution on participation in the fight. But if no fight ensues, it will be difficult for the state to show convincingly that a fight was likely.

Once it is tied so closely to the prospect of a violent response, the fighting words doctrine seems hard to justify. Why should otherwise-lawful speech become unlawful simply because audiences may respond by committing an illegal assault on the speaker? Except perhaps for the rare situation in which the speaker actually intends to incite such a response, it is hard to see why we should hold the speaker responsible for the illegal action of the audience. A more sensible rationale for *Chaplinsky* would be that people simply have the right to be free from certain kinds of verbal assaults. If so, the propensity to provoke a violent response is not really the reason for banning the speech, but only a rough test for when expression has passed acceptable boundaries. The larger question, then, is whether the government has the power to maintain some kind of minimum level of civility.

B. Offensive Language, Captive Audiences, and Public Civility

The Court's most thoughtful discussion of the problem of public civility is found in *Cohen v. California*.[5] The defendant was arrested

---

5   403 U.S. 15 (1971).

for wearing a jacket with the anti-war inscription "Fuck the Draft" in a Los Angeles courthouse. He was convicted of "maliciously and willfully disturb[ing] the peace or quiet of any neighborhood or person ... by offensive conduct." The state courts upheld the conviction on the premise that this language was inherently likely to cause a breach of the peace. The Court had no difficulty in rejecting this implausible rationale, since there was no evidence that anyone but the arresting officer had even noticed the jacket. In any event, the Court said, the state's argument "amount[ed] to little more than the self-defeating proposition that to avoid physical censorship of one who has not sought to provoke such a response by a hypothetical coterie of the violent and lawless, the States may more appropriately effectuate that censorship themselves."

The state court's rationale was so obviously meritless that it could only be understood as a transparent attempt to provide doctrinal support for the traditional taboo on public use of certain words. It was this traditional taboo that was really at stake in the case, leading the Court into a general discussion of the civility issue.

Even in 1971, no one could have argued with a straight face that "four-letter words" could be banned in all books or movies. But the public display of the same words could be considered different. The reader of a book, after all, has made a voluntary decision to expose himself to the author's words, but visitors to the Los Angeles courthouse had not made a deliberate decision to expose themselves to the motto on the jacket. Presumably, people have some right to avoid being involuntarily forced to confront unwelcome communications. For example, no one has the right to park outside someone's house and expose them for hours on end to offensive language on a loudspeaker.

The *Cohen* Court took a cautious approach to this captive audience rationale. The discussion begins with a general discussion of the captive audience problem. The Court observed that, outside the home, the government's power to prevent intrusive expression must be sharply limited if it is not to become an instrument for majoritarian repression of dissidents. Thus, for the captive audience rationale to hold, "substantial privacy interests" must be invaded in an "essentially intolerable manner." Any broader scope for the doctrine would "effectively empower a majority to silence dissidents simply as a matter of personal predilections."

While not finding the privacy claim in *Cohen* frivolous, the Court found it less than compelling. Unlike the person subjected to loudspeakers at home, people confronted with the offensive slogan on the jacket could simply look away. Given what the Court described as the "subtlety and complexity of the factors involved," the Court rejected the privacy claim in *Cohen* for three reasons: (1) the exposure to unwilling "listeners" was brief and took place in a public building; (2) there was no evidence that anyone who was unable to avoid exposure to the jacket actually objected; and (3) the statute itself displayed no concern with the special problem of the captive audience.

Since *Cohen*, the Court has not upheld captive audience claims except where individuals have been unwittingly exposed to offensive communications within the home. For instance, in *Erznoznik v. Jacksonville*,[6] the Court struck down a local ordinance banning films containing nudity from drive-ins where the screen could be seen from the street or another public place. Rather than allowing the "government to decide which types of otherwise protected speech are sufficiently offensive to require protections for the unwilling listeners or viewer," the Court said, "the burden normally falls upon the viewer to 'avoid further bombardment of [his] sensibilities simply by averting [his] eyes.'"

The deeper issue in *Cohen* was the state's power to completely ban the public use of certain words, not to protect captive audiences, but on the theory that the government, "acting as guardians of public morality, may properly remove this offensive word from the public vocabulary." In rejecting this proposition, the Court began by emphasizing the values at stake. Free expression, the Court said, is "powerful medicine in a society as diverse and populous as ours." The First Amendment puts "the decision as to what views shall be voiced largely into the hands of each of us" in the "belief that no other approach would comport with the premise of individual dignity and choice upon which our political system rests." Although the immediate consequence may "often appear to be only verbal tumult, discord, and even offensive utterance," the Court considered these effects necessary byproducts of open debate.

In light of these basic First Amendment values, the Court rejected the argument for banning certain offensive language (such as four-letter words) for several reasons. First, the line-drawing problem seemed irresolvable. Assuming the state cannot ban all language that even the most squeamish person would object to, there seems to be no principled line between acceptable and unacceptable speech: "while the particular four-letter word being litigated here is perhaps more distasteful than most others of its genre, it is nevertheless often true that one man's vulgarity is another's lyric." Second, language serves to communicate not only ideas but emotions, and purging the language of offensive words would impair that emotive function. Finally, banning certain words could have the

---

6   422 U.S. 205 (1975).

effect of banning associated ideas. Indeed, the government might use the censorship of particular words as a pretext for eliminating certain ideas. *Cohen* and similar cases did not involve abusive language toward minorities, but the Court's reasoning would seem to sharply limit the state's power to ban racial epithets, just as much as its power to ban four-letter words.

Under current law, the offensiveness of certain forms of expression provides a basis for government regulation only under narrow circumstances. First, deliberate efforts to incite a violent response from the audience probably can be banned under the "fighting words" doctrine. Second, captive audiences can be protected from offensive speech, but only where the speech constitutes an "intolerable invasion of privacy" (particularly within the home). Indeed, as we saw in the previous chapter, even intentional infliction of emotional distress cannot be made a basis for tort liability, at least when the target is a public figure who is maligned in public discourse. This set of doctrines limits the state's ability to ban hate speech purely on the basis of its offensiveness or emotional impact. As we will see later, there may be some other rationales for regulation of hate speech, but these rationales apply only in certain specific contexts.

II. *R.A.V.* and the Content Distinction

When the state does have the ability to prevent verbal assaults, it may be unable to draw any distinction between racist hate speech and other abusive language. In *R.A.V. v. City of St. Paul,*[7] the Court held that even when regulating unprotected speech, the state has only a limited power to make content-related distinctions. As a result, it struck down a local ordinance specifically targeting hate speech. "R.A.V.," a juvenile, was charged with burning a cross in a black family's yard in violation of St. Paul's "hate speech" ordinance. The ordinance made it a misdemeanor to "place on public or private property a symbol . . . including, but not limited to, a burning cross or Nazi swastika," if "one knows or has reasonable grounds to know" that it "arouses anger, alarm or resentment in others on the basis of race" or other prohibited personal characteristics. As written, the ordinance suffered from obvious overbreadth and vagueness. To save the ordinance from constitutional attack, the Minnesota Supreme Court performed fairly radical interpretive surgery on the ordinance, drastically reducing its scope. Rather than applying whenever a symbol aroused anger or fear, the Minnesota Supreme Court held that the ordinance's prohibition was limited to "fighting words" or "incitement of imminent lawless action." Thus, the only question still

---

[7]   505 U.S. 377 (1992).

remaining in the case was the constitutionality of prosecuting the defendant under this narrowed reading of the statute.

Justice Scalia's opinion for the Court struck down the ordinance for drawing a content-based distinction between various forms of fighting words. He began by rejecting the view that "fighting words" are wholly outside the concern of the First Amendment. Instead, he said, although fighting words have unprotected features, the government still cannot regulate their use "based on hostility—or favoritism—towards the underlying message expressed." He found this precise motivation behind the St. Paul ordinance.

Doctrinally, the most innovative aspect of Justice Scalia's opinion was his recasting of the two-tier theory of free speech. Under that theory, certain categories of expression—such as fighting words, libel, obscenity, and commercial advertising—were completely denied First Amendment protection. As Justice White's dissent in *R.A.V.* points out, the Court had repeatedly stated that these forms of expression were not truly "speech" within the meaning of the First Amendment.

Justice Scalia's opposition to content-based regulation of even "unprotected" speech was a deviation from prior law. But his view probably best fits current First Amendment analysis as a whole. For example, in an earlier era, it made sense to say that an obscene book was not really "speech." Under current law, however, obscenity depends on local community standards, so the same book may be obscene in Memphis and constitutionally protected in Minneapolis. It seems bizarre to say that the book is somehow "speech" in some parts of the country but not others. Similarly, at one point, maybe all uses of the "F-word" would have been considered fighting words, so perhaps that word could have been classified as "non-speech." But after *Cohen,* some uses of the word are clearly protected, and it is less clear how the same word can sometimes be speech and sometimes not. The same expression might be considered fighting words in a face-to-face confrontation but not in a public speech. Again, it is hard to see how the physical setting converts the same utterance from speech to mere conduct.

Thus, by the time of *R.A.V.,* it was probably misleading to say that unprotected speech such as fighting words was simply the equivalent of noncommunicative conduct for purposes of the First Amendment. Moreover, Justice Scalia seems correct that at least some content-based distinctions are impermissible even when dealing with incitements, libel, or fighting words. (Consider, for example, a libel law imposing heightened liability for falsely accusing a public official of being a racist.) Yet, a strict requirement of content neutrality would make no sense when the Court has already found that the content of the message provides a permissible basis for regulation. For instance, falsity is the basis for liability for defamation, so obviously defamation law is far from content neutral. Moreover, there are legitimate grounds to make some content-based distinctions even among categories of libel. Consider a state law that eliminates all liability for defamatory statements about the official actions of state officers and retains liability only for false statements about their private lives. It is hard to see any First Amendment objection to such a law. The hard problem is drawing a line between permissible and impermissible content regulations, in the case of messages that are themselves constitutionally disfavored.

Justice Scalia had some difficulty in explaining when content based regulation of fighting words is or is not allowed. After establishing a general presumption against such content-based regulation, he listed a number of exceptions. For instance, content distinctions are allowed when a subclass consists of the most "extreme" part of a category of unprotected speech (for example, if the state singled out the most perverse forms of obscene speech for regulation). *Virginia v. Black*, which was discussed in Chapter 4, illustrates this. The state was allowed to single out cross-burning within the category of unprotected threats because of its particularly intimidating nature.

The key, Scalia said, is whether the "nature of the content discrimination is such that there is no realistic possibility that official suppression of ideas is afoot." Justice Scalia found that hate speech regulation does involve a realistic possibility of suppression, since it is based on an aversion to the idea of racism. This characterization of the ordinance as targeting ideas was vigorously attacked by Justice Stevens:

> Such a limited ordinance leaves open and protected a vast range of expression on the subjects of racial, religious, and gender equality. As construed by the Court today, the ordinance certainly does not " 'raise the specter that the Government may effectively drive certain ideas or viewpoints from the marketplace.' " Petitioner is free to burn a cross to announce a rally or to express his views about racial supremacy, he may do so on private property or public land, at day or at night, so long as the burning is not so threatening and so directed at an individual as to "by its very [execution] inflict injury." Such a limited proscription scarcely offends the First Amendment.

Proponents of hate speech regulation would obviously agree with Stevens rather than Scalia, but it was Scalia who spoke for the majority of the Court. *R.A.V.* obviously creates a major problem for efforts to regulate hate speech. Of course, many instances of hate speech could be regulated on a more general basis because they involve illegal conduct such as the trespass in the *R.A.V.* case itself. Moreover, to the extent that the state has the power to ban fighting words or to protect captive audiences under current law, *R.A.V.* leaves it free to do so under general regulations that do not specifically target hate speech. What is unclear is how much room the state has to specifically address the problem of hate speech under current law. The next section considers this question in the context of university regulations of hate speech, which had become widespread prior to *R.A.V.*

III. University Regulation of Hate Speech

Racial diversity has been a major goal of many institutions of higher education for the past several decades. Increases in diversity have been accompanied by friction between groups, and in particular, by verbal attacks on members of minority groups. Discrimination laws probably create some duty on the part of universities to prevent their employees and perhaps their students from creating a "hostile environment" for racial minorities. To what extent do a public university's efforts to protect racial minorities from harassment violate the First Amendment, as currently understood? The answer probably depends to a large extent on the particular form of the regulation.

A.   Regulations Keyed to the Racist Content of Speech

A growing body of scholarship attests to widespread concern about the growing problem of racial hate speech in our society. University campuses in particular witnessed a disturbing increase in reports of racial abuse. A much-publicized example is provided by an incident at the University of Wisconsin where white male students followed a black female student across campus shouting "We've never tried a nigger."

Several universities responded with efforts to regulate hate speech. It may be useful to describe some of these regulations. The University of Michigan implemented one of the first, and broadest, regulations of hate speech. The regulation banned any behavior that "stigmatizes or victimizes an individual on the basis of race" or several other factors, and that also involves any threat to or foreseeably interferes with an individual's academic efforts. An interpretative guide listed the following as violations of the policy:

A flyer containing racist threats distributed in a residence hall.

A male student makes remarks in class like "Women just aren't as good in this field as men," thus creating a hostile learning atmosphere for female classmates.

The guide also contained a section entitled "You are a harasser when . . . ," which gave as examples:

You exclude someone from a study group because that person is of a different race, sex, or ethnic origin than you are.

You tell jokes about gay men and lesbians.

You make obscene telephone calls or send racist notes or computer messages.

The Michigan regulation was struck down by a federal district court.

The University of Wisconsin also adopted a broad regulation. The regulation prohibited racist remarks directed at an individual that intentionally demeaned that individual's race or created an intimidating environment. As an example, the rule stated that a student would be guilty of a violation if "she intentionally made demeaning remarks to an individual based on that person's ethnicity, such as name calling, racial slurs, or 'jokes'," with the purpose of creating a hostile environment. On the other hand, a derogatory opinion about a racial group during a class discussion would not be a violation. This regulation was also struck down by a federal district court.

A more limited regulation was adopted at Stanford. It differed from the Wisconsin regulation primarily in being restricted to "insulting or 'fighting' words or non-verbal symbols." These were defined to be those " 'which by their very utterance inflict injury or tend to incite an immediate breach of the peace,' and which are commonly understood to convey direct and visceral hatred or contempt for human beings" on the basis of race or other listed factors. Even this more carefully drafted speech code was struck down under a state law that subjected private universities to the same restrictions in regulating speech as public institutions.

These lower court rulings seem completely in line with *R.A.V.* There is little doubt that much of the impetus to regulate hate speech stems from a desire to combat racist ideology. Justice Scalia's opinion in *R.A.V.* could hardly have made it clearer that he does not view this desire to be a permissible basis for regulating expression, perhaps most pointedly in the following passage:

St. Paul's brief asserts that a general "fighting words" law would not meet the city's needs because only a content-specific measure can communicate to minority groups that the "group hatred" aspect of such speech "is not condoned by the majority." The point of the First Amendment is that majority preferences must be expressed in some fashion other than silencing speech on the basis of its content.

Within the category of fighting words, the St. Paul ordinance targeted speech on the basis of its racist content. *R.A.V.* makes it clear that such content-based distinctions are impermissible. The first generation of hate speech regulations were fatally flawed under this standard.

Matal v. Tam[8] reemphasized the Court's aversion to suppressing speech based on its offensiveness or disturbing effect on its audience. *Matal* involved a band called "The Slants," which attempted to register its name as a trademark. As described by the Court, "Slants" is "a derogatory term for persons of Asian descent, and members of the band are Asian-Americans. But the band members believe that by taking that slur as the name of their group, they will help to 'reclaim' the term and drain its denigrating force." The Patent and Trademark Office (PTO) denied the application based on a provision of federal law prohibiting the registration of trademarks that may "disparage . . . or bring . . . into contemp[t] or disrepute" any "persons, living or dead." The government had argued that it had "an interest in preventing 'underrepresented groups' from being 'bombarded with demeaning messages in commercial advertising,'" while an *amicus brief* referred instead to a government interest in "encouraging racial tolerance and protecting the privacy and welfare of individuals." The Court rejected both interests as illegitimate under the First Amendment:

> [N]o matter how the point is phrased, its unmistakable thrust is this: The Government has an interest in preventing speech expressing ideas that offend. And, as we have explained, that idea strikes at the heart of the First Amendment. Speech that demeans on the basis of race, ethnicity, gender, religion, age, disability, or any other similar ground is hateful; but the proudest boast of our free speech jurisprudence is that we protect the freedom to express "the thought that we hate."

The government's asserted interests in preventing disparagement of racial groups in trademarks involved the impact of this type of speech on minorities. Consequently, *Matal* has potentially broad implications for other efforts to restrict hate speech.

---

8   ___ U.S. ___, 137 S.Ct. 1744, 198 L.Ed.2d 366 (2017).

In *Iancu v. Brunetti*,[9] the Court struck down another provision of the same federal statute, which prohibited registration of "immoral" or "scandalous" matter. In an opinion by Justice Kagan, the Court concluded that the provision was viewpoint-based. She pointed to the dictionaries defining immoral as "inconsistent with rectitude, purity, or good morals"; "wicked"; or "vicious." Scandalous, in turn, is defined as material that "giv[es] offense to the conscience or moral feelings"; "excite[s] reprobation"; or "call[s] out condemnation." She found these terms to be clearly viewpoint based: "Put the pair of overlapping terms together and the statute, on its face, distinguishes between two opposed sets of ideas: those aligned with conventional moral standards and those hostile to them; those inducing societal nods of approval and those provoking offense and condemnation."

Iancu raises serious questions about the validity of a regulation that distinguishes between expression favoring and disfavoring racial or gender equality. It thus reinforces the issues raised by *Matal* about how much room is left for regulation of hate speech. We will discuss later whether regulation could be permissible in special settings or based on alternative theories.

B.   Penalty Enhancement Based on Racist Motivation

Hate speech may involve conduct that is otherwise subject to sanction, such as destruction of property or disturbing the peace. One alternative to a targeted ban on hate speech is to enhance the penalty when an offense is motivated by racial animosity toward the victim. This approach makes some obvious sense. If an employer decides to fire a worker because of discriminatory intent, what would otherwise have been a perfectly legal action becomes unlawful. If the employer decides instead to assault a worker because of discriminatory intent, it seems equally reasonable to say that the attack becomes more culpable. The holding in *R.A.V.* was clearly based on the expressive nature of the prescribed conduct; otherwise, Justice Scalia would not have been at such pains to establish that even "proscribable speech," like fighting words, is not "invisible to the First Amendment." Unlike fighting words, physical assaults are wholly outside the First Amendment.

Despite this seemingly unassailable logic, the Wisconsin Supreme Court held that sentence enhancements based on racial motivation are unconstitutional. After seeing a movie called *Mississippi Burning*, in which a white man attacked a black youth, the black defendant asked a group of other young black men: "Do you all feel hyped up to move on some white people?" When a white youth

---

[9]   ___ U.S. ___, 139 S.Ct. 2294, 204 L.Ed.2d 714 (2019).

walked by, the defendant said: "There goes a white boy; go get him." The white youth was severely beaten, and the defendant received an enhanced sentence because the victim was selected on the basis of race. The Wisconsin court held that the enhanced sentence was unconstitutional because it was punishment based on the "thoughts and ideas that propelled the actor to act." The court argued that anti-discrimination laws punish only objective acts, while selection of victims, "quite simply, is a mental process, not an objective act."

The Supreme Court unanimously reversed the Wisconsin Supreme Court and upheld the use of racial motivation as an enhancement factor in sentencing.[10] The Court distinguished *R.A.V.* on the grounds that the enhancement statute was "aimed at conduct" rather than being targeted at expression like the St. Paul ordinance. Also, the Court said, the state's desire to prevent the special harms associated with bias-motivated crimes "provides an adequate basis for its penalty-enhancement provision over and above mere disagreement with offenders' beliefs or biases." Among these harms were the increased odds of provoking retaliation, causing distinctive emotional harms, and inciting community unrest.

The upshot is that there seems to be no problem with using racial motivation as a basis for enhancing punishment for misconduct. Enhancement is most clearly permissible when the conviction is for violating a conduct-based statute, even though the defendant was also communicating a message. That is, because St. Paul could constitutionally provide an enhancement for racist motivation if R.A.V. had burned trash on his neighbors' lawn, it should also be able to enhance a trespass or illegal burning conviction even when the object burned happens to be a cross.

It is less clear whether the state can enact a general regulation against the use of fighting words, and then have a sentence enhancement based on racial motivation. The Court's primary objection in *R.A.V.* stemmed from the St. Paul ordinance's focus on the content of the message. But a distinction based on motivation differs from one based on content. Under the St. Paul approach, R.A.V. would not have been subject to punishment if he had made death threats without any overt racial references, even if he had chosen his victims based on race. But that situation would be covered by an enhancement statute. Conversely, despite the overtly racial character of R.A.V.'s message, R.A.V. would not have been subject to a penalty enhancement based on motivation, if the victim was chosen for nonracial reasons and the racist message was then simply selected as being most upsetting to that particular victim. Thus, under the hate crime approach, even where expressive but unlawful

---

[10]   *Wisconsin v. Mitchell,* 508 U.S. 476 (1993).

conduct is at issue, application of the regulation is based on the discriminatory *intent* of the speaker, not on the *content* of the speech. At most, the content of the speech serves only as evidence of intent.

C. Regulation   Ancillary   to   Prohibitions   on Discriminatory Conduct

One major reason for concern about hate speech is its relationship with other forms of racial discrimination. In particular, racial harassment may deter access to government facilities and services by members of minority groups. This is a particular concern for universities, whose goal is to encourage broader access. One justification for banning hate speech is to counter the potential effects of racist speech in reinforcing discrimination. *R.A.V.* and *Matal* raise the question whether a regulation of this kind would fail because of a lack of content neutrality. Nevertheless, the university might be able to defend carefully drafted regulations under the compelling interest test, which was discussed in Chapter 2.

In *R.A.V.* itself, the city made an effort to defend its ordinance under the compelling interest test. Justice Scalia agreed that the city had a compelling interest in protecting "the basic human rights of members of groups that have historically been subjected to discrimination." He concluded, however, that content discrimination was unnecessary to protect this interest, since the city could have achieved its goals by a ban on all fighting words rather than focusing on hate speech. By implication, a university arguably could not single out racist hate speech based on content, but instead would have to ban all speech that impaired a person's access to university facilities.

If a University regulation is based on discriminatory intent and effect, however, rather than directly on content, it *may* be possible for the university to target racial harassment. *R.A.V.* specifically recognizes the validity of some selective bans on harassment:

> [F]or example, sexually derogatory "fighting words," among other words, may produce a violation of Title VII's general prohibition against sexual discrimination in employment practices. Where the government does not target conduct on the basis of its expressive content, acts are not shielded from regulation merely because they express a discriminatory idea or philosophy.

To the extent that a harassment ban is truly ancillary to a general university prohibition on racial discrimination, the ban may be said to target behavior on the basis of its discriminatory effect rather than because of its "discriminatory idea or philosophy." Moreover, the fact that a code on racial discrimination singles out verbal racial harassment from the spectrum of fighting words hardly seems to indicate that "official suppression of ideas is afoot." The fact that a discrimination code covers only discrimination-related speech seems no more suspicious than the fact that the National Labor Relations Act regulates only labor-related speech.

R.A.V. also states that a "prohibition of fighting words that are directed at certain persons or groups" would be "facially valid if it met the requirements of the Equal Protection Clause." Thus, it would seem that a rule singling out harassment against members of ethnic groups would pass scrutiny under *R.A.V.*, given the proper factual foundation. Anti-harassment rules are not based directly on the content of the speech, but rather on its intent and effect. A library clerk who hurls racial epithets at members of an ethnic group would be covered, but so would the clerk who singles out members of an ethnic group for any other form of verbal abuse. Thus, anti-harassment regulations are arguably valid under the *R.A.V.* exception for "target-based" regulations.

In summary, *R.A.V.* does leave some room for regulation of hate speech. Where the defendant has also committed an offense unrelated to the content of the speech, such as defacing university property, the penalty can be increased on the basis of racist motivation. Moreover, provided the regulation is narrowly tailored, the university can arguably prevent harassment, defined narrowly to encompass discriminatory efforts to interfere with equal access to university facilities and functions.

It must be recognized, however, that the allowable scope of regulation under current law is much narrower than advocates of hate speech regulation believe necessary, and even within this narrow scope, a great deal of care would be required in drafting. In this next section, we turn to the arguments for significantly revising current First Amendment law to provide more sweeping protection to racial minorities against hate speech.

IV. Critiques of Current First Amendment Doctrine

The extent to which First Amendment doctrine limits the ability of the government to regulate hate speech is vividly illustrated by the unsuccessful effort to block a march by the American Nazi Party in the largely Jewish suburb of Skokie, Illinois. Several thousand survivors of the Holocaust, and many others whose relatives were murdered by the Nazis, lived in Skokie. The American Nazis intended to march through town wearing Nazi uniforms and displaying the swastika on armbands and flags. As the Seventh Circuit observed, there was every reason to believe that the Nazis anticipated and indeed "relished" the fact that many people would find the march "extremely mentally and emotionally disturbing."[11] Although there was some reason to fear violence, local officials declined to stop the march on that basis, and pledged to make every effort to protect the Nazis if the march were held. Moreover, there was no captive audience problem. Since the Nazi march was well publicized, anyone who would be offended could stay away. The Seventh Circuit conceded that the Nazis' beliefs are repugnant to our "core values" and to "much of what we cherish in civilization." Nevertheless, under the First Amendment, "there is no such thing as a false idea"; even the Nazis are entitled to compete in the marketplace of ideas. In a companion case, the Illinois Supreme Court, while admitting that the sight of swastikas is "abhorrent to the Jewish citizens of Skokie" and that the memories evoked are "offensive to the principles of a free nation," concluded with some reluctance that "it is entirely clear that this factor does not justify enjoining defendants' speech."

These rulings were clearly correct under current law. The display of the swastika could not be banned as the visual equivalent of "fighting words" (any more than flag burning could be banned). *Cohen* makes it clear that a violent reaction cannot be presumed, that the offensiveness of a symbol is not a basis for banning it, and that people in public places have little or no claim to be considered captive audiences. *Falwell*, a case discussed in the previous chapter, makes it clear that intentional infliction of emotional distress is permissible so long as it occurs in the setting of public discourse. *R.A.V.* makes it clear that the government cannot single out expressions of racism or anti-Semitism. And of course, *Brandenburg* makes it clear that advocacy of genocide is no basis for suppressing Nazi activities, since there is no likelihood of imminent success. In short, from a lawyer's point of view, the Nazi march represents the prototype of the "easy case."

Yet the issue of the Nazi march hardly seems like an "easy case" to most people—for example, many members of the ACLU resigned out of anger that the civil liberties union had defended the Nazis. Similarly, it is far from obvious to most people that someone who burns a cross in a neighbor's yard in the middle of the night deserves any constitutional protection at all. Understandably, then, there have been strenuous arguments that the treatment of hate speech under current First Amendment law is fundamentally misguided. For the most part, advocates of greater regulation do not contend that the entire notion of the First Amendment is misguided and that the government should have a completely free hand in regulating all

---

[11] *Collin v. Smith,* 578 F.2d 1197 (7th Cir.), cert. denied, 439 U.S. 916 (1978). The companion case was *Village of Skokie v. National Socialist Party,* 69 Ill.2d 605, 373 N.E.2d 21 (1978).

speech. Rather, they contend that hate speech presents a distinctive problem and should be subject to substantially more regulation than is currently allowed. Although these arguments have not prevailed in the U.S. courts, they have been more favorably received in Canada and Europe.

Some of the arguments against current First Amendment doctrine are considered in this section. The issue has given rise to broad scholarly debate, and it is impossible to explore the issues fully in this limited space. We can, however, provide at least a road map to some of the major points of contention.

A.   Uniqueness of Harm

Hate speech can cause two kinds of harm. First, it can have a direct psychic impact on members of minorities groups. Burning a cross in a black family's yard is not simply an annoying trespass; it evokes a history of terroristic acts, as the court observed in *Virginia v. Black*. Second, hate speech can reinforce ideas of racism in the minds of majority group members, further entrenching racism and leading to discriminatory acts.

There are a number of arguments in favor of the view that the psychic impact of racist speech is distinctively severe. Unlike other types of personal attacks, racist speech is based on an immutable personal trait, and a trait that in American society is very important to personal identity. Moreover, having grown up in a society in which racism is widespread, the victim herself may have subconsciously accepted some racist ideas, which are then triggered by the racist insult. Consequently, the racist attack may strike more deeply at the foundations of self-respect. Also, a racist attack is not an isolated incident. For many victims, it may be only a part of a lifetime of repeated humiliations based on race; for all victims, it draws resonance from the entire national history of racial discrimination. Hence, the racial attack has a cumulative effect which may be lacking from other kinds of insults. Finally if members of racial minority groups are disproportionately more likely to suffer from other problems, as a result of personal or historic discrimination, they may simply be in a worse position to cope with any additional trauma.

If indeed these arguments hold water, they suggest that racial slurs do more damage than other verbal insults. If so, the precise balance to be struck between individual harm and First Amendment values could differ for this category of speech. Surely, the harm to a black undergraduate from being stalked by hecklers is greater than the harm to a consumer from a misleading soft drink ad. Why allow the government to regulate soft drink advertising but not racial harassment? This argument might justify a modification of the rules regarding fighting words and captive audiences; at the very least, it would suggest that Justice Stevens' dissent might be preferred over Justice Scalia's majority opinion in *R.A.V.* Thus, some incremental adjustments in First Amendment doctrine might be warranted. Perhaps *Virginia v. Black* was a small step in that direction.

The second type of harm—reinforcement of racist ideas—would require a more far-reaching revision in First Amendment doctrine. This rationale for regulation rests on the assertion that racist speech strengthens the propensity of the audience to entertain racist stereotypes and engage in racist actions. The problem with this claim, from the point of view of the First Amendment traditionalist, is not that it is factually incorrect, but that accepting it as a valid justification for regulating speech would mean abandoning a key doctrinal principle. If it is true that racist speech makes racist behavior more likely, it is also true that subversive speech makes terrorism more likely, and in general, that advocacy of any undesirable idea increases the likelihood of undesirable conduct. Perhaps it could be argued that racist speech is more likely to lead to an imminent racist action because it reinforces and triggers racist ideas that have already been absorbed by the listener. But a similar argument could be made whenever a speaker appeals to norms that are widespread among the audience, whether the norm is racial superiority, resentment of authority, or envy of the rich and powerful.

What is needed is an argument to explain why the harm of racism should be considered legally distinctive, so that the spread of racist ideas justifies regulation when a quantitively similar harm of a different kind would not. One such argument, as we will see, is that racism itself implicates values of constitutional dimension, not merely ordinary governmental interests.

B.   Equality Versus Liberty

The premise is correct: racism does implicate values of constitutional dimension. Race lies at the heart of the Reconstruction-era amendments to the Constitution. The Thirteenth Amendment ended slavery and empowered Congress to eliminate its "badges and incidents"; the Fourteenth Amendment's equal protection clause generally prohibits racial discrimination by government. The Fifteenth Amendment specifically addresses racial discrimination in voting. Racial discrimination, then, is a central constitutional concern.

Moreover, in enforcing these constitutional provisions, the Supreme Court has not been blind to the psychological harm caused by racism. In *Brown v. Board of Education*,[12] the Court's most

---

[12]   347 U.S. 483 (1954).

important ruling on discrimination law, the Court held that segregated schools were inherently unequal because of the stigma imposed on black students, citing studies showing impairment of black students' self-images in segregated schools. Thus, the argument runs, the right to engage in racist speech under the First Amendment is in conflict with the right to racial equality under the Fourteenth Amendment. Both rights have equal constitutional status, and it is wrong to give automatic precedence to the First Amendment right.

One response to this argument is that the Constitution prohibits racial discrimination only by the government, so it has nothing to do with the private speaker. Certainly, the Constitution imposes different obligations on private actors than on the government. In a technical sense, there is no conflict between the Fourteenth Amendment and the First Amendment, because the Fourteenth Amendment requires only the state government to refrain from racism, while the First Amendment allows the private individual to engage in racist speech.

Although this rebuttal has considerable force, it may be too hasty. For instance, there may be a genuine constitutional conflict when the state has an affirmative duty to prevent racist conduct. A school subject to a desegregation order might have a Fourteenth Amendment duty to ensure that black students do not face a hostile environment, but a First Amendment duty to tolerate some degree of free speech by students. Moreover, while it is true that the two amendments are not usually technically in conflict, it is also true that most people view racism as constitutionally disfavored even when the Fourteenth Amendment does not technically apply. For example, the federal law making most forms of racial discrimination illegal was upheld under the congressional power to regulate commerce, but most people would intuitively view the law as more closely related to the anti-racism command of the Fourteenth Amendment than to the economic concerns of the Commerce Clause. Furthermore, the Thirteenth Amendment extends to the "badges and incidents" of slavery, and it is not limited to state action. Thus, it is plausible that private racism implicates constitutional values.

Even granting the premise that the harm done by racist speech implicates constitutional values, it may not follow that a modification of traditional First Amendment doctrine is required. Two aspects of the debate are considered below.

First, supporters of existing First Amendment doctrine reject the relevance of the constitutional norm of equality. Showing that a harm implicates constitutional values may not go very far in justifying regulation. Subversive advocacy implicates constitutional values, since the revolutionary is rejecting the democratic process for legal change embodied in the Constitution. The traditional concept of content neutrality requires that the idea of racial inequality and the idea of revolution be treated equivalently. But it may be argued in response that in reality it is far from neutral to treat verbal attacks on the government the same as verbal attacks on a powerless minority.

Second, except in special circumstances, it may be possible to attack racist behavior directly rather than to try to regulate speech. If so, the conflict may be avoided. Alternatively, regulating speech may simply not be very effective way of countering racism as a practical matter.

As to the issue of neutrality: much of First Amendment law is based on the idea that the government must be neutral among different viewpoints, so that speech advocating racism must be treated the same as speech attacking it, and more generally, speech reinforcing the status quo is to be treated just like efforts to end social subordination. But the concept of neutrality is a slippery one. A century ago, it seemed that neutrality required the government to treat contracts by consumers exactly the same as contracts by giant corporations, and to treat employees and employers as enjoying equal "freedom of contract." But neutrality only means treating similar things the same, without favoritism, and there must be a prior judgment about what things are similar. Such judgments are always potentially open to criticism. Thus, a more sophisticated argument is that racist speech is not simply the mirror image of anti-racist speech; that the two are fundamentally different; and that the propensity to view them as mirror images is itself a product of racism. The same writers would make an identical argument about the propensity to view affirmative action as a form of "reverse discrimination," rather than viewing it as entirely different in kind from traditional racial discrimination.

In part, this argument is a sophisticated rephrasing of the arguments we have already considered: that racial speech does unique harm or impairs special constitutional values. To the extent those earlier arguments hold, racist speech differs in constitutionally relevant ways from anti-racist speech, and it is not a violation of neutrality to treat them differently. But the neutrality critique can be more generally considered to be a claim that the law should distinguish between the powerful and the downtrodden, and that treating the speech of both alike is really no more neutral than denying both the rich and the destitute the right to live in cardboard boxes.

Opponents of this position can, of course, invoke the panoply of traditional arguments in favor of the view that there is "no such thing as a false idea" under the First Amendment. More specifically, they raise two points. First, they say, in practice it is not always easy to determine who is downtrodden and who is not. For example, a sexist comment by a black man to a white woman is hard to classify. Moreover, many groups in American society have made claims of victimization, ranging from racial minorities to religious fundamentalists, making it difficult to limit recourse to the argument for special protection against hostile speech. In reply, advocates of hate speech regulation rely on our ability to distinguish true from false claims of oppression.

Second, critics of hate speech regulations argue that minority groups need freedom of speech, and that majority groups will be unwilling to support this principle without the assurance that they are equally entitled to take advantage of it themselves. Freedom of speech is important for minority groups, but can only survive if it is seen as being a universal right rather than a privilege given unequally to different groups. If progressives regulate speech when they have the power to do so, they open the door for their opponents to restrict progressive speech when given the chance. In response, advocates of hate speech regulation express skepticism about whether dominant groups will abide by this implicit bargain that each side will refrain from restricting the speech of the other.

Thus far, we have considered arguments about whether special restrictions on racist speech are justified in principle. But there is also considerable disagreement about the practical effects of hate speech regulation, and whether those practical effects are really advantageous to minority groups. Opponents argue that hate speech regulation is at best ineffective and at worst counterproductive. In some instances, university hate speech regulations have been used by white students against minority students, and hate speech legislation in other countries has sometimes been used against minority activists for attacking the majority. Moreover, opponents say that hate speech regulations allow racists to wrap themselves in the banner of free speech, portraying themselves as victims of political correctness. Finally, hate speech regulation may create the comfortable illusion that the problem of racism has been solved, decreasing pressure to take more concrete actions to aid minority groups.

All of these assertions are contested by advocates of hate speech regulation. Foreign observers in countries that regulate hate speech seem persuaded that the regulations are helpful, on balance, in fighting racism and ethnic strife. Advocates suggest that the assertion that hate speech regulation is counterproductive is itself paternalistic, since it suggests that the members of minority groups who favor hate speech regulation do not understand their own true interests.

A final, more general dispute relates to whether the arguments in favor of regulating hate speech can be limited as a practical matter, or whether a wide variety of other groups would receive similar protection. Partly as a result of various government antidiscrimination rules, universities typically recognize a wide range of protected classes, including women, racial minorities, the elderly, veterans, gays and lesbians, and the disabled. If all of these groups are given protection from negative speech, the result could be quite sweeping. For example, a disabled veteran might credibly claim to find pacifist slogans highly traumatic, so a university might find itself putting restrictions on antiwar demonstrations.

One of the difficulties in interpreting the debate over hate speech is that is it hard to be sure of precisely what is at stake. Probably the most limited position is that the Court was wrong in *R.A.V.* when it prohibited governments from specifically targeting hate speech even when the same speech could be reached under a different form of regulation. This position questions the Court's views about the form of regulation, but not about the substance of what can be regulated. It would allow a specific ban on racist fighting words, rather than requiring all fighting words to be treated alike. A more aggressive position would hold that First Amendment doctrine should give more weight to the harm done by hate speech in striking a balance between speech and other values. For example, we might allow broader regulation than current doctrine allows of face-to-face racial insults. The broadest position is that hate speech—defined broadly as any speech which impugns an under-represented group—should receive no constitutional protection at all.

Although similar types of arguments can be made in support of all these positions, one may accept the claims only in part, not reaching the most extreme position. Generally, the question of how far one takes the argument seems to be influenced by how one views the other side of the balance. That is, it hinges not on whether one views hate speech as especially bad, requiring special remedial treatment, but on one's opinion of how strongly speech regulation threatens traditional First Amendment values and on the importance one places on those values.

FURTHER READINGS

J.M. Balkin, *Free Speech and Hostile Environments*, 99 Colum. L. Rev. 2295 (1999).

Erwin Chemerinsky and Howard Gilman, Free Speech on Campus (2017).

William Cohen, *A Look Back at* Cohen v. California, 34 UCLA L. Rev. 1595 (1987).

Richard Delgado, *Toward a Legal Realist View of the First Amendment*, 113 Harv. L. Rev. 778 (2000) (reviewing Steven H. Shiffrin, Dissent, Injustice, and the Meanings of America (1999)).

Gary Goodpaster, *Equality and Free Speech: The Case Against Substantive Equality*, 82 Iowa L. Rev. 645 (1997).

Steven J. Heyman, *Free Speech and Human Dignity* (2008).

Charles Lawrence, III, *If He Hollers Let Him Go: Regulating Racist Speech on Campu*s, 1990 Duke L.J. 431.

Mari J. Matsuda, *Public Response to Racist Speech: Considering the Victim's Story*, 87 Mich. L. Rev. 2320 (1989).

Robert C. Post, *Racist Speech, Democracy, and the First Amendment*, 32 Wm. & Mary L. Rev. 267 (1991).

Frederick Schauer, *Expression and Its Consequences*, 57 U. Toronto L.J. 705 (2007).

Philippa Strum, When the Nazis Came to Skokie: Freedom for Speech We Hate (1999).

Eugene Volokh, *Freedom of Speech and Workplace Harassment*, 39 UCLA L. Rev. 1791 (1992).

Jeremey Waldron, The Harm in Hate Speech (2012).

James Weinstein, *Hate Speech Bans, Democracy and Political Legitimacy*, 32 Const. Commentary 627 (2017).

James Weinstein, Hate Speech, Pornography, and the Radical Attack on Free Speech Doctrine (1999).

Chapter 7

SEXUAL MATERIAL

One of the traditional exceptions to First Amendment protection was for a category called obscenity. The first half of this chapter discusses the history of obscenity law as well as current obscenity doctrine. Although obscenity law, in its modern form, is primarily aimed against hardcore pornography, it seems to be notably ineffective in suppressing such material. As a few minutes of exploration on the Internet will confirm, pornography of all kinds is readily available despite obscenity laws. The second half of the chapter considers two other possible methods of controlling sex-related speech: (a) the use of zoning laws to limit the permissible locations for businesses selling pornography, an approach which has been accepted by the courts; and (b) civil rights remedies against materials considered to pose a threat to women, an approach which has been rejected by the federal courts.

I. The Development of Obscenity Law

Chaplinsky v. New Hampshire (the fighting words case discussed in the previous chapter) listed obscenity as one of the forms of speech outside the protection of the First Amendment. Obscenity prosecutions have a long history in the United States, with the first reported judicial opinion dating back to the early Nineteenth Century. Serious efforts to suppress obscenity began in the Civil War era. They resulted in the enactment of bans nationwide on literature tending to "deprave and corrupt" the reader. Because this test was geared to protect the most innocent readers, it resulted in banning notable literary works on the theory that some passages were corrupting. In 1948, the Court divided equally on whether the memoirs of a noted literary critic were legally obscene.[1] Beginning in the late 1950s, the Court began a prolonged engagement with the problem of how to define unprotected obscenity. We will devote some specific attention to its first formulation, the *Roth-Memoirs* test, even though that test has since been modified, because most of the conceptual difficulties in the current *Miller* test were implicit in this earlier formulation.

A. The *Roth-Memoirs* Test

Roth v. United States[2] actually involved two companion cases, one under a federal law banning the mailing of obscene material and

---

[1] *Doubleday & Co. v. New York*, 335 U.S. 848 (1948).

[2] 354 U.S. 476 (1957).

the other under a California obscenity law. According to the Court, no question was presented about whether the particular material was obscene. The only question was whether obscenity in general is "utterance within the area of protected speech and press." Justice Brennan's opinion for the Court concluded that obscenity was not protected speech.

Justice Brennan began his analysis by noting that when the First Amendment was adopted, state laws generally regulated or banned several forms of speech, including libel and in various states either blasphemy or profanity. Justice Brennan described the First Amendment as being "fashioned to assure unfettered interchange of ideas for the bringing about of political and social changes desired by the people." Thus, he said, "[a]ll ideas having even the slightest redeeming social importance—unorthodox ideas, controversial ideas, even ideas hateful to the prevailing climate of opinion" are protected by the First Amendment. But "implicit in the history of the First Amendment is the rejection of obscenity as utterly without redeeming social importance." The defendants argued that the obscenity statutes failed the "clear and present danger" test. But Brennan argued that this test only applied to otherwise protected speech, so obscenity (as a kind of "non-speech") was not covered.

Besides offering this rationale for obscenity law, Justice Brennan attempted to clarify the meaning of obscenity. Sex and obscenity, he said, are not equivalent: "[o]bscene material is material which deals with sex in a manner appealing to prurient interest." He then offered some dictionary definitions of "prurient"—as "[i]tching; longing; uneasy with desire or longing"—and referred to the definition of "prurient interest" under the Model Penal Code as "a shameful or morbid interest in nudity, sex, or excretion." Because of the First Amendment interest in nonobscene discussions of sexual matters, however, Brennan considered it vital to clarify the standards for determining obscenity. The traditional method determined obscenity by the effect of isolated passages on the most susceptible persons. Thus, a work could be held obscene based on a few snippets taken out of context. Brennan rejected this approach. He quoted with approval the instructions given by the trial judge in *Roth*:

> The test in each case is the effect of the book, picture or publication considered as a whole, not upon any particular class, but upon all those whom it is likely to reach. In other words, you determine its impact upon the average person in the community. The books, pictures and circulars must be judged as a whole, in their entire context, and you are not to consider detached or separate portions in reaching a conclusion. . . . You may ask yourselves does it offend the

common conscience of the community by present-day standards.

Justice Brennan spoke for five Justices. The other four feared, for various reasons, that the opinion gave too much scope for censorship. Because their views helped shape the later debate, it is worth reviewing their separate opinions. Two Justices, Warren and Harlan, concurred in the result. Chief Justice Warren argued that the test should focus less on the specific work and more on the defendant's conduct, which helped shape whether the reader would approach the work as pornography or otherwise. In *Roth*, he said, the defendants were in the business of marketing material "openly advertised to appeal to the erotic interest of their customers." They were also "plainly engaged in the commercial exploitation of the morbid and shameful craving for materials with prurient effect." Warren based his vote to affirm the convictions on this conduct. Justice Harlan's concurring opinion argued that each work must be considered on its own merits by the Court to determine obscenity, and that a jury verdict on the subject was not decisive. Justice Harlan also suggested that states should have broader regulatory powers over speech than the federal government. This suggestion has not found later favor as a doctrinal matter, and there is some evidence that the Court is actually more lenient in reviewing federal legislation.

Justices Douglas and Black dissented. Douglas argued that the obscenity laws punished a writer for provoking bad thoughts, not overt acts, and that the First Amendment did not allow speech to be punished without at least showing some relationship to undesirable action. After all, he said, "[t]he tests by which these convictions were obtained require only the arousing of sexual thoughts"; "[y]et the arousing of sexual thoughts and desires happens every day in normal life in dozens of ways."

Roth began a twenty-five-year period of confusion in obscenity law, as the Court confronted numerous allegedly obscene works but was unable to coalesce around a definition of obscenity. In the *Memoirs* case,[3] three Justices (including Brennan) joined in a refinement of the *Roth* test, under which a work could be judged obscene only if (a) the theme of the work taken as a whole appeals to a prurient interest in sex, (b) the material is patently offensive because it violates contemporary community standards relating to the representation of sex, and (c) it is utterly without redeeming social value. Justices Black and Douglas believed that obscenity laws were flatly unconstitutional, so there were five votes altogether to

---

[3]   *A Book Named "John Cleland's Memoirs of a Woman of Pleasure" v. Attorney General*, 383 U.S. 413 (1966).

protect any work not meeting the *Roth-Memoirs* definition of obscenity.

Following up on Justice Harlan's suggestion in *Roth*, the Court concluded that it was obliged to consider the obscenity of each specific work. As a result, the Justices received private viewings of allegedly obscene films on a regular basis, a scene made stranger because the failing eyesight of at least one Justice required a colleague to give a running description of what was occurring on-screen. For the next seven years, the Court issued a series of per curiam reversals of obscenity convictions, but still was unable to find majority agreement on a definition of obscenity. Justice Stewart, for example, confessed that he was unable to define the sort of hard-core pornography that should be considered obscene. He then added, in a famous phrase: "But I know it when I see it."[4]

B.   Obscenity and the Two-Tier Theory

The fundamental intellectual move in Justice Brennan's opinion in *Roth* was to classify obscenity as unprotected speech falling outside the ambit of the First Amendment, which therefore required no more heightened justification to regulate than any other kind of conduct. Critics argued that this was merely an intellectual sleight of hand, avoiding the difficult problem of justifying regulation of pornography. A similar argument is that erotic works are merely sexual stimulants and so should be regulated like other sexual conduct, sparking the response that even obscene works have expressive content and a cognitive element.

In principle, there seems to be nothing wrong with the argument that some types of utterances do not involve the kind of "speech" that the First Amendment was intended to protect. For example, contracts obviously involve language, but no one has ever thought that laws regulating the terms of contracts violated the First Amendment. The question, however, is why obscenity should be placed in this category. It is true that obscene literature is a way of obtaining sexual stimulation, which is a result that can also be produced by non-expressive conduct. Still, televised football games are for some people a way of avoiding boredom, and that, too, is a result that can be produced by non-expressive conduct. Why should vicarious sex be treated differently than vicarious athletics?

The Court has not generally inquired whether particular forms of expression have "redeeming social value." It is not clear that a football game adds anything identifiable to the marketplace of ideas. Yet no one has argued that televised sports events are outside of the First Amendment unless they can be proved to have redeeming social

---

4   *Jacobellis v. Ohio*, 378 U.S. 184, 197 (1964) (Stewart, J., concurring).

value. An even better analogy might be a boxing match, in which the participants are engaging in what would normally be considered antisocial conduct (committing physical assaults for pay). As the Court noted in *Roth*, obscenity bans were historically linked to legal restrictions on profanity, and we saw in the last chapter that those restrictions have been essentially eliminated. Why is obscenity different than other offensive and intellectually vacuous forms of speech, which are generally constitutionally protected?

Implicit in Justice Brennan's *Roth* opinion seems to be a psychological model in which sexual urges are sharply differentiated from other thoughts and emotions. His opinion refers to sex as "a great and mysterious motive force in human life", one which has "indisputably been a subject of absorbing interest to mankind through the ages; it is one of the vital problems of human interest and public concern." Yet if sex were only another human motivation, like anger, curiosity, and hunger, it is hard to see why speech appealing to sex should be judged by a different standard than other speech.

Rather, the Court's assumption seemed to be that sex is a particularly dangerous instinct, in need of careful control (if not repression). Like the drug dealer, the Court seemed to think, the seller of obscene works is triggering a response that his customers cannot fully control and that will undermine their ability to function as responsible members of the community. Just as it is psychologically on a different level than other activities, so sex is on a different level under conventional morality—after all, no one proposes punishing works that appeal to a "shameful interest" in food or athletics or money. What makes the Court view an interest in sex "shameful," it would appear, is the loss of appropriate sexual self-control. Thus, in the obscenity area, a two-tier theory of human behavior, in which sexual urges are seen as especially dangerous, underlies the two-tier theory of speech.

The "conduct" argument can be usefully recast into economic language by viewing obscenity as akin to sale of a commodity. Most forms of speech, as discussed earlier, involve what economists describe as "public goods" because their information content can be transmitted by the purchaser to others. But, given the strong attraction held by sexual materials, it may be possible to market those materials with little or no information content. If so, they are more akin to ordinary consumer goods than to most other forms of speech, and it might be possible to justify providing little or no First Amendment protection on that basis. Although it would offer an alternative way of justifying obscenity law, this economic analysis has certainly never been articulated by the Court. Rather than seeing obscene works as akin to ordinary consumer goods and subject to regulation on that basis, the Court seems to liken them to commercial sex.

C.   The Defendant's Conduct

Each of the opinions supporting regulation of obscenity in the *Roth* case had an effect on the law. Justice Brennan's opinion in *Roth* evolved into the Court's test for obscenity, while Justice Harlan's resulted in the Court's case-by-case review of particular works to determine whether the test was satisfied. Chief Justice Warren's emphasis on the conduct of the defendant bore fruit in a series of cases in which the Court looked beyond the "four corners" of the work to determine whether an obscenity conviction could stand.

Even when a work on its face met the *Roth-Memoirs* test, the state did not have a completely free hand in regulating it. First, the Court ruled that *scienter* is necessary to support a conviction. A bookstore owner cannot be held legally responsible for the contents of all the books in the shop. He could only be convicted of selling obscene material if he knew the contents of the work.[5] Second, private possession of pornography by an individual cannot be criminalized; allowing the police to search a person's library for unacceptable works would be too close to "thought control."[6] At least when combined with the heightened privacy interest in the home, private possession was protected (although searches of homes for other illegal materials is allowed). So even if the works were obscene, the defendant could escape liability.

On the other hand, even if the works were not obscene under *Roth-Memoirs*, the defendant might be convicted anyway for using the wrong marketing techniques. If the works were marketed to minors, a variation of the test would be used, suitably modified for the audience. For example, rather than asking whether the work would appeal to the prurient interest of the community, the jury would decide whether the work appealed to the prurient interest of minors[7] (an easy test to satisfy, presumably, since even dictionary definitions have been known to exert such an appeal). But even works marketed to adults might result in conviction if the marketing materials seemed racy. In *Ginzburg v. United States*,[8] the Court upheld convictions for distribution of some relatively innocuous magazines. Today, movies with similar content would probably get the equivalent of a *PG-13* rating, or at worst an *R*. The Court described the magazine as "commercial exploitation of erotica solely for the sake of their prurient appeal" and found them to be

---

[5]   *Smith v. California,* 361 U.S. 147 (1959).

[6]   *Stanley v. Georgia,* 394 U.S. 557 (1969).

[7]   *Ginsberg v. New York,* 390 U.S. 629 (1968).

[8]   383 U.S. 463 (1966).

"permeated" by the "leer of the sensualist." Also, the publisher had attempted to have them mailed—and thus postmarked—from Pennsylvania towns named Intercourse, Blue Ball, and Middlesex. This "brazen" market strategy showed that the magazines were being marketed solely to appeal to prurient interests, and that the defendant was therefore guilty of "pandering."

The pandering doctrine indicates that obscenity actually ranks below any other form of "unprotected" speech in the Court's esteem. Imagine the equivalent ruling in libel law: a holding that a supermarket scandal sheet loses the protection of *New York Times v. Sullivan* because the slogan "Inquiring Minds Want to Know" appeals to "the prurient interest in gossip." Or in the area of subversive speech, imagine a Cold War-era ruling that an otherwise protected political pamphlet could be banned if deliberately mailed from Moscow, Idaho! Only in the area of obscenity could the Court find such factors relevant.

The Court was soon to revisit and modify the *Roth-Memoirs* test, but all of these rulings regarding the defendant's conduct remain good law today.

II. Current Obscenity Law

Obscenity was a highly controversial issue in the late 1960s and early 1970s, probably because of the major changes in sexual mores which occurred during the sixties. Unlike the Warren Court, the Burger Court was supportive of the conservative side of this "culture war," as we will see.

In 1973, a majority of the Justices were finally able to agree on a test for obscenity. In *Miller v. California*[9] and a companion case,[10] the Court expanded the government's power to ban obscenity. After reviewing the caselaw in the area, Chief Justice Burger's opinion for the Court set forth a three-part test for obscenity:

(a) Whether the average person, applying contemporary community standards, would find that the work taken as a whole appeals to the prurient interest.

(b) Whether the work depicts, in a patently offensive way, sexual conduct specifically defined by the applicable state law. As examples, the Court mentioned depictions of "ultimate sexual acts, normal or perverted, actual or stimulated," or "of masturbation, excretory functions, and lewd exhibition of the genitals." The Court later made it clear that this list was not exhaustive—for example, the

---

[9]   413 U.S. 15 (1973).
[10]   *Paris Adult Theatre v. Slaton*, 413 U.S. 49 (1975).

states can add sado-masochistic materials to the "patently offensive" list.

(c) Whether the work taken as a whole lacks serious literary, artistic, political, or scientific value. For example, the Court pointed out, medical text books "necessarily use graphic illustrations and descriptions of human anatomy."

Note the role of "community standards" in this test. The Court considered that people in rural areas might have different norms about sexual matters than people in urban areas, for example, and saw no reason why the entire nation should be forced to the lowest common denominator. (The Court was not willing to reject the use of local community standards even on the Internet, where the practical problems are obvious, though the issue produced tortuous opinions and a deeply fragmented bench.[11]) On the other hand, the third element (serious redeeming value) is not based on community standards. Moreover, the Court itself retains the power to determine that particular materials are not obscene as a matter of law.

In the companion case, the Court dealt with the claim that consenting adults have the right to purchase obscene material—not an unreasonable argument, since the Court had already held that adults cannot be prosecuted for private possession of pornography. The Court concluded that the legislature was entitled to assume that obscene materials were socially harmful even when sold to consenting adults. Among the government's regulatory interests were "the interest of the public in the quality of life and the total community environment, the tone of commerce in the great city centers, and, possibly, the public safety itself." Thus, obscene materials were a form of pollution, degrading the quality of the community. Moreover, the legislature could reasonably conclude that obscene works harmed their readers. If great books "lift the spirit, improve the mind, enrich the human personality, and develop character," then it must be equally true that obscene books "have a tendency to exert a corrupting and debasing impact leading to antisocial behavior." Experience provides ample evidence, said the Court, that "a sensitive, key relationship of human existence, central to family life, community welfare, and the development of human personality, can be debased and distorted by crass commercial exploitation of sex."

Justices Brennan, Stewart, and Marshall dissented on the ground that the definition of obscenity was intolerably vague, and that the state's only significant regulatory interests were to limit access by children and save unwilling adults from exposure to offensive material. Hence, they would have forbidden state

---

[11] See *Ashcroft v. ACLU*, 535 U.S. 564 (2002).

regulation of sales to consenting adults. Other critics of the Court's position have argued that there is actually evidence that exposure to sexual materials can have valuable psychological effects for some people. In any event, critics contend, the First Amendment leaves it up to individuals rather than the government to decide what materials will improve or debase their minds.

Since 1973, the Court has made only one significant departure from the *Miller* obscenity test. In *New York v. Ferber,*[12] the Court upheld a statute banning "child pornography," which was defined as sexual material involving children as models or actors. The Court found that the state's interest in protecting children from participating in the production of these materials was strong enough to justify banning the materials themselves, so as to dry up the market. Indeed, the Court later found that this interest was strong enough to justify a ban on private possession of child pornography, even though ordinary obscenity is not enough to justify an intrusion into the home.[13] The difference, according to the Court, is that child pornography laws are designed to protect the children who are exploited by the production of these materials, while obscenity laws rely on a paternalistic interest in protecting the audience's morals.

Ferber has turned out to be a limited exception to the *Miller* test. The Court has resisted efforts to expand the category of child pornography. In *Ashcroft v. The Free Speech Coalition,*[14] the Court rejected a congressional ban on "virtual child pornography"— pornography in which adult actors portray juveniles or in which computer-modified images appearing like real children are used. Justice Kennedy's opinion for the Court emphasized that "*Ferber's* judgment about child pornography was based upon how it was made, not on what it communicated." Note, however, that the First Amendment does not protect offers to transfer real child pornography or requests to obtain it, regardless of whether the specific material in question is actually real or fake.[15]

Obscene materials seem to be rated somewhere below zero in terms of First Amendment protection, in that they receive a less favorable response from the Court than other forms of supposedly "unprotected" speech. One clear indication of this basement-level First Amendment position is the Court's willingness to tolerate prior restraints, so long as only obscene materials are enjoined and adequate procedural protections are provided.

---

[12]   458 U.S. 747 (1982).

[13]   *Osborne v. Ohio,* 495 U.S. 103 (1990).

[14]   535 U.S. 234 (2002).

[15]   *United States v. Williams,* 553 U.S. 285 (2008).

The Court's attitude toward prior restraints on obscenity is distinctive. For example, in *Alexander v. United States*,[16] the Court held that the First Amendment allowed the government to seize the defendant's adult entertainment business and destroy the inventory, following a conviction for engaging in "racketeering activities." (Under the statute, a finding of "racketeering activities" required little more than a finding that the defendant's business sold obscene materials on more than one occasion.) Unlike previous cases, the Court said, the government had not seized the materials because of their content but because they were materials used in a racketeering enterprise.

It is hard to imagine the Court tolerating such a remedy if another form of speech were involved. Suppose the statute had included the knowing publication of libelous materials on its list of racketeering activities. It seems inconceivable that the Court would allow a newspaper's printing press to be seized as an asset used in this "racketeering activity." Thus, obscenity is clearly being treated as less protected than other forms of unprotected speech such as libel. In short, the Court apparently sees more value in the work of even the most scurrilous journalists than in adult entertainment. The Court provides less primary protection and is more willing to tolerate side-effects with adult entertainment.

III. The "Zoning" Approach

Whatever the Court's intention in *Miller*, obscenity prosecutions (even accompanied by draconian penalties such as forfeitures) seem to have been singularly ineffective in eliminating pornographic material. In any urban area, and many rural ones, it is easy to find stores offering for sale materials that the *Miller* Court would surely have considered unprotected obscenity. Prosecutors are generally unwilling to bring cases because the trials tend to be lengthy and expensive, given the propensity of defendants to offer expert testimony (especially relating to redeeming value), and also because of the unpredictable attitudes of jurors, who may either be personally unoffended by pornography or believe it to be so widely available as to fall within local community standards. Not surprisingly, communities have turned to other approaches.

A. "Second Class" Protected Speech?

Because of concern over the effect of pornographic businesses on neighborhoods, cities turned to the use of zoning laws. In particular, local governments have been troubled by the propensity of adult entertainment businesses to attract other illicit sexual activities such as prostitution. In this section, we will consider the Court's

---

[16]   509 U.S. 544 (1993).

responses to efforts to "zone" sexually related expression into certain localities, as well as more metaphoric forms of zoning involving the media. Of course, the ready availability of pornography on the Internet means that "brick and mortar" sales are less central to the industry. Nevertheless, the zoning cases remain instructive today.

The Court first confronted one of these zoning ordinances in *Young v. American Mini Theatres, Inc.*[17] Detroit had enacted an ordinance prohibiting adult book stores and movie theatres within a thousand feet of any two other regulated uses, which included adult theatres and book stores, liquor stores, pool halls, pawnshops, and so on. An adult movie theater was defined as one "presenting material distinguished or characterized by an emphasis on matter depicting, describing or relating to 'Specified Sexual Activities' or 'Specified Anatomical Areas,'" which were then listed. (Note that much material fitting this description would not necessarily be obscene under *Miller*.) The Court upheld the ordinance in an opinion by Justice Stevens. The Court held that the ordinance was not unconstitutionally vague, because it could be clarified by the state courts. The Court was not very concerned about the possibility of a chilling effect on speech:

> Since there is surely a less vital interest in the uninhibited exhibition of material that is on the borderline between pornography and artistic expression than in the free dissemination of ideas of social and political significance, and since the limited amount of uncertainty in the ordinances is easily susceptible of a narrowing construction, we think this is an inappropriate case in which to adjudicate the hypothetical claims of persons not before the Court.

Also, the Court concluded that a restriction on the location of movie theaters was part of legitimate zoning of businesses rather than a prior restraint.

The most significant part of the opinion, however, was joined by only three other Justices. This portion of the opinion dealt with the issue of content regulation. Justice Stevens found the Detroit ordinance unobjectionable because the locations where a film could be shown were affected only by sexual explicitness, not by "whatever social, political, or philosophical message [the] film may be intended to communicate." Moreover, Stevens continued, although the government cannot completely suppress erotic materials having some arguable artistic value, these materials nonetheless have lesser First Amendment value. Stevens recalled Voltaire's comment that he disapproved of a speaker's remarks but would defend to the death

---

[17]   427 U.S. 50 (1976).

the right to make those remarks. "[I]t is manifest," Stevens said, that the interest in protecting adult bookstores and theaters "is of a wholly different, and lesser, magnitude than the interest in untrammeled political debate that inspired Voltaire's immortal comment."

Justice Powell, the "swing voter" in the case, refused to join this portion of the opinion. He voted to uphold the ordinance based only on the theory that the city was reallocating the location for adult speech but not affecting the total quantity or availability of this speech. The four dissenters vehemently argued that the test for First Amendment protection cannot be how many people would "take arms" to defend the speaker.

Notably, the Court has been unwilling to consign other forms of speech to the "second class" status given erotic expression. In *Brown v. Entertainment Merchants*,[18] a state had attempted to limit the sale of violent video games to minors. The city had tracked the *Miller* definition of obscenity by limiting the ban to games containing patently offensive depictions of violence that lacked redeeming social value and violated community standards. In the absence of a societal tradition of limiting depictions of graphic violence, however, the Court gave these videogames the full measure of First Amendment protection. In contrast, if the videogames contained graphic sex rather than graphic violence, the state would have been on solid ground. Again we are brought back to the notion that sex presents unique dangers to social order.

B. Secondary Effects

A decade after *Mini Theatres*, the Court returned to the zoning issues, and this time was able to formulate a majority opinion. In *City of Renton v. Playtime Theatres, Inc.*,[19] a city ordinance prohibited adult movie theaters within a thousand feet of any residence, church, park, or school. The plaintiffs had purchased two theaters with the intention of showing adult films. The Court upheld the ordinance, but offered a somewhat different analysis than *Mini-Theaters*, treating the ordinance as content neutral.

Admittedly, the Court said, the ordinance did treat theaters specializing in certain films differently than others. Nevertheless, the Court said, the ordinance was not aimed at the content of the films but at the secondary effects of the theatres on the surrounding communities. It was predominantly intended to prevent crime, protect retail sales, maintain property values, and generally to improve the quality of urban life. "In short," the Court said, the

---

[18]   564 U.S. 786 (2011).

[19]   475 U.S. 41 (1986).

ordinance "is completely consistent with our definition of 'content-neutral' speech regulations as those that 'are *justified* without reference to the content of the regulated speech.' "

Given this kind of content neutrality, the Court said the appropriate test was whether the ordinance is designed to serve a substantial governmental interest and allows reasonable alternative avenues of communication. The Court found this test easily satisfied in light of the governmental interest in preserving the quality of urban life. Additionally, the city was justified in relying on the experience of other cities rather than studying the problem independently. Furthermore, the ordinance left legally open five percent of the entire land area for adult theaters, which the Court considered ample even though the lower courts had found there was actually no commercially available land for this use. Although as a practical matter the ordinance might foreclose adult theaters, their proprietors "must fend for themselves in the real estate market"; if they can't find a suitable location, that's their hard luck but is not constitutionally relevant.

One question raised by *Renton* is the definition of a secondary effect. Apparently, the fact that a message offends its audience or bystanders is not a secondary effect, for we saw in the last chapter that restrictions on offensive speech are strictly scrutinized. Thus, the fact that people who see adult theaters are offended by their existence cannot qualify as a secondary effect. Presumably, a secondary effect is a kind of side effect of speech that happens to be associated with particular types of content, but which could in principle derive from other forms of speech.

An illustration might be helpful. Suppose computer programmers were notorious for their use of drugs, and that bookstores carrying computer-related books attracted drug dealers to the area, increased neighborhood drug use, caused property values to decline, and harmed the quality of urban life. Observing these effects, a city council might desire to control the location of stores with books "Depicting Specified Computer Activities", without in any way disapproving of the books themselves or endorsing the views of Luddites who disapprove of computers. Thus, assuming that all of these facts were well-established, special zoning ordinances for computer book stores would not necessarily suggest that the "suppression of ideas" was afoot.

In Chapter 2, we considered some of the problems involved in defining content discrimination. *Renton* is a notable example of the difficulty the Court has sometimes had in applying the notion of content discrimination. The other problem with *Renton* is suggested by the computer store hypothetical. Would the Court really uphold special zoning for computer bookstores? What about zoning of religious book stores, if those were shown to have undesirable effects on the neighborhood? We don't know the answer with certainty, of course, since the Court has never been confronted with those issues, but it seems unlikely that these zoning efforts would receive a sympathetic hearing from the Court. Its willingness to uphold the zoning ordinance in *Renton* based on a fairly thin record seems to signal that, although the Court has retreated from the candor of the *Mini Theaters* opinion, it continues to regard even non-obscene sexual materials as enjoying a lower constitutional status than other protected speech.

The Court's low regard for sexual speech was underlined in *City of Los Angeles v. Alameda Books, Inc.*[20] The Court held that a city had made a prima facie case in favor of an "adult entertainment" zoning provision. The city's argument was based on a single study, conducted five years before this particular provision was enacted and twenty years before the litigation; moreover, the study did not mention the specific problem involved in the case. The Court found it sufficient that both the city's theory and the defendants' were "consistent with the data in the 1977 study." It is difficult to imagine that the Court would uphold a restriction targeting any other form of speech based on such avowedly inconclusive evidence. For example, as we will see in the next chapter, the Court generally demands stronger empirical support for restrictions on commercial advertising.

The idea of "zoning" speech raises some intriguing possibilities for government regulators. In *FCC v. Pacifica Foundation,*[21] the Court upheld an FCC ruling that in effect had zoned "indecent" speech to late night hours, in order to avoid exposing children to the material. Since *Pacifica*, however, this concept has received a less favorable response, and *Pacifica* now seems to be limited to the specific context of broadcasting. In one later case, the Court struck down a provision requiring that cable operators restrict sexually-oriented material to a separate channel and obtain a prior request from viewers for access.[22] Somewhat more recently, the Court rejected a federal statute seeking to prevent access by children to sexual materials via the Internet, primarily because it created too great an intrusion on the ability of adults to get access to such

---

[20]   535 U.S. 425 (2002).

[21]   438 U.S. 726 (1978).

[22]   *Denver Area Educational Telecommunications Consortium, Inc. v. FCC,* 518 U.S. 727 (1996).

materials.[23] These media issues are discussed in more detail in Chapter 11.

IV. The "Civil Rights" Approach

Some scholars have suggested an alternative approach to regulating sexual materials. Under this approach, proposed by some feminists, a new category of speech would be defined as pornographic and banned as a violation of women's civil rights. This section considers the proposal in some detail, and then provides an overview of the fiery debate that arose about this approach.

A. Proposed Legislation

The civil rights approach was first proposed as a city ordinance in Minneapolis, where it passed the city council but was vetoed by the mayor on First Amendment grounds. The key portion of the ordinance was the definition of pornography. The remainder of the ordinance established remedies for women who are directly or indirectly injured by the production or sale of pornography.

To qualify as pornography under the ordinance, a work must constitute "the sexually explicit subordination of women, graphically depicted, whether in pictures or in words." Thus, as a threshold matter, the work must (a) be sexually explicit and (b) graphically depict the subordination of women. In addition, the proposal contains a list of specific characteristics, at least one of which must also be present in order for a work to qualify as pornography. These characteristics include the presentation of women enjoying pain or humiliation or experiencing sexual pleasure in being raped, or depicting women in postures of sexual submission, tied up, or mutilated, or being penetrated by objects or animals. Additional characteristics on the list are the presentation of women "dehumanized as sexual objects," or the exhibition of "women's body parts . . . such that women are reduced to those parts."

The rationale for this approach is explained in the purpose section of the proposed ordinance, in which the city council made a finding that "pornography is central in creating and maintaining the civil inequality of the sexes." Specifically, the council found, the "bigotry and contempt it promotes, with the acts of aggression it fosters, harm women's opportunities for equality of rights . . . ; create public harassment and private denigration; promote injury and degradation such as rape, battery, and prostitution"; and in general, restrict women's participation in public life, including their equal exercise of the right to free speech.

---

[23] *Reno v. ACLU,* 521 U.S. 844 (1997).

The civil rights approach has something in common with obscenity law. Much of the material targeted by the two approaches is probably the same, and the idea that obscene material contributes to sex crimes has a long history. Moreover, traditional obscenity law is based on the idea that certain materials harm the ability of men to relate to women in an appropriate way, and the same idea is basic to the new approach. But there are also obvious differences. Unlike the traditional approach, the new approach makes no effort to provide protection for artistic works—it is no defense that a work qualifying as pornographic under the ordinance has artistic or literary worth. Also, although sexual explicitness is required in the new approach, there is no requirement that the work offend community standards in this regard.

Although the ordinance in modified form was passed in Indianapolis, it was struck down by the Seventh Circuit in *American Booksellers Ass'n v. Hudnut*.[24] But the Canadian Supreme Court has been somewhat more sympathetic. In *Regina v. Butler*,[25] the Canadian court construed its obscenity statute to ban "degrading or dehumanizing material" that violates community standards. In particular, the opinion by Justice Sopinka explained, degrading or dehumanizing materials "place women (and sometimes men) in positions of subordination, servile submission or humiliation" and "run against the principles of equality and dignity of all human beings." Although adopting the rationale of the civil rights approach, the Canadian court's specific guidelines differed from the proposed ordinances. Most notably, the Canadian court parted with the civil rights approach in several respects: using community standards, exempting private use or viewing of obscene materials, and excluding material with any artistic value. But the Canadian court did reaffirm the core premise of the civil rights approach: If "true equality between male and female persons is to be achieved, we cannot ignore the threat to equality resulting from exposure to audiences of certain types of violent and degrading material."

Specifically, advocates of the civil rights approach point to two kinds of harms caused by pornography. First, they argue, it operates as a powerful form of propaganda, conditioning men to view women as less than fully human and existing only to serve the purposes of men, and infusing sexual overtones in dominance relationships with women. Thus, pornography is a key underpinning of sexism, and thereby of discrimination against women. Second, more specifically, pornography directly contributes to violence against women, both

---

[24] 771 F.2d 323 (7th Cir. 1985), aff'd 475 U.S. 1001 (1986) (per curiam). Chief Justice Burger, Justice Rehnquist, and Justice O'Connor dissented from the summary affirmance and urged that the case be set for oral argument.

[25] 134 Nat'l Rptr. 81 (1992).

those who unwillingly participate in the making of pornographic works and those attacked by men exposed to pornography. We will discuss these rationales in turn.

B. Pornography and Sexism

Writing for the Seventh Circuit in *Hudnut*, Judge Easterbrook found it plausible that pornography, by depicting subordination of women, tended to perpetuate that subordination, leading to inferior work opportunities, domestic assault, and sexual crimes. At least, he found the premise plausible enough that the legislature could justifiably resolve the empirical disputes in this manner. But he found this empirical conclusion irrelevant under the First Amendment. The power of pornography to produce bigotry against women "simply demonstrates the power of pornography as speech. All of these unhappy effects depend on mental intermediation. Pornography affects how people see the world, their fellows, and social relations." But affecting how people see the world and act does not justify regulating speech. Other speech, such as communist or fascist propaganda that warp people's views and conduct, is nonetheless protected by the First Amendment. Nor was Judge Easterbrook convinced by the argument that sexual responses are unthinking, because "almost all cultural stimuli provoke unconscious responses." People can be conditioned in "subtle ways"—"[i]f the fact that speech plays a role in a process of conditioning were enough to permit governmental regulation, that would be the end of freedom of speech."

More fundamentally, according to Judge Easterbrook, the ordinance's effort to distinguish sexist from nonsexist speech unconstitutionally discriminated on the basis of content. Speech that subordinates women is forbidden, regardless of literary value, while speech that portrays women as equal is allowed, no matter how sexually graphic. This, he said, is "thought control", allowing those who espouse the approved feminist viewpoint to use sexual images while others may not.

One possible defense of the ordinance is to argue that the ordinance serves a compelling interest. Although a court would probably agree that gender equality is a compelling interest and that suppressing pornography might advance this goal, the test here is a rigorous one. To survive strict scrutiny, the ordinance must be shown to be necessary to achieve its goal and narrowly tailored to doing so. The evidence on this point is mixed. There is some empirical evidence that pornography desensitizes viewers to mistreatment of women, thereby making them more tolerant of discrimination, harassment, and other forms of subordination. Other studies find no effect of pornographic materials on the attitudes of laboratory subjects on issues relating to gender. One study even found that states with high sales of soft-core pornography tend to have the strongest records of opposing gender discrimination. A court might also be concerned that the ordinance was too sweeping, and that regulation of works with artistic merit is unnecessary to achieving the state's compelling interest in promoting gender equality.

C. Pornography and Violence Against Women

In principle, at least, civil libertarians should have less trouble with the argument that pornography causes violence to women than with the argument that it spreads sexism. Violence is the kind of concrete harm that, in suitable circumstances, has traditionally been thought to justify restrictions on speech. There are two separate claims relating to violence, one concerning coercion of actresses and models, the other concerning the encouragement of crimes against women by consumers of pornography.

The hearings on the Minneapolis ordinance, as well as those in other cities, included testimony by women who had participated in making pornographic films. They reported that they had been subjected to coercion to participate, including actual or threatened violence. If these claims are true, what remedies are permitted under the First Amendment? Unquestionably, criminal prosecutions of the abusers, or civil actions against them by the women, are constitutionally permissible. An assault does not become immune from liability because it is performed by a film maker. Moreover, the woman might be able to recover the profits directly derived from the commission of a crime against her, provided the statute was narrowly tailored to achieving this result. Another theory would be liability for misappropriation of her interest in controlling commercial exploitation of her photographed image. This violation of the "right to publicity" should be actionable under *Zacchini v. Scripps-Howard Broadcasting Co.,*[26] in which the Court allowed a recovery by a performer whose circus act (being shot out of a cannon) was broadcast by a television station without his permission. Surely he would have had an even stronger case if he had been forced naked into the cannon at gunpoint by the television crew.

The more difficult question is the extent to which a remedy should be allowed against distributors of the resulting film. At its most draconian, such a remedy would include suppressing all pornographic works in order to prevent women from being physically coerced into participation. In *Ferber*, the Court accepted a sweeping ban on child pornography in order to protect children from participation in its production. But it seems unlikely that the Court

---

[26]   433 U.S. 562 (1977).

would agree that even purportedly involuntary participation by adult women is *inherently* so harmful to them that the state should be able to ban pornography entirely. A less drastic remedy would be to allow a suit by the woman in question against distributors for profiting from screening her forced participation in sexual activities. Recall from Chapter 5, however, the very limited scope that the Court has left for damage actions for invasion of privacy when material is lawfully acquired by the media. Liability might be possible, however, if the Court was convinced that the material did not relate to any matter of public concern, and that liability was necessary to protect a "state interest of the highest order."

A related argument for suppressing pornography is that it results in acts of violence by the men who purchase it. Under the *Brandenburg* test, defenders of the ordinance would have to show that the material explicitly incites violent acts and is likely to result in those acts. Given the lower value that the Court seems to place on speech relating to sex than on political speech, however, the threshold might be lower than it was in *Brandenburg*, which involved political speech. To the extent that the pornographic material is also legally obscene, the Court would be willing to allow regulation on the ground that the material is unprotected anyway. But if the material is not legally obscene—and particularly if it has some artistic or other value—it seems likely that the Court would require at least fairly clear evidence of causality.

Like the evidence on the effect of pornography on male attitudes, the empirical evidence on this point is mixed. The evidence regarding the effects of violent pornography is stronger than the evidence regarding the effects of other categories of pornography. As to violent pornography, psychological experiments do tend to show a greater expressed willingness to engage in violent acts after exposure to the material. Studies of individuals convicted of sexual offenses, however, have not found any correlation with exposure to pornography. Although some studies do show higher rape rates in states with larger circulations of "soft core" periodicals, international studies show lower rates in nations where pornography is widely available.

D. Problems of Interpretation

One of the major problems in interpreting the pornography debate is the difficulty in determining just what material is under discussion. The difficulties of interpreting the Minneapolis ordinance are themselves worth noting. The supporters of the civil rights approach may have in mind restricting a fairly narrow class of commercially available pornography. Yet, the language of the definition seems to be susceptible to much broader interpretations, which have given rise to considerable concern. One set of concerns relates to the doctrines of overbreadth and vagueness, which we discussed in Chapter 3.

Another interpretative concern about the civil rights approach comes from the opposite direction than Judge Easterbrook's concern about viewpoint regulation. It is the fear that the approach might squelch speech with a socially progressive viewpoint. Where Easterbrook was concerned that only speech with the "politically incorrect" viewpoint on sex would be reached, other critics fear that it will apply to speech that is intended to undermine traditional gender relations. Some critics focus on erotic materials marketed to gays and lesbians, at least some of which seems to fit under the language of the definition. Other critics fear that the civil rights approach could be used against art works that incorporate pornographic images in order to make feminist points.

Despite its partial success in Canada, the civil rights approach seems to face formidable obstacles under American constitutional law. In order to be upheld, not only would a strong empirical justification be required, but a court would also probably have to be convinced that the definition was precise and narrowly tailored to its purpose, and that the purpose did not include promoting an ideological perspective on gender issues.

Ashcroft v. The Free Speech Coalition,[27] the virtual child pornography case, demonstrates the kind of resistance that would greet efforts to move beyond *Miller*. One of the arguments for the ban on virtual child pornography was that it encourages pedophiles. The Court vehemently rejected the legitimacy of this rationale:

> The mere tendency of speech to encourage unlawful acts is not a sufficient reason for banning it. The government "cannot constitutionally premise legislation on the desirability of controlling a person's private thoughts." First Amendment freedoms are most in danger when the government seeks to control thought or to justify its laws for that impermissible end.

The idea that pornography fosters violence or discrimination against women seems unlikely to receive a friendlier response from the Court.

The pornography debate also raises the more general question of whether we should recognize new categories of "unprotected speech"—or more accurately, of disfavored communications. The Supreme Court has been extremely reluctant to do so. But why

---

[27]   535 U.S. 234 (2002).

should the length of the historical pedigree be relevant to the acceptability of a restriction on speech?

Although this argument has real force, there are some reasons to be more tolerant of longstanding restrictions on speech than on innovations. First, for those who believe in the relevance of original intent, it is easier to tie longstanding restrictions to the original understanding of free speech. Second, it has taken a great deal of judicial experience to learn how to define the existing categories in a way that strikes a reasonable balance between other social needs and speech values. This is a costly learning experience, and one we may not want to undertake again lightly. Third, if we have managed to tolerate some category of speech for two hundred years, there may be a presumption that regulation is unneeded.

With all this said, however, the argument against recognizing new categories of unprotected speech—or against radically revamping old ones, as in the case of the civil rights approach to obscenity—can amount to no more than a strong presumption. The fact that we have failed to suppress a type of communication in the past is a strong reason for questioning the legitimacy of doing so in the future, but it should not be completely decisive, especially when circumstances have changed dramatically.

FURTHER READINGS

Amy Adler, *What's Left?: Hate Speech, Pornography, and the Problem for Artistic Expression*, 84 Cal. L. Rev. 1499 (1996).

David Bryden, *Between Two Constitutions: Feminism and Pornography*, 2 Const. Comm. 147 (1985).

Elizabeth Glazer, *When Obscenity Discriminates*, 102 Nw. U. L. Rev. 1379 (2008).

Harry Kalven, Jr., *The Metaphysics of the Law of Obscenity*, 1960 Sup. Ct. Rev. 1.

Catharine MacKinnon, Only Words (1993).

Frederick Schauer, *Causation Theory and the Causes of Sexual Violence*, 1987 Am. B. Found. Res. J. 737.

Jeffrey O. Sherman, *Love Speech: The Social Utility of Pornography*, 47 Stan. L. Rev. 661 (1995).

Nadine Strossen, Defending Pornography: Free Speech, Sex, and the Fight for Women's Rights (2d ed. 2000).

Cass R. Sunstein, *Pornography and the First Amendment*, 1986 Duke L.J. 589.

Chapter 8

COMMERCIAL SPEECH

Until about forty years ago, government had a free hand in regulating advertising. At about the same time as obscenity and libel were defined in *Chaplinsky v. New Hampshire* as categories of unprotected speech, the Court announced in another case that commercial advertising also fell completely outside the scope of the First Amendment. In the mid-1970s, however, commercial speech was brought firmly under First Amendment protection. But even today, commercial speech is not covered by the same First Amendment rules as other speech. It is still considered a sort of "second class" speech and receives less protection than political or artistic expression. In this chapter, we will trace and evaluate this evolution. We will then consider the Court's treatment of two specific types of commercial speech: advertising by lawyers and promotion of high-risk products such as cigarettes and alcohol. These relate to the broader question of how much the government can regulate professional speech.

Because this chapter is the end of Part II, we will end with some concluding thoughts about the law governing disfavored categories of speech. The Court has now had over four decades to elaborate on this legal framework. How satisfactory are the results?

I. The Road to Protected Status

Although commercial speech was not explicitly given constitutional protection until 1976, this development was the result of a long evolutionary process. In this section, we will trace this process and then evaluate the arguments for and against protecting commercial speech.

A. Creation and Erosion of Unprotected Status

The Supreme Court first attempted to resolve the First Amendment status of commercial speech in *Valentine v. Chrestensen.*[1] Prior to that time, a few cases involving commercial advertisers had come up, but either the First Amendment had not been invoked or the Court had ignored the question of whether advertising was entitled to constitutional protection. In *Valentine,* the plaintiff had distributed a handbill advertising a submarine exhibit in violation of a New York City ordinance forbidding commercial leafleting in the streets. He brought suit to enjoin

---

[1]   316 U.S. 52 (1942).

enforcement of the ordinance, but lost because the Court found that the First Amendment allowed regulation of the commercial use of the streets. Relying on this case eight years later, the Court held in *Breard v. Alexandria*[2] that door-to-door salesmen—"solicitors for gadgets or brushes"—could not claim the protection of the First Amendment. *Chrestensen* and *Breard* were subsequently interpreted to deny First Amendment protection to all commercial speech. The *Chrestensen* doctrine was criticized by commentators, and the Court never gave a justification for its denial of First Amendment protection to commercial speech. Nor did it define "commercial speech," a term which turned out to be far from self-explanatory. Nevertheless, the Court virtually ignored the commercial speech problem for some twenty years.

The Court returned to the commercial speech area in *Pittsburgh Press Co. v. Pittsburgh Comm'n on Human Relations,*[3] in which a newspaper had been enjoined from placing job ads in gender-designated columns. The Court seemed unwilling to rely exclusively on the *Chrestensen* doctrine to uphold the injunction. Instead, the Court reasoned that classifying want ads by gender was comparable to running "a want ad proposing a sale of narcotics or soliciting prostitutes." The Court's analogy was not especially helpful; the narcotics ad is prohibited as the prelude to other illegal conduct by the advertiser, whereas the basis for prohibiting gender designation in want ads is that the ads *themselves* cause harm by discouraging certain applicants, without any further action by the advertiser.

The next case in the series also evidenced the Court's uneasiness with the *Chrestensen* doctrine. In *Bigelow v. Virginia,*[4] a Virginia newspaper had been convicted of publishing an ad for a New York abortion referral service. The referral service was legal in New York but illegal in Virginia. (This was shortly before the Court's decision holding abortion to be a fundamental right.) The Court began with the premise that Virginia could not prevent its residents from traveling to New York to obtain the referral service. Given this premise, which the Court apparently derived from the "right to travel," *Bigelow* was easy to resolve. A state surely has no legitimate interest in keeping people ignorant of their constitutional rights or in preventing them from exercising those rights intelligently. Quite apart from the First Amendment itself, the existence of a constitutional right (here, the right to travel) seems to imply the additional right to exercise that right knowledgeably. Any special power the government may have to regulate commercial speech derives from its power to regulate the underlying commercial

---

[2]   341 U.S. 622 (1951).

[3]   413 U.S. 376 (1973).

[4]   421 U.S. 809 (1975).

conduct. In *Bigelow*, according to the Court, the state had no jurisdiction over the underlying conduct of interstate travel.

Rather than rest its decision on this narrow ground, the *Bigelow* Court launched into a broad discussion of the First Amendment values involved in commercial speech. The Court contended that the rather mundane advertisement conveyed newsworthy information to a wide variety of readers with no personal interest in the service, including those interested in abortion law reform. It did not take an acute observer to realize that the old commercial speech doctrine was in serious trouble.

B. *Virginia Board*

The end of the old doctrine was not long in coming. A year after *Bigelow*, the Supreme Court decided *Virginia State Board of Pharmacy v. Virginia Citizens Consumer Council, Inc.,*[5] in which it unequivocally held that the First Amendment applies to purely commercial speech. The case arose from a consumer group's challenge to a ban on advertising of prescription drug prices by pharmacists. The primary issue before the Court in *Virginia Board* was whether the content of commercial speech placed it outside the protection of the First Amendment. The Court's analysis provides the foundation of current commercial speech doctrine.

After concluding that an advertiser's economic motive would not disqualify it from First Amendment protection, the Court examined the interest of the individual consumer in obtaining product information. The Court found this interest to be quite strong: "[a]s to the particular consumer's interest in the free flow of commercial information, that interest may be as keen, if not keener by far, than his interest in the day's most urgent political debate." After considering the interest of the individual consumer, the Court went on to consider the public interest in commercial speech. The state apparently believed that the public interest favored restrictions, on the theory that price competition between pharmacists would undermine professionalism and would ultimately impair the quality of service. The Supreme Court had a different view of the best means of attaining the public interest:

> So long as we preserve a predominantly free enterprise economy, the allocation of our resources in large measure will be made through numerous private economic decisions. It is a matter of public interest that those decisions, in the aggregate, be intelligent and well informed. To this end, the free flow of commercial information is indispensable.

---

[5] 425 U.S. 748 (1976).

Countervailing interests suggested by the state were found to be implausible.

There was little sign in *Virginia Board* of the Court's traditional reluctance to assess the merits of economic legislation. Instead, it did not hesitate in giving constitutional status to its own view of economics, which was that price competition is favorable to consumers. Rejecting the argument that consumers would seek the lowest prices regardless of the quality of service, the Court proclaimed the existence of "an alternative to this highly paternalistic approach." That alternative is "to assume that this information is not in itself harmful, that people will perceive their own best interests if only they are well enough informed, and that the best means to that end is to open the channels of communication rather than to close them." In short, the Court said, "[i]t is precisely this kind of choice, between the dangers of suppressing information, and the dangers of its misuse if it is freely available, that the First Amendment makes for us."

We should probably be deeply suspicious when a court proclaims that the Constitution has "made a choice for us"—language the Court has used on more than one occasion. True, the Constitution does not leave us with any choice on some matters, such as whether a thirty-year-old can serve as President. But the question of whether, in regulating advertising, we must assume that consumers behave entirely rationally is not addressed by the text of the Constitution. Indeed, for almost two centuries, no one seems to have thought that the Constitution had any bearing on the subject. There may be good reasons to reject such justifications for regulating advertising, but that is a choice that the Court is making, not one foreordained by the Founding Fathers.

In any event, after *Virginia Board*, there could be no doubt that commercial speech is protected by the First Amendment. *Virginia Board* was a controversial ruling. Before turning to later legal developments, we should pause to consider the soundness of this decision.

C.   Should Commercial Speech Be Protected?

Justice Stevens once remarked that few of us would send our sons and daughters off to war to protect the right to see sexually explicit films at convenient locations. It is equally true that few would send their children to war to defend the right of pharmacies to advertise the prices of prescription drugs. Few people would consider a ban on price advertising to be a human rights violation and demand international sanctions against a country engaging in this practice. Moreover, since the 1930s, it has been quite clear that commercial activity in general is subject to almost unrestricted government regulation, and the courts have abandoned any effort to assess the reasonableness of economic regulations. From an economic view, government regulations of advertising may produce noncompetitive markets, but that is also the goal of many regulations of economic conduct that are indisputably constitutional. Thus, it is not obvious that commercial speech should be considered a constitutional right. Nevertheless, there is a strong argument to be made in favor of the Court's decision to extend constitutional protection to commercial speech in *Virginia Board*.

The natural starting point for analyzing the constitutional status of commercial speech is to ask whether the subject matter of the speech places it outside the boundaries of the First Amendment. The subject matter of commercial speech is some commercial product or service about whose existence, price, or qualities the speaker wishes to communicate. If product information were outside the pale of the First Amendment, the consumer advocate as well as the commercial speaker would be left unprotected. Car companies could constitutionally enjoin critics from revealing unfavorable facts about the safety of its cars, and magazines like *Consumer Reports* could be freely suppressed. These results are simply unacceptable. Millions of people may buy a single product, and the safety of that product is certainly a matter of public concern. Moreover, information about the quality and price of some products may relate to political issues. For example, a belief that American cars are overpriced influences views on foreign car import restrictions, on inflationary price increases for domestic cars, and on the effects of environmental regulations. Knowledge of product safety and reliability relates to consumer protection legislation.

In short, product information is clearly entitled to constitutional protection in at least some contexts. For example, it seems clear that if a company sued a consumer advocate for criticizing the safety of its product, the speech would be considered to relate to a matter of public concern, and the company would at least have to satisfy the *Gertz* test for defamation in order to establish liability. Indeed, it is even possible that the company would be considered a public figure for purposes of attacks on its products.

In any event, it does seem clear that the content of commercial speech does not by itself disqualify it from First Amendment protection. The question, then, is whether the crass motivation of the advertiser should be considered disqualifying. Suppose that a company publishes an exhaustive and entirely truthful survey of the products of its industry. To make the point clear, assume that the survey was taken by *Consumer Reports* and enjoyed constitutional protection when it was published in that magazine. Can the state ban distribution of the survey of the company to limit competition in the industry?

It is hard to see why the identity of the distributor should give the state more regulatory power. Distribution by the company could strip the survey of its constitutional protection only if the company's profit motivation were a disqualifying factor. The *Virginia Board* Court was clearly correct in rejecting this approach. Economic motivation could not be made a disqualifying factor without enormous damage to the First Amendment. Little purpose would be served by a First Amendment that failed to protect the expression of newspapers, paid public speakers, political candidates with partially economic motives, and professional writers. Furthermore, the economically motivated speaker is often the most likely to raise important issues, since disinterestedness is less common than apathy.

Thus, neither the content of the speech nor the speaker's motivation standing alone seems to provide an adequate basis for stripping commercial speech of all First Amendment protection. The burden would seem to be on those who would argue that while neither factor is enough individually, the two factors in combination have a synergistic effect. *Virginia Board* at least seems consistent with the general trend toward narrowing the areas of "unprotected" speech.

II. The Current Status of Commercial Speech

Virginia Board established that commercial speech is entitled to some degree of constitutional protection, but left open the parameters of that protection, except to indicate that the common sense distinction between advertising and other forms of speech might well warrant distinctive treatment. Since then, the Court has developed a special test for regulations of commercial speech. In order to determine the applicability of this test, it is necessary to begin by defining the category of commercial speech.

A. The Boundaries of Commercial Speech

In general, the Court has been content to define commercial speech as speech doing no more than proposing a commercial transaction. In many situations, this is an easy definition to apply, but problem cases do arise. For example, consider a publication by an association of tobacco companies falsely stating that no scientific evidence exists that smoking is harmful to health. If the ad does not contain any direct offer of sale, is it immune from regulation as commercial speech?

The Court confronted a somewhat similar question in *Bolger v. Youngs Drug Products Corp.*[6] A federal statute prohibited unsolicited mailing of contraceptive advertisements. A condom manufacturer proposed to mail pamphlets promoting its products but also discussing sexually transmitted diseases and birth control. One pamphlet described the use of condoms and provided detailed descriptions of some of the manufacturer's products. The other was entitled "Plain Talk about Venereal Disease" and discussed the use of condoms as a means of preventing disease. The second pamphlet contained no identification of the manufacturer or its products except a statement at the bottom of the last page, which identified the pamphlet as a public service by the manufacturer and also gave the brand name of the manufacturer's product.

The Court noted that these pamphlets could not be considered "merely as proposals to engage in commercial transactions." Moreover, the fact that they were advertisements did not necessarily make them commercial speech. (Remember the ad in the New York Times criticizing the Alabama police that gave rise to *New York Times v. Sullivan*.) Nor is it sufficient that the manufacturer had an economic motive for the mailing, or that the materials identified a specific product. Nevertheless, the Court said, the combination of these factors supported the conclusion that the mailings were commercial speech. The fact that the mailings also discussed issues of broader concern was not enough to exempt them from this classification: "A company has the full panoply of protections available to its direct comments on public issues, so there is no reason for providing similar constitutional protection when such statements are made in the context of commercial transactions."

The *Bolger* Court was fairly cautious in its treatment of the definitional question. On the one hand, the Court seemed somewhat diffident in classifying the ads as commercial speech. On the other hand, it carefully reserved the question of whether all three of the characteristics had to be present in order to justify a finding of commercial speech, leaving open whether "corporate image" advertising could be regulated as commercial speech. (Such image advertising does not relate to a particular product, but is designed to promote sales generally.) Thus, after *Bolger*, we know that commercial speech includes any direct proposal of a commercial transaction, and that it also may include economically motivated ads that identify a specific product. The precise boundary between commercial and noncommercial speech, however, is yet to be defined.

---

[6]   463 U.S. 60 (1983).

B.   The *Central Hudson* Test

The current test for regulation of commercial speech was announced in *Central Hudson Gas & Elec. Corp. v. Public Service Comm'n.*[7] In an effort to encourage electrical conservation, a state utility commission banned promotional advertising by utilities, with a narrow exception for ads encouraging shifts of consumption away from peak periods. The utility claimed that the ban prevented it from advertising products and services that use energy efficiently, such as heat pumps. Thus, the ban prevented the utility from promoting services that would result in decreased use of electricity. In the course of striking down this ban, the Court announced the following standard for reviewing regulations of commercial speech:

> At the outset, we must determine whether the expression is protected by the First Amendment. For commercial speech to come within that provision, it at least must concern lawful activity and not be misleading. Next, we ask whether the asserted governmental interest is substantial. If both inquiries yield positive answers, we must determine whether the regulation directly advances the governmental interest asserted, and whether it is not more extensive than is necessary to serve that interest.

The ban on utility advertising failed the final element of this test, since it was broader than necessary to serve its conservation goal.

This element of the *Central Hudson* test might be confused with a "least restrictive alternative" analysis. In a later case, however, the Court made it clear that the government does not need to demonstrate that it used the *least* restrictive means. Nor, the Court reaffirmed, are regulations of commercial speech subject to the overbreadth doctrine. What the government does need to show is that speech regulations are narrowly tailored to achieve their goals.[8] Thus, it is not *necessarily* fatal to a regulation that the court can imagine a less restrictive means of achieving its goal, or that the court can imagine examples of regulated speech that might not cause the kind of harm the regulation is designed to curb. On the other hand, when there are obviously less restrictive ways for the state to achieve its goal, or when much of the regulation's coverage is gratuitous in terms of the state's asserted interest, it is difficult to maintain with a straight face that the regulation is narrowly tailored.

The *Central Hudson* test can be broken into two parts. We begin by determining whether the speech qualifies as legitimate. The

---

[7]   447 U.S. 557 (1980).

[8]   *Board of Trustees v. Fox,* 492 U.S. 469 (1989).

threshold inquiry is whether the regulated speech is misleading or concerns an illegal activity. If so, it receives no constitutional protection.

The second part of the test applies to the remaining, legitimate advertising. The government can regulate truthful advertising about lawful transactions only if it passes a three-prong inquiry: (a) Is the governmental interest a "substantial" one? (b) Does the regulation "directly" advance the governmental interest? (c) Is the regulation tailored to the governmental interest? This three-prong inquiry is essentially a watered-down version of the compelling interest test, but requires a less substantial interest to justify regulation and less precision in the targeting of the regulation. Thus, even speech that truthfully advertises a lawful activity receives less constitutional protection than other forms of speech. Since the inception of the *Central Hudson* doctrine, some Justices and commentators have protested this aspect of *Central Hudson*. Several Justices have suggested that a "blanket ban" on truthful, non-misleading speech about a lawful product requires especially careful scrutiny, at least when the ban was not based on consumer protection.

In particular, critics of *Central Hudson* have argued that paternalistic justifications for restrictions on speech should never be accepted. Yet, many economic regulations are paternalistic, and it is not immediately obvious why paternalism should be a disqualifying factor if a regulation of commercial speech would otherwise be valid. Some critics have argued that paternalistic speech regulations are less visible to the public than direct government intervention in markets (such as fixing minimum prices). But in fact many other kinds of regulations such as tariffs suffer from the same vice: they are difficult for consumers to observe. Another problem with the paternalism argument is that it is not always easy to define paternalism. In *Central Hudson*, for example, one might say that the regulation paternalistically assumed that consumers would unwisely buy energy-wasting appliances. Alternatively, one might say that the regulation assumed merely that consumers would consider only their individual interests in making purchasing decisions, ignoring the societal repercussions of higher energy use. On this view, the regulation may be said to consider consumers as self-centered rather than considering them paternalistically as being unable to pursue their own individual interests.

Thus, the arguments against paternalism are not free from difficulty. Still, the anti-paternalism argument resonates with other parts of First Amendment doctrine. We will return to the paternalism question in connection with our later discussion of advertising dangerous products.

The Justices' uneasiness over the status of truthful commercial speech was reflected in *44 Liquormart, Inc. v. Rhode Island*,[9] in which the Court struck down a statute forbidding price advertising for alcohol except at the place of sale. The Court was badly divided. Although seven Justices agreed that the advertising ban failed to pass *Central Hudson*, four Justices thought that "special care" was required in reviewing regulations designed to prevent truthful information from reaching the public (including Justice Thomas, who argued that regulations designed to keep consumers ignorant are per se invalid.) Four other Justices believed that the normal *Central Hudson* test applied, while the remaining Justice (Scalia) argued that the Court should revisit the entire area of commercial speech and focus on whether advertising was regulated at the time the First Amendment was adopted.

Although the Court decided several commercial speech cases after *44 Liquormart*, in each case it invalidated the government regulation under the *Central Hudson* test, without questioning the test's validity. In *Greater New Orleans Broadcasting Ass'n, Inc. v. United States*,[10] the Court struck down a federal ban on certain broadcasting ads for casinos, because the statute's operation was "so pierced by exemptions and inconsistencies that the Government cannot hope to exonerate it." In *Lorillard Tobacco Co. v. Reilly*,[11] the Court struck down advertising restrictions on cigars and smokeless tobacco, because the ban on outdoor advertising was too broad and the ban on store displays was not likely to achieve the state's goals.

Similarly, in *Thompson v. Western States Med. Ctr.*,[12] the Court invalidated a Food and Drug Administration (FDA) regulation of tailor-made prescription medications for individuals with special problems. The FDA allowed pharmacies to provide such tailor-made medications at physician request, but had banned the pharmacies from advertising the service. The advertising ban was based on a fear that mass marketing would transform the exemption into a large-scale loophole, undermining the general rule that medications must have prior FDA approval. (The government was right: this is exactly what happened later.) Applying *Central Hudson*, a bare five-member majority held that the restriction was broader than necessary to advance the government's legitimate interest in preventing evasion of the FDA licensing scheme. Only Justice Thomas, in a separate concurrence, called for overruling *Central Hudson*. The Court has not returned to the issue since then. Present indications, then, are that

---

9   517 U.S. 484 (1996).

10   527 U.S. 173 (1999).

11   533 U.S. 525 (2001).

12   535 U.S. 357 (2002).

Central Hudson will remain the applicable test despite the expressed dissatisfaction of some Justices.

C. Should Commercial Speech Be Fully Protected?

As we have seen, the Court has provided a lower level of protection for commercial speech in several respects. Deceptive advertising can be regulated without showing *New York Times* malice or even negligence. Prior restraints are allowed, and vagueness and overbreadth rules do not apply. Under *Central Hudson*, truthful speech can be suppressed under a standard that falls short of requiring a compelling government interest. Given that commercial speech is not outside the First Amendment, the obvious question is whether any justification exists for giving a lower degree of protection to commercial speech.

It is easier to justify certain aspects of the distinctive treatment of commercial speech than others. Some First Amendment doctrines are based on prudential assessments of the effects of government regulation on speech. It can plausibly be argued that the prudential calculus works out differently for commercial speech than for other kinds of speech. On the whole, as the Court has suggested, the commercial speaker is better situated than anyone else to know the truth of its statements about the product, unlike a newspaper that knows less about events than the actual participants. Thus, the newspaper is taking a greater risk of making a mistake than the commercial advertiser. Moreover, given the strength of the financial incentive for commercial advertisers, the Court is also probably right in suggesting that chilling effects are smaller than they are for other speakers. It is also less likely that implementation of rules regarding commercial speech will be distorted by ideological dislike of particular speakers. Thus, a plausible argument can be made that commercial speech is less in need of the special protection afforded by overbreadth, vagueness, and prior restraint doctrines. Of course, this argument is based on fairly crude generalizations about whole categories of speech, but this does not seem to be inherently objectionable given the need to fashion practical and reasonably categorical rules.

The harder question is whether the government should be able to suppress truthful advertising in the interest of consumer protection, or whether, as some Justices have insisted, truthful advertising should receive exactly the same constitutional protection as other speech such as political advocacy. If we consider the core values underlying the First Amendment, it seems fairly clear that commercial advertising does not implicate these values to the same extent as some categories of traditionally protected speech.

As we saw in Chapter 1, one set of First Amendment values cluster around democratic self-governance. Although commercial speech may have some incidental effect in enlightening the audience about economic conditions that may have political salience, this effect is certainly far less prominent than the role played in self-governance by explicitly political speech.

Even if we expand self-governance to include private economic decision-making, commercial speech has a weaker claim to protection than other kinds of speech. From an economic perspective, the most important characteristic of protected speech is that its informational content makes it a public good. Because the producer of the protected speech cannot capture the full social value of the speech, the producer has an insufficient incentive to produce beneficial speech. Therefore, regulations of such speech need to be carefully scrutinized to make sure that they do not reduce further the level of speech production. But the main effect of commercial speech is to cause increased consumption of the specific product being advertised, and the producer is in a position to recover fully the benefits of those increased sales. If Apple runs a magazine ad touting the iPhone, most of the benefit will accrue to the company itself. In contrast, the magazine's reports about telecommunications regulation have public benefits that cannot be fully recovered by the magazine publisher in the form of subscription or advertising revenue. The reason is that the information can be passed on to people who didn't buy the magazine. Commercial speech may have some beneficial spillovers, but they are proportionately smaller than the spillover effects of political speech.

A second cluster of speech values center on self-realization. Again, although commercial speech is not devoid of this kind of value, it is not present on the same scale as with traditional works of art. The photographers and writers who produce advertisements may feel some sense of self-expression through their work, but this self-expression is subordinate to the commercial purpose of the work. The works that fall most squarely within the definition of commercial speech—ads that merely announce the price and availability of a product—are the least likely to possess even a modicum of self-expressive value. The purpose of an ad is not to express creativity but to move product.

True, these are rough generalizations: some advertisements surely have a greater esthetic value than some works displayed in galleries. Yet, overall, it would be hard to argue that the average ad has the same value as the average news report or the average work of art. Moreover, government regulation of advertising is generally unlikely to reflect an attempt to suppress an idea. Because of the nexus between advertising and other regulated activities, commercial speech regulations are more likely to be extensions of legitimate regulations of commercial conduct than efforts at thought control. Undoubtedly, it is for these reasons that restrictions on commercial advertising do not have the aura of being human rights violations (except to those who regard *all* interference with the free market as tyrannical).

Do these considerations justify a lower level of constitutional protection for speech? The answer depends on two subsidiary questions: (1) How sound are these categorical generalizations about commercial speech?; and (2) Should constitutional doctrine draw distinctions between speech categories depending on perceptions of social value? The first of these questions seems impossible to answer except subjectively, and the second turns on our willingness to trust judges to make such judgments about the value of various categories of speech. We will return to the problem of valuing categories of speech in the closing section of the chapter.

III. Specific Types of Advertising

Much of the Court's work in the area of commercial speech has involved two specific types of regulation: (a) regulations of advertising by professionals, such as lawyers, and (b) restrictions on advertising for products or services that have traditionally been thought to present special risks of abuse by consumers, such as alcohol, gambling, and tobacco.

A. Advertising by Lawyers

Traditionally, advertising by professionals such as lawyers has been tightly limited. *Virginia Board* put these traditional limitations on a collision course with the First Amendment. In *Bates v. State Bar of Arizona*,[13] the Court took the predictable next step of invalidating a ban on price advertising by lawyers, finding it virtually indistinguishable from the advertising ban on pharmacists considered in *Virginia Board*. It certainly would have created an awkward appearance for a court composed of nine lawyers to announce that lawyers hold a loftier position under the Constitution than other professionals.

Two of the arguments made on behalf of the state regulation in *Bates* deserve mention. First, the state argued that price advertising by lawyers was misleading without information concerning the quality of the services. The Court withheld judgment on the permissibility of advertising claims concerning quality of service but nevertheless rejected the state's argument. The Court believed that it was "peculiar" to deny the consumer relevant information simply

---

[13]   433 U.S. 350 (1977).

because the information was incomplete. The advertising at issue in the case involved routine legal services such as uncontested divorces, where the quality of service might be less of an issue than in some other settings. (Since *Bates*, the Court has generally struck down state restrictions on quality-related advertising when a lawyer wishes to make objectively verifiable claims, such as a statement that the lawyer was certified as a specialist by a professional organization.) Second, as in *Virginia Board*, the Court was unimpressed by the argument that price competition would destroy the norms of professionalism in favor of cutthroat business practices. Although there is a general consensus that the practice of law has become more like an ordinary business, the reader will have to be the judge of whether the Court's decisions were a contributing factor.

A year after *Bates*, the Court made it clear that it was not lifting all restrictions on solicitation of business by lawyers. In *Ohralik v. Ohio State Bar Ass'n*,[14] the Court upheld a ban on in-person solicitation of accident victims. A lawyer had approached two young accident victims, one in a hospital room where she lay in traction and the other on the day she returned home from the hospital. His conduct was also questionable in other respects: he secretly taped the conversations with the clients, and he refused to withdraw from her case when one of the women asked him to do so. Because of the inherent risk of abuse or overreaching, the Court held, states are justified in banning in-person solicitation. But targeted mailings by lawyers are another matter. In *Shapero v. Kentucky Bar Ass'n*,[15] the Court struck down a state rule barring non-deceptive letters to potential clients known to face particular legal problems. These mailings were not considered to present the same kind of risk of overreaching as in-person solicitations.

None of these cases seemed to reflect much concern for the intangible attributes of professionalism that many lawyers felt were threatened by advertising. The Court's later decision in *Florida Bar v. Went For It, Inc.*[16] was a bit more open to this concern. The plaintiff challenged a Florida rule that prohibited mailings to accident victims until thirty days after the injury. Justice O'Connor's opinion for the Court upheld the rule, mostly on the basis of evidence about the effects of lawyer advertising on public opinion:

> The Florida Bar submitted a 106-page summary of its 2-year study of lawyer advertising and solicitation to the District Court. That summary contains data—both statistical and anecdotal—supporting the Bar's contentions

---

[14]   436 U.S. 447 (1978).

[15]   486 U.S. 466 (1988).

[16]   515 U.S. 618 (1995).

that the Florida public views direct-mail solicitations in the immediate wake of accidents as an intrusion on privacy that reflects poorly upon the profession. . . . Significantly, 27% of direct-mail recipients reported that their regard for the legal profession and for the judicial process as a whole was "lower" as a result of receiving the direct mail.

Justice O'Connor endorsed the purpose of the 30-day ban, which was "to forestall the outrage and irritation with the state-licensed legal profession that the practice of direct solicitation only days after accidents has engendered." The regulation was concerned, she added, "not with citizens' 'offense' in the abstract, but with the demonstrable detrimental effects that such 'offense' has on the profession it regulates." The four dissenters vigorously rejected "the proposition that the Constitution permits the State to promote the public image of the legal profession by suppressing information about the profession's business aspects."

It remains unclear two decades later whether the concern for the image of the legal profession expressed by the majority in *Florida Bar* will bear fruit, or whether it was an aberration. Nothing in *Central Hudson* directly precludes recognition of this state interest, but the dissenters in *Florida Bar* seem to have a point—it seems peculiar to allow the state to suppress speech in order to maintain the public image of the potential speakers.

B.　High-Risk Forms of Consumption

States have often heavily regulated or even banned the sale of products and services considered to be immoral or to pose a serious risk of abuse by consumers. Examples include alcohol, addictive drugs, prostitution, and gambling. If the state does prohibit such sales, it can ban advertisements proposing illegal transactions. But suppose that it chooses to legalize some activities in this class. Can it limit advertising of the once-forbidden product, as a way of either reducing overall demand or protecting specific groups it considers especially vulnerable from exploitation?

The Court's initial response to this question seemed encouraging for state regulators. In *Posadas de Puerto Rico Assoc. v. Tourism Co.*,[17] the Court upheld a statutory scheme that legalized casino gambling, but allowed casinos to advertise only to tourists and not to natives of Puerto Rico. The rationale apparently was that wealthy tourists could afford to lose money gambling but that less affluent local residents could not. The Court upheld this regulatory scheme. Given the history of prohibition of gambling, the Court had no difficulty concluding that the state's interest in reducing demand for

---

[17]　478 U.S. 328 (1986).

gambling was substantial. It also concluded (with very little scrutiny) that the restrictions directly advanced the state's goal and were narrowly drawn to focus on ads to local residents.

Although the Court purported to be applying the *Central Hudson* test, its application of the test was unusually deferential. The Court explained its deferential attitude by saying that it would "surely be a strange constitutional doctrine which would concede to the legislature the authority to totally ban a product or activity, but deny to the legislature the authority to forbid the stimulation of demand for the product or activity through advertising on behalf of those who would profit from such increased demand." Legislative regulation of products such as cigarettes, alcohol, and prostitution has ranged from complete prohibition to full legalization, with restrictions on advertising as an intermediate solution. The Court found little reason to rule out this intermediate response on First Amendment grounds.

A decade later, however, the Court seemed to disavow the *Posadas* approach. In *44 Liquormart, Inc. v. Rhode Island*,[18] the Court struck down a restriction on price advertising for alcoholic beverages. Four Justices rejected *Posadas* as a deviation from the Court's otherwise "unbroken line of prior cases striking down similarly broad regulations on truthful, non-misleading advertising when non-speech-related alternatives were available." Four others agreed that *Posadas* had been too hasty in accepting Puerto Rico's justifications without giving them the "closer look that we have required since *Posadas*."

Thus, it is clear at a minimum that even state regulation of advertising for previously banned products must face full scrutiny under *Central Hudson*. At least some Justices seem attracted to a broader per se rule against "paternalistic" regulations designed to keep consumers from making well-informed but unwise choices. The issue, then, is whether the First Amendment implies a prohibition, or at least an especially strong presumption, against paternalistic regulations.

The general thrust of First Amendment doctrine runs against state claims that speech, if believed, will harm the listener or cause the listener to harm others. Disapproval of content distinctions is based on suspicion of state claims of such harms. Effects on third parties provide a much more solid basis for restricting speech. For this reason, the argument against paternalistic regulation gains strength from the overall structure of modern First Amendment doctrine. After all, the premise of the marketplace of ideas is not

---

[18] 517 U.S. 484 (1996).

merely that truthful ideas will win out, but that it is better for them to win out—that ignorance should be replaced by knowledge.

Regulators might respond, however, that the reasons for this general presumption against paternalism do not apply with full force to commercial speech. Empirically, it is not necessarily true that people are always better off with more information. Sometimes, they do respond irrationally to the information. Indeed, this is one of the main rationales for keeping juries from being exposed to relevant but inflammatory information. For risky products such as alcohol, gambling, or drugs, society apparently finds the fear of irrational consumer responses great enough to be a legitimate basis for a complete ban. If the fear that people are too weak to resist a vice is strong enough to justify making it illegal, why not the lesser step of limiting the ability of advertisers to exploit this weakness? In short, the proponent of regulation might say, there really is a common sense difference between commercial speech and other speech, and that difference justifies relaxing the anti-paternalism rule.

The critic of paternalistic restrictions on commercial speech would probably respond at a more fundamental level, by questioning whether First Amendment doctrines should take into account perceptions of the relative values of different kinds of speech or the relative risks of abuse in government regulations of different kinds of speech. The fundamental dispute then, is about whether First Amendment doctrine should distinguish between various kinds of speech—or to put it another way, about the future viability of the categorical approach.

C. The Problem of Professional Speech

We have already seen that the Court has extended First Amendment protection to business solicitation by lawyers, but has classified that as commercial speech. What about other forms of speech that are part of professional activity? As with protection for commercial speech, extending the First Amendment into this area risks undermining the distinction between general economic freedom and protected personal rights, which has been a basic part of constitutional law since the 1930s. Thus, the irresistible force (the Court's impulse to protect speech) collides with the immovable object (the tremendous breadth of the government's power to regulate the economy). This collision came to the Court in an important 2018 case.

National Institute of Family and Life Advocates v. Becerra [*NIFLA*][19] involved a California law regulating crisis pregnancy centers—pro-life centers that offer pregnancy-related services. The state law required clinics that primarily serve pregnant women to

---

[19] ___ U.S. ___, 138 S.Ct. 2361, 201 L.Ed.2d 835 (2018).

provide certain notices. Clinics that were licensed had to notify women that California provides free or low-cost services, including abortions, and give them a phone number to call. The law's stated purpose was to make sure that state residents know their rights and what health care services are available to them. Unlicensed clinics must notify women that California has not licensed the clinics to provide medical services. Its stated purpose was to ensure that pregnant women know when they are receiving health care from licensed professionals. The state argued that the law was subject to lesser scrutiny as a regulation of professional speech.

In an opinion by Justice Thomas, the Court rejected that argument and struck down the law. According to Justice Thomas, the Court had given lower scrutiny to only two categories of laws regulating professional speech: laws requiring professionals to "disclose factual, noncontroversial information in their 'commercial speech,'" and laws regulating professional conduct, even though that conduct incidentally involves speech. As an example of the latter category, the Court referred to laws requiring doctors to give pregnant women seeking abortions "to inform patients of the availability of printed materials from the State, which provided information about the child and various forms of assistance." The Court considered the latter category inapplicable because the required notice was not limited to cases where the facility actually provided a medical procedure and did not include other types of facilities such as general practitioner's offices where services were offered. The Court did leave open the possibility that some other rationale, not provided to it in this case, might justify treating professional speech as a unique category, because it concluded that the notice requirement could not survive even intermediate scrutiny.

Justice Breyer dissented, joined by Justices Ginsburg, Sotomayor, and Kagan. In Justice Breyer's view, the majority approach raised serious issues "[b]ecause much, perhaps most, human behavior takes place through speech and because much, perhaps most, law regulates that speech in terms of its content, the majority's approach at the least threatens considerable litigation over the constitutional validity of much, perhaps most, government regulation." Historically, Breyer argued, "the Court has been wary of claims that regulation of business activity, particularly health-related activity, violates the Constitution." Indeed, he wrote, "[e]ven during the *Lochner* era, when this Court struck down numerous economic regulations concerning industry, this Court was careful to defer to state legislative judgments concerning the medical profession." Justice Breyer found California's notice requirement to be indistinguishable from notices required of abortion providers that the Court had previously upheld. He intimated that the Court was really choosing sides in the abortion debate rather than behaving even-handedly. It is difficult, however, to escape the impression that the majority thought the state of California was the one taking sides.

The major question for the future involves the second category of regulation described by the Court, that of speech incidentally covered by a regulation of conduct. In many settings, speech by a professional may be the service sought by the client, whether in the form of a diagnosis or health recommendation by a doctor or a legal opinion by a lawyer. If the state awards liability against the professional or even takes away the professional's license on the basis of negligence or incompetence in that setting, is it regulating "conduct" to which the speech is incidental? Or are all such regulations now subject to strict scrutiny? It is hard to believe that the Court intends strict scrutiny to apply in the case of a doctor giving an unfounded diagnosis or bad medical advice, but it is not clear precisely how the Court will escape that conclusion. It also seems unclear whether the government cannot license mental health therapists who offer only "talk therapy"—is that conduct or speech?

Issues such as these raise the question of whether the expansion of First Amendment law is putting in peril other settled constitutional doctrines. It also raises the question whether we are stuck with the alternative of either sharply diminished protection for speech or the same protection as core political speech.

IV. The Future of the Categorical Approach

As we have seen throughout this part of the book, First Amendment doctrine has traditionally identified certain categories of messages as warranting heightened government intervention. Initially, these categories were conceptualized as being entirely outside the scope of the First Amendment. In some sense, they were not considered to be "speech" at all for purposes of the First Amendment; instead, they could be regulated like any other form of conduct. So the world of communicative acts was divided into two types: the various categories of "unprotected speech," which were utterly outside the pale of the First Amendment, and all the rest of expressive conduct, which was protected equally by the First Amendment regardless of the specific nature of the speech.

Although this picture still survives and the terminology of "protected" and "unprotected" speech is still in use, legal developments of the past thirty years have eroded its foundations.

Each of the categories of "unprotected speech" now in fact enjoys considerable constitutional protection. Illegal advocacy can only be prosecuted in extraordinary circumstances, commercial speech is protected by the *Central Hudson* test, defamation suits face huge obstacles under *New York Times*, literature that would formerly have been considered obscene is protected by *Miller*, and whether the fighting words exception even survives is controversial. Moreover, *R.A.V. v. City of St. Paul* and other cases indicate that speech that fails to qualify for protection under any of these tests is still not "invisible" to the First Amendment. Thus, "unprotected" speech is not a constitutional zero under the First Amendment.

On the other hand, although speech outside of these categories usually cannot be regulated on the basis of content, we will see in Part III that there are plenty of specific contexts in which the government is in fact allowed to take content into account. So, if we have two tiers at all today, we seem to have disfavored versus favored categories of speech, with corresponding levels of regulation for each, rather than absolutely unprotected versus absolutely protected speech.

Once we discard the idea that some categories of communication simply are not "speech" at all for First Amendment purposes, we must recognize that First Amendment doctrine provides varying levels of protection to different kinds of speech. Sometimes these distinctions are purely historical. Sometimes they are due to perceptions about the relative hardiness of different forms of speech, as in the exception to the vagueness doctrine for commercial speech. And sometimes the distinctions are due to perceptions about varying risks of government abuse. But current doctrine also draws a number of distinctions based on perceptions about the relative value of different kinds of speech—with obscene speech (and even near-obscene speech) treated as low value, defamatory speech about subjects of public concern being protected more than similar speech about nonpublic concerns, and commercial speech being protected less than political speech.

Some authors propose taking this process further, and generally providing higher protection to speech relating to self-governance than to other speech. As we saw in Chapter 1, this is a sometimes elusive distinction, but it is not without basis in the case law. Attention to the different values at issue in different categories of cases pulls the courts toward content-based differentiations between categories of speech. Courts are tugged the other way, not just by a formalist impulse toward uniformity, but more importantly by a skepticism about the ability of anyone other than the individual listener to assess the value of speech. For most of the past thirty years, the attraction of uniformity has been greater, but there have been enough exceptions to leave the final resolution in doubt. The trend toward uniformity leads to broad principles such as the anti-paternalism principle, while resistance to the trend results in exceptions such as *Central Hudson*, which provides a lower level of protection to speech that seems less central to the concerns of the First Amendment.

An alternative perspective on the categorical approach puts less emphasis on the question of First Amendment value. From this perspective, the categorical approach amounts to a kind of prepackaged strict scrutiny, whereby the Court designates some compelling interests (e.g., preventing violence) and then defines what regulations are narrowly tailored to that government interest. It thus reduces the standard of strict scrutiny to a set of relatively clear-cut rules covering various forms of speech. Regulation of the content of other forms of public speech is impermissible without an individualized demonstration of need. In other words, the categorical approach translates the compelling interest test into a series of clear rules for various types of speech.

This perspective on the categorical approach fits most of the categories of unprotected speech: incitement, true threats, and fighting words (the compelling interest being prevention of violence or fear of violence); defamation (protection of personal reputation); misleading advertising (prevention of consumer fraud); advertising for illegal goods and services (enforcement of underlying criminal laws); and child pornography (protection of children from sexual exploitation).

Two of the categories, however, do not fit this pattern, and instead seem to be based on a sense that the speech in question is not valuable enough to justify full First Amendment protection. The first category includes obscenity and pornography, where the value of the speech is clearly a factor. The second category involves truthful commercial advertising for legal products under the *Central Hudson* test, where a combination of profit motivation and lower First Amendment value seem relevant. These two categories may reflect aberrations or special circumstances that lack broader implications.

With the exception of these two categories, the categorical approach arguably may be defensible without any reference to the value of speech. To the extent that unprotected categories do not rely on assessment of speech value, there may be less pressure to admit First Amendment value as a factor in adjusting levels of constitutional protection within protected categories of speech.

FURTHER READINGS

Mitchell N. Berman, *Commercial Speech and the Unconstitutional Conditions Doctrine: A Second Look at "The Greater Includes the Lesser,"* 55 Vand. L. Rev. 693 (2002).

Victor Brudney, *The First Amendment and Commercial Speech*, 53 B.C. L. Rev. 1153 (2012).

Ronald A. Cass, *Commercial Speech, Constitutionalism, Collective Choice*, 56 U. Cinn. L. Rev. 1317 (1988).

Daniel Halberstam, *Commercial Speech, Professional Speech, and the Constitutional Status of Social Institutions*, 147 U. Pa. L. Rev. 771 (1999).

Alex Kozinski & Stuart Banner, *The Anti-History and Pre-History of Commercial Speech*, 71 Tex. L. Rev. 747 (1993).

Tamara R. Piety, *Against Freedom of Commercial Expression*, 29 Cardozo L. Rev. 2583 (2008).

Martin H. Redish, *Tobacco Advertising and the First Amendment*, 81 Iowa L. Rev. 589 (1996).

Michael R. Siebecker, *Building a "New Institutional" Approach to Corporate Speech*, 59 Ala. L. Rev. 247 (2008).

Rodney A. Smolla, *Information, Imagery, and the First Amendment: A Case for Expansive Protection of Commercial Speech*, 71 Tex. L. Rev. 777 (1993).

Kathleen M. Sullivan, *Cheap Spirits, Cigarettes, and Free Speech: The Implications of* 44 Liquormart, 1996 Sup. Ct. Rev. 123.

Part III
SPEECH IN SPECIAL SETTINGS

Chapter 9

PUBLIC PROPERTY

Part II focused on the question of when particular messages are either so harmful or so valueless that the government should have the power to suppress them. In these situations, the government is acting in its sovereign capacity to protect public safety, welfare, and morals. But the government may also attempt to base restrictions on speech upon managerial powers, such as its power to control the use of its own property or the actions of its own employees. The Court has not exempted these more specific government powers from the limitations of the First Amendment. It has, however, applied those limitations somewhat differently. Consequently, a government may impose greater restrictions on its own employees or on individuals using public property than on the population generally. In part, this seems to be only a matter of common sense: it is one thing to say that the government cannot make it a crime to teach the "flat earth" doctrine; it is another thing to say that it must continue to employ a teacher who insists on teaching this doctrine in geography class.

But the line between censorship and legitimate management of government institutions is not always easy to draw. In this chapter, we will consider the extent of government power to regulate speech on public property. As it turns out, for an important class of government property, the government gains no additional leverage from its ownership interest, but in other situations this interest does become significant.

This chapter considers how the government's ownership of property relates to speech rights. The next chapter will consider the related question of the government's power to control speech based on a special relationship with the speaker rather than with the location.

I. Development of Public Forum Doctrine

Only within the past four decades has the Court been able to articulate a test for speech restrictions on government property. In this section, we trace the test's doctrinal evolution.

A. Access, Equality, and Discretion

Outside of the categories of "unprotected" speech, anyone is free to say whatever they want, but not necessarily on someone else's property. A homeowner controls entry to his or her dwelling, and need not allow use of the premises by individuals who want to engage in free expression. (The Court did briefly flirt with the idea that some kinds of private property such as shopping malls should be covered by the First Amendment, but later abandoned the idea. A few state courts have reached such results under state law.) Similarly, one might think the government should be free on behalf of the majority of the population to control the use of its property, whether in the form of streets, parks, or buildings.

Indeed, this was the position taken by the Supreme Court when it first considered the issue of speech on public property. A century ago, the Court had no difficulty in affirming a state court opinion by Oliver Wendell Holmes holding that the legislature had the absolute right to prohibit the use of streets and parks for expressive activities. The power to close the park or highway, thereby denying all public access, implied the lesser power to limit use of the facility to specified activities. Thus, the state was entitled to prosecute an individual who attempted to preach to the crowds on Boston Common.[1]

If this doctrine were still in effect, there would be no right at all to engage in free speech on public property. But in *Hague v. CIO*,[2] forty years later, the Court took quite a different approach, striking down a law which gave the police chief complete discretion over permits for speakers in public places. In response to the argument that the government had the unrestricted right to control use of its own property, the Court had this to say:

> Wherever the title of streets and parks may rest, they have immemorially been held in trust for the use of the public and, time out of mind, have been used for purposes of assembly, communicating thoughts between citizens, and discussing public questions. Such use of the streets and public places has, from ancient times, been a part of the privileges, immunities, rights, and liberties of citizens. The privilege . . . to use the streets and parks for communication of views on national questions may be regulated in the interest of all; . . . it must not, in the guise of regulation, be abridged or denied.

Current doctrine represents a complex blend of these two different viewpoints, one favoring free public expression and the other favoring governmental property rights. As to streets, parks, and sidewalks, with some minor exceptions discussed later, the government essentially gains no additional authority to regulate private speech from its ownership of these public spaces. It cannot close these facilities to speech activities, cannot discriminate between speakers based on content, and can exercise little discretion in

---

[1] *Commonwealth v. Davis*, 162 Mass. 510, 39 N.E. 113 (1895), aff'd sub nom. *Davis v. Massachusetts*, 167 U.S. 43 (1897).

[2] 307 U.S. 496 (1939).

determining whether to allow a particular expressive activity. It is no wonder that such facilities are now called "public forums." Some other government facilities are treated quite differently. For example, the government need not establish an internal communication system for its employees, and it can regulate the subject matter of the material sent through whatever system it does choose to establish. Other facilities may blend some of the attributes of each of these extreme cases. We will consider later the Court's efforts to define these categories.

Although the Supreme Court has devoted much attention to the specific contours of permissible government regulation on particular types of public property, it has never provided any real analysis of some fundamental questions. *Hague* established the public forum status of parks, streets, and sidewalks, but provided little explanation. Why can't the government eliminate expressive activities from these facilities, all of which have other primary purposes? The *Hague* Court's answer was to cite tradition along with state property law, but the Court did not explain why the state cannot break with tradition or redefine its property laws.

Commentators have articulated two different justifications for *Hague*. The first rationale, stressing the access component of public forum doctrine, suggests that public spaces are simply essential for effective free speech, at least for speakers who cannot afford to pay for halls or media use. To allow the states to block access to these facilities would cause an intolerable reduction in the robust, freewheeling debate about public issues that the First Amendment is intended to protect. The second rationale stresses the risks of discrimination. Local governments are unlikely to close parks, sidewalks, and streets entirely to efforts at public communication, which would require banning all concerts and rallies in the parks, all leafleting on sidewalks, and all parades on streets. There is a high risk that specific decisions to prevent access are motivated by dislike of particular speakers or their messages. More legitimate motives are rendered implausible by the long tradition of putting up with the inconveniences accompanying speech in public places. The Court seems more concerned about the risk of content discrimination than the need for ample access to public spaces by dissidents.

If the Court has never explained the right of access to certain property for speech activities, it has also failed to explain why people using other government facilities can have their speech restricted in ways that would otherwise be forbidden. For example, how can a public body insist that members of the audience address only the items on the agenda? In general, the government has no power to restrict speakers to a particular subject matter, and it would probably be impossible for the government to prove that it had a compelling interest in restricting the speech of audience members. (After all, if they waste time by getting off the subject, the government can always make the meeting a little longer.) One answer might be that the members of the audience waive their right to discuss other topics when they are given the floor at the meeting, but this begs the question of why the government can insist on this waiver as a condition for speaking.

Probably the best answer, however, is by analogy to the government funding issue discussed in Chapter 3. There, we saw that the government could impose restrictions on publicly funded speech to ensure that the speech was germane to the subject of the program, but could not add extraneous conditions based on content. Similarly, the government board in our example can condition access to the microphone on an agreement to limit speech to germane topics. In contrast, because no particular speech can be said to be more germane than any other to the "agenda" of public parks, sidewalks, or streets, the government does not have a similar right to condition access to those forums based on subject matter.

Given, then, that various kinds of public property are available in differing degrees to expressive idea, it remains "only" to decide how much regulation is allowed in different settings. It took the Court almost fifty years after *Hague* to agree on a formulation.

B. Public Demonstrations and the Warren Court

Although the right to engage in speech on public property was established in *Hague*, the contours of this right have been litigated only episodically in the history of the First Amendment. For instance, the primary First Amendment issue in the 1950s was anti-Communist legislation that focused entirely on the content rather than on the location of speech. In the 1960s, however, the focus switched to civil rights demonstrations. The Court struggled to define the limits of state authority to regulate demonstrations on the basis of their disruptive impact.

Many of the decisions from this period seemed ad hoc. In *Cox v. Louisiana*,[3] a minister was convicted for leading a march to a courthouse to protest the arrest of civil rights demonstrators. The Court reversed his conviction for obstructing traffic on the ground that the police had allowed traffic to be blocked by some parades despite the statute, so that in effect the police were administering a de facto discretionary permit system. In a companion case, the conviction was based on a state law against picketing at courthouses. The Court held that this statute was constitutional on its face, based on the state's interest in eliminating any public perception of political

---

[3]   379 U.S. 536 (1965).

influence on judicial decisions. But the Court reversed the conviction nonetheless. The statute prohibited demonstrations "near" a courthouse, and the minister was entitled to conclude that the police did not consider his location to be "near" the courthouse since they had directed him there.[4]

Although it reversed this conviction for picketing near a courthouse, a year later the Court upheld a conviction in *Adderley v. Florida*[5] for a demonstration at a jail. The demonstration apparently blocked a driveway to the jail, and the demonstrators were convicted of trespass after refusing to leave. Finding no evidence of discrimination based on the content of the protest, the Court relied on the premise that the state, "no less than a private owner of property, has power to preserve the property under its control for the use to which it is lawfully dedicated."

In contrast, in *Brown v. Louisiana*,[6] the Court reversed convictions for a silent demonstration in a segregated public library, finding no evidence of a disruption sufficient to uphold a charge of disturbing the peace. Similarly, the Court reversed convictions for disturbing the peace based on a demonstration near the state capitol where a large group of on-lookers had gathered.[7]

By the close of the Warren Court period, public forum doctrine was in considerable disarray. The states' power to restrict speech in public places was clearly neither unlimited nor a nullity, but seemed to vary unpredictably depending on the nature of the criminal charge, the location of the speech, the evidence of disruption, and the behavior of the police on the scene. It took about another fifteen years for the Court to come up with a standard to govern these cases.

C. The Modern Approach

The Burger Court experimented with two different approaches to public forum issues. In *Grayned v. Rockford*,[8] the Court upheld use of an anti-noise ordinance against individuals who had been demonstrating near a school. Justice Marshall's opinion for the Court focused on the incompatibility between noisy speech and the school environment. The Court found this specific demonstration to be incompatible with the functioning of the schools. *Grayned* seemed to suggest that speech would be permitted in any public place unless the government could show that the particular speaker's conduct was incompatible with the normal use of the facility. But *Lehman v.*

---

4   *Cox v. Louisiana*, 379 U.S. 559 (1965).

5   385 U.S. 39 (1966).

6   383 U.S. 131 (1966).

7   *Edwards v. South Carolina*, 372 U.S. 229 (1963).

8   408 U.S. 104 (1972).

Shaker Heights[9] took quite a different approach. A plurality held that a city bus company had the discretion to limit access to advertising space on buses to commercial vendors, stressing that the city was taking reasonable action in its proprietary capacity. Like *Adderley*, but unlike *Grayned*, the decision seemed to stress the government's power to control access to its facility, rather than requiring a showing that particular speech would disrupt operation of the facility. In yet another case, *Widmar v. Vincent*,[10] however, the Court held that a college could not open its classrooms to most after-hours student meetings without also allowing access by religious groups. Having "created a forum generally open to student groups," the university could not enforce a content-based exclusion of religious speech. Thus, the Court seemed to vacillate between two different approaches, one giving the government broad discretion to set the boundaries for expression, the other requiring a specific showing of harm to government operations in each particular case.

In the end, the Court split the difference, putting the burden on the government to justify speech restrictions in some facilities but giving it broad control over the use of others. *Perry Education Ass'n v. Perry Local Educators' Ass'n*[11] articulates the modern approach to public forum doctrine. In *Perry*, one union was the exclusive bargaining representative for teachers in the school district. A collective bargaining agreement granted this union the sole right of access to the school mail system and teacher mailboxes at the expense of a rival union that previously had equal access to the same system. The rival union sued to regain its position of equality.

Justice White began his opinion for the Court by elaborating on public forum doctrine. The crux of the opinion is a three-part division of government property into types of forums. The first category is the traditional public forum. In the quintessential public forum, Justice White said, time, place, and manner regulations are allowed, but the government may not close the forum or engage in content regulation without a compelling state interest. This category took care of the state's ability to regulate demonstrations on streets and sidewalks.

The second category, according to Justice White, is the limited forum. Property that has been opened as a forum for public communication is treated as a public forum so long as it remains open, but the government has the option of closing it off entirely. This "limited public forum" category accounted for *Widmar*, the case about religious groups meeting on campus. The college had no duty to open

---

[9]   418 U.S. 298 (1974).

[10]   454 U.S. 263 (1981).

[11]   460 U.S. 37 (1983).

a forum for student groups in the first place; but once it chose to do so, it could not exclude religious speech by students.

The third category is the nonpublic forum. Public property "which is not by tradition or designation a forum for public communication" is subject to broad state control. Not only are time, place, and manner regulations proper, but the state may also "reserve the forum for its intended purposes, communicative or otherwise, as long as the regulation on speech is reasonable and not an effort to suppress expression merely because public officials oppose the speaker's view." Thus, for example, the government could limit the use of the driveway in *Adderley* to transportation rather than communication. Government decisions about these nonpublic forums receive relatively casual judicial scrutiny:

> Implicit in the concept of the nonpublic forum is the right to make distinctions in access on the basis of subject matter and speaker identity. . . . The touchstone for evaluating these distinctions is whether they are reasonable in light of the purpose which the forum at issue serves. . . . [W]hen government property is not dedicated to open communication the government may—without further justification—restrict use to those who participate in the forum's official business.

Applying this test, Justice White saw little difficulty in upholding the access restriction. In his view, the collective bargaining agreement merely allowed the recognized union to use the faculty mailboxes for official documents in the performance of its official duties as collective bargaining agent. Hence, the only discrimination was between individuals performing official duties and others. As the four dissenters saw the case, however, the discrimination was essentially viewpoint based, since the recognized union was allowed to use the mail system, but those opposing its views were not.

Application of the *Perry* test is illustrated by *Minnesota State Board for Community Colleges v. Knight.*[12] A state law authorized a college system's professional employees and academic administrators to engage in collective bargaining. The statute required administrators to "meet and confer" with professional employees on policy questions relating to college policy and governance which were outside the scope of contract bargaining negotiations. Because the college's professional employees had formed a bargaining unit and selected an exclusive union representative, the statute required college administrators to limit formal discussion of these general policy issues to representatives selected by the union. The Court phrased the issue as "whether this restriction on participation in the

---

[12] 465 U.S. 271 (1984).

nonmandatory-subject exchange process violates the constitutional rights of professional employees within the bargaining unit who are not members of the exclusive representative and who may disagree with its views." Concluding that the "meet and confer" sessions were not traditional or limited public forums, the Court followed *Perry* in allowing participation to be limited to individuals selected by the union.

The *Perry* test is the governing standard for regulation of speech on public property, but it leaves many questions unanswered. In the next section of this chapter, we will flesh out the rules governing speech in traditional forums. We will begin by exploring the application of the *Perry* rule to this category of speech, and then consider the regulatory techniques used to implement controls on speech.

II. Regulation in Traditional Forums

Perry strongly reaffirms the *Hague* principle that speech in traditional public forums is subject to only limited government regulation. Content regulation must be based on a compelling interest, and only reasonable restrictions on the time, place, and manner of speech are allowed. We explore the substance of these standards first, and then consider the techniques the government may use to enforce its regulations.

A.   Content Regulation

Viewpoint restrictions are generally not allowed in public forums. Just as the state may not ban speeches favoring overthrow of the government on private property, it cannot ban them in parks. Nor can it prevent leaflets from being distributed on sidewalks based on content. The Court has found a basis case dealing with a traditional public forum. *Burson v. Freeman*[13] involved a ban on vote solicitation within a hundred feet of a polling place. The plurality found this restriction to be narrowly tailored to the compelling interest of preventing voter intimidation and election fraud. Justice Scalia concurred on the basis that such restrictions were so traditional that the area around a polling place should be considered a nonpublic forum. The ban on solicitation within a hundred feet, it should be noted, was not based on government ownership of the surrounding property; it apparently applied equally to private property within the perimeter. So the government seems to be gaining no additional regulatory leverage from its ownership of the sidewalks even in this unusual exception to the rule against content regulation.

---

[13]   504 U.S. 191 (1992).

The rule against content discrimination in public forums extends beyond viewpoint discrimination to what might seem to be reasonable distinctions regarding the subject matter of speech. As we saw in Chapter 2, the Court's modern jurisprudence regarding the content distinction originated in *Police Dep't of Chicago v. Mosley*.[14] In *Mosley*, the Court struck down an ordinance banning picketing near schools except for "the peaceful picketing of any school involved in a labor dispute." The Court held that this exemption created an impermissible content-based distinction: "[s]elective exclusions from a public forum may not be based on content alone, and may not be justified by reference to content alone."

A later example is provided by *City of Cincinnati v. Discovery Network*.[15] A city ordinance banned news racks containing "commercial publications" from sidewalks, but allowed racks containing newspapers. The goal of the ordinance was to reduce sidewalk congestion. Although the content of the news racks obviously had no relationship with the inconvenience to pedestrians, the city had a plausible argument that it was simply striking a different balance regarding the value of commercial speech. The position that commercial speech has a lower status under the First Amendment does have support in the Court's own decisions, as we saw in Chapter 8. Nevertheless, the city's attempt to invoke the lower status of commercial speech was unavailing, and the Court struck down the ordinance.

Thus, in a public forum, the government has no more power to restrict speech on the basis of its viewpoint or subject matter than it does on private property. Since such restrictions have no nexus with the normal uses of streets, sidewalks, and parks, the government's general regulatory power over the content of speech is not enhanced by its interest in preventing interference with those uses.

Note, however, that the public forum doctrine applies only to events held in parks, streets, etc., not to permanent monuments. In *Pleasant Grove City v. Summum*,[16] the Court held that a city did not create a public forum by accepting donated monuments from private groups. It was still free to reject another proffered monument whose content it did not choose to endorse. Monuments in parks were, the Court said, speech by the government, rather than private parties. Hence, the government had complete freedom over which monuments to include, subject only to possible restrictions under the Establishment Clause.

---

[14] 408 U.S. 92 (1972).

[15] 507 U.S. 410 (1993).

[16] 555 U.S. 460 (2009).

B. Time, Place, and Manner Regulations

If it complies with the mandate of content neutrality, the government does have considerable power to regulate the time, place, and manner of speech in the public forum. The classic example is noise regulation. For instance, in *Ward v. Rock Against Racism*,[17] New York City regulated the volume of amplified music from a bandshell in Central Park. The regulation required the musicians to use amplifiers and a sound technician provided by the city. (Notably, *Ward* was probably the first case to squarely hold that music is protected by the First Amendment.)

In assessing the regulation, the Court affirmed the government's power to impose reasonable restrictions on the time, place, and manner of speech, provided that the restrictions are content neutral, "narrowly tailored to serve a significant governmental interest," and "leave open ample alternative channels for communication of the information." Controlling noise is a content neutral justification, but the lower court had struck down the regulation because the city had failed to prove that the ordinance was the least restrictive alternative. The Court made it clear, however, that the "narrow tailoring" requirement is not defeated merely because "there is some imaginable alternative that might be less burdensome on speech." Thus, the Court said:

> [T]he requirement of narrow tailoring is satisfied "so long as the . . . regulation promotes a substantial government interest that would be achieved less effectively absent the regulation." To be sure, this standard does not mean that a time, place, or manner regulation may burden substantially more speech than is necessary to further the government's legitimate interests. Government may not regulate expression in such a manner that a substantial portion of the burden on speech does not serve to advance its goals.

The Court had little difficulty in finding that the "narrow tailoring" standard was met. The Court also found that the guidelines left ample alternative means of communication, since it did not restrict access to the bandshell but merely reduced volume.

Another illustration of the test for time, place, and manner restrictions is found in *Heffron v. International Society for Krishna Consciousness*.[18] Under a rule at the Minnesota State Fair, anyone seeking to sell or distribute merchandise (including printed material) had to obtain a license and conduct the activity from a fixed location. The rule allowed individuals to walk around the fair and

---

[17]   491 U.S. 781 (1989).

[18]   452 U.S. 640 (1981).

communicate verbally with patrons, but sales, distribution, and fund solicitations all had to take place at a booth rented from the fair organizers. Booths were rented on a first-come, first-served basis.

The state supreme court struck down the rule because an exemption for the Krishnas would not noticeably worsen congestion at the fair. The Court reversed, making it clear that the test for time, place, and manner regulations is facial rather than as applied—that is, the test is not whether applying the restriction to one individual speaker is significantly related to the state's goal, but whether the restriction taken on its face significantly advances the goal. The dissenters were skeptical of the conclusion that allowing the distribution of literature throughout the fair would markedly interfere with pedestrian traffic.

A further illustration is provided by *Hill v. Colorado*.[19] A state law prohibited anyone within 100 feet of a health care facility from knowingly approaching within eight feet of another person, without that person's consent, in order to pass out leaflets, display a sign, or engage in "oral protest, education, or counseling." The statute was prompted by protest activities at abortion clinics. In an opinion by Justice Stevens, the Court upheld the statute as a valid time, place, or manner regulation. Stevens rejected the argument by two dissenters (Justices Scalia and Thomas) that the law was obviously targeted at anti-abortion protesters and that it distinguished on the basis of content by singling out "protest, education, and counseling" from other oral communications. As to why the statute should be considered content neutral, the Court stressed that it applied on its face to all viewpoints and subjects. The fact that the statute did not cover routine social interactions (such as asking the time) was not enough to make it suspect in the eyes of the majority, nor was the fact that the impetus for the statute came from demonstrations supporting a given viewpoint.

Having found the statute content neutral, the Court upheld it because it left open many methods of communicating with pedestrians near clinics, and because it was narrowly tailored to the permissible statutory purpose of protecting unwilling listeners from unwanted communications. The Court was unmoved by the passionate argument of another dissenter, Justice Kennedy, who accused the majority of denying "these protesters, in the face of what they consider to be one of life's gravest moral crises, even the opportunity to try to offer a fellow citizen a little pamphlet, a handheld paper seeking to reach a higher law."

---

[19]   530 U.S. 703 (2000).

In *McCullen v. Coakley*,[20] the Court was again confronted with the issue of abortion protests. A Massachusetts statute made it a crime to knowingly stand on a "public way or sidewalk" within 35 feet of an entrance or driveway to any place, other than a hospital, where abortions are performed. The law was challenged by protestors who approached and talked to women outside such facilities, attempting to talk then out of having abortions. The Act exempted four classes of individuals: (1) "persons entering or leaving such facility"; (2) "employees or agents of such facility acting within the scope of their employment"; (3) "law enforcement, ambulance, firefighting, construction, utilities, public works and other municipal agents acting within the scope of their employment"; and (4) "persons using the public sidewalk or street right-of-way adjacent to such facility solely for the purpose of reaching a destination other than such facility." The legislature also retained a separate provision from an earlier law that proscribes the knowing obstruction of access to a facility. The statute clearly impeded access to a traditional public forum. The protestors argued that it was content-based because it applied only to clinics offering abortions and because the exemption for clinic employees and agents favored one side of the debate over the other side.

The Court rejected those arguments and held that the statute was content-neutral in an opinion by Chief Justice Roberts. As to the first argument, the Court held that the statute was content-neutral on its face, because it referred to the location rather than the content of speech. And it also had content-neutral justifications in terms of maintaining unobstructed access to facilities.

The Court concluded, however, that the buffer zones did not survive middle-tier scrutiny. They imposed serious burdens on speech, "pushing petitioners well back from the clinics' entrances and driveways. The zones thereby compromise petitioners' ability to initiate the close, personal conversations that they view as essential to 'sidewalk counseling'." In the Court's view, the buffer zones burdened substantially more speech than necessary. The existing anti-harassment provision, plus the possibility of injunctive relief against repeated obstruction efforts, provided a more narrowly tailored alternative.

Justice Scalia dissented on behalf of himself and Justices Kennedy and Thomas. Scalia considered the statute to be obviously based on content. "Every objective indication shows that the provision's primary purpose is to restrict speech that opposes abortion." He also stressed that the law covered all abortion clinics in the state, although only the Boston clinic had faced serious

---

[20]   573 U.S. 464 (2014).

problems in maintaining order and access. He argued that this undermined the credibility of the state's claimed interest. In Justice Scalia's view, there was "not a shadow of a doubt that the assigned or foreseeable conduct of a clinic employee or agent can include both speaking in favor of abortion rights and countering the speech of people like petitioners." Justice Alito concurred in the judgment on the ground that the exemption for clinic employees constituted viewpoint discrimination, but agreed with the majority that in any event the statute was not narrowly tailored.

There is a large buffer zone excluding from the Supreme Court's grounds, including the plaza in front of the building, the following activities: "demonstrations, picketing, speechmaking, marching, holding vigils or religious services and all other like forms of conduct that involve the communication or expression of views or grievances, engaged in by one or more persons, the conduct of which is reasonably likely to draw a crowd of onlookers." Is this buffer zone constitutional? Would Justice Scalia have argued that strict scrutiny applied?

As these cases illustrate, the Court's review of time, place, and manner restrictions normally is not particularly vigorous. At one time, it appeared that content neutral restrictions in a public forum were subject to particularly careful review. But it now seems that they are subject to only the same review as any content-neutral restriction on speech. Thus, there seems to be little special obligation on the part of the government to avoid burdening speech in the public forum.

C. Licenses

Normally, the government cannot require that speakers obtain a license. Indeed, Blackstone considered the core meaning of freedom of speech to be rejection of the kind of licensing that had been imposed on printers. But at least some uses of public facilities present a legitimate need for prior notice and approval. The police need to know if someone is scheduling a parade so they can divert traffic elsewhere. A concert in the park may require additional police to maintain order. A licensing system also helps to prevent conflicts between different groups planning parades or other events at the same place and time. Thus, there seem to be legitimate reasons for licensing. But there is also a significant risk that licensing requirements will be abused in order to harass unpopular speakers. The Court's primary concern has been to ensure that licensing does not become a pretext for content discrimination. It has imposed two kinds of requirements to prevent content discrimination.

First, the licensing scheme must not give unnecessary discretion to the licensing authority. A scheme that provides too much discretion is void on its face and may be safely ignored. Rather than applying for a permit and appealing a denial, the speaker is entitled to go ahead and speak without even bothering to apply. The rationale is that the mere existence of such discretionary power has a chilling effect on other speakers, so it is important to allow facial challenges to the ordinance. Similarly, the government cannot impose a discretionary permit fee. In *Forsyth County v. Nationalist Movement*,[21] the Court struck down a discretionary fee because neither the ordinance itself nor prior practice provided any articulated standards. Nothing in the ordinance, the Court said, "prevents the official from encouraging some views and discouraging others through the arbitrary application of fees."

Second, if content plays any role in the permit decision, a full hearing and prompt review of the administrator's decision must be available. The germinal case is *Freedman v. Maryland*.[22] *Freedman* involved a licensing system for movies, a process that was considered constitutional at the time but presumably would not pass muster today. The prescreening process was intended to eliminate obscene films. The Court found this particular licensing scheme to be facially unconstitutional, however, because it did not provide adequate procedural safeguards. The Court specified the required procedures in some detail: Within a specified brief period, the censor must either issue the license or go to court (where the censor had the burden of proving the film obscene). Any temporary restraint on exhibiting the film must be limited to "the shortest fixed period compatible with sound judicial resolution," and the exhibitor must also be assured of a prompt final resolution of the dispute. Without these safeguards, the Court said, the burden of seeking review of the censor's decision might deter exhibitors from even attempting to show certain movies. A licensing scheme lacking these safeguards is facially invalid and may be ignored with impunity.

As the Court has made clear, these procedural requirements apply only when there is a risk of content discrimination. In *Thomas v. Chicago Park Dist.*,[23] the Court upheld an ordinance requiring permits before park events involving more than fifty persons, despite the absence of the procedural safeguards mandated in *Freedman*. The Court approved the ordinance because it covered all park activities, whether or not they were expressive, and because "[n]one of the grounds for denying a permit has anything to do with what a speaker might say."

---

[21]   505 U.S. 123 (1992).

[22]   380 U.S. 51 (1965).

[23]   534 U.S. 316 (2002).

D.　Injunctions

A licensing scheme gives the government considerable power to ensure that speakers comply with valid regulatory requirements. Even stronger medicine is the use of injunctions to prevent illegal activity.

Unlike an invalid licensing scheme, an invalid injunction cannot simply be ignored. *Walker v. Birmingham*[24] upheld contempt of court convictions against Martin Luther King Jr. and other ministers who violated a temporary injunction against violating a local ordinance. The temporary injunction was very likely invalid; indeed, the underlying ordinance was struck down later in a challenge by participants in the same march. But in the interests of maintaining orderly procedures, the demonstrators were required to obey the temporary judicial restraint and pursue an appeal, rather than ignoring the injunction as they could have ignored a facially invalid licensing ordinance. The only possible exceptions seem quite limited: Demonstrators probably can ignore an injunction if the court lacks jurisdiction, if the court order is transparently invalid, or if effective appellate review is unavailable.

Because an injunction must normally be obeyed even if it is invalid, it presents a potent threat to speech. As a result, injunctions are subject to the same procedural requirements as licensing schemes. For instance, in *Carroll v. President and Commissioners of Princess Anne*,[25] the Court reversed an ex parte restraining order against a civil rights rally, because the sponsors were not given notice and an opportunity to be heard before the injunction issued. Likewise, in *National Socialist Party v. Village of Skokie*,[26] the Court held that marchers were entitled to have an injunction lifted because the state had failed to provide sufficiently prompt appellate review.

The most troubling cases have involved injunctions regulating anti-abortion protests. These injunctions typically limit the time, place, and manner of activity by protesters who have previously engaged in illegal conduct at the same location. Although the injunctions are not on their face based on content, the fact that they target identified speakers presents an obvious risk of covert viewpoint discrimination. Consequently, rather than applying the standard *Rock Against Racism* test for content neutral restrictions, the Court held in *Madsen v. Women's Health Center, Inc.*[27] that more careful review was in order. Instead of the normal "narrow tailoring"

---

[24]　388 U.S. 307 (1967).

[25]　393 U.S. 175 (1968).

[26]　432 U.S. 43 (1977).

[27]　512 U.S. 753 (1994).

requirement, the injunction had to be shown to "burden no more speech than necessary to serve a significant government interest."

Although Justice Scalia's dissent complained that this was an illusory distinction, the standard does seem significantly tighter than narrow tailoring. The Court has held that "narrow tailoring" is violated only if a restriction covers "substantially more" speech than necessary, whereas here *any* excess coverage by an injunction is forbidden. Thus, the injunction must be quite precisely tailored to achieve its goals. In crafting an injunction, the judge does not have the leeway given the drafters of a statutory restriction. Justice Scalia also argued that injunctions should be subject to strict scrutiny because of the risk that they may be based on hostility to the speakers' ideas, the undesirability of placing the right to free speech within the control of a single judge, and the greater harshness of injunctions. All of these characteristics of injunctions are quite troublesome, yet Justice Scalia seemed to ignore the countervailing factor that injunctions, unlike general ordinances, apply only to individuals who present a continuing threat of illegal activity and who usually have already violated the law.

In *Madsen* and a later case,[28] the Court has provided detailed guidelines about the permissible scope of these injunctions. First, the court may establish a buffer zone in which picketing is forbidden, in order to maintain unimpeded physical access to the facility. The zone must be carefully limited to areas needed for access purposes. Second, reasonable restrictions on noise levels are permissible. Third, the judge has only limited power to protect people entering the clinic from being approached on an individual basis by protestors. A complete ban on uninvited contact cannot be upheld, because individuals on the street are not a captive audience and have no right to be free from unwanted speech. Nor may the judge require individual protestors to "back off" a specific distance when requested to do so by people entering and leaving the clinic. Such a "floating bubble" around pedestrians would make it too difficult for demonstrators to know how to comply with the injunction. But within the fixed buffer zone, if "sidewalk" counselors previously intimidated and harassed people visiting the clinic, the judge may order them to cease contact on request. In short, the injunction may not be used to prevent psychological pressure on women seeking abortions or on clinic personnel. It must be narrowly tailored to prevent physical obstruction or severe harassment that would prevent access to the clinic. This approach seems consistent with the Court's generally protective attitude toward speech in traditional public forums.

---

[28] *Schenck v. Pro-Choice Network of Western New York,* 519 U.S. 357 (1997).

III. Classifying Forums

Under *Perry*, the extent of the government's regulatory power depends on the classification of the forum. In traditional and "limited" public forums, content regulation is virtually forbidden, while anything short of viewpoint discrimination is permitted in the nonpublic forum. Obviously, it is crucial to correctly classify a particular facility. Yet, as we will see, the classification effort has proved difficult in practice.

A. Streets and Walkways

Generally, the Court has had no difficulty in classifying streets as public forums. Rather than asking whether a particular type of street, such as a suburban residential cul-de-sac, has traditionally served as a forum for free speech, the Court has preferred to treat the problem generically. The only real exceptions are streets on military bases, which the Court has refused to consider public forums even when completely open to the public. As we will see in the next chapter, this holding is part of a long tradition of putting the military beyond the protection of the First Amendment.

Sidewalks have proved more troublesome. In *United States v. Grace*,[29] the Court held that the sidewalks outside its own courthouse were public forums, there being nothing to distinguish them to the ordinary observer from any other Washington sidewalks. But in a later case, the Court had a great deal of difficulty in applying *Perry* to a sidewalk connecting a post office to a parking lot.[30] A badly fractured Court held that the post office could ban solicitation of funds on the sidewalk, but there was no consensus on how to classify the sidewalk.

A later definitional struggle involved walkways (not gate areas) in a public airport terminal. Chief Justice Rehnquist's opinion for the Court in *ISKCON v. Lee*[31] held that the terminal was not a public forum. Airport terminals did not qualify as property "immemorially . . . time out of mind" held for public expressive purposes, nor were the airports intentionally opened by their operators as forums for expressive activities. Thus, they were neither traditional nor limited public forums. The majority was split over whether particular restrictions on speech were reasonable under the *Perry* test for nonpublic forums. The ultimate holding of the case was that leafleting was permitted, but fund solicitation was barred.

---

[29] 461 U.S. 171 (1983).

[30] *United States v. Kokinda,* 497 U.S. 720 (1990).

[31] 505 U.S. 672 (1992).

Justice Kennedy, writing for the four dissenters, argued that airports are one of the few public spaces where it is possible to contact large numbers of people. Regardless of history, he argued, a facility should be considered a public forum if "the objective, physical characteristics of the property at issue and the actual public access and uses that have been permitted by the government indicate that expressive activity would be appropriate and compatible with those uses."

The four dissenters in *Lee* seemed inclined to refocus analysis from the *Perry* test toward the compatibility of the speech with the designated uses of the forum. One of the concurring opinions seemed to accomplish a somewhat similar result by focusing on the "reasonableness" of the restrictions in light of the designed uses of the facility. Thus, *Lee* might have been an indication that *Perry* was not the final word regarding speech on public property. It has been nearly thirty years since *Lee* was decided, however, and no further doctrinal clarification has been forthcoming.

B.   Metaphorical Forums

Public forum doctrine began as a way of analyzing public spaces where speakers sought to engage in expressive activities. It has spread, however, to more metaphorical forums, such as home mailboxes or even a government employer's fundraising drive for local charities.

If there is any place that is traditionally used as a site for communication by members of the public, it is the mailbox. Yet in *U.S. Postal Service v. Greenburgh Civic Ass'ns,*[32] the Court held that a home mailbox is not a public forum. Several charitable organizations wanted to drop leaflets into home mailboxes where there was no other practical way to deliver them to houses, but a federal law bans "unstamped matter" in mailboxes. The Court found "neither historical nor constitutional support for the characterization of a letterbox as a public forum."

This decision seems to reflect confusion about the significance of the public forum doctrine. Surely, the mailbox is a public forum in the sense that the government does not have a free hand to determine what subject matters can be discussed in letters. In that sense, the home mailbox is completely different from the internal mail system involved in *Perry*. But even if the mailbox was considered some kind of limited public forum, it would not be hard to justify the restriction to stamped material as a content neutral requirement necessary to maintain the financial integrity of the postal system.

---

[32]   453 U.S. 114 (1981).

Further confusion was cast on the notion of a limited public forum in *Cornelius v. NAACP Legal Defense & Education Fund*.[33] *Cornelius* involved an annual charitable fundraising drive conducted in federal offices. An executive order excluded legal defense and political advocacy groups, but allowed charitable agencies that provide direct health and welfare services to individuals. The majority concluded that the fundraising drive was a nonpublic forum: "We will not find that a public forum has been created in the face of clear evidence of a contrary intent, nor will we infer that the government intended to create a public forum when the nature of the property is inconsistent with expressive activity." Finding no evidence that the government intended the fundraising drive to be a public forum open to all groups, the majority upheld the government's right to exercise control over access to the federal workplace, even on the basis of content.

Thus, the key factor seems to be an intent to open a forum to general use for communication. It is not, however, fatal to finding a public forum that the use of the facility is limited to certain groups. For instance, by opening after-class use of its classrooms to student groups, a university created a limited public forum. Presumably, it would also be possible to create a public forum limited in some other respect—for example, a public meeting in which remarks are required to be germane to the topic at hand but are otherwise unrestricted.

The Court's difficulties in applying *Perry* are illustrated by *Arkansas Educ. Television Comm'n v. Forbes*.[34] A public television station decided that Forbes was not a serious candidate and excluded him from a televised debate. He sued on the basis that the debate was a public forum. The Court rejected the claim that televised debates are a traditional public forum, because claims of access under public forum doctrine would undermine the editorial discretion of public broadcasters. Hence, public broadcasting was generally immune from public forum analysis. But, the Court continued, candidate debates are different for two reasons. First, unlike other broadcasts, the function of a debate is to provide a forum for the views of the candidates, not the perspective of the broadcaster. Second, "in our tradition, candidate debates are of exceptional significance in the electoral process." (How is this relevant under the *Perry* test?) Hence, candidate debates should be treated as nonpublic forums, allowing reasonable, non-viewpoint restrictions on access. The Court concluded that the decision to exclude Forbes had been made on neutral grounds. It might well have been better for the

---

[33] 473 U.S. 788 (1985).
[34] 523 U.S. 666 (1998).

Court simply to analyze candidate debates as sui generis rather than struggling to apply *Perry*.

A much-debated issue is whether the government can limit access to limited forums to groups complying with anti-discrimination requirements. In *Christian Legal Society v. Martinez*,[35] the four dissenters argued that such a restriction on students groups seeking official law school recognition constituted viewpoint discrimination. But the majority did not reach that issue, considering instead the law school had a viewpoint neutral requirement that groups accept all students, rather than singling out certain types of group policies (such as discrimination against non-members of a religion). The four dissenters accused the majority of embracing a principle of "no freedom for expression that offends prevailing standards of political correctness in our country's institutions of higher learning."

This issue illustrates the difficulty of defining limited forums. When a school has an anti-discrimination rule, is it defining a limited forum open to non-discriminating student groups? Or is it opening a forum to all student groups, but then denying access to some?

C. Assessing *Perry*

As we have seen, the Court has found public forum law vexing almost since the time it first rejected the concept of unlimited government power over public places. *Perry* was a reasonably successful effort to bring order to this somewhat incoherent body of law. The *Perry* approach accounts fairly well for the most important prior rulings, and also fit the intuition that some government facilities really should not be subject to the same rules of openness as streets and parks. Finally, its categorical approach limits the need for case-by-case balancing between the government's needs and the First Amendment interest under particular circumstances.

Nevertheless, definite tensions have emerged in applying *Perry*. Two problems seem particularly significant. First, the concept of a traditional public forum is under stress. Essentially, the Court now defines this category to encompass outdoor areas that are not intimately connected with government facilities. This is not necessarily a hard test to apply but it seems arbitrary. Dissatisfaction with this result is suggested by the willingness of four Justices to adopt a more functional approach in *Heffron* and of a fifth Justice to apply the nonpublic forum analysis with heightened vigor.

The other area of strain involves the distinction between limited and nonpublic forums. If a limited forum is defined by governmental

---

[35] 561 U.S. 661 (2010).

intent, as indicated in *Cornelius*, then this seems to be a purely voluntary category which the government can opt into or out of at its discretion. Thus, this category may be somewhat illusory as a restriction on government censorship. Moreover, flexibility exists in defining the nature of a limited forum, leading to the temptation to custom-craft the definition to exclude particular speech. For example, a college could apparently create a limited forum for student groups to discuss scientific, artistic, and literary issues, in effect precluding use of the facility for political discussions. This seems similar to establishing a nonpublic forum for student discussions of course-related issues, yet *Perry* categorizes the two quite differently. Similarly, because a nonpublic forum can be limited to its designated use, a temptation exists to shape the designation in a way that eliminates potentially disagreeable speech. Since the government is not required to announce explicit rules in advance governing the use of forums, a clever lawyer has considerable leeway in inventing a suitable definition of the forum that happens to exclude the particular speech at issue. Courts are unlikely to allow unlimited manipulation of the *Perry* categories, but it is difficult to see how they will maintain the integrity of the *Perry* scheme as a viable protection for speech.

IV. The Future of Public Forum Doctrine

When public forum doctrine was first created some sixty years ago, it seemed to offer exceptional protection for speech taking place in certain public places. Now, however, much of that protection has been integrated into the overall fabric of First Amendment law. The test for time, place, and manner regulations is nearly the same as the general test for all content neutral regulations. Thus, for content neutral regulations, public forum doctrine generally and the *Perry* test in particular are quite irrelevant. Since viewpoint regulation is strictly scrutinized in all settings, public or private, the existence or sub-classification of a public forum is also irrelevant. So as to both content neutral and viewpoint regulations, the significance of public forum doctrine is to establish a negative: government ownership of property does not exempt it from these general First Amendment rules.

No special public forum doctrine is needed to justify the rule requiring the government to grant access to traditional public forums for speech purposes. A rule eliminating access is content neutral, but cannot pass the standard test. Given the traditional tolerance for speech activities in these settings, it would be hard to explain how a complete ban is narrowly tailored to a substantial government interest. Moreover, given the crucial role these forums have traditionally played in public discourse, it would be hard to say that an absolute ban leaves open ample alternative channels of communication. So, general First Amendment rules would prevent the government from closing traditional public forums to expressive activities.

The continuing significance of public forum doctrine relates to non-viewpoint content distinctions. As to speech taking place on private property or in traditional or limited public forums, subject matter restrictions and the like are subject to strict scrutiny. In nonpublic forums, such restrictions are broadly allowed, subject only to a requirement of reasonable relationship with designated use of the facility. Clearly, the government's general interest in maintaining sidewalks, streets, and parks has no relationship to the subject matter of any speech that may take place there. So even if we applied the same reasonableness test to these traditional forums, we would come out the same way.

In short, for all practical purposes, we could restate public forum doctrine as follows:

> Speech on public property is subject to the same rules as speech in any other location, with one exception: the government may impose reasonable restrictions on the subject matter of speech (or the like) in light of the designated purpose of the facility. Under this test, facilities such as streets, sidewalks, and parks, used for general transportation or leisure purposes by the public, do not qualify for subject matter restrictions. The government may waive its right to impose these restrictions on other facilities, thereby creating a "limited public forum"

This restatement seems to account for most of the *Perry* test without placing so much emphasis on drawing bright lines between different categories of facilities.

We might question whether the ability to impose reasonable subject-matter distinctions is justifiable simply because the government owns the property. Although the government cannot ban speech on particular topics, it does not have a duty to subsidize all topics equally by providing communication facilities at its own expense. Moreover, it clearly has the right to ensure that the facility that it creates is used in a way that is compatible with its basic purpose. It seems better to consider the incompatibility question at a high level of generality, by requiring the government to identify and defend subject matter and similar restrictions, rather than fighting the compatibility issue on a case-by-case basis, with all the resulting unpredictability that would entail.

Thus, the current public forum analysis, as reformulated above, seems sound in terms of overall First Amendment doctrine, although the Court's formulation of the doctrine invites needless definition wrangling. The biggest concern is that lax review of content-neutral restrictions by courts has allowed governments too much room to marginalize dissenting speech.

FURTHER READINGS

Thomas P. Crocker, *Displacing Dissent: The Role of "Place" in First Amendment Jurisprudence*, 75 Fordham L. Rev. 2587 (2007).

Daniel A. Farber and John E. Nowak, *The Misleading Nature of Public Forum Analysis: Content and Context in First Amendment Adjudication*, 70 Va. L. Rev. 1219 (1984).

Harry Kalven, Jr., *The Concept of the Public Forum:* Cox v. Louisiana, 1965 Sup. Ct. Rev. 1.

Nathan W. Kellum, *Permit Schemes: Under Current Jurisprudence, What Permits Are Permitted?*, 56 Drake L. Rev. 381 (2008).

Robert J. Krotoszynski, *Our Shrinking First Amendment: On the Growing Problem of Reduced Access to Public Property for Speech Activity and Some Suggestions for a Better Way Forward*, 78 Ohio St. L.J. 779 (2017).

Kevin Francis O'Neill, *Disentangling the Law of Public Protest*, 45 Loy. L. Rev. 411 (1999).

Robert C. Post, *Between Governance and Management: The History and Theory of the Public Forum*, 34 UCLA L. Rev. 1713 (1987).

Geoffrey R. Stone, *Fora Americana: Speech in Public Places*, 1974 Sup. Ct. Rev. 233.

Keith Werhan, *The Liberalization of Freedom of Speech on a Conservative Court*, 80 Iowa L. Rev. 51 (1994).

Timothy Zick, *Space, Place, and Speech: The Expressive Topography*, 74 Geo. Wash. L. Rev. 439 (2006).

Chapter 10

SPEECH IN THE PUBLIC SECTOR

In the last chapter, we saw how the government's power to control its own property interacted with First Amendment values. In this chapter and the next, we will see how the government's regulatory power varies with the identity of the speaker, rather than the location of the speech. This chapter examines how the government's power over speech is augmented when the speaker is operating in the public sector.

Groups within the public sector are subject to controls that would not be allowed for the general public. Schoolchildren, prisoners, and soldiers are all, in different ways, wards of the state and subject to especially intensive regimentation. To varying extents, the basically authoritarian regimes of these institutions are inconsistent with the broad individual freedom enjoyed by the general public. The government does not have the same "parental" interest in the personal conduct of its civilian employees as of students, nor can it impose the same discipline as it does on the military. But the government does have a strong interest in preventing employees from disrupting the effectiveness of governmental operations. It has a similar interest in ensuring that grant recipients use their funding to further the government's purposes, which are sometimes related to speech. With varying degrees of success, the Court has attempted to define the First Amendment rights of each of these various groups. The most puzzling problem is presented by the final category, government grantees, because of the difficulty of separating valid from illegitimate conditions on government funding.

I. Custodial Institutions

In schools, prisons, and the military, the government has broad power to regulate individual conduct. Given its custodial authority in these institutions, it has an unusually broad interest in controlling speech as well. As we will see, however, its power to regulate speech even in these special institutional settings is not unlimited.

A. Schools

The Court's first significant opinion on the rights of public school students may have been the high-water mark of constitutional protection for this group, with successive later opinions retreating toward greater acceptance of censorship. In *Tinker v. Des Moines*

Independent Community School District,[1] two high school students and a junior high student were suspended for wearing black armbands to protest the Vietnam War. An anti-armband policy had been adopted two days earlier in anticipation of the protests. In an opinion by Justice Fortas, the Court upheld the right of students to engage in at least some expressive activities. There was no evidence that the armbands interfered with school activities, and the Court obviously viewed the restriction as motivated at least in part by ideological disagreement. As the Court pointed out, the school had not banned any other insignia, including Nazi iron crosses worn by some students.

The Court put the burden on the school to show that the armbands posed a concrete threat to normal school activities. Neither students nor teachers "shed their constitutional rights to freedom of speech or expression at the schoolhouse gate." Hence, according to the *Tinker* Court, "undifferentiated fear or apprehension of disturbance is not enough to overcome the right to freedom of expression." To justify a restriction on speech, the school "must be able to show that its action was caused by something more than a mere desire to avoid the discomfort and unpleasantness that always accompany an unpopular viewpoint." Admittedly, the First Amendment would not protect "conduct by the student, in class or out of it, which for any reason—whether it stems from time, place, or type of behavior—materially disrupts classwork or involves substantial disorder or invasion of the rights of others." But in *Tinker*, there was no "evidence that the school authorities had reason to anticipate that the wearing of the armbands would substantially interfere with the work of the school or impinge upon the rights of other students."

Later decisions have been more deferential toward the prerogatives of school officials. In *Bethel School Dist. No. 403 v. Fraser,*[2] a student was suspended for two days for giving a tasteless speech at a student assembly. The speech was a nomination address for a student officer. It was filled with clumsy sexual innuendos of the kind that might earn a movie a *PG-13* rating today. Some of the students in the audience acted up during the speech; others (who apparently were either more inhibited or had better taste) seemed embarrassed. The lower courts reversed the suspension, relying on *Tinker*. The Court upheld the school's action. The opinion emphasized three points: inculcating basic social values is one function of the schools; a "vulgar and lewd speech" like the student's could "undermine the school's basic educational mission"; and unlike

---

[1]   393 U.S. 503 (1969).

[2]   478 U.S. 675 (1986).

Tinker, the penalties were unrelated to the expression of any political viewpoint.

Hazelwood School Dist. v. Kuhlmeier,[3] took the *Fraser* analysis one step further, upholding the power of a school principal to censor the school newspaper. The principal had removed two stories from the paper. One described three students' experiences with pregnancy, and the other described the effect of parental divorce on some students. The Court drew a sharp line between the case before it and *Tinker*. Whether the school must tolerate student speech "is different from the question whether the First Amendment requires a school affirmatively to promote particular student speech." *Tinker* addressed "educators' ability to silence a student's personal expression that happens to occur on the school premises." But the issue in *Hazelwood* was "educators' authority over school-sponsored publications, theatrical productions, and other expressive activities that students, parents, and members of the public might reasonably perceive to bear the imprimatur of the school." (This was an early expression of the government speech theory, which we have discussed previously.) According to the Court, such school activities "may fairly be characterized as part of the school curriculum, whether or not they occur in a traditional classroom setting, so long as they are supervised by faculty members and designed to impart particular knowledge or skills to student participants and audiences." Like the student assembly in *Fraser*, the school newspaper fell into this category of quasi-curricular activities.

With regard to such quasi-curricular activities, the *Hazelwood* Court granted schools broad discretion to control speech. According to the Court, schools are entitled to exercise broad control to ensure that students: (a) learn the appropriate lessons, (b) are not exposed to inappropriate material given their ages, and (c) do not mistakenly attribute the viewpoints of particular speakers to the school. Thus, the standard for quasi-curricular activities is not the *Tinker* test, but a much more deferential one: "educators do not offend the First Amendment exercising editorial control over the style and content of student speech in school-sponsored expressive activities so long as their actions are reasonably related to legitimate pedagogical concerns."

The *Hazelwood* Court applied this test with striking deference to the principal's judgment. Although false names were used in the pregnancy article, the Court thought it possible that the students' anonymity was not adequately protected. The discussions of birth control and other sexual matters might have been considered inappropriate for the younger students. Also, in the divorce article,

---

[3]   484 U.S. 260 (1988).

one student made critical comments about her father, who was not given an opportunity to reply. Perhaps these quibbles might have supplied a reasonable basis for editing the articles, but they have the appearance of being after-the-fact rationalizations. The articles had already been approved by the faculty advisor to the newspaper, who would normally be expected to handle editorial issues of the kind allegedly worrying the principal. Far more likely, the principal thought the paper should stick to applauding the basketball team and avoid controversial subjects that might cause parent complaints.

The Court continued the trend toward restricting student speech rights in *Morse v. Frederick*.[4] A high-school principal allowed students to leave the school in order to watch the Olympic torch being carried through town on the street in front of the school. The principal saw students unfurling a banner at the event stating "BONG HiTS 4 JESUS." Construing this as advocacy of drug use, he ordered the students to take down the banner. When one of them refused, the principle confiscated the banner and suspended that student. In an opinion by Chief Justice Roberts, the Court upheld the suspension. According to the Court, the special characteristics of the school environment and the government interest in preventing student use of drugs, allow schools to restrict student expression that they reasonably regard as promoting drugs. Justices Alito and Kennedy, the swing voters in the case, stated in concurrence that public schools may be ban speech advocating illegal drug use, but they regarded "such regulation as standing at the far reaches of what the First Amendment permits."

In practice, the precise constitutional standard may be less important than the amount of deference given to school officials in applying the test. In *Tinker*, the Court was suspicious of the officials' motivation and demanded concrete evidence to support the armband ban. In *Hazelwood*, the Court was willing to accept a tepid effort to rationalize the principal's censorship decision, without much serious consideration of its validity. Obviously, the Court is being tugged in two directions: toward tougher scrutiny because of the need to prevent ideologically motivated restrictions on speech, but toward greater deference because of the need for school officials to maintain discipline without being continually second-guessed by courts. Over time, with regard to high schools, the balance has increasingly swung toward the need for discipline.

The balance seems to come out quite differently for higher education, where the students are more mature, the need for discipline lower, and the tradition of academic freedom much stronger. For public universities, the First Amendment seems to

---

4   551 U.S. 393 (2007).

apply with its full vigor. Because the purpose of the university parallels the First Amendment goal of robust debate, it is much more difficult to justify censorship. In the high school context, however, the Court seems to place more emphasis on the need for social control. As compared with universities, the Court's vision of secondary education puts more emphasis on fostering values and less on promoting critical thinking.

B. Prisons

Prisons, of course, are entirely dedicated to social control and, at least in theory, fostering societal values. Not surprisingly, the Court has been quite friendly to restrictions on speech in this setting. Parallel to the *Hazelwood* test of legitimate pedagogical objectives, restrictions on prison speech are allowed if reasonably related to legitimate penological objectives. The major difference is that the *Hazelwood* test applies only to a subset of student speech, while the same test applies to all speech within prisons. The reason presumably is that prisons are "total institutions" dedicated to complete control over all aspects of their "clients' " lives, whereas schools may be authoritarian but have more limited objectives. Prisoners, like students, have restricted First Amendment rights— students because of presumed immaturity, prisoners because of past criminal conduct.

Although a criminal conviction does not strip the prisoner of all First Amendment rights, it leaves little intact. In *Procunier v. Martinez*,[5] the Court did strike down a regulation censoring letters written by prisoners. The regulation broadly prohibited letters that would "magnify grievances" or were "lewd, obscene, defamatory, or are otherwise inappropriate." But *Procunier* is an isolated exception. In general, the Court has upheld restrictions on prisoner speech with only the scantest review of the government's justifications.

Thornburgh v. Abbott[6] illustrates the Court's deferential attitude toward prison regulations. Federal prison regulations allowed prisoners to receive publications from outside unless the warden found them detrimental to institutional security. The warden was not supposed to reject a publication "solely" because of its religious, philosophical, political or sexual content. Each issue of a publication was supposed to be reviewed separately. Grounds for exclusion included sexually explicit homosexual content or description of "activities which may lead to the use of physical violence or group disruption." The Court upheld this sweeping censorship scheme. In reviewing prison regulations, the Court

---

[5]   416 U.S. 396 (1974).

[6]   490 U.S. 401 (1989).

remarked, "we have been sensitive to the delicate balance that prison administrators must strike between the order and security of the internal prison environment and the legitimate demands of those on the 'outside' who seek to enter that environment, in person or through the written word." Wardens "may well conclude that certain proposed interactions, though seemingly innocuous to laymen, have potentially significant implications for the order and security of the prison." Thus, the Court said, the *Procunier* level of protection should be limited to outgoing letters.

Applying what it called a "reasonableness inquiry," the *Thornburgh* Court considered several factors: (1) whether the regulations are rationally related to a legitimate, neutral governmental purpose (here, prison security); (2) whether alternative means of expression remain available (the other periodicals prisoners were entitled to read); (3) the effect that accommodation of the claim would have on others in the prison (the potential for a ripple effect when materials circulate within the prison); and (4) the existence of obvious, easy alternatives to censorship (which the Court did not find in *Thornburgh*). In a sop to the prisoners, the Court remanded for an "examination of the validity of the regulations as applied to any of the 46 publications introduced at trial as to which there remains a live controversy." Since the trial had taken place some eight years earlier, it seems doubtful that any pressing demand to read these particular publications still existed by the time of the Court's decision.

Apart from the somewhat ad hoc exception for outgoing mail, the First Amendment seems to provide rather minimal protection for prisoners. The only clear principles are that they must be allowed some contact with the outside world, and that the warden may not squelch whole categories of expression because of their viewpoint or subject.

C. The Military

Unlike students, military personnel are adults; unlike prisoners, they have committed no crime. Yet they may well have the least constitutional protection of any of these groups. In *Parker v. Levy*,[7] the Court saw no impediment to court-martialing an officer who sharply criticized the Vietnam war and suggested that black soldiers were given the most hazardous duty there. The Court viewed the statement as advocating that the black enlisted men who were present violate their orders if they were sent to Vietnam. The opinion stressed that the military is a "specialized society separate from civilian society."

---

[7]   417 U.S. 733 (1974).

The scope of military authority to restrict speech is demonstrated by *Brown v. Glines*.[8] Air Force regulations require prior approval from commanders before petitions can be circulated on Air Force bases. Permission can be denied only if the material poses a clear threat to discipline or morale, and cannot be withheld simply because it is critical of military superiors. An officer was removed from active duty for circulating a petition to Congress complaining that grooming standards had caused racial tension and bad morale. A federal statute guarantees service members the right to communicate with members of Congress, and the Constitution expressly singles out the right to petition for the redress of grievances. Nevertheless, the Court upheld the regulation as a reasonable safeguard against materials that might impair morale. "The rights of military men," the Court proclaimed, "must yield somewhat" to meet the imperatives of discipline. "Because the right to command and the duty to obey ordinarily must go unquestioned," the Court added, "the military must possess substantial discretion over its internal discipline." If military personnel do retain some residual right to freedom of speech, it must nevertheless be recognized that the Supreme Court has never found a military censor it did not like.

II. Public Employees

Perhaps the peculiarly low First Amendment rights of soldiers can be explained at least in part because they are at the intersection of two justifications for restricting speech. Not only are they, like high school students and prisoners, in some sense held in government custody, but they are also public employees. As we will see, the Court has viewed government employment as providing a separate basis for additional restrictions on speech, beyond those that could be constitutionally applied to the general population.

A. Dissenters in the Workplace

Unlike prisoners, most government employees do have private lives, so much of their First Amendment activity falls outside of any interest the government may have as their employer. Thus, it has no power to control which magazines they read at home. But the government does have an interest in regulating speech that relates to their employment itself, in order to maintain the smooth functioning of the workplace. Although the government has no legitimate interest in restricting the street corner speaker who says the governor is an idiot, it does have an interest in eliminating members of her own staff who openly insult the office.

---

[8]   444 U.S. 348 (1980).

In *Pickering v. Board of Education*,[9] a teacher had been fired for writing a newspaper letter criticizing the school board's fiscal policies. The Court saw its task as finding "a balance between the interests of the teacher, as a citizen, in commenting upon matters of public concern and the interest of the State, as an employer, in promoting the efficiency of the public services it performs through its employees." The teacher's statements obviously related to matters of public concern. Because the letter did not undermine the performance of his teaching duties or otherwise interfere with the operation of the schools, the school had no more of a legitimate interest in restricting his speech than that of any other citizen. Although the letter did contain some factual misstatements, they did not rise to the level of unprotected defamation under the *New York Times* test. Hence, the Court concluded, the letter was protected speech.

One issue left open by *Pickering* is the role of subject matter in the analysis. Although the Court characterized the speech as relating to matters of public concern, it was not clear whether this was essential to the holding. Also, it was not clear how broadly the term "public concern" swept—recall from Chapter 5 that in defamation law only a narrow category of speech has been excluded from the "public concern" category. In *Connick v. Myers*,[10] however, the Court made it clear that *Pickering* does apply solely to matters of public concern, and that the term is defined somewhat narrowly.

Connick involved a disgruntled assistant district attorney who circulated a questionnaire to fellow workers. The questions covered a variety of workplace issues: office transfer policy (her particular gripe), office morale, the need for a grievance committee, confidence in supervisors, and whether employees felt pressured to work in political campaigns. She was fired for insubordination. The Court attempted to draw a line between matters of public concern and "matters only of personal interest" such as employee grievances. With the possible exception of the "most unusual circumstances," "a federal court is not the appropriate forum in which to review the wisdom of a personnel decision" relating to employee grievances that lack public concern. Matters of public concern, however, remain protected by the *Pickering* test.

Of the questions distributed by the employee, only the one about political campaigns was found to implicate any public concern: "the issue of whether assistant district attorneys are pressured to work in political campaigns is a matter of interest to the community upon which it is essential that public employees be able to speak out freely

---

[9] 391 U.S. 563 (1968).

[10] 461 U.S. 138 (1983).

without fear of retaliatory dismissal." The Court then proceeded to apply the *Pickering* test. It understood *Pickering* to call for a fairly open-ended balance taking into account the employer's interest, the degree of public concern, whether the speech took place at the office or elsewhere, and the context (the fact that the questionnaire was a response to an earlier personal dispute over transfers). The Court concluded that the questionnaire "touched upon matters of public concern in only a most limited sense" and was "most accurately characterized as an employee grievance concerning internal office policy." Given the employee's limited First Amendment interest, the supervisor did not have to put up with "action which he reasonably believed would disrupt the office, undermine his authority, and destroy close working relationships."

Much of the Court's inquiry was not only ad hoc but intensively based on content. This means, of course, that constitutional protection depends on the exact statement made by the employee, which may sometimes be disputed. In *Waters v. Churchill*,[11] two hospital nurses had a conversation about a possible transfer to the obstetrics department. A supervisor fired one of the nurses, after he concluded that she had talked the other out of a transfer by unfairly maligning the department. She maintained, however, that she had only criticized a hospital transfer policy she considered to be impeding patient care and violating state regulations. A badly divided Court concluded that the hospital's action should be judged, not on what the nurse actually said, but on what the hospital reasonably concluded after an adequate investigation. The plurality opinion by Justice O'Connor emphasized that the government's interest in efficient operation "is elevated from a relatively subordinate interest when it acts as sovereign to a significant one when it acts as employer." Someone who is "paid a salary so that she will contribute to an agency's effective operation" cannot expect to "do or say things that detract from the agency's effective operation." Balancing the employer's interest in an effective discipline system with the First Amendment interests of employees, O'Connor concluded that courts should not second-guess an employer's fact findings, provided the employer has made a reasonable investigation. Since the other members of the Court either wanted more deference to employers or less, O'Connor's view seems to represent the holding in the case.

The Court further restricted employee rights in *Garcetti v. Ceballos*.[12] The plaintiff was a deputy district attorney. He was disciplined for a memo to his superiors in which he had identified

---

[11] 511 U.S. 661 (1994).
[12] 547 U.S. 410 (2006).

what he considered lies in a police affidavit for a search warrant. The Court held that the memo was unprotected speech because it was made in the course of his official day-to-day duties. Hence, the *Pickering* balancing test did not apply even though the subject matter was one of public concern. The majority believed that providing any constitutional protection for such "official" speech would risk too great an interference with employee management. The Court noted, however, that the definition of an employee's official activities for purposes of this rule needed to be realistic rather than based purely on a job description. It also reserved the question whether university faculty might have broader speech rights on the basis of academic freedom.

Garcetti distinguishes internal employment matters from outside speech on public issues. As to the latter category, First Amendment protection remains fairly robust. For example, the government cannot prohibit low-level employees from accepting fees for speeches or publications, because the ban significantly burdened protected speech and was not justified by any reasonable concern about corruption or undue influence.[13] On the other hand, high-level officials such as judges or cabinet officials present a more realistic concern about conflicts of interest, because of their broad policymaking authority.

B.   Partisan Activities

Logically, there seems to be nothing particularly distinctive about partisan political activities by government employees. These activities involve matters of public concern with no specific relationship to the workplace. Thus, one would expect that such employee activities would be strongly protected by the First Amendment under the *Pickering* test, except under unusual circumstances where partisan activities had a direct impact on the workplace. Even high school students, prisoners, and military personnel are immune from punishment for supporting the "wrong" political party although they enjoy less than full constitutional rights. One would expect that a mail clerk or school teacher would have a similar right to support or oppose a political candidate.

This is not too far from the Court's current position, but the Court has developed some special rules to deal with this area, and its treatment of partisan activity by employees was controversial. The reason for this special treatment is that the Court's general approach to free speech collides with the long American tradition of political patronage. Although political parties as we now know them arose only after the Founding period, it did not take long for politicians to

---

13   *United States v. National Treasury Employees Union*, 513 U.S. 454 (1995).

discover the advantages of hiring their friends and firing their enemies. This practice became a way of life in many parts of the country.

Today, the use of government employment to reward political allies or coerce unwilling workers into political activity is restrained to some extent by civil service laws. Moreover, federal employees are prohibited from actively engaging in campaign activities, although they are allowed to vote and express their views of the candidates.[14] This prohibition would present a difficult application of the *Pickering* test, because it restrains core political speech, but the Court was persuaded by the history of abuses that led to the prohibition. Because of these various statutes, political exploitation of government workers is somewhat limited.

Outside the scope of these statutory prohibitions, however, the question remains whether workers have any constitutional protection against political pressure. In 1976, the Court refused to permit a new Cook County Sheriff to fire Republican employees, but there was no majority opinion.[15] Several years later, in *Branti v. Finkel*[16] the Court established a clear standard to govern patronage dismissals. In overturning the dismissal of some county public defenders, the Court held that political affiliation normally cannot be a basis for discharging employees. To justify an exception, the government must show that "party affiliation is an appropriate requirement for the effective performance of the public office involved." For example, a speech writer for the governor could properly be required to belong to the governor's own political party. The Court later extended the *Branti v. Finkel* approach to all hiring, promotion, transfer, and layoff-related decisions.[17]

Thus, under current law, a public employer who wants to consider party affiliation faces a higher standard than *Pickering*. Rather than passing a general balancing test, the employer must satisfy a demanding narrow standard. But this difference in treatment seems appropriate. In a *Pickering* case, the claim is that the employee's speech interferes with the effective operation of the office. The basic argument for patronage is different. No one claims that clerks, secretaries, and police officers will perform their duties more effectively if at any given time they all belong to the same political party. Rather, supporters claim that patronage strengthens

---

[14] See *United States Civil Service Comm'n v. National Ass'n of Letter Carriers,* 413 U.S. 548 (1973); *United Public Workers v. Mitchell,* 330 U.S. 75 (1947).

[15] *Elrod v. Burns,* 427 U.S. 347 (1976).

[16] 445 U.S. 507 (1980).

[17] *Rutan v. Republican Party of Illinois,* 497 U.S. 62 (1990).

the party system, and that a strong party system is good for democracy.

Although these claims might be endorsed by some political scientists, it is hard to see any connection between these government interests and the government's special interest as an employer. (After all, much the same interests would be served if the government were allowed to give tax breaks to party workers, yet no one would argue that such discriminatory taxes are constitutional.) As a matter of common sense, if the government cannot fire an individual for being a Communist or a Nazi (as we saw in Chapter 4), it is hard to see why it should be able to fire her for being a Democrat rather than a Republican, or vice versa. Thus, rather than being subjected to a balancing test, consideration of political affiliation should be prohibited except in narrow circumstances.

Nevertheless, the patronage issue remained controversial. In two related 1996 cases, the Court extended the *Branti* rule to independent contractors such as companies supplying services to the government.[18] Although these decisions garnered strong support, including Justices who had previously dissented from the patronage rulings, Justice Scalia issued a blistering dissent which was joined by Justice Thomas.

III. Government Funding

The patronage cases involving independent contractors are only one step removed from the problem of government funding. As we saw in Chapter 3, the entire subject of conditions on government funding resists easy solutions. The problem is that it is very difficult to determine the legitimacy of the government's interest in the grantee's speech, so as to distinguish an unconstitutional penalty from a mere refusal to expand a subsidy.

For instance, suppose the government establishes grants for art projects. Presumably, the independent contractor cases mean that the grants cannot be limited on the basis of partisan affiliation. Moreover, it is hard to see how the grantee's other speech activities would be relevant except under very special circumstances. Unlike the government employee, the grantee does not work in a government office, need not display a cooperative attitude toward superiors, and is unlikely to be in a position to expedite or hinder the grant program as a whole. But suppose the government limits the grants based on the subject matter of the artistic speech. Presumably at least some restrictions are permissible—for example, the government should be able to finance a Shakespeare series without

---

[18] *O'Hare Truck Service, Inc. v. Northlake*, 518 U.S. 712 (1996); *Board of County Commissioners v. Umbehr*, 518 U.S. 668 (1996).

also paying for Ibsen. In contrast, if the government decides to finance new plays, it would seem illegitimate to exclude plays merely because their political perspective is disfavored by the government. The vexing problem is how to draw the line.

We will begin by examining a few cases in which the Court has struggled with this problem. We will then briefly consider the problem in a broader perspective.

A.   Doctrinal Developments

We can get a sense of the Court's struggle with the conditional funding issue from a series of well-known cases. The first of these cases, *Rust v. Sullivan*,[19] involved a more controversial restriction on federal grantees. A federal statute provided federal funding for family planning services, but mandated that none of the funds "shall be used in programs where abortion is a method of family planning." An implementing regulation provided that grantees could not refer women to abortion providers even on request. Nor could grantees engage in lobbying or advocacy in favor of abortion. Finally, any government-funded facilities had to be physically and financially separate from prohibited abortion activities.

The Court upheld the regulations on the basis that they were merely designed to prevent program money from being used for purposes outside of its scope. "[H]ere the government is not denying a benefit to anyone, but is instead simply insisting that public funds be spent for the purposes for which they were authorized." Generally, the Court said, it is only impermissible to place conditions on the recipient of the subsidy as opposed to restrictions on the use of the subsidy itself. One exception covers universities, where some restrictions on the use of government funds may be suspect. As the Court explained, universities are special: "a traditional sphere of free expression so fundamental to the functioning of our society that the Government's ability to control speech within that sphere by means of conditions attached to the expenditure of Government funds is restricted by the vagueness and overbreadth doctrines of the First Amendment." In dissent, Justice Blackmun argued that the funding provision was an impermissible restriction on speech based on viewpoint, since providers were required to facilitate access to prenatal services but forbidden to do so for abortion services.

So long as abortions are legal in a jurisdiction, abortion information is at the very least protected as a form of commercial speech; hence, a blanket ban on such information clearly would violate the First Amendment. Therefore, Congress could not condition unrelated government benefits on an agreement to refrain

---

[19]   500 U.S. 173 (1991).

from constitutionally protected conduct. It could not, for example, punish a physician who engaged in abortion counseling by raising the tax rate on the physician's income. On the other hand, Congress has no constitutional duty to subsidize information to pregnant women about abortion or anything else. The problem, then, is drawing a line between imposition of a penalty and denial of a benefit.

Rust was followed four years later by *Rosenberger v. Rector*.[20] The University of Virginia used mandatory student fees to finance the costs of printing various student publications. It excluded religious speech from the program because of Establishment Clause concerns. The majority decided that the restriction involved impermissible viewpoint discrimination, and distinguished *Rust* as a government speech case, where the government was essentially paying doctors to speak as its agents rather than subsidizing private speech. In contrast, in *Rosenberger* the majority considered that the university's funding program was essentially a limited public forum.

Clearly, however, not every funding decision must be content neutral. In a third case, *National Endowment for the Arts v. Finley*,[21] the Court upheld a content-based funding program for the arts. A 1990 statute required that grants to artists be judged by artistic merit, "taking into consideration general standards of decency and respect for the diverse beliefs and values of the American public." In an opinion by Justice O'Connor, the Court readily accepted the criterion of artistic merit. O'Connor also concluded that the statute's vague, subjective standards were acceptable given the inherent difficulty of judging grant applications, and that they did not pose any specific threat of viewpoint regulation. In an concurrence joined by Justice Thomas, Justice Scalia argued that exclusion from a subsidy program is not coercive, and that viewpoint discrimination is therefore always permissible except when the government has established a public forum. Justice Souter dissented on the ground that the statute was adopted because the government disapproved of the messages of certain artists.

In the fourth case, *Legal Services Corp. v. Velazquez*,[22] the Court came close to disavowing *Rust* in favor of a decidedly more skeptical attitude toward government funding conditions. The Legal Services Corporation (LSC) was established as a nonprofit corporation to distribute federal funds to local legal aid organizations for the poor. *Velazquez* involved a condition on the use of LSC funds, prohibiting grant recipients from challenging the validity of welfare laws. As

---

[20]　515 U.S. 819 (1995).

[21]　524 U.S. 569 (1998).

[22]　531 U.S. 533 (2001).

interpreted by the government, the statute prohibited a legal aid lawyer from arguing in court that a state law conflicts with federal law or that either a state or federal statute is unconstitutional. Legal aid lawyers could, however, argue that a welfare agency made a factual mistake or misapplied an existing welfare statute. When an issue of constitutional or statutory validity arises after a case is underway, LSC advised that its attorneys must withdraw. The restriction applied to all of the grantee's activities, including those funded from other sources.

Not surprisingly, both the government and the four dissenters thought the case was controlled by *Rust*. Their theory was that the government had chosen to create a program for routine welfare litigation, not law reform litigation. But the majority, in an opinion by Justice Kennedy, gave *Rust* a very restricted reading. Although he admitted that the Court in *Rust* "did not place explicit reliance" on this rationale, Kennedy viewed *Rust* as a case involving speech by the government itself, rather than financing of private speech activities. The crucial point was that, like the program in *Rosenberger* but unlike the program in *Rust*, "the LSC program was designed to facilitate private speech, not to promote a governmental message." Kennedy added that the "private nature of the speech involved here, and the extent of LSC's regulation of private expression, are indicated further by the circumstance that the government seeks to use an existing medium of expression and to control it, in a class of cases, in ways which distort its usual functioning."

More recently, the Court attempted to synthesize its caselaw in *AID v. Alliance for Open Society*.[23] The case involved a funding program for organizations fighting HIV/AIDS. As a condition of funding the government required groups to have adopted an explicit policy condemning prostitution and opposing legalization of prostitution. The law was challenged by a group that believed endorsing these views would limits its ability to work effectively with prostitutes in anti-AIDS efforts. According to Chief Justice Roberts' majority opinion, "the relevant distinction that has emerged from our cases is between conditions that define the limits of the government spending program—those that specify the activities Congress wants to subsidize—and conditions that seek to leverage funding to regulate speech outside the contours of the program itself." Although the Court admitted that the distinction is less than crystal clear, it was confident that the statute before it fell on the unconstitutional side of the line.

---

[23] 570 U.S. 205 (2013).

An application of this approach can be found in *Christian Legal Society v. Martinez*,[24] in which a religious student group challenged the law school's requirement that required recognized student groups comply with the school's non-discrimination policy. The Court found this condition to be in line with the purposes of the school's support for recognized students groups, which was to provide enrichment experiences to all students.

Another concept the Court has sometimes invoked in some cases dealing with speech in the public sector has been government speech. Of course, the government has the right to control its own speech and those who purport to speak on its behalf. Thus, someone who is hired to present the government viewpoint has no First Amendment right to use the opportunity for his or her own viewpoint. But the boundaries of this "government speech" doctrine have been perplexing. The boundaries of the government speech category have been somewhat fluid. In *Walker v. Texas Division, Sons of Confederate Veterans*,[25] the state refused to approve a specialty license plate design featuring a Confederate flag. The Court ruled that license plates constituted government speech, because license plates have long communicated messages from the states such as their state mottos, and the public regards the plates as government-connected. Indeed, the majority thought, the purpose of submitting a design to be considered to be put on license plates was probably to convey the impression of government approval. The dissenters pooh-poohed this analysis, pointing to the vast diversity of specialty plates and the unlikelihood that anyone thought the state endorsed all of their messages.

It seems clear that Texas could not have banned bumper stickers portraying the Confederate flag. It seems equally clear that Texas is not compelled to use the flag as an insignia on state vehicles. Thus, the question is whether the license plate is more like a bumper sticker or a state insignia. That question divided the Court 5–4. One might wonder, however, whether this categorizing effort was really the best way to decide whether rejection of the Confederate license plate design is consistent with First Amendment values. The structure of current doctrine, however, seems to make it difficult for the Court to approach cases in such functional terms.

In *Matal v. Tam*,[26] which was previously discussed in Chapter 6, the Court took a different tack. The Court held that a government trademark could not be considered an endorsement of the speech, rendering the registered trademark a message from the government.

---

[24]   561 U.S. 661 (2010).

[25]   ___ U.S. ___, 135 S.Ct. 2239, 192 L.Ed.2d 274 (2015).

[26]   ___ U.S. ___, 137 S.Ct. 1744, 198 L.Ed.2d 366 (2017).

Indeed, the government did not consider the content of the trademark at all except to determine whether it was offensive or disparaging. Consequently, the Court said, "[i]f the federal registration of a trademark makes the mark government speech, the Federal Government is babbling prodigiously and incoherently. It is saying many unseemly things. It is expressing contradictory views. It is unashamedly endorsing a vast array of commercial products and services. And it is providing Delphic advice to the consuming public." The Court distinguished *Walker* because license plates were manufactured and owned by the state, often designed by the state, and the state maintained direct control over the messages conveyed by the plates.

B.   The Subsidy Puzzle

Unconstitutional conditions on government grants have received extensive attention from academic commentators. Some theories focus on the coercive effect of the funding restriction, by asking whether the government has a kind of monopoly power over recipients, is using a "divide and conquer" strategy against them, or is withholding a benefit that under current social norms is considered an entitlement. Another theory focuses on whether the funding restriction skews the availability of constitutional rights in an unacceptable way—for example, by systematically depriving the poor of access to the same kind of information available to the affluent.

Other scholars have focused on the types of conditions placed upon speech. One theory is that, except where viewpoint discrimination is an unavoidable necessity, the scope of government programs should be defined in viewpoint neutral terms; subsidies can then be awarded on any basis "substantially related" to the purpose of the program. Another theory attempts to separate government activities into different spheres. Depending on whether an institution plays an important role in fostering autonomy or self-governance, it may or may not have a general duty to remain neutral regarding content. Yet another approach would ask whether the speech restriction has the effect of impoverishing public discourse by reducing the availability of diverse perspectives. Despite the richness of this scholarly literature, however, it seems safe to say that no fully satisfying solution to the problem has been found. Indeed, it is quite possible that no truly satisfactory solution exists, and that the problem is only amenable to case-by-case adjudication. Still, we might consider whether any guidelines can be found.

A few points seem to be common ground. First, the government is entitled to hire people to present its own views. An advertising company hired to conduct a military recruiting campaign cannot complain of viewpoint discrimination if it wishes instead to broadcast pacifist messages at government expense. Second, the government cannot condition a completely unrelated benefit on speech activities. For instance, it cannot deprive someone of food stamps or a property tax exemption because of their political views. The hard cases are in the middle, where the government is subsidizing only private speech with a specific type of content.

What can we learn about these in-between cases from the Court's treatment of other government benefits such as access to government facilities or public employment? The basic principle seems to be that the government can condition use of its facilities or employment on forbearance from speech that interferes with the purpose of the government program. Thus, the government must be able to make a plausible claim that particular speech falls outside the legitimate scope of the program.

Unfortunately, government programs do not come with labels disclosing their actual purposes. The difficulty in the subsidy cases is to screen out cases in which the government's definition of the program has been distorted by impermissible hostility to disfavored ideas. There seems to be no easy way to do this, but the public forum cases have some lessons to teach. First, viewpoint-based restrictions are obviously far more suspect than restrictions based on subject matter or on mode of expression (a rule which holds even in nonpublic forums). Second, the broader the scope of the government program, the more suspicious we should be of isolated, narrow exceptions. (Recall the distinction between the limited public forum and the nonpublic forum.) Third, tradition can sometimes affect the plausibility of efforts to recategorize the purpose of a forum. The Court is particularly suspicious of funding-based intrusions on forums traditionally devoted to debate such as universities and courtrooms.

Given the complexity of the issues, it is no wonder that the Court has encountered so much difficulty. Cases seem to focus on whether the government has added its own voice, neutrally enhanced speech in some part of the private sector, or distorted the normal functioning of the "market" for speech. What constitutes a distortion seems to depend on two factors. The first is whether the funding condition affects only the use of government funds, or whether it also hinders other speech activities by recipients. The second is the Court's sense of the "normal" functioning of the forum. This factor in turn involves both a descriptive dimension (how is the program defined? how has it functioned in the past?) as well as a normative dimension (how does the forum relate to other constitutional values, like democratic governance in the case of candidate debates?). Thus, the Court seems to be groping for a baseline for the appropriate functioning of the forum, and then trying to assess whether the government has augmented or distorted that functioning. In principle, this inquiry has the advantage of being explicitly tied to First Amendment values. Whether the Court will find these inquiries to be manageable remains to be seen.

In this chapter, we have considered the extent to which a speaker's rights are affected by a nexus to the government. In the next chapter we consider another "special" class of speakers: the media.

FURTHER READINGS

Mitchell N. Berman, *Coercion Without Baselines: Unconstitutional Conditions in Three Dimensions*, 90 Geo. L.J. 1 (2001).

Randall P. Bezanson and William G. Buss, *The Many Faces of Government Speech*, 86 Iowa L. Rev. 1377 (2001).

Alan Brownstein, *The Nonforum as a First Amendment Category*, 42 U.C. Davis L. Rev. 717 (2009).

Richard A. Epstein, *Foreword: Unconstitutional Conditions, State Power, and the Limits of Consent*, 102 Harv. L. Rev. 4 (1988).

Stephen M. Feldman, *Free Expression and Education: Between Two Democracies*, 16 Wm. & Mary Bill of Rts. J. 999 (2008).

Gia B. Lee, *First Amendment Enforcement in Government Institutions and Programs*, 36 UCLA L. Rev. 1692 (2009).

Richard J. Peltz, *Use "The Filter You Were Born With": The Unconstitutionality of Mandatory Internet Filtering for the Adult Patrons of Public Libraries*, 77 Wash. L. Rev. 397 (2002).

James E. Ryan, *The Supreme Court and Public Schools*, 86 Va. L. Rev. 1335 (2000).

Kathleen M. Sullivan, *Unconstitutional Conditions*, 102 Harv. L. Rev. 1413 (1989).

Symposium, *Unconstitutional Conditions*, 26 San Diego L. Rev. 174 (1989).

Eugene Volokh, *Freedom of Expressive Association*, 58 Stan. L. Rev. 1919 (2006).

Chapter 11

THE MEDIA

In Chapter 10, we saw how First Amendment doctrine deals with particular classes of speakers: those having special connections with the government. In this chapter, we turn to another class of speakers: the media.

The most fundamental question is whether First Amendment doctrine should explicitly distinguish media from other speakers. Arguments for special treatment can be made in either direction, either for extra regulation or for greater constitutional protection. On the one hand, because of their broad impact on the public, the mass media may give a relatively small group of people leverage over public opinion. Some believers in the self-governance model of the First Amendment argue that government has an affirmative duty to ensure that the media foster rather than undermine public deliberation. On the other hand, because the media provide an important channel of communication, the media epitomize the marketplace of ideas. Control over the media could give the government leverage over public opinion. Much of this debate has taken place regarding conventional print and broadcast media, but today the flashpoint tends to be social media such as Facebook and Twitter. The one point of agreement is that the media are a powerful forum, a sort of focal point for First Amendment values.

Media law has also become a flash point for debates between self-governance and marketplace theorists. As elsewhere in First Amendment law, the marketplace model is presently ascendant in media law, but there are important countercurrents. Self-governance advocates have not been without their victories. In this chapter, we will consider how doctrine has evolved in two key areas: (a) conflicts between the press and the criminal justice system (including media access to sources of information); and (b) efforts to guarantee access by speakers to media channels. We will then explore possible future directions for media law as it confronts new technologies.

Lurking in the background is a question about the constitutional text. The "press" does receive special mention in the First Amendment, which might imply that it receives a different level of constitutional protection. Also, the press can operate as a check on government abuses—a sort of institutionalized whistle blower. Thus, an argument can be made for special protection for the press. But so far this argument has not prevailed. Opponents have argued that it would be difficult to provide a workable definition of the press, and that the Constitution should protect the street corner speaker just as much as media institutions. Thus the media tend not to receive special constitutional protection.

As we saw in Chapter 5, the Court has generally taken this view with respect to defamation law, only rarely suggesting that media defendants might enjoy greater protection than others. In this chapter, we will see a similar pattern, in which the media are rarely given a preferred position. Only one clear safeguard has been created for the press, and that is a negative one: the press is subject to the same regulations as other businesses but may not be singled out for special burdens. For example, it is constitutional to subject the media to the normal labor and antitrust laws, but unconstitutional to impose a "paper and ink" tax solely on the press.[1] As we will see, however, the Court has sometimes allowed special regulation of certain media based on their distinctive physical or economic characteristics. Perhaps the most pressing issue today is the extent to which the Court will allow Congress to regulate emerging communication technologies.

I.   The Media and the Criminal Justice System

Criminal justice is both a core function of government and a core interest of the press. Predictably, the two institutions' perspectives sometimes collide. Such collisions may occur when the press has information from confidential sources that prosecutors would like to obtain; when pretrial publicity threatens the fairness of the proceedings; or when media attacks on the judicial system undermine its integrity.

A.   Protection of Sources

"Is this off the record?" is a question that everyone knows from movies and television. Use of confidential sources may not be as frequent in real life, but it sometimes does play an important role in news gathering. For example, "Deep Throat" was the confidential source who provided crucial information to reporters about the Watergate scandal. The identity of these sources would often be useful to police and prosecutors, yet the prospect of disclosure could cut off the flow of information to the press. How is this tension to be resolved?

In *Branzburg v. Hayes,*[2] the Court upheld the convictions of three reporters for refusing to disclose confidential information to a grand jury. In an opinion by Justice White, the Court declined to grant reporters a special testimonial privilege. Justice White rejected

---

[1]   *Minneapolis Star & Tribune Co. v. Minnesota Comm'r of Revenue,* 460 U.S. 575 (1983).

[2]   408 U.S. 665 (1972).

the argument that reporters should be compelled to testify only if they had information relevant to a crime available from no other sources. White saw "no basis for holding that the public interest in law enforcement and in ensuring effective grand jury proceedings is insufficient to override the consequential, but uncertain, burden on news gathering that is said to result from insisting that reporters, like other citizens, respond to relevant questions put to them in the course of a valid grand jury investigation or criminal trial." Justice White failed to find any evidence that requiring grand jury disclosure of confidential sources would cause a "significant constriction of the flow of news to the public." The opinion stressed the undesirability of granting special privileges to the press.

The impact of *Branzburg* was substantially blunted, however, by Justice Powell's concurring opinion, expressing his views as the swing voter in this 5–4 decision. According to Powell, a judge could intervene "if the newsman is called upon to give information bearing only a remote and tenuous relationship to the subject of the investigation, or if he has some other reason to believe that his testimony implicates confidential source relationships without a legitimate need of law enforcement." While purporting to endorse the majority opinion, Justice Powell adopted a balancing test:

> The asserted claim to privilege should be judged on its facts by the striking of a proper balance between freedom of the press and the obligation of all citizens to give relevant testimony with respect to criminal conduct. The balance of these vital constitutional and societal interests on a case-by-case basis accords with the tried and traditional way of adjudicating such questions.

Some lower courts have viewed Powell's balancing test as the controlling law. In addition, about half the states have passed shield laws embodying similar balancing tests.

In terms of general First Amendment doctrine, Powell seems to have the better argument. Disclosure orders are content-neutral regulations that affect speech, and should be subject to at least some type of mid-level scrutiny. Thus, courts should ensure that the order serves a significant government interest and is narrowly tailored to the government's needs. (Indeed, because the order is individually targeted rather than directed equally at the public at large, it may present some of the same special risks as injunctions against protestors. Recall from Chapter 9 that in the abortion protest cases, the Court subjected such injunctions to semi-strict scrutiny.) True, disclosure does not directly prohibit communication with sources, but it does burden the communication in a way that the Court has recognized in other contexts. For example, we saw in Chapter 4 that legislative investigations into political associations are limited because of the impact of disclosure on free association. And in cases involving communications in the executive branch, the Court has certainly recognized the possible chilling effect of investigations by grand juries.

Thus, White's argument that disclosure orders are immune from First Amendment scrutiny seems somewhat in tension with general First Amendment doctrine. On the other hand, White was probably right to the extent that he argued against tying First Amendment protection to press status. Other speakers, such as researchers, political activists or bloggers, should be equally protected when gathering confidential information for purposes of publication.

Besides calling reporters as witnesses, the government may also seek to obtain confidential information through use of search warrants. In *Zurcher v. Stanford Daily,*[3] the Court upheld a search of a campus newspaper office for photographs of a demonstration. The voting pattern was much the same as in *Branzburg*, with Justice Powell once again writing a "swing" opinion emphasizing First Amendment concerns. In response to *Zurcher*, a federal statute was enacted which prohibits searches of newsrooms except in exceptional circumstances.[4]

An interesting twist on the confidentiality issue was presented in *Cohen v. Cowles Media Co.,*[5] in which a source sued for breach of contract when a newspaper voluntarily broke its confidentiality pledge by including his name in a story. The Court rejected the paper's First Amendment defense on the basis that contract law, like antitrust and labor statutes, contains rules of general application to which the press is also subject. This seems to be a sensible decision. *Cohen* makes confidentiality promises by the press more credible and thereby increases its ability to obtain information.

B. Fair Trial/Free Press

Crime is always hot news, whether on television or in print. By the time a defendant comes to trial, nearly everyone in the vicinity— or sometimes in the whole country—may have heard about a particularly dramatic case. How, then, can the defendant hope for a fair trial by an impartial jury, when he has already been tried and found guilty by the press?

In several cases, the Court has reversed convictions obtained under such circumstances. The best-known case was probably

---

[3]   436 U.S. 547 (1978).

[4]   Privacy Protection Act of 1980, 42 U.S.C. § 2000aa.

[5]   501 U.S. 663 (1991).

Sheppard v. Maxwell,[6] in which the Court reversed the conviction of Dr. Sam Sheppard for killing his wife. (This case gave rise to "The Fugitive" television series and movie.) The community where the trial was held had been permeated with publicity about the case, including charges about Sheppard's sexual conduct, doctored photographs, and in general what the Court called a "carnival atmosphere."

Courts are expected to take steps to protect the fairness of the trial. Some of the potential remedies for unfair publicity raise no First Amendment questions. For example, the court can move the trial to another location with a lower publicity level, question prospective jurors about their exposure to publicity, or caution jurors to base their decision solely on what they hear in the courtroom. Some of the other potential remedies, however, do involve restrictions on speech.

One strategy is to cut off information at its source. A key source of information consists of the lawyers in the case themselves. Professional responsibility rules in most states limit the right of lawyers to make press statements designed to influence the trial. In *Gentile v. State Bar,*[7] a badly divided Court reversed a lawyer's punishment under such a rule, finding that the rule was valid as written but had been unconstitutionally interpreted. The lawyer's statements were made at a press conference, where he had argued that his client was being framed to protect a police officer who was implicated in the crime. The case produced an extraordinary split majority opinion, with part of the "opinion of the Court" being authored by Justice Kennedy and part by Chief Justice Rehnquist.

In the Rehnquist opinion, the Court held that the standard articulated in the state rule was sufficiently protective of speech. The rule prohibited statements with a "substantial likelihood of materially prejudicing" a proceeding. If the speaker had been an ordinary citizen, the state could have intervened only to prevent a "clear and present" danger of interference with the proceeding. But the Court applied a lower level of protection for speech by lawyers, who are officers of the court. "Lawyers representing clients in pending cases are key participants in the criminal justice system," said the Chief Justice, "and the State may demand some adherence to the precepts of that system in regulating their speech as well as their conduct." Nevertheless, the other "opinion of the Court" by Justice Kennedy lifted the discipline against the lawyer, on the ground that he could reasonably have believed that he was within one of the "safe harbor" exceptions to the rule. The safe harbor

---

[6]   384 U.S. 333 (1966).

[7]   501 U.S. 1030 (1991).

allowed a lawyer to explain the general nature of the defense, and Kennedy concluded that the lawyer was not put properly on notice that his remarks fell outside the safe harbor. Hence, as applied to this particular lawyer, the rule was unconstitutionally vague. The swing voter, Justice O'Connor, considered the basic rule to be valid but the safe harbor unconstitutionally vague.

The upshot of *Gentile* seems to be that, although this particular lawyer escaped punishment, the states have broad power to restrict lawyers' commentary about pending cases. Experienced lawyers seem to be adroit at skirting the limits of these rules.

The remedy of last resort against pretrial publicity is a gag order directed at the press. It is doubtful that such an order would ever be upheld. In *Nebraska Press Ass'n v. Stuart*,[8] the Court unanimously overturned an order banning press reports of an alleged confession. The majority opinion was by Chief Justice Burger. He insisted that "prior restraints on speech and publication are the most serious and the least tolerable infringement on First Amendment rights," so that a "heavy burden" must be met. In the case at hand, the threat the publicity posed to the fairness of the trial was not shown to be sufficiently grave, and the unavailability of less drastic remedies was not proven. Two of the Justices joining the majority opinion wrote separately to indicate their "grave doubt" about whether a gag order would "ever be justifiable." Similar if not stronger sentiments were expressed by four Justices who concurred only in the judgment. Experience has shown that, no matter how famous a case may be, it is always possible to locate twelve people somewhere who have never heard anything about it. Thus, it should always be possible to avoid the use of gag orders while still providing an impartial jury (though perhaps an exceptionally ill-informed one).

In our world of sensationalized media coverage, pretrial publicity is commonplace in significant cases. Probably, the main damage is not to the trial rights of individual defendants, but to personal reputations and to the dignity of the system as a whole. But the Court considers the criminal justice system to be a matter of public concern, and as we saw in Chapter 5, gives little weight to intangible harms from reporting newsworthy events.

C. Access by the Media

Recall from Chapter 5 that once the press lawfully acquires truthful information, it is essentially exempt from liability for disclosing the information. *Nebraska Press* confirms that the press is also immune from prior restraints against disclosure. Thus, the Court has provided generous support for the right of the press to

---

8   427 U.S. 539 (1976).

publish *once* it has obtained the information. But if the press is blocked from obtaining any information in the first place, the question of publication does not arise. Does the press have any constitutional right of access to information? *Branzburg* seems to indicate that press interviews may receive some constitutional protection, at least if Powell's concurrence is considered to be controlling. Clearly, in any event, the government could not normally prevent the press from interviewing *private* parties, even if Justice White is correct that grand jury disclosure should not be considered a burden on this right.

But what about the press's right to obtain information from the public sector? *Gentile* indicates that lawyers, as officers of the court (and therefore quasi-public actors), have some First Amendment right to communicate with the press, though less so than the general public. Presumably, the government can prohibit its own employees from disclosing confidential information to the public, although in theory the *Pickering* balancing test might conceivably place some limit on such prohibitions. Thus, it seems clear that the government can generally restrict access to its own documents—the Constitution contains no Freedom of Information Act.

Governmental restrictions on media access are most troubling with respect to the criminal justice system. Prisons operated under secrecy may degenerate into Gulags, while secret trials may abuse not only the rights of defendants but also the interests of society. For example, there is widespread concern about racial disparities in the criminal justice system, with implications beyond the treatment of individual defendants. Thus, there is a heightened public interest in freedom of information regarding the justice system. The Court has struggled with the application of the First Amendment in the twin settings of access to jails and access to trials. Each setting has given rise to a pair of decisions, one rejecting the First Amendment claim and the other giving it credence.

The jail issue first reached the Court in *Pell v. Procunier*.[9] The Court upheld jail rules prohibiting interviews with individual inmates. The Court reasoned that the Constitution does not impose upon the government "the affirmative duty to make available to journalists sources of information not available to members of the public generally." But four years later, in a confusing 3–1–3 decision, the Court did give some recognition to the right of journalists to access jails. In *Houchins v. KQED*,[10] a television station wanted to photograph part of a county jail where an inmate had reportedly

---

[9] 417 U.S. 817 (1974). See also *Saxbe v. Washington Post Co.*, 417 U.S. 843 (1974) (companion case to *Pell*).

[10] 438 U.S. 1 (1978).

committed suicide. After the station filed a lawsuit, the jail began a program of monthly public tours, covering other parts of the jail. Cameras, tape recorders, and interviews with inmates were forbidden. Writing for three Justices (himself and Justices White and Rehnquist), Chief Justice Burger concluded that the First Amendment simply contains no right of access to sources of information within government control. But three others, (Justice Stevens, joined by Brennan and Powell), argued that "[w]ithout some protection for the acquisition of information about the operation of public institutions such as prisons by the public at large, the process of self-governance contemplated by the Framers would be stripped of its substance."

The swing voter was Justice Stewart. He agreed with Burger that the Constitution "does no more than assure the public and the press equal access once government has opened its doors." He argued, however, that the press had the right to access on terms equal in substance, not just in form, to those of other members of the public:

> That the First Amendment speaks separately of freedom of speech and freedom of the press is no constitutional accident, but an acknowledgment of the critical role played by the press in American society. The Constitution requires sensitivity to that role, and to the special needs of the press in performing it effectively. A person touring Santa Rita jail can grasp its reality with his own eyes and ears. But if a television reporter is to convey the jail's sights and sounds to those who cannot personally visit the place, he must use cameras and sound equipment. In short, terms of access that are reasonably imposed on individual members of the public may, if they impede effective reporting without sufficient justification, be unreasonable as applied to journalists who are there to convey to the general public what the visitors see.

Thus, Stewart concluded, "the availability and scope of future permanent injunctive relief must depend upon the extent of access then permitted the public, and the decree must be framed to accommodate equitably the constitutional role of the press and the institutional requirements of the jail."

Consistent with *Pell* and with the Burger position in *Houchins v. KQED*, the Court rejected a press challenge to the closure of a trial in *Gannett Co. v. DePasquale*.[11] Justice Stewart's opinion for the Court held that the Sixth Amendment guarantee of public trials was at the discretion of the defendant, finding no "correlative right in members of the public to insist upon a public trial." Even assuming

---

[11]   443 U.S. 368 (1979).

that there might be any First Amendment guarantee of access, he found that this "putative right was given all appropriate deference" by the trial judge.

A year later, in *Richmond Newspapers, Inc. v. Virginia*,[12] the Court distinguished *Gannett* and recognized a First Amendment right to public trials, except when "an overriding interest" in closing the trial is articulated in specific findings by the trial judge. Based on the historical practice of allowing public access to trials, the Court held that such a right of access was implicit in the First Amendment. The seven Justices in the majority produced a total of four opinions. The basic rationale seems to be a kind of "reverse public forum" analysis: if streets and parks are traditionally open as places for speaking, trials are traditionally open as places for observing.

Overall, it is fair to say that the Court has not been hospitable to access rights by the media. Access to confidential sources is protected, if at all, only by the uncertain weight of Justice Powell's concurrence in *Branzburg*. Jails can apparently be closed completely to both press and public, though the press may be able to use public access as a wedge to gain modestly greater rights for itself than those of the general public. Trials alone are presumptively public and accessible to the press. By and large, the press must rely on informal methods of securing information, with little constitutional protection. Even without constitutional protection, however, state and federal legislatures have gone a long way to guarantee access to information, through freedom of information acts, sunshine laws, and other statutes. In addition, once the press does obtain information, it is virtually impossible to prevent publication.

II. Access to the Media

Everyone has the right to free speech, but some speak on lonely street corners and others on televisions sets. Because the mass media play such a dominant role in public discourse, there have been recurrent arguments for providing more diverse perspectives in the media, either by giving access to private speakers or by mandating that the media provide balanced coverage of different viewpoints. Otherwise, it is feared, much of the nation's communication system will reflect only the views of a small privileged minority. Although the Supreme Court has never accepted this argument in principle, the Court in effect allowed it in through the back door by allowing exceptional regulation of the broadcasting media.

---

[12]   448 U.S. 555 (1980).

A. Broadcasting

Since 1934, the federal government has licensed broadcasters in order to prevent interference between stations on nearby frequencies. The FCC has been authorized to confer licenses "as public convenience, interest, or necessity requires." The FCC, with some additional prompting from Congress, traditionally used this authority to pursue a broad variety of goals relating to diversity—for example, by limiting the number of stations that can be owned in common, limiting cross-ownership of different media, and favoring local ownership and management. Most notably, the "fairness doctrine" required broadcasters to devote a reasonable amount of time to discussion of public issues and to give fair coverage of each side.

The Supreme Court upheld the fairness doctrine in *Red Lion Broadcasting Co. v. FCC*.[13] *Red Lion* grew out of a series of broadcasts by a fundamentalist minister attacking one of his critics, who in turn demanded free airtime to respond. Apart from the general fairness doctrine, the case involved two specific regulations, one guaranteeing response time when a station endorses or opposes a political candidate, and another requiring an opportunity to respond to an attack on personal character or integrity. The Court held that the government is entitled to require a licensee to "share his [broadcast] frequency with others and to conduct himself as a proxy or fiduciary with obligations to present those views and voices which are representative of his community and which would otherwise, by necessity, be barred from the airwaves." The First Amendment's purpose is "to preserve an uninhibited marketplace of ideas in which truth will ultimately prevail, rather than to countenance monopolization of that market, whether it be by the Government itself or a private licensee." Without the fairness doctrine, "station owners and a few networks would have unfettered power to make time available only to the highest bidders, to communicate only their own views on public issues, people and candidates, and to permit on the air only those with whom they agreed." The First Amendment provides "no sanctuary" for "unlimited private censorship operating in a medium not open to all."

Red Lion was a rousing victory for the self-governance view of the First Amendment. The Court stressed the role of free speech in public deliberations while deemphasizing the possible liberty interest of the media. The Court has continued to view broadcasting as subject to special forms of regulation. In *CBS, Inc. v. FCC*,[14] the Court upheld another federal statute requiring broadcasters "to

---

[13]   395 U.S. 367 (1969).
[14]   453 U.S. 367 (1981).

allow reasonable access to or to permit purchase of reasonable amounts of time" by candidates for federal office. The case involved the refusal of the major networks to sell certain airtime to the Carter-Mondale reelection committee.

The basic argument in *Red Lion* is that the scarcity of broadcasting frequencies justifies greater regulation, including access mandates. This argument has widely been regarded as problematic for two reasons. First, as the FCC itself has sometimes acknowledged, the argument's factual underpinnings are increasingly insecure, especially given the availability of alternatives such as cable and on-line streaming. Second, even if scarcity exists, it is unclear why this justifies regulation of program content. Content-neutral licensing schemes are possible, such as auctions or lotteries, which have been used to allocate frequencies for non-broadcast purposes. If the concern is that a few people may permanently monopolize the local airwaves, an alternative solution would be to make the licenses relatively short-term and nonrenewable. In other words, it is not at all clear that the fairness doctrine can be defended as "necessary" even assuming that access and diversity are compelling government interests.

B.   Other Media

Some of the broad language in *Red Lion* reads like a sweeping endorsement of government-mandated access to the media. In many cities, there are more television stations than daily newspapers. (Indeed, an antitrust exemption immunizes some newspaper mergers from liability.) If it is wrong for one person to monopolize public discussion on the airwaves, it would seem equally wrong for one person to monopolize control of printed discussion of local matters. Yet, the Court decisively held in *Miami Herald Publishing Co. v. Tornillo*[15] that newspapers are exempt from access mandates. A Florida "right to reply" statute required any newspaper that attacked the personal character of a political candidate to provide equal space for the candidate to respond. As the Court explained, the statute was designed to ensure that diverse views reach the public, given that "[c]hains of newspapers, national newspapers, national wire and news services, and one-newspaper towns, are the dominant features of a press that has become noncompetitive and enormously powerful and influential in its capacity to manipulate popular opinion."

Recall that the Court upheld a similar requirement as applied to television. But the Court, ignoring *Red Lion*, found the Florida statute unacceptable for two reasons. First, due to the cost of

---

[15]   418 U.S. 241 (1974).

dedicating space to a response, a paper might be inhibited in attacking candidates in the first place, resulting in a less vigorous debate over public issues. Second, a newspaper is "more than a passive receptacle for news, comment, and advertising." The publisher's "choice of material to go into a newspaper, and the decisions made as to limitations on the size and content of the paper, treatment of public issues and public officials—whether fair or unfair—constitute the exercise of editorial control and judgment." This exercise of editorial judgment is immune from government regulation.

After *Tornillo*, it seemed clear that *Red Lion* was based on the special circumstances of the broadcasting industry, rather than being a sweeping victory for access to the media. The Court re-emphasized the special nature of broadcasting in another setting just a few years later, holding that the unique intrusiveness of broadcasting justified restrictions on "indecent" broadcasts.[16] So by the mid-seventies, there seemed to be a clear divide: printed media received full constitutional protection while broadcasters were subject to special regulations.

Whether or not it was fully principled, at least this seemed to be a clear, understandable rule. However, the rise of new communication media such as cable television would soon blur the boundaries. In a 1992 statute that built on earlier FCC rules, Congress required cable systems to transmit local commercial and public broadcasting stations, subject to some restrictions. After extraordinarily lengthy and complex litigation, the Supreme Court ultimately upheld the "must carry" provisions.

In its first opinion on the issue in 1994, the Court held that the "must carry" rule was content neutral. It remanded the case so the District Court could develop the appropriate record for applying the *O'Brien* test.[17] Unlike the law struck down in *Tornillo*, the must-carry rule was not triggered by the content of the cable operator's other broadcasting, nor did its application depend on the content of the local broadcasts that would be retransmitted. All the rule said was that speakers meeting a certain description (cable systems) had to provide space for speakers meeting another description (local broadcasters).

But the *purposes* of the law were not unrelated to content, as the legislative history made crystal clear. Congress was afraid that the growing market dominance of cable systems would bankrupt television stations lacking cable access. Consequently, Congress believed, the non-cable portion of the population would have

---

[16]   *FCC v. Pacifica Foundation*, 438 U.S. 726 (1978).

[17]   *Turner Broadcasting Sys., Inc. v. FCC*, 512 U.S. 622 (1994) [*Turner I*].

considerably less access to broadcasting sources. Because of the local and educational programming provided by potentially excluded stations, the result would be a loss to public discourse. This is a very *Red Lion*-ish rationale. Justice Kennedy's majority opinion argued that this rationale was subsidiary to Congress's goal of preventing the destruction of the broadcast industry, rather than an independent reason for must-carry; the dissenters considered the rationale content-based.

On remand, following long and expensive litigation, the District Court found that the must-carry rule was significantly related to achieving its purpose of preserving local broadcasting. The Court affirmed, with roughly the same division of Justices.[18] The majority opinion displayed considerable willingness to defer to Congress's predictions about the future of the communications industry. It is unclear to what extent cable now occupies, in some general sense, a position somewhere between broadcasting and newspapers in the First Amendment spectrum. Suppose, for example, that Congress had made well-documented findings that newspapers were no longer carrying program listings for non-cable stations because of pressure from cable companies, and that the absence of such listings would doom some local broadcasters. Would the Court uphold a statute requiring newspapers to carry these program listings (or to open their pages to free advertising by local broadcasters)? In theory, such a statute should be subject to the *O'Brien* test, just like the must-carry rule, but it is doubtful that the Court would apply the same approach to the print media.

III. The Future of Media Law

Communications law is one of the most rapidly evolving areas of the law today. Communications are also among the most rapidly evolving areas of technology. Cable has changed from a back-up system for people with bad television reception into the dominant method of receiving programming. The Internet, which began as a government-funded curiosity, is now a major avenue of communication. Billions of dollars are invested based on speculation about how cable, computers, and telecommunications will evolve.

Traditionally, the law has found it difficult to respond to new technologies. Passing new statutes is a clumsy process, hampered by a whole series of roadblocks deliberately created by the Framers of the Constitution. Court decisions are bound by precedent and issued by a group of often-elderly lawyers, who typically did not necessarily attain their positions of distinction by being intellectually adventuresome. It remains to be seen whether the legal system can

---

[18]   *Turner Broadcasting Sys., Inc. v. FCC*, 520 U.S. 180 (1997) [*Turner II*].

adequately adapt to such a high pace of technological and social change.

Particularly, it remains to be seen how adequately First Amendment law will respond to this challenge. There are, of course, conflicting opinions about what would constitute an "adequate" response, based on conflicting models of the First Amendment itself. We will briefly consider those conflicting models, and then examine the early signs about the Court's response to these emerging technologies.

A. Conflicting Models

Broadcasting and print represent not merely two different technologies, but two different legal models. In the print model, private publishers are completely autonomous, protected against almost all forms of government interference with the content of their publications. In the broadcasting model, stations are trustees acting in the public interest, and are subject to FCC regulation to ensure that they live up to their duties. These two regulatory regimes also reflect two very different visions of the relationship between the government and the media.

The classical viewpoint, which underlies most First Amendment jurisprudence, sees the government as the great enemy of free expression. The central goal of most First Amendment doctrine is to limit the government's ability to interfere with speech. In accordance with this goal, the emphasis is on ensuring the liberty of the speaker. This liberty is not necessarily the ultimate goal, in and of itself, but it is assumed that values like the search for truth and democratic self-government will best flourish when every speaker decides for himself what to discuss. This is a marketplace of ideas in more than one sense, since it places most speech in the private sector and leaves it to the market to determine what will be said and by whom.

Advocates of this viewpoint see broadcasting regulation as a historical oddity. Licensing arose when First Amendment rights were not well entrenched and were especially tenuous for new technologies. Over time, the licensing scheme became so embedded in the structure of the industry and in public folkways that change seemed unthinkable. By the time modern First Amendment doctrine arose, it seemed too late to rewrite broadcasting law. But new technologies do not suffer from this unfortunate history and its attendant (and perhaps spurious) scarcity rationale. So they should be treated on the model of the print media, and broadcasting regulation should be left aside as an anomaly. According to advocates of this viewpoint, First Amendment law should relate primarily to process rather than end results. Protect the free operation of the marketplace of ideas, and then diversity, access, and vigorous public debate will follow.

But others believe that we should keep our eyes firmly on the ultimate goals of First Amendment law, rather than assuming the invisible hand of the marketplace will automatically produce desirable results. These First Amendment revisionists do not oppose freedom of speech, but they contend that affirmative government action is needed to create a robust public discourse. Pointing to the unimpressive content of much of the popular media, they argue that a well-functioning democracy requires better informed citizens. Today, they might also point to manipulation of public opinion via false or inflammatory posts on social media.

Both visions have their appeal. The dominant, classic vision appeals to our distrust of government in the area of speech. It celebrates our ultimate trust in individuals to decide for themselves what to listen to or see. The revisionist vision appeals to widespread concerns about the current state of the marketplace of ideas, and about whether the public is really sufficiently thoughtful to govern. But there is ground for concern about both visions. The classic vision seems to assume blindly that new communication technologies will automatically develop benignly. Revisionists seem overly confident of the good intentions of government regulators and inclined to patronize ordinary citizens who may not share their tastes or values. If, until now, the classic vision has been dominant, *Red Lion* at least is a reminder that our First Amendment tradition contains some dissident strains more favorable to the revisionists.

B.   Straws in the Wind

It is too early to say where the Court is heading with regard to new technologies. The early indications suggest that it will not use broadcasting as the model, but that it may well allow some innovative regulations never applied to the print media.

With respect to cable, *Turner* seems to firmly reject the broadcasting model, which would allow the government a general power to ensure access and diversity. But the Court has not necessarily adopted the print model either. In *Denver Area Educational Telecommunications Consortium v. FCC*,[19] in which the Court upheld portions of federal regulation of indecent cable programming, the plurality opinion by Justice Breyer explicitly refused to transplant either broadcasting or print law to cable. "Both categorical approaches suffer from the same flaws," he said, in that "they import law developed in very different contexts into a new and changing environment, and they lack the flexibility necessary to

---

[19]   518 U.S. 727 (1996).

allow government to respond to very serious practical problems without sacrificing the free exchange of ideas the First Amendment is designed to protect." In his concurrence, Justice Souter added that the Court should be reluctant to establish firm doctrines when communications technology was still in such a state of flux.

The Court also steered away from the broadcasting model in *United States v. Playboy Entertainment Group*.[20] In contrast to the sympathy shown to the zoning approach in *Pacifica*, the Court was much less friendly to efforts to protect children from exposure to sexually explicit material on cable television. The Telecommunications Act required cable operators either to scramble sexually explicit channels in full or to limit programming on those channels to certain hours, because of the possibility that "signal bleed" from incomplete scrambling would allow children to see portions of the programming. Justice Kennedy's opinion for the Court held the provision to be content-based and struck it down. He emphasized that the statute was concerned with the "direct impact that speech has on its listeners" rather than with secondary effects. Playboy had offered a "plausible, less restrictive alternative," namely, requiring cable operators to block undesired channels at the request of individual households, combined with advertising and other efforts to notify households of this option. The government failed to show that this alternative would be ineffective at protecting children. Justice Kennedy emphasized that cable "expands the capacity to choose; and it denies the potential of this revolution if we assume the Government is best positioned to make these choices for us." Justice Breyer wrote for the four dissenters, agreeing with the majority's general approach but concluding that the proposed alternative would not be effective. The presumption against regulation seemed much stronger for all of the Justices than it has typically been in broadcasting cases.

The Court refused to adopt the broadcasting model for the Internet in *Reno v. ACLU*,[21] another "indecency" case. The Court distinguished broadcasting as involving a history of extensive government regulation, a scarcity of available frequencies (at least initially), and a particularly invasive medium. Most significantly, the Court said, the Internet "can hardly be considered a 'scarce' expressive commodity." Rather, the Court observed:

> This dynamic, multifaceted category of communication includes not only traditional print and news services, but also audio, video, and still images, as well as interactive, real-time dialogue. Through the use of chat rooms, any

---

[20]   529 U.S. 803 (2000).

[21]   521 U.S. 844 (1997).

person with a phone line can become a town crier with a voice that resonates farther than it could from any soapbox. Through the use of Web pages, mail exploders, and newsgroups, the same individual can become a pamphleteer.

Consequently, the Court found "no basis for qualifying the level of First Amendment scrutiny that should be applied to this medium." But despite this rejection of the broadcast model, the Court did not assume that a ban on indecency was automatically unconstitutional, as such a ban surely would have been if applied to the print media. Rather the Court carefully analyzed the extent to which less restrictive alternatives were available and dissected the careless drafting of the statute. Thus, the Court seems in actuality to have adopted a more contextual analysis than it would have done for the print media, even while eschewing the broadcasting model.

Thus, the Court seemed inclined to feel its way through the "brave new world" of telecommunications, without committing itself to blindly following precedents from older technologies. The Court seemed sympathetic to regulatory goals such as assuring access and diversity, and protecting children from inappropriate speech, it was quite leery of allowing direct regulation of content. More recently, in *Packingham v. North Carolina*,[22] the Court analogized social media to traditional public forums, casting even more doubt on content regulation, though the case itself involved access to social media rather than content. Still, the Court has yet to confront the quasi-monopoly status of some social media firms and their consequent control over important channels of public communications. It remains to be seen how the Court will respond to government intervention in this domain, whether content-based or otherwise.

FURTHER READINGS

C. Edwin Baker, *The Independent Significance of the Press Clause Under Existing Law*, 35 Hofstra L. Rev. 955 (2007).

Stuart Minor Benjamin, *Proactive Legislation and the First Amendment*, 99 Mich. L. Rev. 281 (2000).

Jim Chen, *The Last Picture Show (On the Twilight of Federal Mass Communications Regulation)*, 80 Minn. L. Rev. 1415 (1996).

Owen M. Fiss, The Irony of Free Speech (1996).

Thomas G. Krattenmaker and Lucas A. Powe, Jr., Regulating Broadcast Programming (1994).

Seth F. Kreimer, *Censorship by Proxy*, 155 U. Pa. L. Rev. 11 (2006).

---

[22]   ___ U.S. ___, 137 S.Ct. 1730, 198 L.Ed.2d 273 (2017).

Ronald J. Krotoszynski, Jr., *The Irrelevant Wasteland*, 60 Admin. L. Rev. 911 (2008).

Gregory P. Magarian, *Substantive Media Regulations in Three Dimensions*, 76 Geo. Wash. L. Rev. 845 (2008).

Justin Marceau and Alan Chen, *Free Speech and Democracy in the Video Age*, 116 Colum. L. Rev. 991 (2016).

Barry McDonald, *The First Amendment and the Free Flow of Information*, 65 Ohio St. L.J. 249 (2004).

Cass R. Sunstein, Republic.com (2001).

Alexander Tsesis, *Social Media Accountability for Terrorist Propaganda*, 86 Fordham L. Rev. 605 (2017).

Chapter 12

ASSOCIATIONS, PARTIES, AND POLITICAL CAMPAIGNS

The previous chapter considered the application of the First Amendment to one type of group undertaking, the media. This chapter considers more broadly the application of the First Amendment to groups. We begin by exploring the basic right of freedom of association, and then turn to the particularly important associations known as political parties. We close with a discussion of campaign financing, focusing particularly on the regulation of organizations such as political action committees and corporations.

I. Freedom of Association

The final clause of the First Amendment prohibits laws abridging "the right of the people peaceably to assemble and to petition the government for a redress of grievances." Even without this textual anchor, it would be obvious that the First Amendment must protect not merely the individual speaker but also organized activities, ranging from political parties and media organizations to protest committees and dissident groups. Effective speech often requires more resources than a single individual can bring to bear, and political impact often depends on numbers. Thus, the First Amendment would lose much of its value if it protected only isolated individuals but left the government a free hand to prevent organized activity.

The argument for protecting freedom of association is strongest, then, when the organization's activities themselves are within the scope of the First Amendment. In tracing the history of First Amendment doctrine relating to subversive speech in Chapter 4, we witnessed the emergence of constitutional protection for political association. The Court took steps in *Scales* and *Noto* to ensure that individuals would not be subject to "guilt by association." Even when the association itself strays into unprotected criminal activities, individuals can only be punished for intentional support for the association's illegal purpose. The effect is to create a safety buffer for individuals who might otherwise be afraid to join dissident organizations for fear of being tainted by organizational actions they do not support.

Thus, the case for protecting freedom of association is strongest when the organization's activities revolve around political speech. In this section, however, we will focus on groups whose main purposes are nonpolitical.

A. Regulating Group Membership

Most of the modern cases involving state regulation of group membership arise in the context of state discrimination laws. *Roberts v. United States Jaycees*[1] is illustrative. Two Minnesota chapters of the Jaycees were sanctioned by the national organization for violating a national bylaw prohibiting women from being members. The local chapters filed a civil rights complaint against the national organization under a state anti-discrimination law. The national organization responded with a federal lawsuit claiming that the state could not force it to accept women as members of its local chapters. The Supreme Court held that compelling the national organization to accept women would not violate its constitutional rights. Justice Brennan's opinion for the Court distinguishes between two different senses of freedom of association. One line of cases holds that "choices to enter into and maintain certain intimate human relationships must be secured against undue intrusion by the State because of the role of such relationships in safeguarding the individual freedom that is central to our constitutional scheme." Brennan refers to this as the *intrinsic* feature of the right to associate, since it involves protection of association for its own sake. Another line of cases recognizes a "right to associate for the purpose of engaging in those activities protected by the First Amendment—speech, assembly, petition for the redress of grievances, and the exercise of religion." Brennan refers to this as the *instrumental* feature of association.

Regarding the intrinsic aspect of association, Justice Brennan observed that human groups span a broad range from intimate personal relationships such as families to business corporations. Families involve "deep attachments and commitments to the necessarily few other individuals with whom one shares not only a special community of thoughts, experiences, and beliefs but also distinctively personal aspects of one's life." Among the traits of families are "relative smallness, a high degree of selectivity in decisions to begin and maintain the affiliation, and seclusion from others in critical aspects of the relationship." Generally, only relationships with similar qualities are protected as intrinsic associations, according to Brennan. The Jaycees failed to qualify. Except for restrictions on gender and age, membership was completely unselective, and the local chapters had several hundred members. The local chapters, which had the better claim to be considered intimate associations, actually had decided in favor of

---

[1]   468 U.S. 609 (1984).

admitting women; only the more impersonal national organization was opposed.

Regarding the instrumental aspect of association, Justice Brennan observed, "collective effort on behalf of shared goals is especially important in preserving political and cultural diversity and in shielding dissident expression from suppression by the majority." Hence, the Court has recognized a right to "associate with others in pursuit of a wide variety of political, social, economic, educational, religious, and cultural ends." The Jaycees qualified for protection as an instrumental association, because national and local organizations had taken public positions on a variety of issues, and members regularly engaged in civic, charitable, lobbying, and other protected activities. But limitations on the right to associate for expressive purposes may be imposed "by regulations adopted to serve compelling state interests, unrelated to the suppression of ideas, that cannot be achieved through means significantly less restrictive of associational freedoms." The Court concluded that the government's compelling interest in eliminating gender discrimination justified regulation of the Jaycees. The Court was skeptical that admission of women would change the content or impact of the organization's speech, and in any event, found that any effect on protected speech was "no greater than is necessary to accomplish the State's legitimate purposes."

Several years later, the Court extended the *Roberts* holding in *Board of Directors of Rotary International v. Rotary Club of Duarte.*[2] Again, the case arose from a conflict between a local group and the national organization. The national Rotary revoked the charter of a local club because it had admitted women. The local club and two female members filed suit in state court challenging the action as a violation of state civil rights law. As in *Roberts*, the Court found no violation of the right to intimate association. The size of local clubs ranged from fewer than twenty to nearly a thousand, with an annual turnover of about ten percent. Rather than carrying out their activities in private, local clubs sought publicity. Also, as in *Roberts*, the Court found no significant impact on the clubs' expressive activities, and held that any "slight infringement" was justified by the state's compelling interest in eliminating discrimination.

In some later cases, however, the Court was more receptive to expressive association claims in discrimination cases. Consider *Hurley v. Irish-American Gay, Lesbian, and Bisexual Group.*[3] The state courts had ruled that the annual St. Patrick's Day parade was a "public accommodation," and that exclusion of a gay and lesbian

---

[2]   481 U.S. 537 (1987).

[3]   515 U.S. 557 (1995).

group from the Boston parade was therefore a violation of state civil rights law. The Supreme Court unanimously reversed. Justice Souter's opinion for the Court considered the parade to be an expressive activity: "Spectators line the streets; people march in costumes and uniforms, carrying flags and banners with all sorts of messages (e.g., 'England get out of Ireland,' 'Say no to drugs'); marching bands and pipers play, floats are pulled along, and the whole show is broadcast over Boston television." Admission of the gay and lesbian group to the parade would alter the message presented, unlike cases such as *Roberts* in which compelled admission "did not trespass on the organization's message itself."

Hurley has several noteworthy features. First, any mention of the compelling interest test is conspicuously absent. Having found a substantial intrusion on the parade's expressive rights, the Court ended the analysis without a glance at any state interests. Second, the Court observed that the parade sponsors had no desire to exclude individual gay people from the parade, but simply objected to the inclusion of an explicitly gay contingent. Thus, the real question was not *who* was in the parade, but *what* message they would convey. *Hurley* was therefore factually distinguishable from the Jaycee and Rotary cases, where the sole issue was membership.

In *Boy Scouts of America v. Dale*,[4] the Court took *Hurley* one step farther. An openly gay scout leader had challenged his expulsion from the Boy Scouts. The state courts held that the Boy Scouts were covered by a state law prohibiting discrimination in "public accommodations" on the basis of sexual orientation. In an opinion by Chief Justice Rehnquist, the Court held that the state had violated the organization's right to expressive association. Rehnquist concluded that the Scouts were an intensely expressive organization, dedicated to instilling its system of values in boys, and that one of those values was opposition to homosexuality. Although he denied that an expressive association "can erect a shield against antidiscrimination laws simply by asserting that mere acceptance of a member from a particular group would impair its message," here the individual's "presence in the Boy Scouts would, at the very least, force the organization to send a message, both to the youth members and the world, that the Boy Scouts accepts homosexual conduct as a legitimate form of behavior." Four Justices joined a dissenting opinion authored by Justice Stevens.

What gave *Dale* the potential to undermine antidiscrimination laws is not so much its holding, which was simply that an expressive association need not include in a leadership position a member who openly opposes its message. (Compare the rule that the government

---

4   530 U.S. 640 (2000).

can discharge a "policy-level" employee on the basis of political views contrary to his superiors.) Rather, the potential threat stemmed from the Court's great deference to the organization's assertion that it had a contrary message and that the individual's presence would interfere with that message. In reality, the organization's only explicit message was being "morally straight," which it had at best loosely tied to any teachings about sexual orientation. Indeed, the organization allegedly did not revoke the membership of heterosexual Scout leaders who openly disagreed with the Scouts' policy on sexual orientation, and different sponsors of scout troops had different positions on the issue. But the Court was unwilling to probe the national leadership's litigation position regarding the organization's views. Perhaps the majority simply found it obvious that the Boy Scouts would not accept homosexuality. If, however, the teaching of the case is that an expressive organization needs only to make a colorable claim of interference with its message in order to prevail, the potential for disrupting anti-discrimination laws is obvious.

Five years after *Dale*, the Court seemed less willing to defer to an association's own assessment of its expressive needs. *Rumsfeld v. Forum For Academic Institutional Rights, Inc. [FAIR]*,[5] was a challenge brought by law schools and law faculty to a federal statute requiring equal access to military recruiters. The law schools contended that allowing military recruiting undermined their message of nondiscrimination on the basis of sexual orientation, because at that time the military had a "Don't Ask, Don't Tell" policy against homosexuality. The federal statute actually took the form of a funding cutoff, but the Court made it clear that a direct mandate would have been equally permissible.

The Court brusquely rejected their claim that the plaintiffs' associational rights were impaired: "The law schools *say* that allowing military recruiters equal access impairs their own expression by requiring them to associate with the recruiters, but just as saying conduct is undertaken for expressive purposes cannot make it symbolic speech, so too a speaker cannot 'erect a shield' against laws requiring access 'simply by asserting' that mere association 'would impair its message.' " The Court simply found the law school's claimed associational interest implausible: "Recruiters are, by definition, outsiders who come onto campus for the limited purpose of trying to hire students—not to become members of the school's expressive association. This distinction is critical." In short, a "military recruiter's mere presence on campus does not violate a

---

[5]   547 U.S. 47 (2006).

law school's right to associate, regardless of how repugnant the law school considers the recruiter's message."

FAIR suggests that *Dale* is limited to expressive organizations, not those serving other purposes such as commercial profit, and to "members" rather than arms-length relationships. Two important questions remain unanswered. First, to what extent are employees (or at least some employees) to be considered as more akin to members than to the recruiters involved in *FAIR*? And second, may the government condition funding to an expressive organization on compliance with antidiscrimination rules regarding members?

B.   Collective Action

Sometimes a group of people combine to take an action that any of them would have a constitutional right to perform individually. It is little surprise that their collective action is also normally protected by the Constitution. But the Court has sometimes further held that of association protects organizational activities, even though those same activities are apparently not constitutionally protected when undertaken by single individuals.

One of those activities is the financing of litigation. The Court first held that associational rights included litigation in *NAACP v. Button*,[6] in which the state of Virginia banned organizations from retaining lawyers in a case unless they were parties or were otherwise financially affected. The NAACP was seeking to provide lawyers for civil rights litigants, but was not directly a party to the litigation. The Court characterized the litigation undertaken by the NAACP as an "effective form of political association," and was unable to identify any compelling interest that might justify the ban. In dissent, Justice Harlan insisted that the ban was content neutral and supported by the state's interest in the integrity of legal representation.

Although *Button* seemed influenced by the state's hostility to civil rights organizations and the public interest nature of the litigation, the Court soon found association rights to be present in a case exhibiting neither factor. In *Brotherhood of Railroad Trainmen v. Virginia State Bar*,[7] the Court held that a union had the constitutional right to represent its members in personal injury litigation arising from workplace accidents. On the other hand, a personal injury lawyer's solicitation of clients was held not to be subject to this rule in *Ohralik v. Ohio State Bar Ass'n*,[8] but rather to

---

[6]   371 U.S. 415 (1963).

[7]   377 U.S. 1 (1964).

[8]   436 U.S. 447 (1978).

be an ordinary example of commercial speech. This pattern of results is a bit perplexing.

If there were a constitutional right for an individual to hire a lawyer, then obviously there should be a constitutional right for a group of people to do the same thing collectively. But the Court has never held that individuals do have the constitutional right to hire lawyers for civil litigation, so it is unclear why a group should gain a constitutional right through association that none of them has individually. Perhaps the implication is that if a state voluntarily chooses to legalize an action when undertaken by a single individual, it cannot classify a collective decision to undertake the same action as illegal, at least without showing some concrete injury. But such a rule would invalidate the antitrust laws, which make it illegal for a group of sellers to agree on prices even though each of them has the right to set their own price. Notably, the antitrust laws do not require proof that a particular price-fixing conspiracy actually harmed consumers.

For similar reasons, the Court's decision in *NAACP v. Claiborne Hardware Co.*[9] is also somewhat puzzling. The case arose from a boycott of white stores by blacks in a Mississippi county, which was intended to force businesses and civic leaders to agree to a series of civil rights demands. The Court had never held that an individual's right to boycott a business is constitutionally protected. Thus, it is hard to see why a collective decision to engage in the same activity should be protected, though the Court so held.

Indeed, no general constitutional right to boycott seems to exist. When a labor union refused to load or unload ships engaged in trade with the Soviet Union as a political protest against the Soviet Union's invasion of Afghanistan, the Court found no difficulty in holding the boycott illegal.[10] Presumably a similar boycott of Soviet imports by a human rights group would have been constitutionally protected. Admittedly, the Court has a long tradition of putting labor-management relations at the fringe of the First Amendment. Still, it is not clear why the NAACP should have the right to engage in activity that is forbidden to the AFL-CIO—except perhaps on the reasonable assumption that the government's sanctions against the NAACP were motivated by racism or ideology, whereas the ban on union boycotts was part of a neutral scheme for regulating labor relations.

---

[9]   458 U.S. 886 (1982).

[10]   *International Longshoremen's AFL-CIO v. Allied International, Inc.*, 456 U.S. 212 (1982).

Perhaps this kind of judgment about governmental good faith also underlies *FTC v. Superior Court Trial Lawyers Ass'n,*[11] in which the Court upheld the application of the antitrust laws to another boycott. That boycott was organized by lawyers in private practice who acted as court-appointed counsel in criminal cases in the District of Columbia. (If the lawyers had all worked for the same private employer, a strike would not have been considered an illegal restriction on trade.) They were protesting the low fees for criminal representation. Alternatively, perhaps the Court considers commercial speech to be protected, but not commercial association. In any event, the Court's decisions in this area remain a riddle.

II. Political Parties

No such puzzles attend the First Amendment status of political parties. Although they were outside the purview of the Framers when the First Amendment was written, there is no question that their activities fall within the core of the First Amendment. Yet, they are also part of the electoral process, a process that is established and regulated by the government. The difficult problem is drawing a line between legitimate state efforts to structure the electoral process and illegitimate intrusion on the rights of the parties.

A. Internal Party Affairs

For any one state to attempt to dictate the procedures for a national political party has the obvious potential for chaos. If one state's statute required a two-thirds majority for a national presidential nomination, another state might counter with a simple majority rule, resulting in nationwide confusion. Even regulation of the party's local activities within a single state, however, may abridge its associational rights. For instance, a state lacks the authority to prevent governing bodies of political parties from endorsing primary candidates.[12]

Two cases from the 1980s illustrate the limits of state regulatory power. In *Democratic Party v. Wisconsin,*[13] a state law required national political parties to seat only delegates who were pledged to abide by the Wisconsin primary. The party's national organization required that primaries be limited to registered Democrats. Contrary to the party rules, Wisconsin held an "open" primary in which voters did not need to make a public declaration of their party affiliation. The party's rule was intended to restrict cross-over voting, which had allowed Republican voters to play a decisive role in some

---

[11]   493 U.S. 411 (1990).

[12]   *Eu v. San Francisco County Democratic Central Committee,* 489 U.S. 214 (1989).

[13]   450 U.S. 107 (1981).

controversial Democratic primaries. The Court held that the state could not constitutionally require party delegates to abide by the results of the open primary. Freedom of association "necessarily presupposes the freedom to identify the people who constitute the association, and to limit the association to those people only." The national party "chose to define their associational rights by limiting those who could participate in the processes leading to the selection of delegates to their National Convention." The state was unable to show any compelling interest in interfering. Wisconsin was free to conduct an open primary, but not to insist that the delegates be bound by the result.

The converse situation was presented in *Tashjian v. Republican Party.*[14] The state insisted on a closed primary while the party wanted an open one. Maintaining that "the act of formal enrollment or public affiliation with the Party is merely one element in the continuum of participation in Party affairs," the Court held that inviting the participation of independents was an aspect of freedom of association. By placing limits on the "group of registered voters whom the Party may invite to participate," the state limited the "Party's associational opportunities at the crucial juncture at which the appeal to common principles may be translated into concerted action, and hence to political power in the community." The state asserted several justifications for the statute, most notably the desire to prevent splintered parties and factionalism. Although these concerns about the effects of open primaries were shared by some notable political scientists, the Court held that it was up to the party itself, not the state government, to determine its own long-term interests.

B. Ballot Access

State legislatures are dominated by the major political parties. Perhaps not coincidentally, state election laws often make life difficult for independent candidates, write-ins, and new parties. The Court's initial decisions seemed skeptical of such legislation. For example, the Court struck down Ohio laws requiring petitions by new parties to be signed by fifteen percent of qualified voters and requiring independent presidential candidates to file seven months before the election.[15] But later decisions seem more sympathetic to state efforts to prevent erosion of the two-party system.

In *Burdick v. Takushi,*[16] the Court upheld a Hawaii statute prohibiting write-in votes in general elections. The motivation for

---

[14] 479 U.S. 208 (1986).

[15] *Anderson v. Celebrezze,* 460 U.S. 780 (1983); *Williams v. Rhodes,* 393 U.S. 23 (1968).

[16] 504 U.S. 428 (1992).

write-in campaigns was apparent: a third of all elections for the state legislature were unopposed, but many voters preferred to cast blank ballots rather than endorse the unchallenged candidate. The Court announced a two-track test for assessing ballot restrictions. When election provisions impose "severe" restrictions, they are subject to strict scrutiny. But if an election law imposes only "reasonable, nondiscriminatory restrictions" on voters' rights, "the State's important regulatory interests are generally sufficient." Because Hawaii provided several easy paths to a place on the ballot, the Court considered the write-in ban relatively mild, and found the state's interest in preventing post-primary factions to be a sufficient justification.

Similarly, in *Timmons v. Twin Cities Area New Party*,[17] the Court upheld a ban on "fusion" ballots. Fusion is a practice going back to the Nineteenth Century in which a minor party agrees to list another party's nominee as its own. This allows the minor party to enter into a coalition with larger parties, and historically has been an important factor in the long-term viability of third parties. The Court did not find the ban on fusion ballots to be a "severe" restriction on third-party rights. It was also unimpressed by the argument that fusion is necessary for minor parties to thrive. "Many features of our political system—e.g., single-member districts, 'first past the post' elections, and the high costs of campaigning—make it difficult for third parties to succeed in American politics." The Constitution does not "require States to permit fusion any more than it requires them to move to proportional-representation elections or public financing of campaigns." The Court found a number of valid interests behind the ban, including prevention of voter confusion.

The most notable portion of the *Timmons* opinion discusses the constitutional status of the two-party system:

> States also have a strong interest in the stability of their political systems. This interest does not permit a State to completely insulate the two-party system from minor parties' or independent candidates' competition and influence, nor is it a paternalistic license for States to protect political parties from the consequences of their own internal disagreements. That said, the States' interest permits them to enact reasonable election regulations that may, in practice, favor the traditional two-party system, and that temper the destabilizing effects of party-splintering and excessive factionalism. The Constitution permits the Minnesota Legislature to decide that political stability is best served through a healthy two-party system.

---

[17] 520 U.S. 351 (1997).

The scope of government support for the two-party system seems to be the fundamental question in the ballot access cases.

At first blush, the *Timmons* Court's position seems to be paradoxical: states must allow *some* access for third-parties and independents, but not enough to allow them to threaten the two established parties. This raises two questions: How did the two-party system get to enjoy this quasi-constitutional status? And why not allow the states to eliminate independents and third-parties entirely, ending any threat to the two-party system? In short, it is unclear how the Court's vision of a balance between major parties and their competitors finds a constitutional grounding.

The explanation for the Court's rulings seems to have relatively little to do with individual First Amendment rights. Rather, the Court seems to have in mind a model of democracy. In this model, the dominant role is played by the two major parties, but the threat of outside competition helps keep those parties responsive to public opinion. This is a plausible vision of American democracy, though not an inevitable one. The ultimate stakes seem to be the overall stability and responsiveness of the system, rather than the individual expressive or associational rights of voters, candidates, or parties. Perhaps it would be more straightforward to say that completely insulating the major parties from challenge would give too much power to party hierarchies at the expense of popular democracy. This is a judgment less connected to the First Amendment than to the constitutional guarantee of a "republican form of government." Perhaps if that clause of the Constitution had not been held judicially unenforceable early in the nation's history, the Court would have adopted this more straightforward analysis of the issues.

III. Campaign Financing

After the Watergate scandal, Congress passed far-reaching campaign reforms in 1974. The reforms were motivated by concerns about corruption and conflicts of interest during the Nixon Administration. There was also a general belief that campaigns were becoming too expensive, forcing elected officials to spend too much of their time on fundraising rather than official duties. Another concern was that large contributors were gaining disproportionate influence over American politics.

Although some campaign reforms tried to regulate the independent speech of a candidate's individual supporters, the primary impact of campaign reform has been on group activities by organized campaigns, political parties, and political action groups. Thus, it seems appropriate to discuss campaign financing issues in connection with the general topic of associational rights.

The Supreme Court has profoundly shaped our current politics through its rulings on campaign finance. This area of law has given rise to a spate of cases as legislatures have attempted to find ways of regulating campaign contributions despite judicial obstacles. In a general book on the First Amendment, it would be inappropriate to try to cover all of the doctrinal nuances. Instead, we will begin by discussing the Supreme Court's landmark decision in *Buckley v. Valeo*,[18] and then focus on the two most significant post-*Buckley* cases.

A.   The *Buckley* Decision

Understanding *Buckley* requires some additional detail about campaign finance legislation. The Federal Election Campaign Act of 1974 included restrictions on political contributions and expenditures that applied broadly to all phases of and all participants in the election process. The 1974 law prohibited individuals from contributing more than $25,000 in a single year or more than $1000 to a single candidate for an election campaign, and also from spending more than $1000 a year "relative to a clearly identified candidate." A second set of provisions imposed disclosure and reporting requirements. A third set established a system for public funding of presidential campaigns. The Court upheld the latter two sets of provisions and invalidated much of the first set. Because of the complexity of the case, which involved multiple challenges to many different provisions of the statute, the opinion was issued *per curiam*, with different Justices authoring different sections anonymously.

We will focus on the Court's treatment of the expenditure and contribution limits. The key to the Court's analysis was its determination that strict scrutiny applied. The government had argued that spending money was conduct rather than pure speech, so that the regulations should be considered the equivalent of restrictions on symbolic speech. The Court firmly rejected the suggestion that "the dependence of a communication on the expenditure of money operates itself to introduce a nonspeech element or to reduce the exacting scrutiny required by the First Amendment." Moreover, the government interests underlying the statute did not satisfy the requirement of being unrelated to the suppression of free expression. These interests included "restricting the voices of people and interest groups who have money to spend and reducing the overall scope of federal election campaigns." Thus, the rationale for the statute "arises in some measure because the communication allegedly integral to the conduct is itself thought to be harmful." Having decided that full First Amendment scrutiny was

---

[18]   424 U.S. 1 (1976).

warranted, the Court proceeded to analyze the expenditure and contribution limits separately.

The expenditure limits, according to the Court, were "substantial rather than merely theoretical restraints on the quantity and diversity of political speech." The $1000 limit on individual expenditures "would appear to exclude all citizens and groups except candidates, political parties, and the institutional press from any significant use of the most effective modes of communication." The restrictions on spending by campaigns and parties were less severe, but would still have required restrictions on the scope of past federal campaigns. The Court found the interests invoked by the government to be insufficient to justify the spending restrictions. The danger of corruption was not sufficient to justify the expenditure limitations, as independent expenditures did not pose a major danger of real or apparent corruption. Moreover, in order to avoid vagueness, the statute had to be construed to apply only to ads that "in express terms advocate the election or defeat of a clearly identified candidate." As so construed, however, the statute was too narrow to block evasion of the contribution limitations.

The Court was even less impressed by the argument that the expenditure limits were necessary to neutralize the effects of wealth on political campaigns. According to the Court, "the concept that government may restrict the speech of some elements of our society in order to enhance the relative voice of others is wholly foreign to the First Amendment," which was intended "to secure 'the widest possible dissemination of information from diverse and antagonistic sources' and 'to assure unfettered interchange of ideas for the bringing about of political and social changes desired by the people.'" (The internal quotations are from *New York Times v. Sullivan*, the defamation case discussed in Chapter 5.) The Court's view that equalization is an impermissible regulatory objective has been a primary source of controversy about the case.

The Court was less hostile to the contribution restrictions. Unlike restrictions on expenditures, "a limitation upon the amount that any one person or group may contribute to a candidate or political committee entails only a marginal restriction upon the contributor's ability to engage in free communication." Such a contribution "serves as a general expression of support for the candidate and his views, but does not communicate the underlying basis for the support." Thus, a contribution limitation places "little direct restraint on his political communication, for it permits the symbolic expression of support evidenced by a contribution but does not in any way infringe the contributor's freedom to discuss candidates and issues." In short, the Court seemed to consider contribution restrictions to involve primarily associational rather than speech rights, and to burden those rights only marginally. The Court found ample justification for the restriction:

> The increasing importance of the communications media and sophisticated mass-mailing and polling operations to effective campaigning make the raising of large sums of money an ever more essential ingredient of an effective candidacy. To the extent that large contributions are given to secure a political *quid pro quo* from current and potential office holders, the integrity of our system of representative democracy is undermined. Although the scope of such pernicious practices can never be reliably ascertained, the deeply disturbing examples surfacing after the 1972 election demonstrate that the problem is not an illusory one.

"Of almost equal concern," the Court added, is the "appearance of corruption" due to public awareness of the potential for abuse created by large contributions.

The upshot was that the Court upheld the contribution limitations but found the expenditure limitations clearly unconstitutional. Supporters of campaign reform protested that the decision left the carefully structured statute in tatters. For instance, one effect of *Buckley* is to accentuate the advantage of wealthy candidates who can spend unlimited amounts of money on their own campaigns, while less affluent candidates must operate under the restrictions of the contribution limits when raising money.

One effect of *Buckley* was to increase the importance of campaign spending by organizations such as political action groups (PACs), corporations, and other groups. In *California Medical Ass'n v. Federal Election Comm'n*,[19] the Court upheld limits on contributions to PACs. A 1971 federal statute limited contributions to multi-candidate political committees to $5000 per person. Following the *Buckley* analysis, the Court concluded that the provision validly furthered the government's interest in preventing actual or apparent corruption. If Congress could restrict contributions directly to a single campaign, it could also restrict contributions to a pool used to finance multiple campaigns. In contrast, in *Federal Election Comm'n v. National Conservative PAC*,[20] the Court struck down limits on PAC expenditures. True, the Court conceded, PACs "are not lone pamphleteers or street corner orators in the Tom Paine mold; they spend substantial amounts of money in order to communicate their political ideas through sophisticated media advertisements." And the law limited the

---

[19]   453 U.S. 182 (1981).

[20]   470 U.S. 480 (1985).

spending of money, not the views of the PAC. Still, in the context of a national political campaign, "allowing the presentation of views while forbidding the expenditure of more than $1,000 to present them is much like allowing a speaker in a public hall to express his views while denying him the use of an amplifying system."

B. *McConnell v. Federal Election Commission*[21]

McConnell is the second key case on campaign finance. In 2002, Congress passed its most important campaign finance legislation in three decades, the Bipartisan Campaign Reform Act (BCRA). BCRA is a massive, complex piece of legislation, leading to an equally massive, complex set of opinions by the Justices. Our focus will be on two of the major provisions. Section 323 attempts to eliminate "soft" money donations. It prohibits national political parties from soliciting, receiving or spending any money except in compliance with federal funding limits—in effect, forcing them to rely entirely on "hard money" that is subject to federal regulation. Section 203 attempted to deal with a problem created by *Buckley* concerning corporate speech. Congress had attempted to ban all use of corporate and union funds (except through PACs) for campaign ads. But the *Buckley* Court, in order to avoid overbreadth concerns, had construed the statute to apply only to ads containing "express advocacy" of a candidate. Section 203 expanded the ban to include all "electioneering communications."

Like the original 1974 statute, the 2002 version was immediately challenged on First Amendment grounds. Many observers expected the Court to strike down substantial portions of BCRA, if not the entire statute. But the Court's response was surprisingly sympathetic to efforts at campaign reform. The lead opinion was jointly authored by Justices Stevens and O'Connor.

As to the soft money ban in section 323, the Court reviewed evidence that candidates and donors exploited the ban to provide campaign funds for the use of specific candidates, bypassing the contribution limits. The evidence connected soft money to failures to enact generic drug legislation, tort reform, and tobacco legislation. Moreover, the Court said, the interest in preventing corruption extends beyond buying votes to buying access to officials, and the evidence showed that "various corporate interests had given substantial donations to gain access to high-level government officials."

The Court also upheld section 203, rejecting the claim that it was overbroad. The Court observed that "in the future corporations and unions may finance genuine issue ads during those time periods

---

[21] 540 U.S. 93 (2003).

[preceding elections] by simply avoiding any specific reference to federal candidates, or in doubtful cases by paying for the ad from a segregated fund."

McConnell was notable in several respects. The Court seemed more willing to defer to Congress on questions about the practical impact of campaign finance reform. It also recognized "soft" corruption as a problem—that is, situations where donations provide influence over or privileged access to an official, although there is no explicit agreement to swap campaign funds for favored treatment. Finally, it accepted as legitimate concerns about the use of union or corporate treasuries to influence elections. But this more accepting attitude toward reform proved to be short-lived.

C. *Citizens United*[22] and Beyond

Although *McConnell* seemed to represent a more tolerant attitude toward campaign finance regulation, it was soon followed by several smaller cases that took a more skeptical stance. Justice O'Connor had been the crucial swing vote in *McConnell*, and with her replacement by the more conservative Justice Alito, it seemed likely that campaign finance regulation was in trouble.

In the most important of these post-*McConnell* case, the new majority made it clear that it was prepared to make abrupt changes in campaign finance law. In *Citizens United*, the Court reached out to decide a question that the parties had not raised and overruled *McConnell*'s limits on corporate campaign spending. In the course of doing so, the Court seemingly stripped Congress of any power to regulate corporate political activities with the possible exception of direct contributions to candidates.

The majority found corporate campaign expenditures completely unproblematic. First, the Court made clear, anything short of quid pro quo bribery is simply not a problem. "That speakers may have influence over or access to elected officials does not mean that those officials are corrupt. And the appearance of influence or access will not cause the electorate to lose faith in this democracy." Second, it is equally unproblematic that corporations divert money earned from economic endeavors to the political sphere. "All speakers, including individuals and the media, use money amassed from the economic marketplace to fund their speech, and the First Amendment protects the resulting speech." Third, corporations are not only entitled to equal respect with individuals as speakers, they are actually superior sources of political advocacy. Extolling the value of corporate political activity, the majority said that restrictions on corporate speech "muffle the voices that best

---

[22]   *Citizens United v. FEC*, 558 U.S. 310 (2010).

represent the most significant segments of the economy." The majority had no hesitation in overruling prior precedent so as to free corporations to make their special contribution to electoral politics.

Prior to *Citizens United*, the Court seemed to attempt to balance the interest in eliminating possible inhibitions on political speech with concerns about special interest influence, distortion of the political process, and political equality. In *Citizens United*, the Court seemingly abandoned any other concerns to maximize the amount of speech on political issues regardless of the source or of any secondary effects.

The public seems not to agree with the Court that purchasing influence over officials is unproblematic and that corporations have the same rights to free speech as human beings. It remains to be seen, however, whether judicial deregulation of campaign finance will significantly impact public confidence in government or in the political process.

The *Citizens United* Court did seem to be willing to support disclosure requirements (upheld in *Citizens United*) and public financing (although not at the expense of the right of the wealthy to outspend their opponents). More recent cases generally have also been hostile to campaign finance reform. In *Arizona Free Enterprise Club v. Bennett*,[23] the Court struck down an Arizona law intended to equalize the position of candidates accepting public financing. Such a candidate would receive matching funds for any amount by which an opponent's expenditures, plus independent expenditures, exceeded the initial level of state funding. The same Justices who formed the majority in *Citizens United* struck down the matching mechanism as a burden on the expenditures made on behalf of the competing candidate. Then, in *McCutcheon v. FEC*,[24] the Court struck down a federal limit on the total amount of contributions to candidates and political organizations in any one election cycle (about $125,000 per couple). The Court found this an impermissible effort to equalize political influence.

A 2015 case was a departure from the strong trend of invalidating campaign finance regulations under the Roberts Court. In *Williams-Yulee v. Florida Bar*,[25] the Court upheld a limit on solicitation of campaign contributions by judges in judicial elections. Chief Justice Roberts opinion speaks of the "vital state interest" in safeguarding "public confidence in the fairness and integrity of the nation's elected judges." Unlike elected officials, Roberts emphasized,

---

[23] 564 U.S. 721 (2011).
[24] 572 U.S. 185 (2014).
[25] ___ U.S. ___, 135 S.Ct. 1656, 191 L.Ed.2d 570 (2015).

judges are not supposed to be responsive to the preferences of their constituents, and allowing them to solicit campaign contributions would create a temptation to sway decisions in favor of prospective donors.

The dissenters argued that the majority did not seem to be demanding as much precision in the fit between ends and means as in some other cases of strict scrutiny. On the other hand, once avoiding the appearance of partiality is accepted as a compelling state interest, is it possible to draw rules as precise as those that the dissenters demanded?

The dissenters seemed sanguine about the possibility that judges might become as responsive to contributors as other office-holders, or that their involvement in solicitation might create an appearance of favoritism in later rulings. To the extent that the governmental interest is public confidence in the institutions of government, isn't the dissent right that this interest is neither more nor less important as applied to judges as to others? On the other hand, could the majority argue that there is a special interest in giving litigants (as opposed to the general public) confidence that there cases are being decided impartially?

Williams-Yulee may turn out to be an isolated exception to the Court's enthusiasm for deregulating campaign finance, or it may be a harbinger of at least a subtle shift. In any event, the Court to date has shown no inclination to overrule *Buckley*'s limitations on contributions to individual candidates. But the options for campaign reform seem to be shrinking. The current majority accepts only *quid pro* corruption (bribery) or the appearance of quid pro quo corruption as legitimate bases for corruption. It staunchly rejects any more general concerns about the corrosive effect of large amounts of money on politics, such buying access to elected officials, making officials responsive primarily to the desires of large donors, or increasing the already high level of public mistrust of government and the democratic process. It would be ironic if, as critics of *Citizens United* fear, the result of First Amendment enthusiasm for uninhibited political debate is to hand political power to a small circle of wealthy individuals and corporate managers at the expense of broader democratic participation. In any event, the available tools for would-be reformers seem largely limited to disclosure requirements, public financing, and limits on contributions to individual candidates or political organizations.

IV. Concluding Thoughts on Quasi-Public Speech

In our society, free speech often takes place in institutional settings. The topics discussed in Part III of this book have not involved lonely pamphleteers distributing their work from door to door. Rather, they involved access to government financed facilities; denizens of high schools, prisons, and military units; public employees; representatives of the mass media; and massive political organizations. Is there is a connecting thread that has caused the Court to view these settings as special?

If there *is* such a common thread, it may be that all of these institutions are intimately connected, in one way or another, with the operation of the government itself. Some of the institutions directly involve government support or financing; other institutions such as the media and political parties play major functions in controlling the government. Often, these latter institutions have co-evolved with government regulation—the government, after all, organizes the elections in which political parties participate, and establishes the preconditions for the successful operation of electronic media. In an earlier era, the Court gave the government special regulatory powers over "businesses affected with the public interest." The institutions discussed in Part III all fit this general description to varying degrees.

The analytical tools developed in the context of the purely private speaker are sometimes useful in the context of the quasi-public speaker. Much of the doctrine in the area, however, seems to be an effort to bend doctrines such as content neutrality to fit the quasi-public setting. The result has been a whole series of complicated rules governing various kinds of quasi-public speakers—allowing broad content control in schools, subject-matter but not viewpoint discrimination in nonpublic forums, control of contributions but not expenditures in political campaigns, "compelling interests" for regulating elections that seem less than earthshaking, and so forth.

It is tempting to suggest that the Court should move beyond these ad hoc accommodations toward some more general theory of quasi-public speech. It is unclear, however, what the contours of such a more general theory would be, or whether the common elements of these various institutions are really substantial enough to support a unified analysis. The distinction between regulation of the public versus internal governmental affairs often seems to be helpful, as does the general maxim against suppression of unpopular ideas. But each institution has its own peculiarities, and in the end a unified approach may be unhelpful in dealing with the problems unique to each area.

FURTHER READINGS

Ashutosh Bhagwat, *Associational Speech*, 120 Yale L.J. 978 (2011).

Bruce E. Cain, *Party Autonomy and Two-Party Electoral Competition*, 149 U. Pa. L. Rev. 793 (2001).

Dale Carpenter, *Expressive Association and Anti-Discrimination Law after* Dale: *A Tripartite Approach*, 85 Minn. L. Rev. 1515 (2001).

Edward B. Foley, *Equal-Dollars-Per-Voter: A Constitutional Principle of Campaign Finance*, 94 Colum. L. Rev. 1204 (1994).

Richard L. Hasen, *Three Wrong Progressive Approaches (and One Right One) to Campaign Finance Reform*, 8 Harv. L. & Pol'y Rev. 21 (2014).

Deborah Hellman, *Defining Corruption and Constitutionalizing Democracy*, 111 Mich. L. Rev. 1385 (2013).

Paul Horwitz, *Three Faces of Deference*, 83 Notre Dame L. Rev. 1061 (2008).

Samuel Issacharoff, *Private Parties with Public Purposes: Political Parties, Associational Freedoms, and Partisan Competition*, 101 Colum. L. Rev. 274 (2001).

Lawrence Lessig, *What an Originalist Would Understand "Corruption" to Mean*, 102 Cal. L. Rev. 1 (2014).

Daniel Hays Lowenstein, *Associational Rights of Major Political Parties: A Skeptical Inquiry*, 71 Tex. L. Rev. 1741 (1993).

Barry P. McDonald, *Campaign Finance Regulation and the Marketplace of Emotions*, 36 Pepperdine L. Rev. 395 (2009).

David McGowan, *Making Sense of* Dale, 18 Const. Comm. 121 (2001).

Robert Post, Citizens Divided: Campaign Finance Reform and the Constitution (2014).

Part IV
RELIGION

———

Chapter 13

FREE EXERCISE

The opening clauses of the First Amendment concern religion: "Congress shall make no law respecting an establishment of religion, or prohibiting the free exercise thereof." These few words have given rise to tremendous controversy. What is an "establishment" of religion? Does it mean only a formal state church, like the Church of England? Or does it mean any form of government preference or support for a specific religion, or any preference or support for religion in general? And what about "free exercise"? Clearly, a law targeting a specific religious practice is generally impermissible. But what about a general law that happens to forbid a particular religious practice, like a ban on alcohol as applied to sacramental wine? Even broader issues lurk behind these, about the role that religious motivation and sectarian groups play in American public life, and about religious diversity as a form of multiculturalism.

In terms of social importance, not to mention scholarly attention, few areas of First Amendment law have loomed as large as the religion clauses. The topic of almost every chapter in this book is complex enough to warrant a book in its own right. Nonetheless, probably none has been the subject of so many recent books as the role of religion in American public life. In these final two chapters, we will only touch the surface of the profound issues in this area. The goal of these chapters is simply to identify the issues, sketch the major opposing positions, and analyze the Supreme Court's efforts.

This chapter focuses on the Free Exercise Clause. We begin by examining the special constitutional standing of religion, including the reasons for its inclusion in the Constitution. The next two sections then focus on a central issue in Free Exercise law: the extent to which religious practices are entitled to exemption from general legal requirements. This is followed by a section surveying other Free Exercise issues, and the chapter then closes with an assessment of the current status of the right to free exercise.

I. The Constitutional Status of Religion

Why was "religion" singled out for special treatment in the Constitution? Should it receive special constitutional treatment? And what does "religion" mean in this context, anyway? We address these questions in turn.

A. Religious Freedom in American History

When English settlers arrived in America, their prior experience with religious issues had been incendiary—literally so, in that many still remembered a history that included burning "heretics" at the stake. From the time Henry VIII pulled away from Rome, religious conflict had been in the forefront of English life, beginning with the bitter struggles between Catholics and Protestants for the remainder of the Tudor dynasty. The Church of England became the established church, but Protestant dissenters ultimately were responsible for deposing and executing Charles I. When Cromwell's reign was over, the Church of England was reestablished. Only in 1688 did Parliament foreswear persecution of other Protestants, but even then, Anglicans had a preferred legal position.

The American colonies varied in their attitude toward religious freedom. The Puritans of New England, having fled religious persecution in England, lost no time in persecuting other religious groups. They expelled Baptists and Quakers, making Congregationalism the established church. Other states such as New York and New Jersey basically ignored religious sects. At the other extreme from the Puritans, the founders of several colonies emphasized freedom of religion. William Penn founded Pennsylvania and Delaware, as Roger Williams founded Rhode Island, to be refuges for religious dissidents. Maryland was founded by a Catholic proprietor, who promised to allow "free exercise" of religion by all Christians. Unfortunately, Maryland soon reverted to a more intolerant regime.

The Carolina colony was founded with the help of philosopher John Locke. Locke was one of a group of great thinkers, beginning with Spinoza, who developed the concept of religious freedom. After some initial waffling, Locke espoused the position that religious tolerance was the only way to prevent explosive conflicts. He stressed the need to distinguish civil government, concerned only with earthly interests, from religion, concerned only with spiritual matters. Although Locke's views were far-reaching for his time, his support for religious freedom was not unqualified. He thought the state could try to persuade religious dissenters to change their ways, and he did not oppose the English established church. Locke also had no doubt that religious practices must give way before any legitimate secular regulatory interest.

Locke's followers, such as Jefferson, played a prominent role in the struggle for religious freedom in America. As Jefferson put it, "it does me no injury for my neighbor to say there are twenty gods, or no god. It neither picks my pocket nor breaks my leg." Jefferson favored religious freedom as a means to eliminate sectarianism: he hoped that Unitarianism would ultimately become the universal American faith. Jefferson, unlike Locke, was willing to extend religious toleration to Catholics and atheists, and was staunchly opposed to any establishment of religion. His good friend James Madison shared his inclination to create a strict division between the temporal and spiritual spheres. Their allies included Baptists and other new sects, who felt smothered by the older established churches. These dissenting groups, however, may not have completely shared the same conception of religious liberty.

After the American Revolution, almost all the states adopted new constitutions, and all but one of the new constitutions protected religious freedom. The new federal Constitution prohibited religious tests for public office. It also allowed affirmations as an alternative to oaths in several provisions. Yet it did not provide any more general protection for religious freedom. This was one of the grounds for opposition to the Constitution raised by the Anti-Federalists, who feared that state protections for religious freedom would be overridden by the national government. Madison, who initially opposed a Bill of Rights, sponsored its introduction in the new Congress. He was partly motivated by pressure from Baptist constituents seeking more protection. Previously, he had argued that such constitutional protection was unnecessary because of the federal government's limited powers. He had also maintained that the "multiplicity of sects which pervades America" was "the best and only security for religious liberty in any society; for where there is such a variety of sects, there cannot be a majority of any one sect to oppress and persecute the rest."

Madison's draft of what became the First Amendment provided: "The civil rights of none shall be abridged on account of religious belief or worship, [n]or shall any national religion be established, nor shall the full and equal rights of conscience be in any manner, nor on any pretext, infringed." The language adopted by the House was that "Congress shall make no law establishing Religion, or prohibiting the free exercise thereof, nor shall the rights of conscience be infringed." In turn, the Senate version provided: "Congress shall make no law establishing articles of faith or a mode of worship, or prohibiting the free exercise of religion." The final language was written by the Conference Committee. We will return later to a consideration of the original understanding of this final language. Whatever else it may or may not mean, however, it clearly does indicate that religion has a special status under the Constitution. In the next section, we consider the possible rationales for this special treatment.

B. Free Exercise Values

One argument for giving special protection to religion is the
desirability of religion itself. But if the purpose of the Free Exercise
Clause is to promote religion, it is puzzling that the Establishment
Clause seems to inhibit direct government assistance to that end. So
most efforts to justify religious liberty as a constitutional principle
eschew reliance on the premise that religious belief is desirable, and
instead seek more secular justifications. (Within various religious
traditions, there may also be theological arguments for tolerance
toward other religions, of course.) The question legal scholars have
asked is why even the nonreligious should be willing to provide
freedom for religious believers. The suggested answers are varied
and subtle, but for present purposes can be divided into three rough
categories.

One approach stems from Locke and other classic philosophers
of liberalism, represented today by John Rawls and Ronald Dworkin.
At the heart of these theories is a vision of the state as having limited
powers. Individuals are free to form their own basic plans in life,
living out their own vision of the good. The function of the state is to
establish a fair set of ground rules, including rules for allocating the
resources people need to pursue their visions, as well as methods of
protecting the rights of each individual from infringement by others.
Religion plays a particular role in this vision. Historically, religion
has offered many of the most compelling visions of the proper human
life. The religious diversity of modern society has meant that people
with differing fundamental values have had to learn to live together
in peace. The upshot is that religion is considered a core example of
the kind of personal autonomy that the liberal state is pledged to
protect.

From this perspective, the right to be a fundamentalist
Christian and the right to gay marriage are similar: both involve
central aspects of personal autonomy. Although originally deriving
from liberal philosophers like Locke, a more pluralist spin can be put
on the argument, in which the point is not personal autonomy but
respect for the views of minority cultures, whether they be religious
sects or ethnic groups. (From this perspective, the religion clauses
have an equal protection function, preventing discrimination against
religious minorities.) This pluralist argument might also stress the
importance of intermediate institutions such as churches, which
stand between the isolated individual and the Leviathan of state
power.

A second approach focuses on the potential threats of religious
dissension to social peace. Madison's view seems to have been that
religious freedom would cause the fragmentation of religious groups,

which would tend to subdivide into numerous quarreling sects. This atomization of religion would prevent any religious group from achieving enough political hegemony to threaten others. A similar argument for religious toleration is that suppression merely drives dissident religions underground, provides them with martyrs, and sets the stage for increasingly bitter conflict. It is better, according to this theory, to defuse the situation through an attitude of genial tolerance. A related argument is that we ought not to force people into corners where they will be forced to rebel or practice civil disobedience. All of these arguments focus on the contribution of religious tolerance to social stability.

A third approach focuses on the quandary of religious believers in a secular society. By the standards of the secular society, many religious beliefs appear irrational, and their adherents seem to be gripped by compulsions that make little sense to outsiders. From the purely secular point of view (or often, from the perspective of another religion), the deeply religious may seem a bit crazy. So, just as we make accommodations for the mentally incompetent, we should make similar accommodations for the religious. It is worth noting that, despite the superficially anti-religious tone of this argument, it has actually been made by serious religious believers, not just skeptics. So long as the mentally ill pose no threat to themselves or others, we allow them to live their lives in peace. Surely, the argument goes, we ought to extend at least the same right to those with sincere religious convictions, even if those convictions make no sense from our own point of view. Otherwise, we risk pitting ourselves against well-intentioned, sincere fellow citizens who are doing no harm to anyone else.

All of these arguments have their difficulties. The philosophical "autonomy" argument is inconsistent with religions that view their beliefs as compelled by God rather than voluntary. It is also difficult to define precisely the line between core exercises of autonomy and mere personal preferences that do not receive special constitutional protection. The argument from social peace resonates strongly with the European experience of the early modern age, but may be less relevant to contemporary America. And the "religion as madness" arguments seem a bit too disrespectful to be fully satisfying as a justification for giving religion a privileged status. Nevertheless, taken together, the arguments may combine to make a strong case for religious tolerance.

C. Defining "Religion"

If religion is going to have a special status under the Constitution, it becomes important to define religion. This turns out to be somewhat difficult for two reasons. First, many purely secular beliefs touch on some of the same questions as religion—for example, the Big Bang theory in astronomy describes the origins of the universe, a traditional subject of religious discourse. If such secular positions were considered "religious," the Free Exercise Clause would merge into the Free Speech clause. Similarly, the Establishment Clause would become universal in scope—government would be unable to support any viewpoint whatsoever. But it seems unlikely that federal funding for a space telescope violates the Establishment Clause. Second, it is not easy to find a common thread running through all recognized religions. For example, many devout Buddhists do not believe in God; many Orthodox Jews do not believe in an afterlife; and some other religions emphasize mystic experiences rather than standards of conduct.

The Supreme Court has confronted the issue of defining religion three times. In *Torasco v. Watkins*,[1] the Court struck down a state law that prevented a Secular Humanist from being appointed as a notary public because he refused to declare his belief in God. The Court listed not only Secular Humanism but Buddhism, Taoism, and Ethical Culture as religions. A few years later, in *United States v. Seeger*,[2] the Court construed the conscientious objection provision of the draft law to apply to a non-theist. The statute required that the objection to war involve the objector's "relation to a Supreme Being." The Court characterized as religious any "belief that is sincere and meaningful [which] occupies a place in the life of its possessor parallel to that filled by the orthodox belief in God of one who clearly qualifies for the exemption." In *Welsh v. United States*,[3] the Court extended *Seeger* to an individual who did not call his own views "religious" and said they were formed by reading history and sociology. Nevertheless, the Court found that these views played the same role in his life as religious views do for the traditional believer.

In formulating this view, the Court referred to the views of Protestant theologian Paul Tillich. He viewed the essence of religion to be "ultimate concern"—meaning, roughly speaking, the fundamental wellspring of a person's motivations and emotions. If we probe deeply enough, in Tillich's view, all people have an ultimate concern that generates the meaning of their lives. It is at this core that the individual must say, with Martin Luther, "Here I stand. I can do no other." Tillich viewed this core as the essence of religion.

This approach has the advantage of transcending all distinctions of creed while still excluding many secular beliefs; it also explains why religion should have special constitutional status in a

---

[1]   367 U.S. 488 (1961).

[2]   380 U.S. 163 (1965).

[3]   398 U.S. 333 (1970).

democratic society that respects individual identities. But Tillich's position may be more problematic as a legal test than as a philosophical position. It seems ambiguous, and it could require a probing psychological inquiry that may be beyond the capacity of the judicial system.

The alternative to a global definition seems to be a case-by-case approach, in which judges examine claimed religious beliefs by analogy to accepted religions, and attempt to determine if the resemblance is "close enough." Or, to put it another way, with religion as with pornography, perhaps we must ultimately rely on the ability of judges to "know it when they see it." Given the difficulty of defining religion, it is fortunate that the problem does not arise more frequently in litigation.

II. Exemptions for Religious Conduct

If there are any American believers in classical Greek religion, the Free Exercise Clause obviously protects their right to pray to Zeus and Athena. But what about other aspects of religious worship? The ancient Greeks sacrificed goats and made burnt offerings to the gods. Suppose their hypothetical modern followers were prosecuted under a general animal cruelty statute or for violating an air pollution rule? Presumably, the general rules were not created with the ancient Greeks' religion in mind. Still the effect would be to ban an essential aspect of pagan religion. Does the right to "free exercise of religion" include the right to exemptions from general laws that burden religious practices? As we will see, the Court has not followed a steady course in addressing this question.

A.　The Era of the Compelling Interest Test

Until 1963, the Court had never applied the Free Exercise Clause to exempt a religious practice from a general rule of state law. A new era began with *Sherbert v. Verner*.[4] A Seventh-Day Adventist was fired because she refused to work on Saturday. She also turned down several other possible jobs for the same reason. She was denied unemployment compensation on the ground that she had failed to accept suitable work without "good cause." In an opinion by Justice Brennan, the Supreme Court held that this denial of benefits violated the Free Exercise Clause. Because of her religious practice, the Court said, she suffered the economic equivalent of a financial fine, forcing her to choose between abandoning her religion or forfeiting her benefits. The Court then considered whether the state had a compelling interest in denying benefits, and found none—not surprisingly, given that most other states would have granted the benefits. Later cases applied *Sherbert* even when the individual

---

4　374 U.S. 398 (1963).

acquired her religious scruples only after accepting a job or where the scruples were apparently based on idiosyncratic religious interpretations.[5]

Probably the most notable application of *Sherbert* was *Wisconsin v. Yoder*.[6] In accord with the practices of the Old Order Amish, the defendant had refused to send his children to school after the eighth grade. He was convicted for violating Wisconsin's compulsory education law, which required school attendance for an additional two years. In an opinion by Chief Justice Burger, the Supreme Court reversed the conviction. The Court began by observing that the defendant's conduct was rooted in religious belief, not on a "subjective evaluation and rejection of the contemporary secular values accepted by the majority, much as Thoreau rejected the social values of his time and isolated himself at Walden Pond." The Court agreed that the state had a compelling interest in assuring its citizens sufficient education to participate intelligently in the political system and to function in society. But the Court was unconvinced that an additional two years of education would do much to advance those purposes, at least in the case of the Amish, who had a good record for preparing their children for life as part of their self-sufficient society.

Yoder illustrates the concerns that some commentators had about the *Sherbert* approach. As the distinction between the Amish and the Thoreau disciple made clear, the Court was granting an exemption specifically to religious individuals that it would not extend to others with equally heartfelt but secular beliefs. (Is this consistent with the definition of religion in *Seeger*?) Similarly, while Sherbert had a constitutional right to turn down Saturday work because of her religion, a woman with an equally strong commitment to caring for a disabled child would have had no constitutional protection. Rather than eliminating discrimination against religion, critics argued, the *Sherbert* approach preferred religion and provided what amounted to mandatory affirmative action for religious minorities. This, they said, was not only beyond the requirements of the Free Exercise Clause, but a violation of the Establishment Clause. The Establishment Clause violation was compounded, they argued, because the Court not only preferred religion over nonreligion but some religions over others. *Yoder* emphasizes the long track record of the Amish as upstanding members of society, with an implied contrast to religious communes and other upstart groups. Moreover, while purporting to uphold the right to free

---

[5] *Hobbie v. Unemployment Appeals Commission*, 480 U.S. 136 (1987); *Thomas v. Review Board*, 450 U.S. 707 (1981); *Frazee v. Illinois Dept. of Employment Security*, 489 U.S. 829 (1989).

[6] 406 U.S. 205 (1972).

exercise, the Court was actually forcing the children in question to participate in a religious society that they might well want to escape, upholding the rights of the Amish Order but perhaps infringing those of individual children.

Despite these criticisms, the *Sherbert* compelling interest test remained the law for twenty-seven years. During this period, the Court struggled with defining the contours of the test. Recall that the government only had to provide a compelling justification when a state law burdened religion. The Court devoted some effort to refining the concept of burden. It refused to find a "burden" in two notable cases involving Native Americans. In *Bowen v. Roy*,[7] the Court held that the government could assign social security numbers to welfare applicants and use them over the applicants' religious objection, though it might not be able to require the applicants themselves to apply for the social security numbers. In *Lyng v. Northwest Indian Cemetery Protective Association*,[8] the Court found no free exercise objection to a plan to build a road on government property through a sacred site used for Indian rituals. Like the assignment of the social security number, building a road on the government's own property was simply a matter of the government's internal operations. Although the Court conceded that the road "could have devastating effects on traditional Indian religious practices," it did not "coerce individuals into acting contrary to their religious beliefs." Hence, it was not covered by the Free Exercise Clause, and the government had no need to demonstrate a compelling interest.

If the government had been required to demonstrate a compelling interest in *Lyng*, it might well have won the case anyway, simply because the Court seemed willing to accept almost *any* state interest as compelling in this context. In *United States v. Lee*,[9] the Court apparently considered the social security system more inviolate than public education. Like *Yoder*, *Lee* involved the Amish, but in *Lee*, the Court found no basis for an exemption. A member of the Old Order Amish, who employed several other Amish workers, refused to pay social security tax because "the Amish believe it sinful not to provide for their own elderly and needy and therefore are religiously opposed to the national social security system." The Amish actually had an excellent record of providing for their elderly without the assistance of the federal government. Nevertheless, the Court held that the government had a compelling interest in forcing them into the social security system, apparently on the theory that

---

[7] 476 U.S. 693 (1986).

[8] 485 U.S. 439 (1988).

[9] 455 U.S. 252 (1982).

allowing any exemptions from social security would unravel the entire system.

Perhaps the nadir of the *Sherbert* test was *Goldman v. Weinberger*.[10] The Court rejected a free exercise challenge to an air force regulation that prohibited a Jewish military doctor from wearing a yarmulke (skullcap). Apart from the usual invocation of the military's interest in maintaining discipline and order, the government was unable to come up with any concrete suggestion about how the yarmulke would interfere in the slightest with his military activities. Indeed, one lower court judge suggested that the government's compelling interest was precisely the need to teach soldiers to obey even completely pointless orders. Nevertheless, the Court deferred to the military's judgment.

By 1990, the status of the compelling interest test was somewhat ambiguous. On the one hand, *Sherbert* contained broad, powerful language creating a right to religious exemptions. On the other hand, when push came to shove, the Court never seemed to grant exemptions except in the context of unemployment compensation (apart from *Yoder*). Something had to give. In the end, it was the *Sherbert* rule.

B. *Smith* and Religious Exemptions

The era of the compelling interest test came to an end in 1990 with Justice Scalia's majority opinion in *Employment Division v. Smith*.[11] Two Native Americans had been fired by a private drug rehabilitation organization because they used peyote, a hallucinogen, as a sacrament in a ceremony of the Native American Church. Their applications for unemployment compensation were denied under a state law disqualifying employees discharged for work-related "misconduct." When the case first came before the Supreme Court, the Court remanded for a determination of whether sacramental peyote use violated Oregon's criminal law. On remand, the Oregon court held that the criminal statute did apply to the conduct in question. When the case returned to the Supreme Court, the Court focused on the issue of criminality, apparently reasoning that if the state was entitled to criminalize certain conduct then it could also penalize that conduct by denying unemployment benefits.

Justice Scalia conceded that the state could not ban forms of conduct "only when they are engaged in for religious reasons, or only because of the religious belief that they display." Thus, the state could not prohibit bowing before a golden calf. But the state's drug law was not aimed at religious practice and was concededly

---

[10]   475 U.S. 503 (1986).
[11]   494 U.S. 872 (1990).

constitutional as to most drug users. Reviewing the case law, Justice Scalia concluded that the Court had "never held that an individual's religious beliefs excuse him from compliance with an otherwise valid law prohibiting conduct that the State is free to regulate."

Smith recognized two exceptions. First, as in *Yoder*, the Court had sometimes granted exceptions in cases that "have involved not the Free Exercise Clause alone, but the Free Exercise Clause in conjunction with other constitutional protections." *Yoder* was such a hybrid case, since it involved the right of parents to direct the education of their children, a right that itself enjoys some constitutional protection. Second, as in the *Sherbert* line of unemployment cases, the Court had required religious exemptions when the government had already provided for individualized treatment. *Sherbert* and its progeny "stand for the proposition that where the State has in place a system of individual exemptions, it may not refuse to extend that system to cases of 'religious hardship' without compelling reason." But these decisions had "nothing to do with an across-the-board criminal prohibition on a particular form of conduct."

Justice Scalia offered a series of arguments against use of the compelling interest test. Use of the test had sometimes involved a determination of whether a practice was "central" to a religious practice (thereby making the regulation a severe burden). But Justice Scalia insisted that the courts had no business making such theological assessments. Thus, the compelling interest test would have to apply to "all actions thought to be religiously commanded," central or not. In a highly diverse society, this could require religious exemptions from a huge range of civic obligations, "ranging from compulsory military service, to the payment of taxes, to health and safety regulation such as manslaughter and child neglect laws, compulsory vaccination laws, drug laws, and traffic laws, to social welfare legislation such as minimum wage laws, child labor laws, animal cruelty laws, environmental protection laws, and laws providing for equality of opportunity for the races." In other First Amendment contexts, the compelling interest test produces "equality of treatment," but here it would produce a "constitutional anomaly": the "private right to ignore generally applicable laws." Better, he said, to leave religious exemptions to the legislatures, despite the admitted risk that they might tend to favor more mainstream religions.

The *Smith* decision was received with dismay in many quarters. Congress almost unanimously adopted the Religious Freedom Restoration Act (RFRA), which was intended to overturn *Smith* and restore the compelling interest test. In *City of Boerne v. Flores,*[12] however, the Court held RFRA unconstitutional as applied to the states. All of the Justices agreed that Congress could not use its power to pass civil rights legislation simply on the basis of disagreement with the Court's rulings, though three Justices continued to express doubts about the validity of *Smith* itself.

It should be noted, however, that *Bourne* applied only to state governments because it was based on federalism. Consequently, RFRA remains in effect with regard to the federal government. In *Burwell v. Hobby Lobby Stores,*[13] a five-Justice majority held that RFRA immunized a closely held corporation from being required to provide contraception coverage to female employees. The majority concluded that RFRA protected the religious scruples of the owners, who sincerely objected to providing insurance for actions by employees that violated their religious views. The majority found that the federal government had a less restrictive alternative: extending to for-profit corporations an optional mechanism already provided to non-profit religious organizations. Justice Kennedy concurred to emphasize the narrowness of the decision in applying only to contraception (indeed, on the facts, only to forms of contraception that operate after intercourse has already occurred). He also stressed the existence of an off-the-rack accommodation already devised by the government, showing that universal compliance was not critical to the health care law. The four dissenters expressed concern that the Court had opened the door for corporations to object to coverage for a wide range of medical procedures and to claim religious exemptions from anti-discrimination and other laws. They also suggested that publicly held corporations might well try to take advantage of the ruling. *Burwell* makes it clear that, as a practical matter, *Smith* has no significance as applied to the federal government, given the existence of RCRA.

State governments, however, are given great leeway under *Smith* to prohibit religious practices, even those essential to religion. But *Smith* remains a controversial decision. We describe the debate over *Smith* in the next section.

C. *Smith* and Original Intent

Given Justice Scalia's advocacy of originalism, it is ironic that this has been one of the major grounds of criticism of his *Smith* opinion. In her dissent in *City of Boerne,* Justice O'Connor mustered much of the historical evidence against Scalia's view, drawing on the work of constitutional historians. For instance, several state

---

[12] 521 U.S. 507 (1997).

[13] 573 U.S. 682 (2014).

constitutions protected religious exercise except when it harmed specific state interests. In New York, the exception was for "acts of licentiousness" and "practices inconsistent with the peace or safety of this State." In Maryland, it was for any disturbance of "the good order, peace or safety of the State", infringement of "the laws of morality," or injury to "others, in their natural, civil, or religious rights." The Northwest Ordinance provided that no person "demeaning himself in a peaceable and orderly manner" shall be "molested on account of his mode of worship or religious sentiments." These formulations seem to contemplate conduct, not just private worship.

Justice O'Connor devoted particular attention to James Madison's views, given his central role in the adoption of the First Amendment. In the debates over the Virginia Declaration of Rights, Madison's proposed language would have protected the "full and free exercise" of religion, "unless under color of religion the preservation of equal liberty, and the existence of the State be manifestly endangered." Later, in supporting a Bill for Establishing Religious Freedom drafted by Jefferson, Madison drafted his famous "Memorial and Remonstrance Against Religious Assessments." In the "Memorial and Remonstrance," Madison argued that free exercise entails a "duty toward the Creator":

> This duty is precedent both in order of time and degree of obligation, to the claims of Civil Society . . . [E]very man who becomes a member of any Civil Society, [must] do it with a saving of his allegiance to the Universal Sovereign. We maintain therefore that in matters of Religion, no man's right is abridged by the institution of Civil Society, and that Religion is wholly exempt from its cognizance.

Similarly, Jefferson held that the federal government was constitutionally forbidden "from intermeddling with religious institutions, their doctrines, discipline, or exercises."

Justice O'Connor also observed that the "practice of the colonies and early States bears out the conclusion that, at the time the Bill of Rights was ratified, it was accepted that government should, when possible, accommodate religious practice." For example, Quakers were often exempted from the duty to swear an oath of allegiance, and most states exempted conscientious objectors from conscription. In addition, she noted, "North Carolina and Maryland excused Quakers from the requirement of removing their hats in courts; Rhode Island exempted Jews from the requirements of the state marriage laws; and Georgia allowed groups of European immigrants to organize whole towns according to their own faith."

As Justice Scalia pointed out in his own *Boerne* concurrence, Justice O'Connor's arguments are far from ironclad. The state constitutions typically applied only to regulations made "for," "in respect of," or "on account of" religion, a description that might not apply to neutral laws of general application. Moreover, the provisos about "good order" and so forth could be read broadly, since "peace" and "order" were often taken to encompass the obligations to obey general laws in Eighteenth Century usage. Nor are the religious exemptions granted by early legislatures decisive, since they do not show that the legislators felt constitutionally obligated to provide the exemptions. Still, these early exemptions do shed light on conceptions of religious freedom during the Founding period.

D. *Smith* and Constitutional Values

Justice Scalia might have been right that the historical record is inconclusive. But the question remains whether, as its critics insist, *Smith* is inconsistent with the text of the Free Exercise Clause and its underlying goals. As Justice Scalia conceded in *Boerne*, criticism of *Smith* "has, of course, great popular attraction." After all, he added, who "can possibly be against the abstract proposition that government should not, even in its general, nondiscriminatory laws, place unreasonable burdens upon religious practice?" Even the resolutely secular might well agree, provided that the exemptions encompass a sufficiently broad range of "ultimate concerns." What is most disturbing about *Smith* to its critics may be that it seems to give little credence to these values, treating the most heartfelt religious convictions as entitled to no more respect from government than any passing consumer whim.

But Justice Scalia is right that this "abstract proposition" does not completely resolve the issue. Apart from the historical evidence, two arguments can be mustered against the compelling interest test and in favor of *Smith*.

One argument is that exemptions violate the Establishment Clause. Indeed, in *City of Boerne*, Justice Stevens argued in a concurrence that RFRA violated the First Amendment by providing the religious "with a legal weapon that no atheist or agnostic can obtain." Such a "governmental preference for religion, as opposed to irreligion" violates the First Amendment, according to Justice Stevens. But whether exemptions "favor" religion depends on our assessment of the baseline. In *Smith*, for example, if we view the baseline as being the ban on peyote, then the exemption provided an advantage to religious users of peyote that would not be available to others. But we might view the baseline as being a legal regime that accommodates both pressing secular needs (psychiatric uses of drugs) and the practices of mainstream religions (sacramental wine during Prohibition.) Then the refusal to exempt the Native American Church seems discriminatory. So the preference argument turns on the choice of baselines. As we will see in the next chapter, the Court has actually been fairly hospitable to government accommodation of religion, which deprives this argument against *Smith* of some force.

A second argument, which seems less persuasive despite Scalia's heavy reliance on it, is that the compelling interest test was unmanageable. Scalia's opinion in *Smith* suggested that the test would open a floodgate of litigation, and that it was impossible to apply the test in a principled way. Related concerns are that the availability of exemptions would lead to fraudulent claims or would create an incentive to join minority religions. Experience under the *Sherbert* regime and under RFRA did not confirm these fears, with the possible exception of prison litigation. True, there was a wide range of cases, including some that might be viewed skeptically, but the practical impact on state government did not seem overwhelming, nor did the judicial rulings seem any less principled than in any other area of civil rights or constitutional law.

The biggest fear about *Smith* is that it allows the state to crush minority religions out of sheer indifference. State regulations that serve no pressing purpose may turn out to be deathblows to core religious practices, but may remain in place because nobody cares enough to bother adjusting them (or worse, because the religion in question just seems too weird to be taken seriously). One way to deal with at least the most extreme cases would be to consider religiously mandated practices to be the equivalent of symbolic speech. As we saw in Chapter 3, ordinary conduct like sleeping in the park or burning a piece of paper enjoys a modest level of constitutional protection under the *O'Brien* test when undertaken for communicative purposes. The test requires that the government regulation be narrowly tailored to some significant goal. We might also apply this test to symbolic religious actions. This is a notably less rigorous standard than the compelling interest test, but seems closer to the Court's actual practice in the *Sherbert* era. As we will see at the close of this chapter, despite its sweeping language, *Smith* itself may also offer some room for protecting religious minorities.

III. The Current Status of Free Exercise

For now, whatever its critics may think, *Smith* is clearly the law. But it would be mistake to view *Smith* as the death knell of the Free Exercise Clause. As we will see, reports of the death of the Clause have been somewhat exaggerated. It should also be noted that religious freedom laws remain relevant despite *Boerne*: RFRA itself is still applicable to the federal government (though not the states); a post-RFRA federal statute applies to the religious claims of prisoners and to those of churches in land-use cases; and about a dozen states have passed their own versions of RFRA. In addition, some state supreme courts have refused to follow *Smith* in interpreting their state constitutions. But outside of these special circumstances, *Smith* remains the governing standard.

A. Targeted Regulation of Religion

Smith dealt with a law that on its face had no application to religion. Quite a different rule applies to targeted regulations. Apart from the Free Exercise Clause, such regulations may run afoul of other constitutional limitations. Some rules targeting religion may violate the Free Speech clause. In *Rosenberger v. Rector and Visitors of the University of Virginia*,[14] the Court struck down a University of Virginia rule denying expense payments to student religious groups for printing costs, when such payments were generally available to other student groups. The Court found that the University had selected for "disfavored treatment those student journalistic efforts with religious editorial viewpoints." As the dissent pointed out, however, the University refused to fund advocacy by other religious groups or by anti-religious groups. The Court responded that it is "as objectionable to exclude both a theistic and an atheistic perspective on the debate as it is to exclude one, the other, or yet another political, economic, or social viewpoint."

Under some circumstances, the Establishment Clause also provides some protection from regulations targeting religion. In *Larson v. Valente*,[15] the Court struck down a Minnesota statute that imposed reporting requirements on religious organizations soliciting more than half of their funds from nonmembers. The Court began with the premise that the "clearest command of the Establishment Clause is that one religious denomination cannot be officially preferred over another." By in effect requiring some religions to register but not others, Minnesota was engaging in such a preference, and it was unable to point to a compelling interest for doing so. This no-preference principle has some application to the exemption problem. Often, a particular sect has enough power to win an exemption. Under the no-preference principle, in order to be constitutional, the exemption must be broad enough to cover all similarly situated religions, not just one.

Most significantly, the Free Exercise Clause continues to apply to rules that target religious practices for regulation. In *Church of the Lukumi Babalu Aye, Inc. v. Hialeah*,[16] a post-*Smith* decision, the

---

[14] 515 U.S. 819 (1995).

[15] 456 U.S. 228 (1982).

[16] 508 U.S. 520 (1993).

Court struck down local ordinances that were targeted against a church's use of animal sacrifice. All nine Justices concluded that the ordinances were unconstitutional. Justice Kennedy's majority opinion applied the *Smith* standard, found that the ordinances were not "neutral and of general applicability" but rather were enacted with the intention and effect of suppressing a religion, and applied strict scrutiny. The ordinances flunked strict scrutiny. They were underinclusive with respect to the two interests cited in support of them: protecting public health and preventing cruelty to animals. Justice Scalia, joined by Chief Justice Rehnquist, filed a separate statement agreeing with much of the majority opinion, but objecting to the inquiry concerning the subjective motivation of the city council. Several other Justices concurred but argued that *Smith* was wrongly decided.

Church of the Lukumi indicates that *McDaniel v. Paty*[17] also remains good law. In *McDaniel*, the Court invalidated a state prohibition on ministers serving as delegates to the state's constitutional convention. Although many states had rules limiting the participation of ministers in government when the Constitution was enacted, the Court unanimously held the statute unconstitutional. Such a law can hardly be considered a neutral law of general application.

Church of the Lukumi opens the door to the same kinds of attacks on intentional discrimination under the Free Exercise Clause as have been allowed by racial minorities under the Equal Protection Clause. Despite the difficulties of proving discriminatory intent, this can be a powerful weapon. Civil rights litigators have become skilled in using historians and political scientists as expert witnesses to prove discriminatory intent. Moreover, the discriminatory intent need not coincide with the original enactment of the ordinance. In the voting rights area, it is well settled that a law is unconstitutional if it either was passed with discriminatory intent or else was kept in place for discriminatory purposes. By analogy, it should also be possible to attack a state law that was passed for neutral purposes, if the legislature later rejected reform efforts because of hostility to the specific religions seeking exemptions. Although obviously more difficult to litigate than the *Sherbert* test, the intent test does provide some leverage for religious groups in litigation.

The Court followed, and perhaps expanded, this exception to the *Smith* doctrine, in *Masterpiece Cakeshop v. Colorado Civil Rights Comm'n*.[18] A same-sex couple had visited Masterpiece Cakeshop, a bakery in Colorado, to make inquiries about ordering a cake for their

---

[17]   435 U.S. 618 (1978).

[18]   ___ U.S. ___, 138 S.Ct. 1719, 201 L.Ed.2d 35 (2018).

wedding. The baker told them he would not create a cake for their wedding because of his religious opposition to same-sex marriages. The couple filed a charge with the state civil rights commission alleging discrimination on the basis of sexual orientation. At one hearing, members of the commissions made several skeptical or perhaps disparaging statements. At a later hearing, one of the commissioners went further. He said, "I would also like to reiterate what we said in the hearing or the last meeting. Freedom of religion and religion has been used to justify all kinds of discrimination throughout history, whether it be slavery, whether it be the holocaust, whether it be—I mean, we—we can list hundreds of situations where freedom of religion has been used to justify discrimination. And to me it is one of the most despicable pieces of rhetoric that people can use to—to use their religion to hurt others." There was also some question as to whether the Commission had successfully distinguished the case from some earlier rulings in which it had upheld the right of owners to refuse to bake cakes with religiously based, anti-gay sentiments. Based on these circumstances, the Court concluded that the "neutral and respectful consideration" to which to which the shop owner "was entitled was compromised here," and the commission's "treatment of his case has some elements of a clear and impermissible hostility toward the sincere religious beliefs that motivated his objection."

The Court's rationale explicitly left for another day the larger question whether wedding vendors or businesses can decline service to same-sex couples where the record does not contain any hostile comments about religious objections or claims that religious objectors are singled out for especially harsh treatment. But several passages in the majority opinion suggest resistance to any broad, religiously based exemption for merchants. The opinion emphasized that American "society has come to the recognition that gay persons and gay couples cannot be treated as social outcasts or as inferior in dignity or worth, " such that "the exercise of their freedom on terms equal to others must be given great weight by the courts." It also said that while "religious and philosophical objections are protected, it is a general rule that such objections do not allow business owners to deny protected persons equal access to goods and service under a neutral and generally applicable public accommodations law." And it said that any principle favoring bakers like Phillips would have to be "sufficiently constrained, lest all purveyors of goods and services who object to gay marriages for moral and religious reasons in effect be allowed to put up signs saying 'no goods or services will be sold if they will be used for gay marriages,' something that would impose a serious stigma on gay persons." With Justice Kennedy retiring shortly after this decision was released, the import of these words is less clear than it might have been had he stayed on the Court.

B.   The Inviolability of Theological Claims

If there is one clear principle of constitutional law, it is that no branch of the government can rule a theological statement true or false. For instance, in *United States v. Ballard*,[19] the defendants had been convicted for mail fraud, having represented themselves as divine messengers with healing powers. The Court held that the trial court properly refused to submit the truth of these religious claims to the jury.

It remains more controversial whether the defendants' sincerity in making the claims could have been submitted to the jury—the conflicting considerations being the incongruity of secular courts deciding the sincerity of religious beliefs, and the undesirability of creating a religious safe harbor for con men. Current law seems clear that anyone seeking to take advantage of a religious exemption, whether grounded in statute or constitutional law, *can* be required to establish the existence of a sincere religious claim.

The *Ballard* rule applies only when one element in implementing a law is the truth or falsity of a statement. It does not apply to ordinary regulation of conduct. For instance, the state has the right to prohibit the sale of dangerous or ineffective drugs. Simply because the defendants' belief in the product is based on religion, the government does not have to share the same belief. But what the government cannot do is to punish the making of religious statements as such. Thus, the statement "God approves of this drug" cannot be considered false advertising. For constitutional purposes, there is no such thing as a punishable false theological statement.

For similar reasons, the courts are leery of involvement in ecclesiastic disputes. Thus, it was unconstitutional for a state court to determine whether a man had properly qualified as a Catholic chaplain, in the course of determining whether he was entitled to funds under a will.[20] The state court had no jurisdiction to determine this matter of ecclesiastical law. Similarly, when local churches seek to withdraw from a national body, it is unconstitutional for the courts to attempt to decide whether the national body has deviated from the faith.[21] Nor can the local courts resolve disputes over church property by considering whether church authorities properly complied with ecclesiastical law or whether a church tribunal improperly exercised

---

[19]   322 U.S. 78 (1944).

[20]   *Gonzalez v. Roman Catholic Archbishop of Manila,* 280 U.S. 1 (1929).

[21]   *Presbyterian Church in the United States v. Mary Elizabeth Blue Hull Memorial Presbyterian Church,* 393 U.S. 440 (1969).

jurisdiction.[22] Such disputes must be decided on the basis of neutral property rules that do not entangle the court in theological issues.[23]

The civil inviolability of theological assertions seems so fundamental that it could be derived from several parts of the Constitution. Rejecting the truth claims of one religious group in favor of another would be giving preferred status to the latter, in violation of the Establishment Clause. It also would violate religious liberty under the Free Exercise Clause.

C. Selection of Ministers

The Court seemed to carve out another exception from the *Smith* rule in *Hosanna-Tabor Evangelical Church*.[24] The case involved a teacher in a religious school who was allegedly fired in retaliation for filing a lawsuit in which she had claimed that the school discriminated against her on the basis of her disability. The Court held that she qualified as a minister because she performed some religious duties and was part of a special category of teachers at the school who were labeled "ministers" after some theological training. The majority was unimpressed by the arguments that teachers outside this category performed the same duties when needed and that her religious duties took only 45 minutes of her work day.

The Court recognized a "ministerial exception" prohibiting ministers from suing their churches for firing them. In the Court's view, "requiring a church to accept or retain an unwanted minister, or punishing a church for failing to do so, intrudes upon more than a mere employment decision." Rather, "such action interferes with the internal governance of the church, depriving the church of control over the selection of those who will personify its beliefs."

Notably, the Court bypassed the opportunity to use the *Smith* framework. It would not be hard to argue that the case involved a hybrid right—freedom of association (of the kind involved in *Dale*, discussed in the last chapter) plus freedom of religion. The Court could then have applied the compelling interest test, concluding that the interest in eliminating discrimination against the disabled was insufficiently compelling. Instead, the Court chose to forgo the use of *Smith*.

The Court distinguished *Smith* on the ground that *Smith* involved "only outward physical acts." In contrast, the case before it "concern[ed] government interference with an internal church decision that affects the faith and mission of the church itself." The breadth of this exception from *Smith* remains unclear. On its face, it

---

[22] *Serbian Eastern Orthodox Diocese v. Milivojevich*, 426 U.S. 696 (1976).

[23] See *Jones v. Wolf*, 443 U.S. 595 (1979).

[24] 565 U.S. 171 (2012).

seems to apply only to a church's decision to discharge a minister. But it is also possible that this case marks a possible move away from *Smith* as a guiding rule, at least when the Court thinks that a core church interest is at stake.

D. Exemptions from Neutral Laws After *Smith*

How much room does *Smith* leave to attack the application of neutral laws to religious conduct? More than one might think. Consider two examples.

One recurring issue is the administration of medical assistance such as blood transfusions contrary to the patient's religious beliefs. Assume a neutral state law authorizes administration of life saving treatment over a patient's refusal. Does *Smith* eliminate any Free Exercise Claim? Perhaps, but not necessarily. The hybrid right analysis offers a possible escape. The right to bodily integrity has been recognized as a component of substantive due process, including the right under at least some circumstances to refuse life-prolonging medical assistance. Even if this due process right would be insufficient on its own, it provides a foothold for a Free Exercise hybrid claim.

A second example is also widespread. Many landmark preservation cases involve church buildings that are no longer effectively serving their purposes. States are reluctant to allow modification to these historic buildings. Provided that the state law has some hardship exemption, the preservation law may fall into the "individualized determination" exception to *Smith*. Another possible argument is that the Takings Clause and the Free Exercise Clause could combine into a hybrid claim. (As noted earlier, a federal statute might also support the church's challenge.)

Thus, at least if they are interpreted liberally, the twin exceptions from the *Smith* rule may be quite broad. Still, they are not unlimited. For example, the right to use drugs has never been given any constitutional recognition, so a hybrid claim in *Smith* itself would have been difficult. Moreover, *Smith* does little to define the parameters of the exceptions, so it remains to be seen whether they will be broadly interpreted.

One factor that may influence the interpretation of these exceptions is whether they are perceived as principled. In the *Smith* opinion itself, the exceptions are presented with little justification. They have the appearance of being clever ways of distinguishing past cases that Justice Scalia lacked the votes to overrule. So understood, the exceptions are unlikely to be read broadly except by judges wanting to undermine *Smith* itself. But good arguments can actually be made in favor of both exceptions.

Consider the exception for hybrid claims. This can be defended in two ways. First, one of the rationales for *Smith* was that a contrary rule would simply leave an unlimited universe of conduct open to religious exemption claims. Requiring a nexus with another constitutional right somewhat narrows the universe of possible claims. Second, the fact that a claim involves religious exercise means that a strong interest in individual autonomy is involved. Since many other constitutional rights are based at least in part on this interest, the religious aspect indicates that the overall claim lies within the core of the other constitutional right, not on the periphery. For instance, freedom of association is designed to protect intimate and expressive organizations, and religious organizations seem to be a paradigm case. Thus, the two rights really do reinforce each other.

The other *Smith* exception involves individualized hardship provisions. Here, again, there is a principled argument for the exception. It is quite difficult to police such individualized determinations to ensure that they are untainted by bias toward a particular religion. A compelling interest test helps screen out discriminatory denials. For example, it is hard to believe that in *Sherbert* the state uniformly denied compensation to people with unmanageable secular work conflicts. Yet, it would be difficult to prove intentional discrimination against work conflicts caused by religious beliefs. Also, the determination of hardships in religion cases is sometimes entangled with determinations about the religion itself. For example, if a church seeks a variance from landmark preservation, part of its argument involves the incompatibility of the building with the church's mission and priorities, which are not secular matters. So there is an arguable basis for the "individualized treatment" exception from *Smith*.

Even if these exceptions are defensible, their scope remains unclear. Over two decades after *Smith*, lower courts have yet to agree on how to apply the case. One court refused to apply the hybrid test because the judges found it nonsensical; others apply it where there is a colorable, non-Free Exercise claim; still others require that the non-Free Exercise claim be independently viable.[25] A regulation banning police officers from wearing beards was held not to be a "neutral law of general applicability" because it also contained a medical exemption.[26] But another court held that a law banning discrimination against unmarried couples was general enough, even

---

[25] See *Kissinger v. Board of Trustees*, 5 F.3d 177 (6th Cir. 1993); *Brown v. Hot, Sexy, and Safer Productions*, 68 F.3d 525 (1st Cir. 1995); *Swanson v. Guthrie Ind. School Dist.*, 135 F.3d 694 (10th Cir. 1998).

[26] *Fraternal Order of Police Newark Lodge No. 12 v. City of Newark*, 170 F.3d 359 (1999).

though it contained exemptions.[27] So far, the Supreme Court has shown no interest in straightening out the confusion.

At this point, the reader may be convinced that the religion clauses are not only controversial but recondite. As we will see, however, the Establishment Clause makes the Free Exercise Clause look simple.

FURTHER READINGS

Richard F. Duncan, *Free Exercise Is Dead, Long Live Free Exercise: Smith, Lukumi, and the General Applicability Requirement*, 3 U. Pa. J. Const. L. 850 (2001).

Abner Greene, *Religious Freedom and (Other) Civil Liberties: Is There a Middle Ground?*, 9 Harv. J. L & Pol'y 161 (2015).

Ronald J. Krotoszynski, Jr., *If Judges Were Angels: Religious Equality, Free Exercise, and the (Underappreciated) Merits of Smith*, 102 Nw. U. L. Rev. 1189 (2008).

Douglas Laycock, *The Remnants of Free Exercise*, 1990 Sup. Ct. Rev. 1.

Brian Leiter, Why Tolerate Religion (2012).

Christopher Lund, *Free Exercise Reconceived: The Logic and Limits of* Hosanna-Tabor, 108 Nw. U. L. Rev. 1183 (2014).

Ira Lupu and Robert Tuttle, *The Mystery of Unanimity in* Hosanna-Tabor Evangelical Lutheran Church v. EEOC, 20 Lewis & Clark L. Rev. 1265 (2017).

William F. Marshall, *In Defense of* Smith *and Free Exercise Revisionism*, 58 U. Chi. L. Rev. 308 (1991).

John Thomas Noonan, The Lustre of Our Country: The American Experience of Religious Freedom (1998).

Steven D. Smith, *Blooming Confusion: Madison's Mixed Legacy*, 75 Ind. L.J. 61 (2000).

Eugene Volokh, *A Common-Law Model for Religious Exemptions*, 46 UCLA L. Rev. 1465 (1999).

---

[27] *Thomas v. Anchorage Equal Rights Comm'n*, 165 F.3d 692 (9th Cir. 1999), vacated on other grounds, 220 F.3d 1134 (9th Cir. 2000) (en banc).

Chapter 14

THE ESTABLISHMENT CLAUSE

From a lawyer's point of view, the Establishment Clause may be the most frustrating part of First Amendment law. The cases are a tangle of divergent doctrines and seemingly conflicting results. The Court seems unable to settle on a governing test, and what efforts it has made in that direction often turn out to be vague and unhelpful.

As we will see, there are several reasons for this situation. Part of the doctrinal chaos is due to the diversity of views on the Court. Because there are multiple judicial viewpoints, the outcomes of cases are determined by shifting coalitions, causing an incoherent pattern of decisions. Also, the Establishment Clause involves government support for expressive activities, which generally presents analytic difficulties. We have already seen in the free speech context how difficult it is to distinguish legitimate from illegitimate subsidy schemes. Here, the difficulty is compounded because any interpretation of the Establishment Clause must also come to grips with the Free Exercise Clause, as well as with the Speech Clause's prohibition on viewpoint discrimination. Not only must the government avoid promoting religion, it must also avoid discriminating against or inhibiting religion. At times, the government seems to be walking a Teflon tightrope, with little hope of avoiding a fall.

Presenting a convincing, coherent vision of the Establishment Clause is a task beyond the scope of this book. A more feasible goal is to provide an orientation to the problems that make the Establishment Clause so challenging. Section I covers the basics: the origins and purposes of the Clause, plus a quick overview of doctrinal evolution and current schools of thought. Section II describes three tests that have had some support on the Court, while Section III traces the twisted doctrinal evolution in some crucial areas (religion in public and private schools, and religious symbolism on government property). Section IV probes the most vexing Establishment Clause problem: to what extent can the government accommodate the burdens placed on religious practice by its programs, without impermissibly aiding religion? Since this chapter is also the end of the book, the chapter closes with a few brief thoughts about the present state of First Amendment law.

I. The Basics

To understand current disputes over the Establishment Clause, it is necessary to know something about how the debate has developed. We will "begin at the beginning" with the history leading up to adoption of the Clause, looking also at the conflicting lessons that have been drawn from that history. Then, we will try to get a quick sense of how the modern Supreme Court's view of the issues has evolved. Finally, we will examine the two most prominent schools of thought among contemporary commentators on this issue.

A. The Origin of the Establishment Clause

The history of religious freedom was sketched in Chapter 13, and much of what is said there is also helpful in discussing the Establishment Clause. Only a little needs to be added relating to the Establishment Clause.

In the colonies, statutes often regulated conduct for religious reasons. For instance, Massachusetts banned "unnecessary walking" on the Sabbath, and Connecticut provided for public whipping as punishment for "cursing or reproaching the true God." Connecticut also required every household to keep a Bible. New England states were especially aggressive in financial support for churches. In most, local residents were entitled to vote on which sect to support, and dissenters were allowed to subscribe to another Protestant church instead. Opponents of the system included Baptists and followers of Roger Williams, who believed that the church was corrupted by state support. Nevertheless, these systems did not entirely disappear until the early Nineteenth Century.

The most notable struggle over establishment took place in Virginia. Thomas Jefferson criticized the Virginia legal regime for limiting the rights of dissenters. For instance, non-believers in the Trinity could not hold any public office, and might even be faced with a loss of property rights. Jefferson, a deist, viewed this as a form of "religious slavery." Following independence, a struggle took place between advocates of establishment (most notably Patrick Henry) and opponents such as Jefferson, Mason, and Madison. The advocates kept trying to expand the Anglican church's privileges, while the opponents tried to eliminate them. In 1784, the supporters brought forward legislation requiring each individual to support a Christian sect, whether Anglican or another chosen by the individual. A contribution to the schools was allowed as a fallback option for individuals who could find no appropriate religious beneficiary.

Mason and others asked Madison to draft a response, and he replied with his famous "Memorial and Remonstrance Against Religious Assessments." He argued that a true religion would not need the support of law, that no one should be taxed to support a religious institution of any kind, and that establishments were incompatible with religious freedom. He also criticized the Virginia

Bill for supporting only Christian churches: "Who does not see that the same authority which can establish Christianity, in exclusion of all other Religions, may establish with the same ease any particular sect of Christians, in exclusion of all other Sects." Madison also held that any forced religious contribution was a "signal of persecution" that "degrades from the equal rank of Citizens all those whose opinions in Religion do not bend to those of the Legislative authority."

The upshot was the enactment of the Virginia Bill for Religious Liberty drafted by Thomas Jefferson. The preamble proclaims that "Almighty God hath created the mind free; that all attempts to influence it by temporal punishments or burthens, or by civil incapacitations, tend only to beget habits of hypocrisy and meanness, and are a departure from the plan of the Holy author of our religion, who being Lord both of body and mind, yet chose not to propagate it by coercions on either." The preamble continued that:

> [T]o compel a man to furnish contributions of money for the propagation of opinions which he disbelieves, is sinful and tyrannical; that even the forcing him to support this or that teacher of his own religious persuasion, is depriving him of the comfortable liberty of giving his contributions to the particular pastor, whose morals he would make his pattern. . . .

Accordingly, the statute provided that "no man shall be compelled to frequent or support any religious worship, place, or ministry whatsoever."

The drafting history of the Establishment Clause a few years later was rather tangled. As noted in Chapter 13, Madison's proposal merely disallowed the establishment of "any national religion." At various stages in the House, this language became "no religion shall be established by law," then "Congress shall make no laws touching religion," and finally "Congress shall make no law establishing religion" (along with accompanying changes in the language regarding free exercise). Different language was proposed in the Senate. On the whole, the Senate language was narrower. The initial Senate version said "Congress shall make no law establishing One Religious Sect or Society in preference to others." Finally, the Senate settled on "Congress shall make no law establishing articles of faith or a mode of worship." The Senate language would have allowed support for "religion in general" but not preferences between religions. But this language was unacceptable to the House. In Conference Committee, the House succeeded in obtaining the ultimate language included in the Bill of Rights. Discerning any meaning from this drafting history may be like reading tea leaves.

Following adoption of the Establishment Clause, the government took somewhat inconsistent attitudes toward religion. Appeals to God in official addresses were common, as were official calls for days of thanksgiving and prayer. The First Congress hired chaplains, and the government sometimes provided support for other religious activities. On the other hand, Jefferson adamantly opposed all of these as unconstitutional. For instance, he refused to proclaim a day of thanksgiving because it would "indirectly assume to the U.S. an authority over religious exercises which the Constitution has directly precluded from them." Although the proclamation would carry no formal penalty, it would carry "some degree of proscription perhaps in public opinion." Madison waffled, but ultimately agreed with Jefferson about rejecting even ceremonial references to religion and on the unconstitutionality of government chaplains.

Several different viewpoints underlay the Establishment Clause. Evangelicals, following Roger Williams, worried that governmental connections would corrupt the church and that aid would favor more entrenched churches over newcomers such as the Baptists. Jefferson wanted a "wall of separation between church and state," primarily because he feared that religious irrationality would engulf government. Madison favored separate spheres for religion and government to prevent "usurpation on one side or the other" or "a corrupting coalition of alliance between them." He favored religious pluralism as a way of preventing particular religious factions from becoming powerful enough to oppress others. Federalism concerns also played a role, because some supporters of the federal Bill of Rights feared that the government would interfere with state establishments. Apparently they viewed religion as a local rather than national concern.

Not surprisingly, later writers have found conflicting lessons in this history. The most limited view would allow government support for religion so long as no specific religion is preferred. The current consensus, however, seems to be that the historical record on balance does not support this view. The other historical studies seem to split roughly into two groups. Those who stress the views of Jefferson, and to a lesser extent Madison, conclude that the Establishment Clause was intended to eliminate all federal jurisdiction over any religious matters, making the government strictly secular and leaving religion to the churches. Just as opponents of affirmative action say that government should be color blind, the lesson drawn by these individuals is that government should be religion blind, neither favoring nor hindering religious practices. Other writers put more stress on the evangelical supporters of religious freedom, finding support in some of Madison's views as well. These writers believe that, rather than attempting to prevent any government connection to religion, the Establishment Clause was primarily intended to protect religious minorities from coerced support of religion, while leaving the government otherwise free to recognize the importance of religion in personal and public life. Besides these differences in emphasis, writers also disagree strongly about how to read particular documents and how to interpret the views of individual thinkers.

B. Doctrinal Evolution

These divergent interpretations of history have found their way into Supreme Court opinions, which reflect similarly contradictory visions of the Establishment Clause. The Supreme Court's early opinions seemed to oscillate between conflicting visions.

The first Establishment Clause case was *Everson v. Board of Education.*[1] Justice Black's majority opinion staunchly supported separation of church and state, but then went on to uphold public busing to parochial schools as a safety measure. Justice Black, in typically vigorous prose, summarized the Establishment Clause as follows:

> The "establishment of religion" clause of the First Amendment means at least this: Neither a state nor the Federal Government can set up a church. Neither can pass laws which aid one religion, aid all religions, or prefer one religion over another. Neither can force nor influence a person to go to or remain away from church against his will or force him to profess a belief or disbelief in any religion. No person can be punished for entertaining or professing religious beliefs or disbeliefs, for church attendance or non-attendance. No tax in any amount, large or small, can be levied to support any religious activities or institutions, whatever they may be called, or whatever form they may adopt to teach or practice religion. Neither a state nor the Federal Government can, openly or secretly, participate in the affairs of any religious organizations or groups and vice versa. In the words of Jefferson, the clause against establishment of religion by law was intended to erect "a wall of separation between church and State."

Nevertheless, Black also stressed the need to "be careful, in protecting the citizens of New Jersey against state-established churches, to be sure that we do not inadvertently prohibit New Jersey from extending its general state law benefits to all its citizens without regard to their religious belief." He considered free transportation to school to be one of those general benefits. The four dissenters argued that the *Everson* holding was a breach in the wall

---

[1]   330 U.S. 1 (1947).

of separation. They emphasized that the Constitution was intended "to take every form of propagation of religion out of the realm of things which could directly or indirectly be made public business and thereby be supported in whole or in part at taxpayers' expense."

Just five years later, in *Zorach v. Clauson,*[2] the Court upheld what it took to be an accommodation of the needs of religious children. New York City had a "released time" program under which students could be released from study hall for religious lessons outside of the school building. In upholding the program, Justice Douglas stressed that "[w]e are a religious people whose institutions presuppose a Supreme Being." When the government "encourages religious instruction or cooperates with religious authorities by adjusting the schedule of public events to sectarian needs, it follows the best of our traditions" by respecting the "religious nature of our people" and accommodating "their spiritual needs." To ban accommodation would be to "show a callous indifference to religious groups."

In the two decades after *Everson*, the Court seemed to oscillate between these two attitudes. It sometimes stringently enforced separation, as by striking down school prayers, which had been widespread until then. But it also allowed special treatment for religion in the form of tax exemptions, and some kinds of assistance to parochial schools such as free textbooks. Finally, in 1971, the Court attempted a synthesis of its case law in *Lemon v. Kurtzman.*[3] *Lemon* struck down two state laws providing partial funding for teacher salaries at parochial schools. In an effort to make sense of the prior cases, the Court announced a three-part test: "First, the statute must have a secular legislative purpose; second, its principal or primary effect must be one that neither advances nor inhibits religion; finally, the statute must not foster 'an excessive government entanglement with religion.'" The salary supplements were unconstitutional because they involved excessive entanglement. In order to ensure that the money did not go for religious instruction, the state had to engage in intrusive supervision of parochial school activities. Moreover, the legislation also caused religious issues to become entangled in politics due to bitter disputes over this novel form of assistance to church-related activities.

For most of the next twenty years, *Lemon* was clearly the governing test. In more recent years, its status has been less clear. To date, it has never been overruled, and it still receives favorable mention in some majority opinions. But sometimes the Court seems to forget about it entirely. The Rehnquist Court's approach seemed

---

2   343 U.S. 306 (1952).

3   403 U.S. 602 (1971).

quite different in spirit from Burger Court opinions such as *Lemon* and the Roberts Court seems likely to hew to that path.

The shift is illustrated by two cases involving the same New York program for remedial education. Taking advantage of federal funding, New York placed public teachers into parochial schools to offer special educational programs for low-income students. In 1985, the Court declared the program unconstitutional in *Aguilar v. Felton*.[4] The Court found several flaws in the program: (1) because they worked in the parochial school, the public school teachers might be co-opted into the school's religious mission, particularly if they shared its religious orientation themselves; (2) providing materials for use in parochial schools directly subsidized them by eliminating expenses they would otherwise bear themselves; (3) the presence of public employees on church property created a graphic symbol of interdependence between church and state; and (4) the necessary government monitoring of the teachers involved excessive entanglement. But in 1997, the Court reopened the *Aguilar* litigation and overruled its prior opinion in a decision reported as *Agostini v. Felton*.[5] The Court no longer believed that there was a significant risk that public employees would be drawn into the school's religious mission, nor did it continue to categorically object to "direct" aid to parochial schools. Extensive monitoring would not be necessary once these concerns were dismissed, so the entanglement issue was eliminated. On the whole, the *Agostini* Court seemed more anxious to prevent the exclusion of religious children from an important public service than to prevent government assistance to religious institutions.

The Court continues to remain badly divided on Establishment Clause issues, as illustrated by *American Legion v. American Humanist Association*,[6] The case involved a 32-foot tall cross commemorating World War I. Six Justices filed opinions in the case. Justice Alito wrote the majority opinion, holding that the monument's age and historical context muted any message of religious endorsement. In a portion of the opinion joined only by Chief Justice Roberts and Justice Kavanaugh, he wrote that the *Lemon* test had failed to provide an effective unifying framework for Establishment Clause cases and that the Court had since followed a more context-based approach that looked to history for guidance. Justice Thomas argued that the Establishment Clause should not apply to the states and in any event should not prevent the government from using sectarian symbols. He also joined a separate opinion by Justice Gorsuch arguing that the case should be dismissed

---

[4]   473 U.S. 402 (1985).

[5]   521 U.S. 203 (1997).

[6]   ___ U.S. ___, 139 S.Ct. 2067, 204 L.Ed.2d 452 (2019).

for lack of standing because the offense felt by onlookers at religious symbols did not constitute injury in fact. Justice Kavanaugh wrote separately to indicate that each category of Establishment Clause case had its own doctrinal approach. Justice Kagan also concurred, emphasizing her view that *Lemon* retained significance: "Although I agree that rigid application of the *Lemon* test does not solve every Establishment Clause problem, I think that test's focus on purposes and effects is crucial in evaluating government action in this sphere—as this very suit shows." Justices Ginsburg and Sotomayor dissented, emphasizing that the cross has always been a religious symbol and even in the war context has been used only for the graves of Christian soldiers. In short, while there seems to be a clear majority that *Lemon* is either unworkable or inapplicable to some types of cases, the balance of power on the Court seems to be with Justices taking a more ad hoc approach and unwilling to embrace any overriding standard.

C.   Separationists Versus Accommodationists

The New York special education program provides an apt setting to discuss the main division between Establishment Clause scholars today. One viewpoint is that such a program is an equalizing measure. Unless disadvantaged students can receive these special services while attending parochial school, they are put to a cruel choice. Either they may attend public school and obtain desperately needed help, or they may attend parochial school and follow their religious teachings at the price of foregoing the help. The condition on receiving assistance, then, is that they must attend either a public school or a non-religious private school. Some might argue that this burden on religion violates the Free Exercise Clause. But in any event, accommodationists maintain, it is a sufficient burden that the government should be able to alleviate if it chooses to do so. For the government to withhold this assistance is not to be neutral toward religion. Instead, its effects actively discourages religion. Thus, according to accommodationists, the program ensures government neutrality in the choice between public and parochial school.

From a different perspective, however, the program seems far from neutral. The effect of providing assistance is to make the parochial school a more attractive option than it otherwise would be. Moreover, the assistance is not for some subsidiary services but for core educational purposes, little different than sending public school teachers to take up the burden of covering particular subjects such as foreign languages. This assistance frees up funds that can then be used to finance the school's purely religious activities, or to lower tuition and attract additional students. According to separationists, the result can only be to encourage religious divisiveness, as parochial schools compete with others for their share of the available public funding. Moreover, as parochial schools become dependent on public assistance, they inevitably suffer some loss of independence: he who pays the piper calls the tune. Finally, by creating a sort of joint educational venture with parochial schools, the government sends a message of support for religious practices that alienates nonbelievers. Given the essential role of religious indoctrination in parochial schools, separationists say, the government might as well finance Sunday Schools.

Both of these viewpoints exert a powerful appeal, and neither can be easily dismissed. Both viewpoints can claim some support in the historical record. Moreover, it is difficult to see how either viewpoint could be adopted in its purest form. The ultimate in separationism would be to require churches to pay for their own police and fire protection, so that no public funds would be used in any way to support their activities. But no one has ever taken that position. The ultimate in accommodationism would be to require the public schools to provide religious instruction, so that students would not have to give up their right to attend public schools in order to obtain a religious education. (Besides, members of a specific religion may be too few or too poor to support a parochial school.) But no one goes quite this far either. Thus, we need to draw a line somewhere in the spectrum of government actions that make religious activities more feasible. It is little wonder that the Court has struggled with finding the place to draw that line.

II. Current Judicial Approaches

The Justices have articulated several tests for identifying the limits of the Establishment Clause. As mentioned above, the *Lemon* test now has an uncertain claim to acceptance, but no clear successor has emerged. Each of these approaches, including whatever is left of *Lemon*, offers some positive points but also poses significant problems.

A. Secular Purpose and Effect

As *Agostini* illustrates, the entanglement prong of the *Lemon* test seems to be fading from the scene. The Court no longer seems worried about political divisiveness as such, and seems willing to deal with problems of government supervision as they arise. But the secular purpose and effect prongs seem more viable.

The Equal Protection Clause prohibits statutes that are facially neutral but actually designed to discriminate against racial minorities. Discriminatory intent is not a permissible basis for legislation. By the same token, a desire to further religion seems inconsistent with the Establishment Clause. For example, it would seem to be unconstitutional for the government to pass a law forbidding the raising of hogs in order to promote Jewish and Islamic religious practices. For just the same reason, a law mandating the eating of pork, passed in order to punish members of those religions, would violate the Free Exercise Clause even under *Smith* because of its motivation.

Nevertheless, the purpose requirement has its problems. First, establishing the motivation of a collective body can be a difficult undertaking, and some have argued that it is essentially impossible. Second, much of criminal law and family law were originally supported by religious beliefs, and they still may draw support from that source. Yet it cannot be illegitimate for legislators to support laws that are otherwise valid merely because they also have religious motivations. Third, it is unclear what counts as a secular purpose. In particular, if the legislature believes that it is merely compensating for a burden on religious practice, it is unclear whether this should be considered a purpose to further religion or merely an attempt to remain neutral.

A somewhat similar problem attends the secular effect prong of *Lemon*. Recall *Agostini*. Is the primary effect of the New York program to provide services to all children regardless of their school choices, or is it to underwrite parochial schooling for certain children? One factor is the net effect of the program as a whole. If inclusion of parochial schools merely offsets a competitive advantage that the program gives other schools, it may be accommodationist. But if the net effect of including parochial schools in a program is to make them more attractive relative to other public or private schools than they would be if the program did not exist at all, the program appears preferential. This test would allow special education programs to be extended to religious schools, but probably not tuition vouchers. Another factor is whether the program provides an incentive for anyone to adopt a religious affiliation in order to qualify. More broadly, we could consider the program to have a secular purpose so long as it applies equally to secular and religious entities. This would allow both special education and vouchers.

Despite these difficulties, *Lemon* retains some appeal. It is similar to the requirement that to avoid strict scrutiny, a regulation of speech must serve purposes unrelated to the suppression of free expression. Similarly, *Lemon* requires that a law serve purposes unrelated to the promotion of religion.

B. Endorsement

Perhaps the greatest problem with the *Lemon* is not conceptual but practical. It turned out to be hard for different judges to agree on how to apply the test to particular circumstances. Also, the test did not seem particularly helpful in dealing with religious symbolism, where "purpose and effect" seem intangible. For this reason, Justice O'Connor proposed an alternative test. In her concurring opinion in *Lynch v. Donnelly*,[7] a religious symbolism case that we will discuss later, she laid out her endorsement test. Her premise was that the Establishment Clause "prohibits government from making adherence to a religion relevant in any way to a person's standing in the political community." Although entanglement can result from this connection between religion and political standing, the primary and "more direct infringement is government endorsement or disapproval of religion," which "sends a message to nonadherents that they are outsiders, not full members of the political community, and an accompanying message to adherents that they are insiders, favored members of the political community."

This test has some appeal. Surely it is basic to our understanding of democracy that all citizens are equal without regard to religion. Also, the endorsement test does seem responsive to the problem of religious symbols. Suppose the Minnesota legislature passed a resolution making Lutheranism the "official state religion"—perhaps a dubious honor, given that the state's legislature has also seen fit to make blueberry the "official state muffin." The purpose might be nonreligious (merely to commemorate the historic role of Lutheranism in Minnesota history) and the practical effects seem unclear. Yet such a declaration seems quite contrary to the Establishment Clause. The endorsement test fits these facts neatly.

Yet, O'Connor's test has serious problems. First, it has proved difficult to apply, as we will see in the section on religious symbolism. It has an unavoidably subjective aspect, which is especially unfortunate because this particular subjective reaction probably varies with a person's religious standpoint. Whose reaction determines whether the message is one of endorsement? It is not easy to specify what kind of person operates as the bellwether (the reasonable member of a minority religion? the average citizen? the most sensitive person?), or what information they have available (in particular, how well do they understand the legal context?). Second, although the endorsement test is not really precluded by Establishment Clause history, endorsement does not seem to have been the primary concern of the Framers. Third, like *Lemon*, the endorsement test has difficulty evaluating issues of religious accommodation.

---

[7]   465 U.S. 668 (1984).

C.   Coercion

As an alternative to the endorsement test, several Justices have proposed a focus on coercion. As explained by Justice Kennedy in *Allegheny* (another religious symbolism case we will discuss later), the principle is that "government may not coerce anyone to support or participate in any religion or its exercise."[8] Again, this is an appealing principle: surely it is at least part of the core of the Establishment Clause. This theory also helps explain why the Establishment Clause applies to the states. Like other parts of the First Amendment, the Establishment Clause is incorporated into the concept of "liberty" under the Fourteenth Amendment. Incorporation is harder to explain if we think of the Clause as pertaining primarily to the secular nature of government rather than to individual freedom. Nevertheless, this approach, too, has significant problems.

The first problem is defining coercion. Of course, we could limit "coercion" to mean a direct mandate to engage in a religious practice subject to criminal penalty or civil fine. But this definition is unappealingly narrow. For instance, it does not cover the use of general tax receipts to subsidize a particular church (paying a general tax isn't a religious practice). Yet we know that the use of taxes to support religion was at the core of the original concept of establishment. Justice Kennedy dealt with this problem by adding a separate prohibition on "direct benefits to religion in such a degree that it in fact 'establishes a [state] religion or religious faith, or tends to do so.'"

Also, at least in its narrower sense, coercion does not readily cover other practices now commonly thought to violate the Establishment Clause, such as state-supplied prayers for use in the classroom when participation is voluntary. To avoid these problems, Kennedy expands his view of coercion to include psychological pressures and economic incentives, as well as instances of "[s]ymbolic recognition or accommodation of religious faith" that would "place the government's weight behind an obvious effort to proselytize on behalf of a particular religion." But at this point, the meaning of "coercion" starts becoming a bit misty.

A second possible criticism is that under this interpretation, the Establishment Clause seems to verge on being superfluous. After all, the Free Exercise Clause already prohibits coercion against religious practices. One explanation might be that free exercise covers coercion to refrain from religious conduct and establishment covers coercion to engage in religious conduct. But we know that the Free Speech Clause guarantees not only the right to speak but the right to refrain

---

[8]   *County of Allegheny v. ACLU*, 492 U.S. 573 (1989).

from speaking. Similarly, it would seem that the Free Exercise Clause should cover not only the right to engage in religious practices but the right to refrain from doing so. But then, what is the Establishment Clause for? At most, under this interpretation, it merely seems to serve as an adjunct to the Free Exercise Clause, reinforcing the rule against state coercion of religion.

Finally, in part because the concept of coercion is pliable, the test has not always been easy to apply. Reasonable people may differ on what is coercive, and where the majority group sees only an invitation, a religious minority may see an offer it cannot refuse.

III. Doctrinal Evolution: Moving Beyond Chaos?

With three different tests in the field, shifting groups of Justices embracing each test, and some degree of difficulty in applying each test, it is little wonder that the Court's Establishment Clause jurisprudence has been a mess. The weaknesses of these tests, it should be said in fairness, owe less to any analytical inadequacies of the Justices, than to the inherent difficulty of identifying any approach that is both workable and broadly acceptable. We will briefly examine the cases in three areas to identify some major themes and point out some of the pitfalls. Due to space limitations, the treatment will be far from exhaustive.

A.   Religion in Public School Programs

We begin with the area where the Court's decisions have been the most coherent. The "wall of separation" remains at its highest on the grounds of the public schools. The Court has been quite vigilant in prohibiting any involvement of the schools in religious activity. The keystone cases are *Engel v. Vitale*[9] and *Abington School Dist. v. Schempp*.[10] One case involved a voluntary nondenominational prayer written by the state; the other involved mandatory Bible readings. The Court insisted that, voluntary or not, school prayer is improper. Even a small intrusion of religious teaching in the form of Biblical verses was said to be a "trickling stream [that] may all too soon become a raging torrent." These rulings now command wide support in legal circles, both judicial and academic. The prohibition on directed school prayer (even voluntary prayer) now seems to be one of the benchmarks for Establishment Clause theories. Indeed, proposed constitutional amendments designed to allow "prayer in the schools" typically forbad the government to supply the prayer.

Other cases have been more controversial because the religious nature of the material was less obvious. In one case, the state argued

---

⁹   370 U.S. 421 (1962).

¹⁰   374 U.S. 203 (1963).

unavailingly that the Ten Commandments were being displayed not because of their religious message, but because of their fundamental role in the evolution of Western legal systems.[11] Perhaps the Court doubted that many second graders could understand this fine distinction. In perhaps the closest case in this area, the Court struck down a "moment of silence" law (which seemed religiously neutral on its face), because of what seemed to be a specific purpose to encourage prayer.[12]

Beginning with the famous Scopes trial in the 1920s, the theory of evolution has been at the forefront of religious disputes concerning the public schools. In *Edwards v. Aguillard,*[13] the Court could find no secular purpose for a law that required the inclusion of "creation science" in biology classes. Justice Scalia protested in dissent that the constitutionality of the law should not depend on the mental states of some of the legislators. Most notably, in *Epperson v. Arkansas,*[14] the Court struck down a law that prohibited teaching the theory of evolution. The Court found it clear that "fundamentalist sectarian conviction was and is the law's reason for existence."

Some critics have argued that by precluding the perspective of creationism, the state had in effect "established" the religion of "secular humanism." But this cannot be correct. The government must make determinations about what methods for establishing facts are reliable and which are not. It is not an establishment of secular humanism for the courts to allow DNA tests in criminal trials while excluding readings of tea leaves and astrological charts. It would, however, be an establishment of religion to require that whenever DNA evidence is admitted, the testimony of a "spiritual medium" must also be admitted. Nor do such evidence rulings violate the rights of jurors who are required to listen to scientific information they may consider unholy rather than spiritualist information they trust.

Similarly, in determining constitutional issues, the court must determine what is a rational basis for legislation. It is not a violation of the Establishment Clause for the court to consider immunization a rational method of controlling disease and burning witches an irrational method of doing so. Similarly, the government is entitled to insist that students learn scientific information rather than religious alternatives. If the subject of biology is going to be taught at all, it should be taught on the basis of the same nonreligious considerations that a court would use to determine which evidence to

---

[11] *Stone v. Graham,* 449 U.S. 39 (1980).

[12] *Wallace v. Jaffree,* 472 U.S. 38 (1985).

[13] 482 U.S. 578 (1987).

[14] 393 U.S. 97 (1968).

admit at trial or what basis for legislation is rational. Whether the school could simply drop biology, or excuse religious objectors from some or all of the class, is a harder question. But unlike the phone company, the public schools are not common carriers, required to transmit all messages without discrimination.

The Court's more recent confrontations with religion ceremonies in the public schools have often involved "extra-curricular" prayer. In *Lee v. Weisman*,[15] a high school principal invited a rabbi to give a commencement address, first giving him guidelines on how to prepare inoffensive prayers for public occasions. The rabbi's prayer was suitably inoffensive, not to mention bland, but nevertheless led to litigation. Justice Kennedy wrote the opinion for the Court holding the prayer to be a violation of the Establishment Clause. Applying his coercion test, he concluded that commencement was a semi-obligatory occasion in a student's life, and that students would feel psychologically coerced to stand during the prayer or at least to maintain a respectful silence. In dissent, Justice Scalia ridiculed Kennedy's view of "coercion" and argued that nonsectarian prayer on public occasions, which some have called the American civic religion, helps to overcome sectarian friction and create public unity. But Scalia's idea that high school graduation is a completely optional event seems unrealistic. In any event, if government guidelines for prayer do not exceed the proper role of government under the Establishment Clause, it is hard to imagine what does.

Santa Fe Indep. School Dist. v. Doe[16] extended *Weisman* to cover student-lead prayers. In the face of litigation, the school district had abandoned an earlier system in which students elected a "student council chaplain" to deliver a prayer before each home football game. Under the district's new procedure, students would vote to decide whether to have an "invocation" delivered before each game, and if so, would elect a student to deliver it. In an opinion by Justice Stevens, the Court invalidated the policy on its face, viewing the outcome as largely controlled by *Weisman*. The Court rejected the argument that this was private rather than public speech, concluding that the policy implicitly endorsed religion. The majority also considered that attending high school football games is not entirely a free choice for high school students, given peer pressure. The dissenters (Rehnquist, Scalia, and Thomas) conceded that the policy might be unconstitutionally applied but argued that it should not be struck down on its face.

The Court seems to have had less difficulty with sponsorship of religion in the public schools than with other Establishment Clause

---

[15]   505 U.S. 577 (1992).

[16]   530 U.S. 290 (2000).

problems. The main reason is that all of the tests seem to point in the same direction. School-sponsored observances are transparently designed with particular religious views in mind. They cannot be justified as accommodations for religious students because of their direct impact on nonreligious students, who are necessarily exposed to prayers, creation science, or whatnot for the benefit of their religious classmates. Thus, they easily fall afoul of *Lemon*. They also appear to provide symbolic support for particular religions only. It was no coincidence that it was the Judeo-Christian Ten Commandments rather than the Buddhist Eightfold Way that Kentucky chose to display. And, given the generally authoritarian nature of public schools and the existence of compulsory education laws, any official connection with religion easily is labeled as coercive.

Clearly, the key to this analysis is to distinguish school-connected activities from truly voluntary private activities. In *Good News Club v. Milford Cent. Sch.*,[17] an elementary school had refused to allow a Christian organization for schoolchildren to use a room. It was conceded that the program of after-school room use for student activities was a limited public forum. The Court held that the exclusion was unconstitutional, notwithstanding that the group planned to engage in prayer and other religious activities. The majority concluded that giving access to the group would not violate the Establishment Clause because the meetings were held after school hours, not sponsored by the school, and open to any student who obtained parental consent, not just to members of the group. Thus, under current law, activities sponsored even loosely by the public schools must be rigorously neutral, but truly private activities may be religious—and excluding those private activities may violate the Free Speech clause. School sponsorship, then, is the critical threshold issue.

B. Aid to Parochial Schools

For most of the past fifty years, the Court was able to produce only a confused tangle of rulings about state aid to parochial schools. Some of the distinctions in the cases seemed to verge on the comic. The state could supply buses to take children from home to school and back, but not buses to take them on field trips. It could supply textbooks, but not globes and atlases. Some of these and similar distinctions could be justified as exercises in line-drawing, but the overall doctrine seemed chaotic. More recent decisions suggest that the Court moving toward a more coherent doctrinal framework and one more accepting of assistance to religious schools.

---

[17] 533 U.S. 98 (2001).

In *Mitchell v. Helms*,[18] a divided Court upheld a federal statute that provided supplies for parochial and other private schools on a per capita basis. Six Justices agreed that previous cases, which had limited provision of instructional materials such as maps to parochial schools, were inconsistent with recent doctrine and should be overruled. But these six Justices split in their analysis. The plurality opinion of Justice Thomas, joined by Chief Justice Rehnquist and Justices Scalia and Kennedy, placed heavy stress on the fact that the same aid was available to all schools on a nondiscriminatory basis. Thomas was unimpressed by the showing that some of the materials had been used for purely religious purposes. In a concurrence, Justice O'Connor (joined by Justice Breyer), said that the plurality had put too much weight on the "neutrality" of the aid program, but she concluded that the diversion to religious purposes was de minimis. The three dissenters, led by Justice Souter, argued that the program constituted impermissible direct aid to religious activities.

In one of its most important Establishment Clause rulings, the Court upheld a school voucher program in *Zelman v. Simmons-Harris*.[19] The parties agreed that the program had a purely secular purpose; the local public schools were a disaster, and the legislature wanted to provide some viable alternatives for poor students. A scholarship program provided tuition aid for some students to attend private schools, as well as funding for suburban schools accepting those students and for new "charter" schools in the public system. It also provided some tutorial aid for eligible students who chose to remain enrolled in their usual public schools. The majority opinion by Chief Justice Rehnquist found this to be a program of "true private choice," in which a neutral government program provides aid directly to a broad class of individuals, who in turn direct the aid to institutions of their own choosing. The majority was unimpressed by the fact that 96% of the participating students who attended private schools went to religious schools, or by the fact that none of the suburban public schools had agreed to participate. Justice O'Connor's concurring opinion stressed the broad range of alternatives available to participating students, including the public charter schools. The four dissenters, led by Justice Stevens, protested that "the overwhelming proportion of large appropriations of voucher money must be spent on religious schools if it is to be spent at all, and will be spent in amounts that cover almost all of tuition."

Thus, the Court seems to be moving away from any concern about the pervasively religious nature of parochial schools. When neutral programs of financial aid have a nonreligious purpose, they

---

[18]   530 U.S. 793 (2000).

[19]   536 U.S. 639 (2002).

will be upheld by the current majority if: (a) they provide aid directly to the schools themselves for educational or student services, and no more than a *de minimis* amount is diverted to purely religious activities; or (b) they provide aid via "truly free" parental choice. The exact contours of these doctrines remain to be worked out, but the mood is distinctly friendly to aid to parochial schools. The change in the Court's emphasis may be in part due to change in social realities, since religious schools are no longer completely dominated by a single sect, now face competition from other private schools, and seem to be an important alternative for students in failing school systems. No doubt considerable litigation will continue, however, particularly on the "secular purpose" requirement, on diversion of direct funding, and on the definition of "truly free choice."

The more pressing issue raised by these cases, however, relates to the kinds of conditions that the government may place on these grants. Justice Breyer emphasized in his *Zelman* dissent that recipient schools in the voucher program were required to meet certain criteria. They were required to accept students of all religions. They were also forbidden to "advocate or foster unlawful behavior or teach hatred of any person or group on the basis of race, ethnicity, national origin, or religion." These standard might impact different religions to varying extent, raising Establishment Clause concerns. Religious schools can also be expected to argue that the voucher program is a limited public forum, making content discrimination impermissible. Yet, without such restrictions, voucher programs would lose considerable political support.

The Establishment Clause analysis might also be affected by the elimination of such restrictions, because only students belonging to particular religions would be in a position to benefit, parental choices might be much more limited, and the purpose of the program would look more accommodationist than purely educational. The funding conditions on these programs are sure to lead to further litigation, which courts are likely to find difficult to resolve.

Further questions were raised about the power to exclude religious groups from government aid by *Trinity Lutheran Church v. Comer*.[20] A Lutheran childcare center, which had merged with a church, applied for funding as part of a state program to install safer surfaces made of recycled tires at playgrounds at nonprofits. The government rejected the ground because of its strict policy against providing any funding to churches. In an opinion by Chief Justice Roberts, the Court held that this government policy was unconstitutional. According to the Court, because the policy "expressly discriminates against otherwise eligible recipients by

---

[20] ___ U.S. ___, 137 S.Ct. 2012, 198 L.Ed.2d 551 (2017).

disqualifying them from a public benefit solely because of their religious character," it was subject to "the most exacting scrutiny." The opinion concluded:

> The Missouri Department of Natural Resources has not subjected anyone to chains or torture on account of religion. And the result of the State's policy is nothing so dramatic as the denial of political office. The consequence is, in all likelihood, a few extra scraped knees. But the exclusion of Trinity Lutheran from a public benefit for which it is otherwise qualified, solely because it is a church, is odious to our Constitution all the same, and cannot stand.

Footnote 3 of the opinion, which was joined only by the Roberts, Kennedy, Alito, and Kagan, limited the scope of the opinion: "This case involves express discrimination based on religious identity with respect to playground resurfacing. We do not address religious uses of funding or other forms of discrimination." Justices Thomas and Justice Gorsuch wrote separately to express disapproval of this footnote. Justice Breyer, concurring in the judgement, emphasized the health and safety nature of the benefit in the case.

In dissent, Justice Sotomayor (joined by Justice Ginsberg), argued that the decision represented an important breach in the separation of church and state:

> To hear the Court tell it, this is a simple case about recycling tires to resurface a playground. The stakes are higher. This case is about nothing less than the relationship between religious institutions and the civil government— that is, between church and state. The Court today profoundly changes that relationship by holding, for the first time, that the Constitution requires the government to provide public funds directly to a church. Its decision slights both our precedents and our history, and its reasoning weakens this country's longstanding commitment to a separation of church and state beneficial to both.

The biggest immediate question posed by *Trinity Lutheran* relates to school voucher programs. The Court had previously held that it is constitutional to include religious schools in such programs. But it is constitutional to exclude them? If so, states will be left with a choice between having no voucher program at all or making it available to parochial schools as well as secular ones.

Unquestionably, the Court's current position of upholding programs that provide aid without regard to religion will seem objectionable in principle to many observers, not to mention a strong minority of Justices. Their fears of excessive entanglement and religious friction may yet turn out to be justified. But for better or worse, the Court's current direction seems clear.

C. Religious Symbolism

Although there have only been four Establishment Clause cases dealing with religious symbolism, they have generated more than their share of confusion. The first case was *Lynch v. Donnelly.*[21] A city put up an annual Christmas holiday display, which included a Christmas tree, a wishing well, Santa, colored lights, and a creche depicting the nativity of Jesus, all owned by the city. In an opinion by Chief Justice Burger, the Court held that this was not a religious display, but merely a depiction of the historical origins of a secular winter holiday. In a concurring opinion, Justice O'Connor advanced her endorsement test for the first time. She concluded that the creche did not carry a message of endorsement because of the overall setting. Apparently, the presence of Santa, holiday lights, and the tree neutralized the religious implications of the creche. The dissenters protested in vain that the creche was a specifically Christian religious display and inevitably communicated a message of exclusion to nonbelievers.

In *County of Allegheny v. ACLU,*[22] the Court issued two rulings about holiday displays. It held unconstitutional the display of a creche on the main staircase of a county courthouse, even though the display was privately owned. Five Justices applied the endorsement test, concluding that the display of the creche without the sanitizing context of Santa and the reindeer carried a message of endorsement. But another majority found no objection to the display of a menorah in a nearby public building, next to a Christmas tree and a sign saying "Salute to Liberty." Two of the Justices using the endorsement test decided that in context the menorah was part of a message supporting pluralism and freedom of belief, rather than a religious endorsement.

Later, in *Capitol Square Review Board v. Pinette,*[23] another fractured Court held that allowing the Ku Klux Klan to erect a large cross in a public square outside the statehouse would not violate the Establishment Clause. (Justice Thomas noted wryly that most people would not view the Klan's use of the cross as religious.) The plurality opinion by Justice Scalia argued that private religious speech cannot violate the Establishment Clause when it takes place in a public forum. Three concurring Justices applied the endorsement test, but found that a reasonable observer would not attribute the message to

---

[21] 465 U.S. 668 (1984).

[22] 492 U.S. 573 (1989).

[23] 515 U.S. 753 (1995).

the government, because the square was used for expressive purposes by so many different groups.

As with the parochial school cases, the problem here is not that the individual positions of the Justices are senseless, but that the ultimate outcomes seem to rest on fine and somewhat subjective distinctions, which have given no end of trouble to the lower courts. One lower court judge tartly remarked that the endorsement test, by requiring such a careful consideration of how objects were displayed, seemed more suitable for application by interior designers than the judiciary.[24]

Although the Court was willing to inquire into legislative purpose in order to ensure religious neutrality in *Alleghany County*, it severely limited its inquiry into presidential purpose in *Trump v. Hawaii*.[25] This case involved the third effort by President Trump to ban travel from certain countries, the first two having been struck down by the lower courts. The bans were challenged under the Establishment Clause for litigation reasons. They were allegedly motivated by religious animus against the potential immigrants, but those immigrants lacked standing in U.S. courts. Their family members had standing but their own religious practice was not directly affected, making an Establishment Clause claim the best litigation option.

The majority applied only a modest degree of scrutiny despite significant evidence of anti-Muslim motivation. Because it found immigration matters to be a "fundamental sovereign attribute exercised by the Government's political departments largely immune from judicial control", the Court applied only what it called a truncated form of judicial review. Prior statements by President Trump provided at least strong suggestions that the bans were aimed at Muslims. The majority said that it would consider this evidence but would "uphold the policy so long as it can reasonably be understood to result from a justification independent of unconstitutional grounds." It found "persuasive evidence that the entry suspension has a legitimate grounding in national security concerns, quite apart from any religious hostility." In dissent, Justice Sotomayor accused the majority of "ignoring the facts, misconstruing our legal precedent, and turning a blind eye to the pain and suffering the Proclamation inflicts upon countless families and individuals, many of whom are United States citizens." *Trump v. Hawaii* seems to carve out an area of minimal constitutional scrutiny cases involving government support of the borders, but probably does not

---

[24] *American Jewish Congress v. Chicago*, 827 F.2d 120 (7th Cir. 1987) (Easterbrook, J., dissenting).

[25] ___ U.S. ___, 138 S.Ct. 2392, 201 L.Ed.2d 775 (2018).

affect Establishment Clause analysis more generally. The separation of powers aspects of the case, and the degree to which it frees the President from normal constitutional scrutiny, are discussed in detail in Chapter 8.

The Court has continued to find line drawing difficult in considering arguable governmental endorsements of religion. In *Town of Greece, NY v. Galloway*,[26] the town board began public meetings with prayers by local ministers, some of which were sectarian. Given the long tradition of legislative prayers, the plurality opinion by Justice Kennedy did not find problematic the city's failure to broaden the roster of invitees to include more non-Christians or by the sectarian nature of the prayers. Concurring, Justice Scalia and Thomas found that the prayers were not comparable to coercive state establishments of the Founding era, even assuming that the Establishment Clause was incorporated into the Fourteenth Amendment. The dissenting Justices pointed out that citizens were required to attend board meetings on occasion in order to obtain zoning variances or other actions, and that non-Christians in the audience would undoubtedly perceive a message of exclusion from the succession of Christian ministers.

IV. The Accommodation Problem

Probably the most fundamental problem under the Establishment Clause is how to handle efforts to accommodate religion. Allowing a Jewish law student to reschedule a Saturday exam at a state university may not seem like an establishment of religion. But other accommodations seem more questionable. Where is the line to be drawn?

A. War Between the Clauses?

One reason this problem has seemed so intractable is that the two religion clauses seem to tug in opposite directions. Consider *Lyng v. Northwest Indian Cemetery Protective Ass'n*.[27] The issue in *Lyng* was whether the Forest Service could build a road through an ancient ceremonial site still used by Indians, thereby destroying their ability to practice their religion. The Court seemed sympathetic to their plight but held that the Free Exercise Clause did not limit what the government could do with its own property. Even so, re-routing the road would certainly seem consistent with the spirit of the Free Exercise Clause if the government chose to do so. But consider the Establishment Clause concern that would be created by a voluntary government decision to preserve the land. Under *Lemon*, it might well be said that the primary purpose and effect of the decision would

---

[26] 572 U.S. 565 (2014).

[27] 485 U.S. 439 (1988).

be to advance a particular religion. The decision could also be said to send a message of endorsement of religion—presumably, the government would not reroute a road for a practice that it disapproved of, like a nude beach. The coercion test would present no problem—but that is little consolation: the coercion test would also present no problem if the government decided to start building churches.

There is a tug of war between these two clauses. On the one hand the Free Exercise clause seems to prevent the government from burdening religion. On the other hand the Establishment Clause seems to be telling us not to make any special deals for religious groups. Because we are not sure of the proper baseline, we do not know when an accommodation for religion "advances" it and when it merely "accommodates" a burden created by the government. The Free Exercise Clause seems to give religion preferred status as an especially important human activity, while the Establishment Clause prohibits the government from doing anything in its favor. Everything that is constitutionally required by one clause seems to violate the spirit if not the letter of the other. It is this apparent tension between the two classes that has made the area such a minefield.

B.   Possible Resolutions

Although there are various ways to escape this dilemma, we will focus on three. Each of them avoids the dilemma by giving particular prominence to certain values at the expense of others, thereby defusing the conflict.

The first approach is secularism, which in effect pushes the Establishment Clause to its maximum possible extreme while restricting Free Exercise. For the secularist, the Constitution creates a nonreligious government whose concerns do not extend to religion, either pro or con. So the government cannot properly accommodate religious practices, since to do so would treat religion differently than equally heartfelt nonreligious conduct. The Free Exercise Clause provides no impetus to accommodation, since the secularist agrees with Justice Scalia that the Clause only prohibits deliberate efforts to suppress religion. Under this approach, which seems to be somewhat similar to the approach in France, there is little room for legislative discretion in religious matters.

The second approach is pluralism, which effectively elevates the Free Exercise Clause over the Establishment Clause. From the pluralist perspective, the religion clauses are designed to create a world of thriving religious diversity. To promote such diversity, the Free Exercise clause requires mandatory government exemptions, along the lines of *Sherbert v. Verner*, but usually with an even broader definition of what constitutes a burden on religion. Essentially, the government must ensure that the net effect of its actions maintains or increases religious diversity. Although the Establishment Clause is not completely disregarded, it turns out to prohibit accommodation only in exceptional cases. The secularist and pluralist have only one thing in common: neither would leave religious matters to legislative discretion. From the view of religious groups, this may seem like the ideal approach, at least if they expect to benefit as much or more than competing religions. But they may become uncomfortable when this approach is extended to minority religions of which they disapprove.

The final approach is majoritarianism. It reads the Free Exercise Clause narrowly, as in *Smith*, so that accommodation is never constitutionally required. But it also reads the Establishment Clause narrowly, so that the government has a fairly free hand in making voluntary accommodations for religious groups. Here, rather than secularism or religious liberty, it is majority rule which receives privileged status. Some observers view this as the most likely direction for the Court to take. It may be unfair to say that this approach eliminates the conflict by eliminating the religion clauses. It does, however, avoid any collision between clauses by curtailing the scope of both clauses. The effect is to leave it up to the political process, by and large, to decide when to accommodate religious beliefs. Those who lose out in the process would find little refuge in court.

C. Impermissible Accommodations

The reason that accommodations are often appealing is that the status quo is itself lacking in neutrality. For instance, if a law school schedules exams for Saturday but not for Sunday, is it thereby favoring Christians over Jews? Although the *Smith* Court was unwilling to provide exemptions under the aegis of the Free Exercise Clause, it specifically opened the door to legislative exemptions. Thus, at least at present, the secularist position seems to be ruled out. Assuming exemptions are at least sometimes permitted, it may be better to ask when accommodations become impermissible. A few pragmatic observations are in order.

The first is that the same factors favoring exemptions under the Free Exercise Clause should be relevant to determining when they are permissible under the Establishment Clause. Under *Smith*, exemptions can still be claimed when religious claims are tied to other constitutional rights, or when individualized consideration of hardship is permitted. The easiest cases under the Establishment Clause should be those that come close to fitting within these categories. So accommodation should be most readily available when a colorable (if not successful) free exercise claim is present.

A second point is that accommodation becomes more suspect the harder it is to identify precisely what burden imposed by the government has been accommodated. There is a tendency to view parochial schools as an accommodation to the fact that the government uses taxes to support nonsectarian public schools. But this seems questionable. Everyone pays taxes for schools and other services; apart from being marginally poorer, the religious person's ability to utilize private schools is unaffected by the existence of public schools. Many other citizens also pay taxes though they do not send children to public school. (Also, the existence of public schools raises property values, even for owners who do not use those schools.) Moreover, as argued earlier, the government can hardly be criticized for teaching secular subjects in the public schools, and its doing so cannot be considered a burden on anyone's religion.

A third point is that an accommodation must be generally open to all religions, rather than favoring any. This seems to be one moral of *Board of Education of Kiryas Joel v. Grumet*.[28] A community of traditionalist Jews, the Satmar Hasidim, sent most of their children to parochial schools, but sent disabled children to surrounding public schools in order to obtain federally funded special education. (This was during the period between *Aguilar* and *Agostini*, when it was considered unconstitutional to provide these services on the premises of religious schools.) The Hasidic children, however, were subjected to harassment in the public schools. As an accommodation, New York passed special legislation creating a village school district, so that the children would not need to attend school in the outside community. There was no assurance that a similarly situated school district with another religion would receive similar treatment. Thus, the accommodation was too ad hoc to be permissible.

A final point is that the accommodation should not run afoul of the coercion principle. Forcing an employer to pay an employee's cab fare to get to church may be "accommodating" the employee's religious needs, but it is flatly inconsistent with the Establishment Clause. For this reason, the Court was right in *Estate of Thornton v. Caldor, Inc.*[29] to strike down a state law requiring employers to give the day off to any employee claiming a particular day was his Sabbath. Requiring the employer to provide a day off was in essence a forced contribution by the employer to the employee's religious practices. Note that the federal government and some states do require employers to accommodate religious requirements of

---

[28]   512 U.S. 687 (1994).

[29]   472 U.S. 703 (1985).

employees, but only to the extent that doing so does not impose an unreasonable burden.

V. Concluding Thoughts on Current First Amendment Law

We have now finished a rather lengthy, but nevertheless incomplete, tour of First Amendment law. I will not attempt, at this late point in the book, to produce a unified theory that somehow makes sense of all the diverse, complex doctrines we have considered. But I would like to close with a brief sermon on the inadvisability of missing the forest for the trees.

From a lawyer's perspective, the least settled and coherent aspects of any legal field are the most interesting. It is these areas that give rise to litigation and that challenge the lawyer's ability to advise clients. These unsettled areas are also the growth zones of the law, typically indicating where the legal system is attempting to cope with changing social realities. Hence, they are also the primary focus of legal scholarship. All of this is as it should be. But there is a risk of distortion in this exclusive focus; on gray areas; as one wag once said, a lawyer is someone who knows a lot about twilight but not much about noon or midnight.

Despite the vast diversity of opinion about the First Amendment, there are also striking areas of consensus. Until fifty years ago, the most burning issue about free speech was the government's power to suppress groups with radical ideas, who might threaten the established order. The question is so clearly settled today that it takes only a few pages to review the current law. Nowhere on the scholarly horizon or among the federal judiciary do we see an effort to reopen this issue, though we are not lacking for extremist groups with violent potential. To a constitutional scholar from an earlier era, the complete absence of any serious debate about this point would probably be the biggest surprise in current First Amendment law.

But this is only the beginning of the areas of agreement. For example, as contentious as the religion clauses are today, there seems to be little on-going legal debate about traditional school prayers, which everyone agrees are unconstitutional. Likewise, although there is debate about whether *New York Times v. Sullivan* found the right formula, only a few would argue that libel law is simply outside the bounds of the First Amendment, though any lawyer would have thought so sixty years ago. Nor is anyone making the argument, plausible though it was early in the last century, that the government's ownership of property or status as an employer give it carte blanche to control speech. Innovative as these doctrines were at the time, they now seem essentially undisputed.

Beyond this, there seems to be widespread agreement on the core principle that the government is powerless to outlaw ideas. Even where new arguments are made for regulating speech, such as the feminist attack on pornography, they are always tied to the form or context of speech, not merely the hateful idea expressed. Even the broadest proposal for regulating pornography stops well short of banning all sexist ideas, and the same is true for proposals to regulate hate speech. Equally, conservative arguments for restricting speech in schools never simply rely on the bald proposition that the government should keep children from being exposed to bad ideas. Perhaps, at the beginning of the Twenty-first Century, we have finally learned to respect the most intangible yet basic freedom of all: freedom of thought.

FURTHER READINGS

Vincent Blasi, *School Vouchers and Religious Liberty: Seven Questions from Madison's Memorial and Remonstrance*, 87 Cornell L. Rev. 783 (2002).

Alan E. Brownstein, *Evaluating School Voucher Programs Through a Liberty, Equality, and Free Speech Matrix*, 31 Conn. L. Rev. 871 (1999).

Noah Feldman, *The Intellectual Origins of the Establishment Clause*, 77 N.Y.U. L. Rev. 346 (2002).

John H. Garvey, What Are Freedoms For? (1996).

Frederick Gedicks, *Incorporation of the Establishment Clause Against the States: A Logical, Textual, and Historical Account*, 88 Ind. L.J. 679 (2013).

Frederick Gedicks and Rebecca Van Tassell, *RCRA Exemptions from the Contraceptive Mandate: An Unconstitutional Accommodation of Religion*, 49 Harv. Civil Rights-Civil Liberty J. 343 (2014).

Kent Greenawalt, Religion and the Constitution—Volume 2: Establishment and Fairness (2008).

Philip Hamburger, Separation of Church and State (2002).

John C. Jeffries, Jr. and James E. Ryan, *A Political History of the Establishment Clause*, 100 Mich. L. Rev. 279 (2001).

Douglas Laycock, *"Nonpreferential" Aid to Religion: A False Claim About Original Intent*, 27 Wm. & Mary L. Rev. 875 (1986).

Leonard W. Levy, The Establishment Clause: Religion and the First Amendment (1986).

Martha Nussbaum, Liberty of Conscience: In Defense of America's Tradition of Religious Equality (2008).

Suzanna Sherry, Lee v. Weisman: *Paradox Redux*, 1992 Sup. Ct. Rev. 123.

TABLE OF CASES

INDEX
